FINANCE AND LAW: TWINS IN TROUBLE

FINANCE AND LAW: TWINS IN TROUBLE

Edited by
LUDO CORNELIS

intersentia
Cambridge – Antwerp – Portland

Intersentia Ltd
Sheraton House | Castle Park
Cambridge | CB3 0AX | United Kingdom
Tel.: +44 1223 370 170 | Email: mail@intersentia.co.uk

Distribution for the UK:
NBN International
Airport Business Centre, 10 Thornbury Road
Plymouth, PL6 7 PP
United Kingdom
Tel.: +44 1752 202 301 | Fax: +44 1752 202 331
Email: orders@nbninternational.com

Distribution for the USA and Canada:
International Specialized Book Services
920 NE 58th Ave. Suite 300
Portland, OR 97213
USA
Tel.: +1 800 944 6190 (toll free)
Email: info@isbs.com

Distribution for Austria:
Neuer Wissenschaftlicher Verlag
Argentinierstraße 42/6
1040 Wien
Austria
Tel.: +43 1 535 61 03 24
Email: office@nwv.at

Distribution for other countries:
Intersentia Publishing nv
Groenstraat 31
2640 Mortsel
Belgium
Tel.: +32 3 680 15 50
Email: mail@intersentia.be

Finance and Law: Twins in Trouble
Ludo Cornelis (ed.)

ISBN 978-1-78068-172-6
D/2015/7849/1
NUR 820

GPRC
Guaranteed
Peer Reviewed
Content

British Library Cataloguing in Publication Data. A catalogue record for this book is available from the British Library.

CONTENTS

INTRODUCTION

Ludo Cornelis*

Since the start of the financial crisis in 2007, which turned into an economic crisis soon afterwards, it was obvious, even for lawyers, that public law had something to do with the genesis of the crisis and that public law has available to it adequate instruments to make a reoccurrence of such a crisis unlikely.

Financial law, tax law, criminal law, and so on, are designed to regulate the behaviour of financial institutions and other corporations. Since public law was unable to avoid the 2007 crisis, only one finding is compelling: its instruments did not work properly or, worse, were badly designed or applied.

Since 2007, a lot has been done from a financial, tax and criminal law point of view, confirming this finding.

But what about private law? Some of the authors started thinking and talking, in 2010–2011, about a possible connection between private law and the outbreak of a financial/economic crisis. Not much was – and still is – to be found in case law or legal writings about such a link.

Our prima facie feeling, in our capacity as both teaching professors at various Belgian universities and legal practitioners, was that private law and the emergence or absence of a financial/economic crisis are linked. However, we were unable to immediately define these links or to determine their scope and effects.

That lack of understanding made us curious and ambitious. We wanted to know more about it and, if possible, outline the connections between private law and the crisis experienced by the world since 2007: did private law institutions, mechanisms or instruments in their current design contribute to the crisis? Does private law provide institutions, mechanisms and/or instruments which might have prevented the genesis of a financial/economic crisis? If so, why did these institutions, mechanisms and/or instruments fail to do so? Is there a need for new or modified institutions, mechanisms and/or instruments to improve the impact of private law on events that may lead to a new financial/economic crisis?

Raising questions is the easiest part of a job; finding answers in a legal no man's land is much harder. We decided to proceed with a working group of members accepting the challenge of the questions raised in their research areas.

Not every colleague invited to join the team accepted the invitation. Some declined it because they thought private law would have nothing to do with events such as a financial/economic crisis. Others asserted that private law had worked pretty well all over the years and is unable to do more or better. They appeared to be sceptical, if not hostile, about the purpose and focus of the working group.

We learned a lot from these responses. First, we understood that it would be wrong to expect overall approval or applause from all lawyers, many of them taking for granted issues we intended to investigate, leaving beaten tracks. Second, we needed to prepare ourselves to deal with all the possible (harsh) critics. An understanding of the reasons leading to the 2007 financial crisis required better insights into economics, sociology, politics and so on; in a word, our team had to read and study hard.

Fortunately, most colleagues enthusiastically accepted the invitation to join the team.

From our first meeting, a conference day was planned for 29 March 2013. It left us almost two years for preparation, making sure at the same time that failure was not an option: we promised each other a result.

All team members started reading about the 2007 financial crisis and its economic effects. As mentioned, our readings dealt more with economics, sociology, politics, psychology and so on than with law, private law in particular. We organised several meetings where all the members of the working group discussed the readings and tried to translate the results into legal terms. These meetings led to further reading and, in particular, further bilateral or multilateral discussions.

In the course of our meetings, the team determined the programme of the conference day step by step, leaving to each member the final responsibility for his or her contribution, after (at times passionate) discussions within the team.

Gradually our team discussions and reflections made it clear(er) that private law and the absence or the outbreak of a financial/economic crisis are strongly intertwined.

We understood that private law provides as many useful institutions, mechanisms and/or instruments against the emergence of such a crisis as public law does.

It may be difficult to admit for experts in private law, but the 2007 crisis should not only be attributed to a failure of public law, but also to private law.

Evidently we soon realised that we would not be able to (dis)cover all connections between private law and the phenomenon of a financial/economic crisis. Choices had to be made. Many topics were left for future investigations by us and others, who hopefully are inspired by our approach and first steps.

Although addressing Belgian law, we also believed it worthwhile to prepare our papers in English to make it accessible for persons familiar with other legal systems to benefit from our approach and findings or to keep aloof from them.

The conference day was an unpretentious success: our findings were presented and discussed with the attendants, giving inspiring food for further thought.

Our debriefing meeting had to take place without one of the founding fathers of our working group, who was called in the meantime to become the Belgian Minister of Finance, a time-consuming office.

Several months more were spent on fine-tuning and finalising our papers.

We are happy to present them now to you together with Intersentia, who took the risk of sharing with us the criticism and blame that our opinions and/or positions may induce.

Our book starts with contributions setting and dealing with the financial scene, and ends with proposals to improve its functioning. These contributions deal more with public than with private law issues. It cannot be otherwise: private law depends on the political, social and economic organisation designed by public law. It has to comply with public law and therefore one needs to know how public law deals with finance and economics.

Finance and economics refer to income and assets of persons and families suffering from a financial and economic crisis, as has been and is still the case with the subprime crisis.

While Mr Thomas Piketty was working with a team of economists on his spectacular and eye-opening *Le capital au XXIème siècle* (Paris, Seuil, 2013) and while another group of experts in different fields was preparing its *magnus opus Changing inequalities in rich countries* (Oxford, OUP, 2014; two volumes), we came to the conclusion that family law, dealing *inter alia* with income and assets at family level, had to be addressed in this book.

Agreements, without doubt, are a powerful (financial and economic) tool, governed by private law. Our readings made us understand that famous economists pointed to the 2007 financial and economic crisis as being a systemic risk. We wondered how the concept of systemic risk has to be translated into legal terms.

We thought about public order (public policy), said to be a fundamental principle within private law, but one with unclear content and scope. A look into these intriguing words became a must.

With financial markets having been compared to a casino world, we also decided that speculation needed screening and analysis from a private law perspective.

Financial instruments such as credit debt obligations (CDO) or credit default swaps (CDS) appear to be (complex) agreements. We thought it useful, by way of example, to dig into the 'regularity' of credit default swaps.

The rich are becoming richer; the poor becoming poorer. We investigated mechanisms in private law contributing to the accumulation of wealth. The legal rules dealing with return on investments consolidate that movement. The way private law deals with interest rates is therefore a major issue and concern.

From our findings in family law and discussions with regard to public order, speculation, credit default swaps and interest rates, it appeared that the legal issues encountered (in public and private law) are not simply connected with, but are fully determined by, the political, social and economic organisation, becoming a 'system' available within a particular society at a particular time.

A general overview of the different modern opinions, addressing the relationship between enterprises (the captains of finance/industry) and the society they are part of, is therefore more than helpful.

Enterprises are most often incorporated as commercial companies. By virtue of company law they have to make profit(s). Commercial companies in combination with agreements are redoubtable instruments of private law, allowing their shareholders – in good times – to leverage the prospects of benefits. When tools or tricks are used that make it likely that the party will one day be over, the wild search for maximum and early profits may be at the expense of (civil) society. Is profit-making really a perfect excuse for risky businesses conducted within a commercial company? The question had to be addressed.

The 2007 financial crisis came about due to a lack of (financial) liquidity: financial guarantees are at the heart of the financial rules determining the liquidity of financial institutions. It is no wonder, then, that this issue, with its recent legal developments, inspired another contribution.

As already mentioned, the papers presented in this book do not by any means cover any and all connections between private law and the phenomenon of a financial/economic crisis. It was not our aim to do so. Our aim was different. We wanted to become aware of these connections, for ourselves and for others, and be willing to raise the questions we have tried to address to the best of our (current) knowledge.

Endnotes

* Ludo Cornelis is Professor at the Free University of Brussels and an Attorney at the Brussels Bar.

SETTING THE SCENE: FINANCIALISM AS A SINGLE STORY

Michel FLAMÉE*

Chimamanda Adichie is an exceptional Nigerian author. In a speech at the TED conferences in 2009 she said:

> 'Power is the ability not just to tell the story of another person, but to make it the definitive story of that person. [...] The "single story" creates stereotypes, and the problem with stereotypes is not that they are untrue but that they are incomplete. They make one story become the only story.'

We are still enslaved to the 'story' of the financial and economic crisis of 2007–2008. Economists, political scientists, sociologists, psychologists, philosophers, anthropologists and biochemists have studied the causes of the crisis. Yet lawyers are derided for being remarkably quiet on this subject.

The question is whether legal rules are lacking, whether they have not been properly applied, or even whether they have helped to trigger or exacerbate the crisis.

Perhaps the silence of lawyers may be attributed to the fact that they still do not have a full picture of the multiplicity of factors that contributed to the crisis. In this introduction I would like to explain my view of these circumstances, which is based on my own experience in a supervisory capacity, though it only reflects my personal conviction.

1. THE ORIGIN OF THE FINANCIAL CRISIS

In the past five years numerous experts in a number of countries have conducted many technical studies. In Britain, Lord Adair Turner produced a particularly clear report known as the Turner Review.

1.1. THE TURNER REVIEW

Our system is based on the concept of a 'free market economy', with companies subject to rules laid down primarily in competition law, but subsequently also in financial law.

Over the past twenty years, the following theory – the story – regarding the financial markets has been unchallenged:[1]

> 'But the predominant tendency of financial markets theory of the last 20 to 30 years has been to assert that:
> (i) efficient and liquid financial markets deliver major allocative efficiency benefits by making possible a full range of contracts, thus enabling providers and users of funds more effectively to meet their preferences for risk, return and liquidity;
> (ii) markets are sufficiently rational as to justify a strong presumption in favour of market deregulation; and
> (iii) that even if markets are theoretically capable of irrational behaviour, policymakers will never be able to judge when and how far they are irrational with sufficient confidence to justify market intervention.'

Confronted with these principles, this 'story', the regulators developed a system which they believed would generate a deep, liquid capital market, accompanied by a legal framework which only needed to organise sufficient adherence to commitments and respect for property, a framework that only needed to counteract fraud. In line with these ideas, the regulators had a role to play specifically in organising the exchange of information, where the aim is to ensure that all investors gain access to comparable information simultaneously.

The Turner Review finds that these three fundamental principles proved erroneous.

So the question is: how have we reached this point? Does it demonstrate the failure of capitalism as a system?

1.2. CAPITALISM IS EVOLVING

There are many definitions of capitalism, described in many disciplines and countless studies.

To simplify the argument, I only want to refer to a timeline that most people are familiar with. When capitalism began, family businesses predominated, but development led to larger enterprises needing proper management. However, managerial capitalism fairly rapidly gave way to investment capitalism.

In a family business, the directors and the management still had an overall view of all the processes in the business, but industrialisation created a need to enlist competent outsiders who were then appointed first as managers and later as directors of corporate structures.

But it did not stop there. Very soon, the need for investment funding led to the development of investment capitalism, with all the corresponding rules. The successive amendments to corporate legislation bear witness to these changes.

However, the past two decades have brought a new phase in which investment capitalism developed into what we might call 'financial capitalism', or even 'financialism', with corporate objectives and working methods which are fundamentally different from those of yesteryear.

Until the investment capitalism stage, the operation of the investee business and its importance in the real economy were the criteria for assessing the decisions taken, but with the advent of financial capitalism, the concept of 'shareholder value' became predominant, and the link with the real economy was severed. This development is referred to as 'financialism'.

1.3. BRIEF ACCOUNT OF FINANCIALISM

> 'Financialism is an economic system where the primary activity consists of creating and manipulating financial instruments. Financial instruments – loans, mortgages, stocks, bonds, and so on – are in their original form firmly linked to economic reality: the mortgage finances home ownership, the stock certificate represents ownership of a company that owns physical assets, the bond secures debt incurred to build a factory.
>
> However, when financialism sets in, financial instruments become progressively further removed from their role in supporting commerce in the real world and develop a life of their own, a weird shadow dimension, a hall of mirrors, a distorted alternate reality that intersects and reacts with the real economy in unpredictable and destructive ways. George Soros described this phenomenon as "reflexivity". Derivatives have a lot to do with it. Leverage and the abuse of easy credit are contributing causes. The shadow banking system is a symptom.'[2]

Financialism originates from tools belonging to at least four disciplines, which fall within the broad scope of this seminar:

1. *In economics* a very strong tendency has emerged, culminating in statements by the Nobel Prize winner Milton Friedman, who said that the only aim of a business must be to generate profits.[3] This is seen as its sole corporate function to which all other aims are subordinate.
2. *In the technological development* of resources that support the running of a business, mathematical models now make it possible to offer not only figures giving an idea of the value of a business, but also an increasingly accurate – or at least convincing – prediction of how those figures will change in the future.
3. *In accounting* there has been a fundamental change from historical accounting to risk-driven assessment, and to the practice of discounting future figures on the observation date, whereby the figures already take account of future developments. Consequently, far less importance is attached to the real economic context of the business and its continuing usefulness to society. Instead, what counts is the value gained on paper: although that gain has not yet actually been achieved, it is apparent in the discounted figures and can then be cashed in as quickly as possible by shareholders selling the shares in a liquid market. The seller no longer cares whether the built-in future increase in value can or will ever be realised.
4. *From the managerial point of view* these developments emerged first in the United States. They were reflected there in the way in which market regulation developed and in the method of organising the governance structures of businesses. The concept in which directors and managers took on personal responsibility for the survival and development of the business in which they worked gave way to a regime in which directors and managers are seen as purely carrying out the policy decisions of the shareholders. Here it should be borne in mind that the shareholders have only one aim, namely to make a profit as quickly as possible, with all the associated volatility for their shareholdership itself.

In the United States this led to techniques in which managers, partly for self-preservation, did their utmost to drive up the financial results of the business.

They actually ceased to focus on their company's core business (e.g. Enron) but tried to maximise the financial income that the business can vaunt, and the return that it can offer its shareholders.

For that purpose they used numerous leverage techniques, which produced excellent results on paper but would ultimately undermine the business.

An institutional answer actually emerged concerning the degree to which their legal relationship with one another and with the shareholders could still prompt the management and directors to be cautious about the shareholders' objectives. Whereas, a few decades ago, traditional institutional investors such as bankers and insurers invested in industrial companies with industrial development potential, the nature of institutional shareholders has changed. Private equity funds, hedge funds and even pension funds have become major shareholders, thus gaining that power in the business. And from the moment that they can exercise power, maximising shareholder value means that all sorts of techniques are introduced into the day-to-day management: the company's debt ratio is increased to its maximum in the short term, the intrinsic capital of the business is cut wherever possible, and operational activities are reorganised to generate the maximum rapid sale value.

This leads to a sort of managerial Ponzi scheme in which the eventual owner of the property rights will be left with a virtually worthless business that will go bankrupt.

The same techniques were transposed to the financial sector. Schemes which were originally devised to cover risks were gradually separated from their economic reality.

A CDS became a naked CDS, and therefore an instrument for gambling. The same economic risk could be covered by multiple CDSs, because there was good money to be made as soon as the default event occurred. Moral hazard became an integral part of the financial devices.

But this technique enhances the shareholder value at a time when the settlement date is not yet in sight, and so long as disposal is still possible because of the Ponzi effect, based on deep liquidity.

These structures became even more complex in CDSs-squared, which were so complicated that even an experienced financier could no longer understand how they would ultimately be settled.

But so long as there were buyers, there was a lot of money to be made, and it was assumed that the developers would not be blamed. In fact, most of these transactions took place between professional contracting parties who were therefore assumed to know just how risky these investments were.

In addition, a number of macro-economic effects were not taken into account, such as the reduction in property values and – in an environment where credit had expanded inordinately owing to its leverage in relation to the real economy – events such as the crisis of confidence triggered by the subprime incident.

1.4. DESCRIPTION OF THE DANGER IN THE FINANCIAL SECTOR

As explained above, both the new accounting rules and the development of mathematical models enabled financial institutions to inflate their figures.

1. *The mechanics of accountability:* The Turner Review[4] demonstrates particularly clearly how the regulations allowed uncontrolled credit expansion, thereby endangering financial institutions:

> 'Most of the holdings of the securitised credit and the vast majority of the losses which arose, were not in the books of end investors intending to hold the assets to maturity, but on the books of highly leveraged banks and bank-like institutions.
>
> This reflected an evolution of the securitised credit model away from the initial descriptions. To an increasing extent, credit securitised and taken off one bank's balance sheet, was not simply sold through to an end investor, but:
>
> - bought by the propriety trading desk of another bank; and/or
> - sold by the first bank but with part of the risk retained via the use of credit derivatives; and/or
> - "resecuritised" into increasingly complex and opaque instruments (e.g. CDOs and CDO-'squareds'); and/or
> - used as collateral to raise short-term liquidity.
>
> In total, this created a complex chain of multiple relationships between multiple institutions, each performing a different small slice of the credit intermediation and maturity transformation process, and each with a leveraged balance sheet requiring a small slice of capital to support that function.
>
> Some banks were truly doing "originate and distribute", but the trading operations of other banks (and sometimes of the same bank) were doing "acquire and arbitrage". The new model left most of the risk still somewhere on the balance sheets of banks and bank-like institutions but in a much more complex and less transparent fashion.

Five key features of this new model played a crucial role in increasing systemic risks, contributing to the credit boom in the upswing and exacerbating the self-reinforcing nature of the subsequent downswing:
(i) The growth of the financial sector.
(ii) Increasing leverage – in many forms.
(iii) Changing forms of maturity transformation.
(iv) A misplaced reliance on sophisticated maths.
(v) Hard-wired procyclicality.'

2. *An example of reinforcing factors*: In a particularly interesting paper on whether the regulation of the method of remunerating managers increases the inclination to take decisions which are risky for the company, Lazonick[5] concludes that giving stock options encourages managers to artificially enhance the value of the business at the time of exercising those options.

   In some circumstances this appears to be a 'weapon of value destruction', as is the purchase of own shares, rather than a measure to inhibit the taking of risks detrimental to the company.
3. *Why the blind faith in financialism?* The technical causes of the crisis are gradually becoming clear. The practice of financialism spread in the context of economic convictions about shareholder value, propagated partly by Milton Friedman. This development was also eagerly accepted and promoted by the American government, which proceeded with extensive financial deregulation. At a time when the population faced a rising toll of body-bags following the attack on Iraq, the relaxation of the rules on credit was helpful in maintaining the impression of increasing prosperity, until the bubble burst.

2. GLOBALISATION OF THE CRISIS

These developments took place in the American context and more generally in the Anglo-Saxon context, but inevitably spread to Europe.

The international scale and operation of financial institutions is one of the key factors here, but the main factor is the globalisation of the type of practices adopted by financial institutions, regardless of their size, and the volatility and mobility of their managers in a 'globalised' context.

As a result of globalisation, practices common in the United States and the United Kingdom generated substantially bigger profits than the more traditional practices in other economic regions; as soon as that happened, it was more or less inevitable that those practices would become prevalent everywhere. The training of people destined to take on management functions in financial institutions also centred on the new dominant 'story' of financialism.

Technically, securitisation and the sale of claims packaged accordingly was a way of reducing the balance sheets of US banks, increasing revenue leverage, and flooding the European financial market with instruments which – moreover – appeared to be very creditworthy in view of the opinions of rating agencies.

All this was further reinforced by globally active businesses recruiting management and directors specifically trained in the Anglo-Saxon context, who therefore saw no problem at all in introducing practices that they considered totally justifiable.

If young managers are trained for a couple of decades in the conviction that the market forces regime – in which deregulation is the key word – and free self-regulation provide the best conditions for the development of a prosperous society, then they can hardly be expected not to support that view if they are also offered attractive remuneration for perpetuating this system.

In many businesses, these developments took place in good faith; a number of market players refined these techniques to their current utmost limit in the pursuit of profit. We must be aware of that.

In their contribution to the book *The Embedded Firm*, De Graaf and Williams[6] quote Alan Greenspan who, in October 2008, told the United States House Committee on Oversight and Government Reform: 'Those of us who have looked to the self-interest of lending institutions to protect shareholders' equity, myself included, are in a state of shocked disbelief', and Judge Richard Posner, one of the founders of the Law and Economics movement in the 1970s, who said: 'Some conservatives believe that the depression is the result of unwise government policies. I believe it is a market failure. The government's myopia, passivity and blunders played a critical role in allowing the recession to balloon into a depression, and so have several fortuitous factors. But without any government regulation of the financial industry the economy would still, in all likelihood, be in a depression. We are learning from it that we need a more active and intelligent government to keep our model of capitalist economy from running off the rails. The movement to deregulate the financial industry went too far by exaggerating the resilience – the self-healing powers – of laisser-faire capitalism.'

The dominance of the shareholder is expressed most clearly in a takeover. The arduous struggle for successful introduction of the takeovers directive, owing to the differences of approach between the Anglo-Saxons and the more continental legal systems, resulted in a regime that offers multiple interpretations.

The Winter Report[7] stressed that the shareholders' right to take the ultimate decision on whether or not to accept the takeover bid and the price offered, as expressed in recital 16 to the EU takeovers directive, reflects the Anglo-Saxon shareholder value approach.

However, the shareholders' dominance over the company is nowadays being called into question.

In the European context, the division of power between the various stakeholders in a company has been the focus of special attention, yet in reality the shareholder has increasing power.

Only recently, in analysing the departure of Duco Sickinghe, journalists writing in *De Tijd*[8] commented:

> 'He managed to make Telenet profitable. In addition, the weakened share became so cheap that opportunistic investors gradually returned. After a year, the share was already trading at a good profit. And things only got better. In 2007, Liberty Global upped its stake from 28% to just under 50%. From then on the Liberty approach prevailed: take on debts and reduce the capital at the same time.
>
> And at the same time make a profit. In 2008, the company's cashflow margin topped the giddy heights of 50% for the first time. In 2008, Sickinghe – who by now had become an excellent investors' masseur – announced that Telenet planned to continue rewarding loyal shareholders year after year in a tax-efficient way. Shareholders became the favourite stakeholders in the Telenet strategy. There were no major takeovers involved, even though rumours emerged over the years, e.g. about tying the knot with Mobistar. "Telenet prefers to bid for itself", read the headline in *De Tijd* in 2012.
>
> Another headline, dating from 2010: "The shareholder's benefactor". That shareholder was Liberty Media, which was getting shares for nothing thanks to the constantly increasing leverage. The small shareholders were in it together with Liberty, and they benefited too. Will they continue to do so after the Duco era? The Liberty strategy cannot last forever. Telenet still has precious little capital and mounting debts.'

That is a textbook example of the developments just described, albeit in industry rather than in the financial sector.

3. WHAT SHOULD BE DONE?

What should lawyers do? In the short term, technical measures are possible, but more fundamental thinking is also required. So lawyers need to do think about both cyclical and structural aspects.

3.1. PRIMARY RESEARCH: CYCLICAL TECHNICAL SURVEY

In order to work out what measures to adopt, we first need to take a helicopter view in which lawyers re-examine the rules on how managers, directors and shareholders should deal with one another.

Supervisors are working to tighten up both the financial rules, in terms of a whole series of ratios, and the corporate governance issues.

The big question is whether compliance with those ratios justifiably instils confidence. According to the ratios, the Belgian Dexia group was perfectly solvent when it slid into the abyss.

The measures which national supervisory authorities are taking in that area are based on the rules of European bodies (the ESAs, European Supervision Authorities: EBA, EIOPA, ESMA) and international organisations (Basel Committee, IAIS, IOSCO).

In practice, those rules are greatly influenced by the largest market players, who in this case are from the Anglo-Saxon world; their idea of a politically correct economy is thus being imposed on the rest of the world which is passively accepting their idea.

Their views therefore influence the way in which the texts should be worded and how they are adapted to the non-Anglo-Saxon context.

This means that the training of lawyers, economists and commercial engineers should give them a thorough insight into the broader social context leading to the prevailing rules, so that they realise how rules which are inappropriate to their own cultural approach should be understood and interpreted by managers and directors, and their client/shareholders.

In the organisation of the economy, lawyers are usually only involved in the final stage, in devising the legislation. However, their contribution must not be confined to just transposing concepts developed by economists, statisticians and actuaries on the basis of pure technical efficiency. This is quite apart from the fact that those other professions are also subject to a public consultation obligation.

The added value that lawyers can offer is undoubtedly their sensitivity to the changing interpretations that may be applied to a particular rule in the future.

Trained mathematicians sometimes tend to assume that they offer a solution, which once agreed upon will create stability. Heisenberg's principle, whereby the observed object is influenced by the observer, applies here.

In the financial sphere, all financial regulation will be digested after a time by the market players, and will therefore influence their behaviour in a way that is not obviously predictable. This needs to be borne in mind when the rules are being devised; rules which therefore need to undergo constant critical scrutiny.

Another question here is whether broad concepts such as 'public policy' can be used in that process and in the application of the rules by the courts.

Until recently, the concept of public policy in the financial sphere was very difficult to define.

That is undoubtedly still the case, but certain contours are beginning to emerge in the regulatory practice of supervisors.

The two elements given prominence by the regulators at international level are the maintenance of financial stability and the emphasis on inter-generational responsibility, to which should be added intra-generational responsibility, or in other words solidarity.

When issuing and applying financial regulations, lawyers will therefore have to understand and express how and when the maintenance of financial stability will affect relations between market players.

International organisations are trying to define this concept in more detail; it is a concept that is viewed mainly from a macro-economic angle.

The macro-economy then influences what can be classed as proper behaviour and honourable practice in the financial sphere.

Inter- and intra-generational responsibility is a concept that is much trickier to define, and essentially concerns the very heart of our social structures, such as new approaches to the solidarity obligation, e.g. in the context of the family. There is no doubt that the turn of the century prompted some fundamental thinking on this subject. Hayek said that once a particular level of social development has been reached, there is no going back.

That is the challenge facing the financial sector. Having seen how capitalism was an engine of progress in the industrial sphere, do we want to continue to accept that the principles of competitiveness, growth and profit allocation in the financial sphere can be regulated according to exactly the same model as in the industrial world?

The crisis that has now dragged on for five years shows that the rules on the subject need to be reviewed or at least refined.

Financiers provide a service for the real community, and thus perform a public service. In assessing the proper behaviour of stakeholders in financial institutions, the interests of one stakeholder, more specifically the shareholder and his desire for value, must not be allowed to prevail over the interests of the other stakeholders, and of society as a whole.

Cyberspace has made it possible to develop virtual worlds such as Second Life. Nevertheless, few will doubt that, while these virtual worlds allow extravagant fantasies within their own limits, that must not have a detrimental effect on the real world.

The same applies to developments in the financial world. Financing techniques have become opaque and have grown inordinately, obscuring their character as a useful tool. This requires a response, e.g. institutionally, by revising the structure of financial institutions (but there is little consensus on that, and a lot of lobbying) or, for example, by restricting certain types of activity (such as naked trading).

Be that as it may, the financial world also needs a multidisciplinary appraisal – that is including by the lawyers among us – bearing in mind that it should aim at a service-oriented architecture.[9]

3.2. SECONDARY RESEARCH: STRUCTURAL, FUNDAMENTAL SURVEY

Hector Sants, CEO of the British Financial Services Authority, talking about the requirements that will have to be imposed on financial institutions, said that '[t]here must be clear recognition of the need for institutions to contribute to the common good'.[10]

Legally, the question is therefore whether the common good, to which Sants refers, can be defined in terms of 'public policy' or in terms of other more specific legal concepts in the regulations.

But the question goes beyond that.

The crisis started as an economic and technical problem caused by granting credit without adequate links to the real economy, and thus without security in the form of hard economic assets, but it then developed into a monetary crisis. The trigger was creditors' lack of confidence in the ability of sovereign states to fulfil the guarantees that they had offered concerning support for the financial sector. This crisis centred on the European Union, and more particularly the eurozone.

It was exacerbated by the lack of united, appropriate responses by the political structure that Europe has become to the events exported to the European Union by a politically stronger entity, namely the US.

Politicians try to devise answers to the world order under the direction of the G20. However, the question is whether those answers are good enough to cope with the more fundamental problems that will increase the pressure on large parts of the financial system. The issues here are population ageing and the cost associated with mounting environmental problems, not to mention the imbalances which ensue as emerging countries strive for the same comfortable lifestyle as the now declining developed economies, and the fact that, in their efforts to control the crisis, the authorities constantly turn to quantitative solutions (increasing solvency requirements for financial institutions), thereby overlooking the fundamental question of whether these quantitative obligations are actually enough to make the system robust.

It is noticeable that some are already reducing the pursuit of the 'common good' to the slightly modified continuation of the current system, without asking whether civil society will tolerate further crises, some of which are already looming on the horizon.

On the other hand, it is argued that the current crisis is far more significant than previous ones. Some observers[11] think that the crisis represents a social revolution just as great as the change from an agricultural to an industrial society. The reason is the unprecedentedly marked global character of financialism, which means that there is no single traditional nation – or even a regional authority – that can adequately counteract the effects of this financialism.[12]

What about the future? There are two likely scenarios: either the politicians will carry on patching up the system until it breaks, or they will conduct a new, fundamental inquiry into the universal rights that people nowadays can expect to enjoy in the face of the actual threats hanging over us (ageing, environment, etc.).

The globalisation of the quest for short-term profits can be countered by global promotion of the fundamental rights to which everyone is entitled in the financial sphere. In legal terms, this means extending the range of human rights in addition to the existing socio-economic rights which pre-date financialism, taking particular care to ensure that these fundamental rights are actually enforceable by law. That is a challenge for politicians and lawyers. I hope it is not utopian.

We can be assured that the world will soon look very different from how it appears today. The established certainties about financial, monetary and fiscal law and their interconnections no longer exist. Their story has to be rewritten in the light of the experiences of the past five years.

The younger generations are entitled to a future which they can view with confidence. That is the foundation that will enable them to contribute useful innovations to our society.

To conclude with the words of Chimamanda Adichie, this book is just one storyline. Not the only one, nor the definitive one – which is just as well.

Endnotes

* Michel Flamée is a Former Vice-Chairman of the Belgian Financial Supervisory Authority and a Former Chair of the International Association of Insurance Supervisors

1. FSA, *The Turner Review*, p. 40, www.fsa.gov.uk/pubs/other/turner_review.pdf.
2. Tom Armistead, 'Jungle Ethics Financialism vs. Free Market Capitalism', 8 June 2009, http://seekingalpha.com/article/141852-jungle-ethics-financialism-vs-free-market-capitalism.
3. The views of Milton Friedman and their implications are discussed in detail in a study by Leo E. Strine Jr., 'Human Freedom and Two Friedmen: Musings on the Implications of Globalization for the Effective Regulation of Corporate Behavior' (2007), Scholarship at Penn Law, Paper No. 187, http://lsr.nellco.org/upenn_wps/187/.
4. *The Turner Review*, p. 16, www.fsa.gov.uk/pubs/other/turner_review.pdf.
5. 'Why executive pay matters to innovation and inequality', in C.A. Williams and P. Zumbansen (eds.), *The Embedded Firm*, Cambridge University Press, pp. 413–439.
6. 'The intellectual foundations of the global financial crisis: analyses and proposals for reform, in C.A. Williams and P. Zumbansen (eds.), *The Embedded Firm*, Cambridge University Press, pp. 392–393.
7. For an interesting American analysis of the EU Takeovers Directive, see: 'The EU Takeovers Directive: a shareholder or stakeholder model?', in C.A. Williams and P. Zumbansen (eds.), *The Embedded Firm*, Cambridge University Press, pp. 233–255.
8. *De Tijd*, 9 March 2013.
9. Under the aegis of the Free University of Brussels, Koen Byttebier and Michel Flamée created the Chair of 'Stewardship of Finance' to address this challenge, with our colleague Paul Jorion as the first incumbent, taking a much appreciated approach to ideas about both primary and secondary research. For example, following the measures taken in Cyprus in response to the crisis there, his blog (www.pauljorion.com/blog/?p=51610) contained a contribution from P. Sarton du Jonchay, entitled 'Cyprus, the monetary revolution on the march'. The author raised questions about international monetary law and in particular the impact of taxation in this context.
10. Speech by Hector Sants at the FSA Chartered Institute of Securities and Investments Conference on 17 June 2010, available at www.fsa.gov.uk/library/communication/speeches/2010/0617_hs.shtml.
11. See for example Alain Touraine, *Après la crise*, Seuil, 196 pages.
12. In this connection, see the remarkable latest BRICS declaration (BRICS summit on 27 March 2013).

PUBLIC ORDER AND OTHER VERMIN

Ludo CORNELIS*

1. INTRODUCTION

It took me some time before I understood that the financial and economic crisis, which started almost seven years ago in the American subprime market and brought the most important financial institutions and insurers to and over the edge of collapse, was made possible with contracts such as for example collateral debt obligations and, naked or not, credit default swaps.

Well-known economists like Stiglitz[1] and Krugman[2] speak about a crisis of the financial and economic system. That crisis affected negatively the lives of millions of citizens all over the world. Only the most affluent persons,[3] 10–25% of the population, for obvious reasons,[4] were spared and were able to go on with business as usual.

To rescue and to preserve the financial and economic system, and therefore the assets of the most affluent, billions, even trillions of dollars, yen, euros and other currencies were spent. The money, however, did not come out of the pockets of the financial troublemakers, nor even out of the pockets of the most affluent.

It was put on the table by public authorities, which, however and strangely enough, did not take control over the – rescued – financial and economic system. In order to proceed with the bailouts, sovereign states had to increase their already heavy public debts, making it more and more unlikely[5] that their taxpayers would ever be able to pay their debts.

This – for creditors – precarious situation leads to much higher interest rates, resulting in the service of interests as frightening as the reimbursement of the principal for current and future generations.

Politicians, with the help of the most affluent in society, tend to say that the financial and economic crisis is nearly over. As a matter of fact, it is not and will last as long as public finance has not recovered from the bailouts. It will take a long time and many other unpleasant events may make it even harder to achieve that result.

Financial and economic activities are part of human activities. Human activities are at the centre of (human) communities.[6] Within a community, each and every activity is shaped and regulated to make sure that it will not affect, in the short and in the long run, the essential elements of the (social) system, called a community.

How then was it possible to rush into a financial and economic crisis, endangering the financial and economic system of the world community, if not at least of the Western communities, without legal alarms going off in time? Should the law not serve and protect the community against disasters of this kind?

The fact that none of the legal alarms went off in the face of financial and/or economic developments which created a risk for the financial and economic system and therefore of the whole community, should be a nightmare for every lawyer, whatever his/her position.

The financial and economic crisis has been analysed by economists,[7] politicians,[8] sociologists,[9] philosophers,[10] anthropologists,[11] psychologists,[12] historians,[13] mathematicians,[14] chemists,[15] experts in finance,[16] etc. Lawyers however failed to do so, with a few exceptions.[17]

On the contrary, huge numbers of lawyers were involved when the knock-out of the financial and economic system needed to be avoided. Often, they were the same lawyers who had a few years earlier advised financial institutions and insurers on the very contracts and other legal acts that had propelled them in the direction of this financial and economic mess in the first place.

Could the lack of interest in an in-depth legal analysis of the causes of and remedies for the financial and economic crisis be explained by a desire to conceal the fact that existing legal alarms were possibly switched off and not re-activated?

Hoping that another and better explanation accounts for the absence of an in-depth legal study of what went wrong in the 2000s, the mere fact that contracts and other legal instruments (such as CDOs and CDSs) were at the heart of unconsidered and uncontrolled raids for profit[18] makes it mandatory that lawyers take the time to discuss the benefits (if any) and drawbacks of a financial and economic crisis engineered by legal instruments.

This chapter is intended to be a first step in that direction, the good news being that legal alarms to prevent raids of the kind experienced do exist. The bad news is that it is much harder to find out and to understand why those legal alarms remained inactivated.

This paper is limited to Belgian law, which the author is familiar with, and it could be a straightforward objection that other jurisdictions should have been included. At least two reasons justify the approach adopted.

First, having had the opportunity, some years ago, to lecture on comparative law, I know that it is not unusual that the same legal concepts (inter alia contract, liability, public order, etc.), although common to different jurisdictions, eventually have a (more or less) different content and/or scope.

A detailed and critical knowledge of the legal system under consideration is furthermore required to detect the available legal alarms, to determine their nature and finally to figure out the reasons why they were not activated in time.

The study of these questions, albeit limited to Belgian law, may inspire qualified lawyers of other jurisdictions to apply this analysis to their own legal system. This would be the best outcome of this chapter.

2. PUBLIC ORDER: A LEGAL ALARM

According to article 6 of the Belgian Civil Code, particular agreements may not be detrimental to statutes that deal with public order and public decency.[19]

Belgian lawyers are more familiar with the legal effects of a breach of a statute that deals with public order than with the concept and scope of 'public order' itself.

They believe, in general, that everything has been said about public order since the Belgian Supreme Court[20] adopted in 1948[21] the definition proposed by Henri De Page, a legal scholar.[22] Since then Belgian lawyers have thought that a statute deals with public order when it concerns, in public law, essential interests of the State and society, and in private law, when the statute determines the fundamental legal foundations of the economic and/or moral order.[23]

Satisfied with that 'definition', they even think that it is a hopeless task to improve it. It is left to the courts, i.e. to individual judges on the merits, to clarify the concept.[24] At best, public order is assimilated to the general or public interest.[25]

When, for example at the time of conclusion of a contract, parties breach a statute of public order, their contract (as a whole or in part) is void and may be invalidated by the courts.

Under Belgian law a distinction is made between different invalidities. In the case of a breach of a statute of public order, the contract is said to be affected by an absolute invalidity.[26] Absolute invalidity means that each interested person (not only the contracting parties) can claim for annulment of the contract. Subject to the rights of defence of the parties, even judges can raise *ex officio* the issue of absolute invalidity, when litigation is referred to the court. The absolute invalidity of a contract can moreover be claimed at all levels of court proceedings. Furthermore, it cannot be cleared by a confirmation or informed approval by the parties. In general, the statute of limitation provides for a period of at least ten years when an absolute invalidity is at stake.[27]

The characteristics of absolute invalidity underpin the (social) importance of statutes, with a content related to public order: contracting parties have to undergo and to act in line with those statutes; they are not allowed to deviate from them.[28]

In (legal) theory it is clear and, by definition, not open to discussion that statutes of public order have priority over the will of contracting parties.

It appears meanwhile that Belgian lawyers try to constrain the impact of statutes of public order and also with respect to the general concept of imposing public order on private law matters, particularly contracts.[29]

Although they confirm, time after time, the (theoretical) priority of public order over the will of the parties, they are, at the same time and whenever possible, looking for possibilities to weaken the (possible) impact of public order on the freedom of will, setting limits on its content and scope.

Many examples can be found.

While article 6 (as well as other provisions of the Belgian Civil Code) contains a reference to the general concept of public order, most Belgian lawyers only read in this provision a reference to statutes and/or general principles of law, dealing with matters of public order and to the related case law, astutely restricting the scope of that legal provision.[30]

How is this restriction to be explained?

When one has to determine whether a contract or other legal act complies with the general concept of public order, an appropriate and reliable definition of public order is required.

When one thinks that it is enough to determine whether a statute is to be qualified as being of public order, the intention of the legislator alone has to be determined to that effect. It is then not necessary to know what public order is all about.

By reading article 6 of the Belgian Civil Code as if it only refers to statutes of public order, Belgian lawyers avoid and probably refuse to dig into the intricate but interesting general concept of public order.[31]

The same reluctance appears from the fact that Belgian lawyers most of the time restrict the application of article 6 to the conclusion of contracts.[32] The wording of that legal provision is however broader. It states that contracts cannot depart in general from statutes that deal with a matter of public order. The performance and/or the termination of contracts, i.e. contractual obligations/duties require legal acts. Those acts fall also within the scope of article 6, but Belgian lawyers, in general, simply do not acknowledge it.[33]

It is nevertheless the poor definition of the concept of public order, which apparently satisfies most Belgian lawyers, that illustrates most of all that it is meant to remain an underdog in private law, an area that private law lawyers wish to dedicate to the freedom of will.

The definition of (a statute of) public order, proposed by Henri De Page[34] and since then approved by the Supreme Court[35] is indeed a poor and hollow one.

According to this definition, an essential interest of the State or the community in public law relates to public order, and therefore a statute dealing with a matter of this kind has to be qualified as a statute of public order.

With all due respect, the wording of that part of the definition is rather ambiguous. It does not determine how an essential interest of the State or of the community is to be distinguished from a non-essential interest. One may even be tempted to question whether it is appropriate to make such a distinction: are not all interests of the State or of the community essential interests? Furthermore how should a situation where an (essential) interest of a society (for example in the long term) conflicts with short-term interests of the State be dealt with? The definition does not address that issue.

The result is not better when it comes to private law, where (a statute of) public order is associated with the fundamental legal foundations of the economic and/or moral order.

Here too the question is how a fundamental foundation is to be differentiated from a non-fundamental one? What test is to be used to that effect? Another – unavailable – test is needed to be able to ascertain the foundations of an (economic and/or moral) order. Incidentally, why should only the economic and/or the moral order matter in private law? What about the social, cultural, ecological, environmental orders, and so on?

The financial and economic crisis moreover recalled and highlighted that an economic order may conflict with a moral order: what is the test that should be applied in dealing with and resolving such a conflict?

The definition in its application to private law is ultimately based on a misconception: it takes for granted that (fundamental) legal foundations determine the economic and/or moral order. This is contrary to the learning which is gained by living in a community. It is human activities which develop within the community that determine its economic and also moral order. After the appearance of such an economic and/or moral order, the community if satisfied by such an order may feel the need to translate those orders into legal rules, thus leading eventually to the creation of a legal system. Public order pertains amongst others to the economic and/or moral order as applied within a particular community; the legal rules, adopted to preserve inter alia such orders are their result, not their cause. The Belgian definition of public order does not adequately reflect the sequence of events leading, first, to inter alia an economic and moral order and, only afterwards, to their legal transcription.

When Belgian legal scholars pay attention to the significance of public order in (private) law they do, in general, not challenge the definition, proposed by the *Cour de cassation*, but instead approve it.[36] They state that it is difficult, if not impossible, to improve on it. In their opinion, it can be left to the judge to determine in each case on the merits what public order is about. According to them, there is no need to proceed to an in-depth analysis of public order. They consider public order to be rather a matter of fact, than of law.

No wonder, therefore, that the understanding of public order according to this approach changes from one legal scholar to another and from one judge to another.[37]

Furthermore the delegation to individual judges of the power to decide what is and what is not related to public order in each particular case speaks volumes about the vulnerability of its definition.

This delegation weakens further the importance and impact of public order on private law: the decisions of judges on the merits only bind the parties involved. No general rules for instance can be inferred from them.[38] Case law is therefore by its nature, fragmentary. As a result, it is difficult to understand why a particular situation is in one case judged by one court to be in breach of public order and not in others. In case law, public order becomes a *fait divers*.

Another question arises: if the judge on the merits is believed to be able to determine what public order is about and, at the same time, to apply that concept, as he/she sees it, to the case brought to court, why do other lawyers and, in particular legal scholars, assert that they are unable to say more about public order than what is to be found in the (poor) definition of the *Cour de cassation*?

All these escape routes that make it possible to turn around the concept and not to address the in-depth analysis of public order reinforce the finding that the relationship between public order and (Belgian) lawyers is, at best, ambiguous.

On the one hand, they declare (but are they serious?) that nobody can act in breach of public order, but on the other hand, are far from enthusiastic about public order, using each and every opportunity to reduce its (theoretical) importance.

Is the conclusion different when public order is associated with the public or the general interest?[39] The association of public order with the public or the general interest appears to be of no help at all. To replace a poorly (if at all) defined concept, such as public order, with another poorly (if at all) defined concept, such as the general or the public interest, does not move things forward. It appears to be a skilful manoeuvre to abruptly shut down discussions on public order, making it pointless to even enter into a discussion. Lawyers clearly know how to proceed when they encounter a question they dislike.

Moreover, it takes very little time to find out that Belgian law does not provide a definition of what is covered by the general or public interest. A satisfactory test to distinguish the public (general) interest from private interests is also missing.

The idea to replace the concept of public order with the concept of public (general) interest thus comes to a dead end or appears to be a vicious circle, as one may even consider that the best way to define the public (general) interest is to associate it with public order.

To fathom the mystery of public order (and, at the same time, that of public-general interest) much more is required: the boundaries of the legal system and the comfort it provides to lawyers must be given up, at least for a moment. To determine public order, attention must be paid to the roots of what a (human) community is and what it requires.

3. THE HISTORY OF PUBLIC ORDER

Legal history had something else in mind with regard to public order than the (current) achievements with regard to the concept under Belgian law.

The authors of the *Code civil*, in 1804, had a clear view on public order:[40] they placed article 6 at the outset of the Civil Code not by mere accident, but because they wanted to emphasise that human activities leading to contracts or other legal acts are always subordinated to the organisation of the community in which they take place.

They addressed public order as a general concept and principle dominating private law and, especially, contracts and other legal acts, although at the same time they took into account that public order can be the subject of statutes.

Putting this legal provision at the outset of the *Code civil*, they also made it clear that public order is, in a certain way, a point of interconnection between public and private law, allowing public law concerns to find their way into private law.

The authors of the *Code civil*, in doing so, wanted to avoid parties with agreements or other legal acts being able to negatively impact on the community as structured by public law. In case of (direct or indirect) conflict between an agreement or another legal act and the structure adopted by the community, the agreement (or other legal act) should have no legal effect, as the structure of the community always has to prevail.

They have set a legal alarm in place that should activate or be activated when the anticipated or actual effects of agreements or other legal acts are not or no longer consistent with the structure the community has adopted and is looking for. This legal alarm was called 'public order'.

The same idea reappears in article 1133 of the *Code civil*. According to that provision, the cause (the motives, the reasons) of any contractual obligation has to comply with public order and with public decency.[41] Belgian courts, however, only consider the determinant motives when they apply this legal provision.[42] Motives that are found to be not determinant are not taken into account, even if they may conflict with public order. This case law again reduces the impact of public order on agreements and other legal acts. On the other hand, the same courts find that the subject of each contractual obligation has also to comply with public order and public decency,[43] although no legal provision is to be found in the *Code civil* to that effect.

The authors of the Civil Code could have been more precise when in article 6 they addressed the relationship between public and private law. They for instance could have stated that public order (and/or public decency) introduces public law concerns into the sphere of private law. The truth is that they were quite plain on the matter. Clever lawyers, as practitioners of private law generally are most of the time, have no problem in determining what the authors of the *Code civil* intended by article 6.

They therefore know that they are no longer acting consistently with the legislator's intention when they leave it to the courts to decide, on a case-by-case basis, the requirements of public order, while no appropriate and reliable definition has been made available to do so.

Clever lawyers also know and understand that the concept of public order refers to the (political, social, ethical, moral, cultural, economic, etc.) structure of a community however small or big it may be. Once that structure has been conceived and put in place by the community members and/or their representatives, lawyers can enter the scene and work out rules of public law to protect and preserve that (already existing) structure. The structured organisation of a particular community is its public order, consolidated by public law, and it prevails over private law.

The same clever lawyers know and understand that they do not need to focus on so-called mandatory law to find out what public order is about, but that this concept, first of all, requires an in-depth knowledge of the (political, social, ethical, moral, cultural, economic, etc.) structured organisation of the community they are serving.

All this was so obvious to the authors of the *Code civil* when they drafted articles 6 and 1133 that they thought it superfluous, or overlooked the need, to define what public order means and guarantees within a community.

This imperfection of the *Code civil* does not alter the fact that 'clever' lawyers know (and always have known) that the concept of public order is only helpful in the legal field when an appropriate and reliable definition is made available. In its absence, as is the case unfortunately in Belgian law, the legal alarm that public order is meant to be is indeed switched off.

In other words, without an appropriate and reliable definition, public order is left to its own fate, a situation that cannot be applauded.

4. ARE THERE BRAVE LAWYERS LEFT?

How is this (troubling) reserve of lawyers to be explained when public order turns up?

Do they consider it to be too burdensome to determine what public order means within their community? Are they too lazy, too shy or too modest to take plain positions about public order and its impact on their community? Do they think their training does not allow them to say something significant about the political, social, ethical, moral, cultural, economic, etc. order of the community they are part of?

Taking into account the energy which lawyers can spend on legal issues or when they have to work out (innovative) legal instruments, the answers are clearly to be found elsewhere. In general, lawyers are neither shy nor modest: they are trained to be leaders in legal issues, and public order for sure is part of the legal issues they face. Most of the time, their training also includes political, social, ethical, moral, economic, etc. issues. Accustomed to work with legal technicalities, the technicality of public order cannot scare or paralyse them.

Could it be that they are reluctant vis-à-vis public order due to a (kind of) conflict of interest? Lawyers know better than anyone that public order is related to mandatory rules, arising from statutes, case law, general principles of law, and eventually the concept of public order itself. Mandatory rules address situations, activities, situations and/or events within the community. Practising law without having to think about mandatory rules makes life a lot easier for lawyers. When their principals are in trouble or are looking for new possibilities, address new 'challenges' and expect solutions from 'their' lawyers, public order, being a legal alarm, not only makes life harder for them, but also puts them at risk.

On the one hand, when looking for the results expected by their principals, lawyers have to take public order and its impact into account. In these circumstances, public order may make it impossible to work out the solutions the principal wants to achieve. On the other hand, any mistake with regard to public order may amount to a legal malpractice with an ensuing liability risk.

Public order becomes an inconvenience, even a nuisance not only for the principals who do not want to take care of public order, but also for practising lawyers.

Together with their clients, they may feel more comfortable with an unclear, and eventually obscure, concept of public order. Leaving public order in a grey area allows solutions to be found in the same grey area to the benefit of the principals. Moreover, when the lawyer's contribution comes under investigation, it leaves room for discussion, loopholes for malpractice and the ensuing liability risk of the lawyer.

From this point of view, it looks as if lawyers, when they neglect public order, for example by withholding an appropriate and reliable definition, are more concerned about their own situation and/or advantages than about the structured organisation of the community they are expected to serve.

The declining interest of lawyers in public order, even their unspoken hostility, is but a symptom of a dramatic development in their behaviour, although they claim it is still in line with what they are expected to do from a community point of view.

Of course, when questioned, the vast majority of lawyers will dispute this finding. They know that a finding of this kind undermines their position within the community as it affects the confidence the community may place in them.

The finding may however be a point of no return for lawyers. Either they remember that law and the administration of justice are public services designed, organised and financed to the (exclusive) benefit of the community, or they consider that law and the administration of justice are but tools to be used by them to the benefit of their principals and ultimately to their own benefit.

Taking for granted that law and the administration of justice are but tools available to the benefit of lawyers and their principals is a major mistake, distorting the two public services concerned. It interferes with their objectives and does so to the detriment of the community.

This is not to say that lawyers cannot take care of their own interests or those of their principals.

They are entitled to do so, but only as long as their practice is in accordance with the applicable legal rules. What matters is the application of the legal rules, within the framework of the administration of justice when litigation is at stake. Taking care of the interests of the principals or of the lawyer's own interests is clearly subordinated to the legal rules, when they are applicable.

To reverse the order of priority, putting private interests before public order, for instance the application of legal rules of that nature, puts the lawyer in an off-side position.

In other words, in order to comply with the public services they are expected to provide to the community (law, administration of justice), lawyers need an appropriate and reliable definition of public order.

Only when such a definition is made available can public order show its teeth and be enforced.

5. ANY FUTURE FOR PUBLIC ORDER?

At this very moment, the wings of public order are silently clipped in private law. In public law, on the contrary, the concept appears to be better accepted and more vigorous.

Public order (and also public decency) appears frequently in international treaties. The Union Treaty and the European Convention for the Protection of Human Rights and Fundamental Freedoms (ECHR) are such examples.

They hold that national legal provisions imposing restrictions within the Union on the free movement of goods, workers, services, capital or payments, on the freedom of establishment[44] or on human rights and fundamental freedoms[45] may be justified and therefore upheld because of inter alia public order (or public decency) prevailing in a Member State.

There should be no doubt about it: fundamental (European) treaties confirm that (national) public order supersedes the rights and/or freedoms granted to individuals and to the legal entities individuals are using.

When an exception is made to a rule, it means that the idea making the exception is more important than the idea laid down in the (general) rule.

To be clear: public order (public decency) prevails over individual rights and freedoms, even when sanctified in fundamental international treaties.

It is therefore no surprise that in recent case law of the European Court of Justice, regulatory measures enacted by a Member State dealing with additives in victuals, with the financial stability of its social security system, with the avoidance or by-passing of taxation, with restrictions of games of chance etc. are upheld based inter alia on the general concept of public order even if the regulation at stake hampers the free movement of goods, workers, services, capital or payments or is a burden to the freedom of establishment.[46]

The approach is the same in the case law of the Belgian Constitutional Court when the principles of (legal) equality and the prohibition of discrimination are applied. According to the Constitutional Court, a regulation in favour of the security of the country, of the public security, for the avoidance of criminal offences or for the protection of human decency is to be assessed taking into account the general principle of public order in a democratic community.[47] A regulation that is discriminatory to some extent can be justified and upheld if this is required for the sake of public order.

More than one lesson can be drawn from public law when it comes to public order. First, in public law nobody seems to be afraid of the concept, even in the absence of an overall definition. Its content and scope seem to be a common good in public law, making it possible to apply the concept in all (and very different) areas. Second, public order is not restricted to legal provisions. On the contrary, it appears to be a general principle or concept, required by and part of the organisation of a democratic society. Conceived as a general principle, it covers all possible situations, acts or events.

Despite practitioners of private law not being used to the feeling, as they believe – in general – that private law is more important than public law, humility has to emerge. How can it, indeed, be explained that public order is at the zenith in public law and almost outlawed in private law? How can practitioners of private law be taken seriously when they state that it is very hard, if not impossible, to outline an appropriate and reliable definition or test of public order, while its content and scope are almost a common good in public law? How can they claim that public order should be relevant only with regard to legal provisions or rules, leaving unanswered the question of how private law has to deal with the general concept of 'public order', while that concept is at the heart of public law? How can they pretend that public order is a question to be considered at the conclusion of contracts alone, while it governs all human activities at all stages in public law?

Are the practitioners of private law saved by the bell or can they come up with a smoking gun? Unfortunately for them, only in their dreams.

It is of course an easy thing to suggest that private law surpasses or should surpass public law. The origins of private law point to another conclusion. If there is something such as private law, its origins are always to be found in public law and more in particular in the public services of legislation and of the administration of justice. The foundations of private law, in other words, are locked in public law.

Due to its (public law) origins, private law has to contribute to the public order put in place by public law.

Can practitioners of private law, who nevertheless still want to believe that public law should be superseded by private law, get out of trouble by stating that the discussion is coming to nothing as long as no appropriate and reliable definition of public order is available. Furthermore can they hold that it is an illusion to await or expect such a definition, public order being but an open and vague concept? Is it true that public order is an open, vague concept of the same nature as many others in private law such as reasonableness, fairness, good faith, abuse of right?

Being the champions of vague and open concepts, designed by them to make everything and its contrary possible at the same time,[48] depending on the circumstances, practitioners of private law can indeed make the argument that public order, in the absence of an appropriate and reliable definition, leaves it to the individual judge to determine what public order requires, what the same individual judge also has to do when he/she applies reasonableness, fairness, good faith or any other open, vague concept.

Their argument sounds good: in private law, they claim that there is no need to add another open, vague concept (public order) to those already available. With those already available concepts every result can still be achieved as it is the individual judge who will appreciate and determine the result he/she finds reasonable, fair, just, in good faith, etc. in accordance with public order. It all boils down to the decision of the individual judge, whatever may be the open, vague concept referred to. No tears may be shed therefore on the loss of one open, vague concept (public order), as long as many others are left, ready and able to do the job that each and every open, vague concept can take care of.

At the outset, indeed, this argument makes sense. However, all depends on the content and scope, assigned to the concept of public order. If public order is but a synonym of reasonableness, fairness, good faith, abuse of rights or any similar open, vague concepts, then the argument for sure should conclude the discussion.

So, is there any ground for it? In Belgian law, no legal scholar or case law has yet defended this point of view. On the contrary, the (poor) definition of public order, taken into account by the Belgian *Cour de cassation* does not associate public order with reasonableness, fairness, good faith, abuse of right, or any other similar open, vague concept.

Looking closer at that (poor) definition in order to detect possible links with the considered open, vague concepts it seems, however, obvious that reasonableness, fairness, justice, good faith, the prohibition of any abuse of rights, to an extent still to be determined, are part of the moral order governing a community. If there is an overlap between public order and the other (open, vague) concepts, it is thus only a partial one. Political, social, cultural, economic concerns are not as such addressed when it comes to reasonableness, fairness, justice, good faith, etc.

If this were the only observation on the interconnection between public order and other (open, vague) concepts, practitioners of private law would have no trouble finding out that political, social, cultural, economic concerns may be underlying moral/ethical judgements. They will claim that their argument is to be upheld: public order is but another presentation of other open, vague concepts and therefore private law should not bother about it.

To fully understand the difference between public order and other (open, vague) concepts, one has to consider the reasons why those other (open, vague) concepts have surfaced and operate in private law.

Reasonableness, fairness, justice, good faith and other similar open, vague concepts have been elaborated in private law not only by legislators and courts, but also by legal scholars and practitioners as (legal?) instruments that allow the individual judge, in interaction with the litigating parties, to regulate their situation in conformity to the best of his/her knowledge and belief.

Concealed by the open, vague concept is to be found a delegation of powers, not easy to justify, ultimately from legislators to individual judges and also to the practitioners of private law, who – with the help of those open, vague concepts – have the opportunity to strive for a decision in favour of their principals.

At the same time, this approach requires a lot of confidence in the individual judge and in his/her capacity to 'judge', as the decision depends on the best of his/her knowledge and belief. Knowledge and beliefs differ from person to person and this is not different when that person is a judge.

Having been a practitioner of private law for more than thirty years, I have learned that judges are eager to figure out decisions balancing the interests of the litigating parties in the way they, to the best of their knowledge and belief, consider and feel reasonable, fair, just and in line with good faith. There is nothing surprising about this finding: the case is brought to court by the parties and their lawyers because the parties disagree on the balance of mutual interests. Reasonableness, fairness, justice, good faith and similar concepts, in most if not all cases, deal with a litigated balance of interests. With those (open, vague) concepts the judge arrives at a balance of interests that he/she believes to be appropriate, taking all the available information into account.[49]

As such, political, social, cultural, economic concerns emerge rarely in court. Even moral and ethical concerns at a community level are not often part of the discussions in court and therefore, of the court rulings.

The administration of justice focuses mainly on the interests of the parties involved and the balance they should respect, once the court (the judge) has rendered its judgement.

Public order, on the contrary, has other aims. The aim of public order is not by any means to increase the power of individual judges or to focus on balancing the interest of the litigating parties. Quite the contrary, its aim is to put the courts (the judges), the parties and their lawyers under a duty to take into consideration – at all times and without any exceptions allowed – the structured organisation of the community (becoming, in legal terms, its public order), which supersedes any balance between the interests in dispute, and also the findings of judges, to the best of their knowledge and belief.

Reasonableness, fairness, justice, good faith and similar concepts are tailored at the level of the parties' interests and decided upon in court by the judges, when they administer 'justice'. With regard to public order, the parties, their lawyers and judges are ruled by concerns that refer to the community and its structured organisation. Those concerns have nothing to do with the interests of the parties at stake or with the best knowledge and belief of the judge, who has to administer 'justice'.

Reasonableness, fairness, justice, good faith and similar concepts thus cannot replace public order in private law: they deal with concerns that are wholly different.

6. BACK TO THE FUTURE WITH PUBLIC ORDER

Public order serving other purposes than the open, vague concepts lawyers are used to in private law, its objectives remain out of reach or, at least, remain hazardous in the absence of an appropriate and reliable definition.

For the reasons explained,[50] the definition considered by the Belgian *Cour de cassation* cannot be called appropriate and reliable.

One or more test(s) have to be determined to distinguish acts, events, situations, etc., in accordance with public order and those in conflict with it, despite the (general) opinion that it would be a 'mission impossible' to improve the definition of the *Cour de cassation*.

How to handle this challenge?

It may be a good idea to refer to dictionaries in order to remember what the words 'public' and 'order' mean in different languages.[51] They confirm that public order refers to the organised structure/the structured organisation of a community or society, based on rules, called also a system. This specification shows the way, but of course needs further explanation.

It seems obvious that public order first of all requires a community/society. This brings to the table an issue that has been heavily discussed over the years: which came or has to come first, the community (the group) or the individual? It may be a question still confounding philosophers or some right-wing politicians, but this discussion has long since lost its importance or at least became a lost battle.

One cannot have one's cake and eat it: even in small groups of individuals, each and every one of them has to respect the targets, operations and processes determined within the group. If an individual within the (small) group refuses or fails to do so, it will not take much time before the others let him/her know that the question is simple: in or out. If an individual wants to benefit from the achievements of the group, he/she will have to contribute and, in any case, will not be allowed to endanger the common goods/services achieved by the group (the community). It works like that in small groups and the same applies to large communities.

In other words, if an individual wants to benefit from what a community has put in place, he/she has to contribute to the community and will not be allowed to endanger common goods/services produced by that community. If an individual is not disposed to do so, because of his/her opinion about individual freedom, he/she has to turn away from the community and should take care of him/herself without counting on the efforts and achievements of the community.

Even in Western countries, individuals who think freedom is the ultimate value can find places where they can live without any surrounding community, its organisation and achievements.

In Western countries, individuals who, for the sake of their freedom, are ready to turn their back to every community and to organise their lives and those of their families, without support of common goods/services, are however very rare.

For those who want to remain within the community in order to benefit (by day and by night) from its common goods/services, the die is cast. Their membership in the community includes that they accept its organisation and that they are willing to contribute to its achievements. Being a member of the community and having the benefit of common goods/services it provides, and at the same time claiming the freedom not to contribute and even to put its organisation in danger, are contradictions a community should not tolerate.

Membership of a community and individual freedom moreover are not part of the same playing field. Membership of a community leaves room for individual freedom, subject to its consistency with what the community stands for. On the contrary, when individual freedom is privileged and is allowed to supersede the community, nobody can expect the other community members to contribute to the achievements and common goods/services the community is looking for. Such goals will have to be met by each individual person, making any organisation impossible.

To put it simply: individual freedom leads to individual orders. A structured and organised community, on the contrary, is a prerequisite of public order. A community always requires organisation. Without organisation, there will be no community, but rather a gathering of individuals living apart, together.

The organisation is determined by the targets, processes and operations a community selects. The selected targets, processes and operations will rule all activities, situations and events within the community, irrespective of their political, social, economic, religious and cultural nature. Each activity, situation or event will have to meet the targets, processes and operations selected by the community to that effect. Political, social, economic, cultural, religious activities, situations and events have their own particular targets, processes and operations, again selected by the community.

As a result, the organisation amounts to a set of (political, social, economic, cultural, religious) rules, structuring the activities, situations and events within the community concerned and becomes a system at an overall level.

The added value of a community lies in its achievements, taking the form of (common) goods/services which the community provides to all its members. Those goods/services may relate to political, social, economic, cultural, religious activities, situations or events, but – in any case – all members will be allowed to benefit from them. In general, these common goods are considered to be out of reach if it is left to individuals to produce them.

Their achievement requires a structured organisation at the level of the community.

Once a community has settled on a set of rules that are determined by already selected targets, processes and operations and resulting in common goods/services, it starts to worry about the survival of its structured organisation. These worries lead to still other common goods/services, especially legislation and the administration of justice. Rules of a political, social, economic, cultural, moral, religious and ethical nature are thus transformed into legal rules, to be applied when their conditions are fulfilled. Through legal rules and the administration of justice, a community aims to protect its structured organisation for the benefit of all its members. To that effect the legal rules are associated with sanctions and compulsory treatment, in case of breach.

The foregoing lines may be theoretical and even boring. They still give the opportunity to remember that legal rules only matter because of the underlying political, social, economic, moral, cultural concerns and choices that lead to a structured organisation a community has selected, adopted and put in place.

In other words, when a legal rule is to be analysed, the lawyer should keep in mind the political, social, moral, ethical, cultural, economic rules, often interconnected, put in place, to achieve targets, processes and operations, selected by the community. No legal rule stands thus by itself; its foundations always refer to political, social, moral, ethical, cultural, economic concerns and choices, made by the community and leading to common goods/services provided to all its members.

It may be true that the law, due to case law, regulations and deregulations, has become difficult to understand and to handle. The wilderness it became however did not change its very nature: an instrument, conceived as a common good/service, to protect the structured (political, social, economic, moral, ethical, cultural, etc.) organisation of a particular community.

Every legal rule is connected with and determined by the structured organisation of the community, having adopted that particular legal rule. Whatever the prevailing circumstances and individual interests may be when a legal rule is applied, its application has always to be consistent with the underlying structured organisation.

Having pointed out that public order only makes sense within a community and that a community is necessarily a structured organisation, the most important and difficult part is still ahead.

As public order depends on selected targets, processes and operations in order to provide common goods/services[52] to the community members when they engage or are engaged in whatever activities, situations or events, it becomes important to know more about those (selected) targets, processes and operations. Their selection, of course, is a question of politics. To understand the process of selection and its results, one has to know who has or will have the power to make the selection on behalf of the community.

In Western democracies based on the fundamental rule of the universal[53] and single[54] right to vote, the power to select targets, processes and operations belongs to the majority of the community members. Elections lead to representatives, who have to act in the name and on behalf of the majority of the community members, it being understood that their decisions and choices will apply to the whole community, including its minorities.

What can, in general, be learned about this majority of community members? In short, a lot: the strongest, most affluent and most intelligent (and even the stronger, more affluent and more intelligent) individuals never constitute as such a majority within a community. Compared to them, it is the less strong, affluent and intelligent individuals who secure the majority of votes. As a result, their representatives, of course, will have to take care of the less strong, affluent and intelligent individuals. Their voters expect protection from them inter alia against the stronger and the strongest, the more and the most affluent, and the more and the most intelligent, as those minorities obviously would take decisions to their benefit and thus to the detriment of the less strong, affluent and intelligent majority, if they had the power to do so within the community concerned. When representatives neglect (too much) the concerns of their voters, the majority will turn to other representatives who promise to take better care of its concerns.

On paper, democracy improves the living conditions of the majority of the community members and has to result in less – material – inequality between the majority and the minorities. In the real world, things are more complex as the still growing – material – inequality between community members, even in Western democracies, demonstrates.[55]

On the one hand, the stronger and the strongest, the more and the most affluent and the more and the most intelligent individuals often join the majority and, taking advantage of their strength and experience, are able to influence the decision-making process of the representatives. It is even not unusual for them to present themselves for election and become elected or at least to have strong ties with representatives they support.

On the other hand, the stronger and strongest, the more and most affluent and the more and most intelligent individuals join forces and start lobbying the representatives to avoid decisions they dislike or to have decisions made in their favour.

Finally, the balance of power between the majority and the minority within a community is determined by the fact that each of them, albeit to a different extent, needs the other to keep the community operational. The minorities of the stronger and strongest, the more and most affluent and the more and most intelligent individuals know that only the majority keeps 'things'[56] running. The majority of the less strong, rich and intelligent individuals knows that their community needs the contribution of the minorities to be ongoing and balanced.

As long as the representatives of the majority within the community have the overall power to determine its targets, processes and operations, the community can be called a democracy, even with minorities of stronger and strongest, more and most affluent and more and most intelligent individuals influencing the decision making of the representatives in different ways.

Unfortunately, this no longer is the situation in a lot of Western democracies, if not in most of them.[57] For different reasons and in different ways, it has for almost thirty years been accepted as a matter of fact that a (small) minority of the most affluent[58] has, through corporations and other legal entities organised at the international level, concentrated disproportionate (financial/economic) power. This power exceeds at a national level the power(s) of the represented majorities.

The shifting of power from majorities to a (small) minority of the most affluent (and their followers) has dramatically changed the balance of powers. The bailouts due to the financial and economic crisis of 2007–2013,[59] and the incapacity afterwards of Western leaders to impose on the financial sector regulation to prevent a repeat of the crisis, are but some examples of that changed balance of powers.[60]

It is a major challenge for Western democracies to reverse the current situation and to reallocate the overall powers to the represented majority, where they belong. Everything is still in place for such reallocation: the majorities only have to make it clear to their representatives that they must have the guts to address the issue and to use their powers in the interest of the actual and future majorities within communities, called democracies.

In a democracy, the representatives take care of and protect the majority of the less strong, affluent and intelligent individuals. They do so by determining the targets, processes and operations within the community, and their decisions and choices will apply to all community members. Before a community can think about flat screens, iPads, leisure, holidays, etc., representatives necessarily focus on the fundamental living conditions of the (voting) majority: physical and psychological integrity; security of each person, his/her family and their goods; healthcare; education; and so on.

They improve or guarantee those living conditions when they design, put in place, manage and finance 'common goods/services', placed at the disposal of all community members.

When taking care of those fundamental living conditions, the representatives will moreover take into account that humans are far from perfect and that they aspire to self-determination (although being eager to benefit from the advantages the community is providing them).

It is well known that human nature is flawed.[61] That flaw is the result of the struggle for life and of the survival of the fittest, over the ages. Even educated humans, under circumstances, can become cruel, unpredictable and dangerous, not only in respect to other living species and for 'Mother Earth', but also to other humans. Propelled by this flaw, humans never have enough and always want more. The distinction between what belongs to me and what belongs to the other or to the community is, in human eyes, rather unclear and subject to change.

That flaw is present in each and every human: from the most affluent to the poorest, from the strongest to the weakest, from the most intelligent to the least. To keep it under control, a lot of education and social and self-control are needed. Impossible to eradicate, the flaw often emerges and tends to take control over human behaviour. In order to improve their own position in whatever area, humans may be prepared to intentionally cause harm to other humans or to the community. When it comes to fraud, humans – acting under control of the flaw – proceed with an unlimited imagination. No community can approve or allow fraudulent behaviour as it obstructs its structured organisation and does place it in danger. Its representatives, therefore, must take serious note of the flaw, work out processes to keep it under control and operations to sanction humans when they give in to it.

In their short time on earth, humans question the meaning of life and of human activities.[62] The best answer yet provided is that each human should be allowed to determine how he/she wants to organise his/her lifetime, within the community he/she belongs to. Self-determination (others call it freedom), reviewed as a valid answer to human finiteness, entrusts humans control over their lifetime: they can plan their lives and make dreams come true. It moreover makes humans responsible for their acts, words and decisions.

The level of self-determination depends, however, on the structured organisation of the community. Indeed, the community (its representatives) determines the living conditions of its members and, in doing so, provides leverage to self-determination.

It should be obvious that the use made of self-determination has to be in line with the structured organisation of the community that provides to each member the living conditions which allow him/her to enjoy the pleasure of self-determination.

In a democracy, ruled by the majority of its members, the living conditions are designed, organised, managed and financed as public services.[63] The representatives of the majority have to put and to keep public services in place to the benefit of the community (and most of all, of their voters) guaranteeing their security, their safety, their health, their education and so on. Of course, the design, organisation, management and funding of those public services require many choices. Within each target (security, safety, health, education, etc.) many other secondary or subordinated targets are to be considered. This also applies to the processes and the operations of public services. The choices made will determine not only the scope of the public services, but also their quality.

The community, the balance of powers between its (voting) majority and its minorities, the elected representatives and the selected targets, processes and operations all boil down into specific public services, put in place to the benefit of all community members. Some public services guarantee survival, physical as well as psychological integrity, security, safety, healthcare, education, mobility, etc., determined by the level of development of each community. Others deal with the flaw in human nature, protecting each member from the flaw that affects all other members and vice versa. The array of public services allows the community members to determine, with more possibilities at hand, what to do with their lifetime, however always in accordance with the organisation of that community.

The structured organisation that a community has to set up and maintain in order to be able to provide its members with public services, in accordance with selected targets, processes and operations, is its public order.

Three different issues are to be distinguished. The first refers to the structured organisation that public services need, from the very start, in order to be designed, put in place, managed and financed. At the same time, the second element refers to the benefits, made available to all community members by the designed, organised, operated and financed public services. Finally, the third element determines the balance between the structured organisation of the community and the self-determination left to the decision of each community member.

The paramount importance of the structured organisation makes it necessary that the structured organisation always supersedes individual decisions and/or interests, even the ones of the most affluent (or of the legal entities they use), as the survival of the community, in the long run, depends on it.

Human activities of whatever nature are only tolerated in any particular community when consistent with its structured organisation, i.e. the public services it is putting at the disposal of its members. Acts, including legal acts, hampering or impairing the organisation, the operation and/or the financing of public services, require and justify an immediate response of the community concerned, by means of other public services, designed to that effect (such as law and the administration of justice).

It would be a fallacy to believe that the concept of public order becomes redundant once it is understood and accepted that it is linked to the design, the organisation, the operation and the financing of public services.

A good understanding of the public services made available is of course a great help, but public order is more than that. It is the (legal) remedy imagined and put in place to determine when a human act (including a legal act) is incompatible with the structured organisation of the community. This assessment has to deal not only with the immediate effects of the act considered, but also with its effects on a long term and, very importantly, its effects on the structured organisation should the act become generalised.

As a result, public order is not to be conceived as the exclusive hunting ground of legislators. It is true that they determine, in democracies, the structured organisation of the community and, moreover, can adopt statutes, stating explicitly that they deal with matters of public order.

Courts and, more generally, lawyers indeed still have the duty to determine whether or not any particular act is consistent with public order (assessed also in the long term and/or when generalised). It is impossible for legislators to make an assessment of (individual) acts, taking into account all the surrounding circumstances. This is the task of lawyers and, at the same time their justification within their community. They have to act as whistle-blowers: infringements of public order have to be detected by them and submitted to the attention of their principals, of the courts and/or of legislators. They of course have to refrain from any participation in acts breaching public order. If a principal wants his/her lawyer to act against public order, the latter has to end his/her appointment. Should a lawyer 'forget' those principles, he/she may be jointly liable, together with the principal, for the damage caused to the community.[64] A lawyer in distress with public order should (be able to) turn to his/her bar or other professional organisation not only to get reassurance about what to do, but also to avoid the legal profession as such getting involved in activities that hurt public order.

7. RETHINKING SOME POSITIONS IN PRIVATE LAW

This chapter is not the place to deal with all matters that require rethinking of positions taken for granted in the law of contracts, obligations (duties) and torts and eventually inconsistent with public order.

In this chapter only a few examples are addressed of situations where private law does not properly take into account the concept of public order.

The first example tackles credit default swaps, a 'financial' instrument, developed by lawyers to please financial institutions and also from time to time insurers.[65] Credit default swaps (CDSs) are contracts. Their complex denomination disguises what they are all about and this disguise is not a stroke of (bad) luck. To understand CDSs some explanations are therefore needed.

When a person grants a credit to another person, he/she, in doing so, accepts at the same time, a financial risk on its debtor. The debtor may indeed be unable to reimburse the credit when due and/or to serve the agreed interest, when matured. To get rid of that (financial) risk, the creditor may be ready to pay an amount to a person or legal entity, who accepts to take over the already existing risk on the debtor. Against payment that third party (the protection seller) will, in the case of a (to be defined) default of the debtor, pay the creditor (the protector buyer) the (possibly agreed) amount(s) and thereafter try to recover from the debtor.

This situation is well known in insurance law and handled as a credit insurance, a regulated instrument, only to be offered by a (licensed) insurance company, which, to that effect, has to comply with a vast array of regulations in order to make sure that it will be able, except in extraordinary situations, to honour its (contractual) obligations when an (insured) risk materialises.

Instead of turning to credit insurances, financial institutions, having a lot of financial risks on their books, 'invented' another mechanism with exactly the same effects, but, with the help of lawyers, they called it credit default swaps.

Financial institutions have important credit claims on their books. In order to replace those credits by liquidity, more interesting for their shareholders and upper management, they, first, imagined credit debt obligations (CDOs). To that effect, they assign their credit claims to special purpose vehicles (SPV), incorporated and financed by them. The SPV pays a transfer price to the financial institution, allowing the financial institution to make a profit. It is not unusual for the funding of the transfer price to be provided by the financial institution or by a company belonging to the same group of companies. In many cases only the claim is assigned, while the guarantees against the final debtor remain with the assigning financial institution.

Within the SPV the bunch of assigned claims is cut up and packed in credit debt obligations (CDOs), a new 'financial instrument' with a risk level depending on the underlying (slices of) credits and their associated contractual regime.

Once the creditworthiness of the CDOs has been assessed by (in the meantime famous) rating agencies, the CDOs are sold by the SPV as securities with a high return (part of the interests that the final debtors have to pay) to other financial institutions, who, in turn, present them to their clients.

A lot can already be said about the (in)validity of credit debt obligations and the associated contractual clauses, but here and now only credit default swaps (CDSs) are investigated.

The purchaser of CDOs obtains a 'financial instrument', with a high return, promised by the SPV, but, at the same time, takes over from the SPV and the original financial institution, the financial risk of default of the ultimate debtor. The purchaser, of course, knows nothing about the ultimate debtor and, in general, he/she has not acquired any collateral, settled by the debtor. As the expected high return depends on the performances by the unknown debtor(s), potential purchasers of CDOs may feel uncomfortable and wish that risk to be under control.

With a CDS, the financial risk inherent to CDOs is shifted from their purchasers, who pay a 'premium' to that effect, to another party (in general a financial institution or even – from time to time – an insurer), who undertakes to make contractual payments if the financial risk (a default from the ultimate debtor), occurs.

Here the shoe begins to pinch: in a CDS the protection seller is not a regulated insurer, although its activity, despite the misleading name given to the 'financial' product, is nothing less than a credit insurance and thus a regulated product. With a CDS, the protection seller receives premiums from the protection buyers, but thinks he does not have to deal with the legal duties applicable to insurers, namely to put in place and maintain assets, able to cover (except in extraordinary events) the financial risks taken over from the CDS protection buyers. In other words, with the CDS business the protection sellers act in breach with insurance law as it engages in an insurance activity without licence and moreover in breach of the technical rules, that apply to insurers.[66]

Security within the community being a public service, organised by that community for the benefit of its members, does not only concern their person and families but also their goods and other assets. The security of goods and other assets is achieved inter alia with the concepts of property and binding force of contracts. Both concepts are part of the public order, founding inter alia the structured organisation of the community.

The regulation made applicable to insurers goes even further: it aims to ensure that the insurer will be able to honour his (contractual) duties when the insured risk materialises. If that risk relates to goods or other assets, the insurer must be able to pay the insured amount or the damage caused to them. To that effect, an insurance licence is required, as well as regulated assets, in a proportion related to the risks insured.

Credit default swaps, being none other than repacked and disguised credit insurances, conflict with the regulation on insurance activities. They result in activities in breach of legal provisions of public order. The contracts, called credit default swaps therefore are (absolutely) void, notwithstanding any *lex contractus*. A choice of a legal system applicable to the CDS that would accept the validity of the CDS has itself to be disregarded as being part of a void contract and moreover as being itself in conflict with public order. The choice of a *lex contractus* is indeed but another trick to avoid the effect of public order (including legal provisions of that nature) at the place where the contract is intended to have legal effects. The legal effects of an absolute nullity have yet been outlined: the statute of limitation is at least ten years.[67]

The second example relates to tax avoidance. For a long time, Western democracies have suffered from the plague of tax avoidance, tolerated for reasons difficult to understand and even less easy to justify.[68] The situation is no different in Belgium.

A distinction is made between tax fraud and tax evasion.[69] When a person or a legal entity has to pay taxes but nevertheless, for whatever reason and/or with whatever cunning device, refuses to pay the taxes due, he/she breaches tax law. This infringement, when discovered, will, most of the time, be qualified as a criminal offence, will give rise to additional taxation, and, at the same time, will amount to a (fraudulent) fault under articles 1382–1383 of the *Code civil*.

Tax evasion relates to a person or a legal entity that avoids tax liability. He or she stays outside the legal conditions required for taxation. No infringement, no breach of tax law occurs as a result. Under Belgian law, the opinion prevails that tax avoidance is in itself legal, but with some exceptions resulting from the theory of abuse of right and/or from specific legal provisions. The prevailing opinion, however, does not take into consideration the requirements of public order, 'absent' in the discussion.

When a person or a legal entity wants to avoid taxation, he/she will proceed with legal acts, prompted (at least in part) by the desire to pay no or less tax. The reasons[70] inducing a person or a legal entity to indulge in tax avoidance have to be taken into account and assessed in relation to public order.

It has to be remembered that most, if not all, taxes are dedicated to the financing of public services, provided by the community to its members. In setting up tax dodges, persons and legal entities wish to preserve their activities within the community and/or assets from taxation. If they succeed, they achieve a return on such activities and/or assets, out of reach of the ordinary taxpayer.

There is unfortunately more to be said about the legal acts that always accompany tax avoidance: the members of the community, who proceed with and benefit from tax avoidance, shield activities and/or assets they own from taxation. To that effect, they on the one hand do not contribute to the financing of the vast public services, while on the other hand still enjoy those public services as members of the community. The resulting gap in the funding of public services has to be made good by the ordinary taxpayers or by the downsizing of the public services, if the tax burden on taxpayers is considered to be too heavy. Tax avoidance, in other words, has a negative impact on public services, counterbalanced by personal 'profits' of the tax avoiders.

The most popular route for tax avoidance leads to tax havens, where taxation is as light as possible. Persons or legal entities, skilled in tax avoidance, transfer assets to tax havens, most of the time using 'sophisticated' mechanisms such as special purpose vehicles, transfer pricing schemes, netting, etc. Practised on a very large scale, tax avoidance each year over the last forty years has guided thousands of millions of US dollars, euros and other currencies to tax havens. This process continues to be active.

Of course those funds do not remain stored in accounts in the tax havens. Tax avoidance has indeed become an industry: almost all important banks and financial institutions have branches or subsidiaries (SPVs) in tax havens. They collect the evaded funds and with some transfers, introduce them to the international financial markets. 'Poor' countries, which have trouble with the funding of their public services, call upon those international financial markets. They borrow large amounts at high and compound interest rates to finance their public services, in order to keep the organised structure of their community afloat. The tax avoiders, still members of the prejudiced community, as well as their families, friends and employees, benefit without any disruption from the public services, financed by the ordinary taxpayers and by public debt. Those ordinary tax payers moreover will have to take care of that public debt: a situation that is more than painful.

The interests served and the reimbursements of debt once again through opaque international financial markets, flow back to the accounts in tax havens, and are immediately re-engaged in other financial transactions.

There can be no doubt about it: tax avoidance and the surrounding industry that takes advantage of it place the (democratic) community at risk. They are incompatible with its public order.

Tax avoidance is one of the most obvious explanations for the growing financial and resulting material/social inequalities between a (small) minority, beneficiaries of tax avoidance, and a (large) majority. This growing inequality is due not only to the increasing wealth of that (small) minority, but also to worsened living conditions of the (large) majority. However, even the most affluent and powerful, whether royals or majority shareholders of corporations, should notice and understand that this increasing inequality is putting the structured organisation of (democratic) communities under an intolerable pressure. A major correction should not be long in coming if nothing changes.

From a legal point of view, the remedies are available as all legal acts linked to tax avoidance and its surrounding industry conflict with public order. All persons or legal entities involved with the setting up of tax avoidance, its organisation, its operation and management, act in breach of public order with each of their acts dedicated to tax avoidance. Those legal acts place in danger the financing of the public services a community has decided to provide to its members, obstruct the community to do so or to do so at the appropriate quality levels. Being legal acts, they are null and void or at least inapplicable/unchallengeable to the prejudiced community. Their nullity is an absolute one; the statute of limitations is at least ten years.[71]

Here too contractual provisions making the law of a tax haven applicable to the (invalid) legal acts are of no help, as they are part of the organisation of tax avoidance.

Acts in conflict with public order have another interesting particularity. Breaching public order amounts to negligence if a normal and reasonable person acting in the same circumstances, would have refrained from doing so. In that case, a general duty to take care would have been disregarded. It is rather unlikely that a normal and reasonable person living within a community would engage in an activity that conflicts with the public order of his/her community. Acting in breach of public order will thus, in most cases, qualify as a negligence (a fault) under the articles 1382–1383 of the *Code civil*.

Subject to accountability (free will), the breach of a general duty of care causing a (foreseeable) damage triggers, in Belgian law, the legal duty (obligation) to repair all the damage caused to other persons or legal entities.[72]

When public order is breached, the resulting damage affects the structured organisation of the community. It is the task of its (elected) representatives to claim at once its compensation from the person(s) or entity(ies) liable for that damage. Here the statute of limitations is in general five years.[73]

8. CONCLUSIONS

Lawyers, especially when they practice private law, often give the impression that they are not interested in discussions about public order, its impact on the validity or the enforceability of legal acts and the possible liability that may result from its breach. A (poor) definition of public order makes it easy or easier for them to mask their (poor) involvement.

Their reticence may proceed from a conflict between the personal interests of practitioners of law, guided by their principals, on the one hand, and the interests of the community deemed to be served by them, on the other hand. This conflict of interest is not sufficiently taken into account by legislators and/or courts.

Awareness about this conflict of interest may result in an appropriate and reliable definition of public order, to be applied in private law, that is more than needed when the validity of legal acts or a possible liability resulting from a breach of public order is at stake.

Contrary to the prevailing opinion, this chapter undertakes the search for such an appropriate and reliable definition of public order.

Its (first) results, subject to further investigation, tend towards the finding that an appropriate and reliable definition is not out of reach. That definition is not to be found as such in the legal system. Public order appears to deal with questions and answers about the structured organisation of a particular community. Its definition is linked to that structured organisation. Consequently, it is necessary to pay attention to each of the words used: what is meant by a 'community', when can a community be called a democracy, how has the balance of powers between the majority and the minorities to be determined, what can be expected from elected representatives, which targets, processes and operations have to prevail in a (democratic) community and for what reasons?

The answers to those questions lead to public services designed, organised, operated and financed by the (elected) representatives to the benefit of all the community members.

Public services require, by definition, a structured organisation that has to be in place to achieve the levels of quality looked after and, once put in place, they become an essential part of that structured organisation. Those public services also deal with the human flaw, replacing selfishness by solidarity, public services being made available for all members of the community. With public services placed at their disposal, the community members can moreover make a much better use of the self-determination they pursue, giving to their lifetime the meaning and content they privilege.

The structured organisation of a (democratic, by preference) community leads thus to public services and the design, organisation, management and funding of public services determine the public order within the community considered.

Acts of whatever nature, coming from whatever person or legal entity, including the most affluent and powerful, that endanger the (democratic) community, its structured organisation and thus the public services it has put in place or it wishes to provide to the benefit of its members, conflict with public order and require their elimination in order to preserve the community.

No wonder then that the public services of law and/or of the administration of justice have been conceived to declare acts incompatible with public order null and void or, at least, unenforceable and that they may give rise to a liability in tort towards the community.

A democratic community is entitled to expect from all its lawyers that they contribute to the preservation of its public order. Benefiting from the public services the community has put in place and maintained, they have been trained to detect and to act against acts and developments inconsistent with the structured organisation, selected and determined by the (voting) majority, represented by its legislators.

The financial and economic crisis, which was generated a long time before 2007, is for lawyers nothing more than a wake-up call. It gives the opportunity to recall that lawyers are to serve the community before any other interest. Bringing about an appropriate and reliable definition of public order is part of their tasks. They also should acknowledge the existence of a general principle of law prohibiting acts inconsistent with public order. There is no way around this approach if lawyers still wish to contribute faithfully to their (democratic) communities.

Endnotes

* Ludo Cornelis is a Professor at the Free University of Brussels and an Attorney at the Brussels Bar.

1. J. Stiglitz, *Freefall, free markets and the sinking of global economy*, London, Penguin Books, 2010, 416 p.; in French: J. Stiglitz *Le triomphe de la cupidité*, Mayenne, LLL, 2010, 474 p.
2. P. Krugman, *Pourquoi les crises reviennent toujours?*, Paris, Seuil, 2009, 201 p.; P. Krugman, *Sortez-nous de cette crise… maintenant*, Paris, Flammarion, 2012, 284 p.
3. M. Sandel (*What money can't buy. The moral limits of markets*, London, Allen Lane, 2012, 244 p.) speaks about the affluent.
4. They, first of all, benefited from the bailouts, preserving their assets.
5. J. Attali, *Tous ruinés dans dix ans? Dette publique: la dernière chance*, Paris, Fayard, 2010, 263 p.
6. The word 'community' (instead of 'society'), is used as it refers to what is common to its members. The word 'community' therefore expresses better the idea of inclusion, while the word 'society' refers rather to a closed social system, viewed from the outside.
7. Inter alia P. Krugman, *supra* note 2; J. Stiglitz, *supra* note 1, but also D. Cohen, *La prospérité du vice, une introduction (inquiète) à l'économie*, Paris, Albin Michel, 2009, 309 p.; D. Cohen, *Homo economicus. Prophète (égaré) des temps nouveaux*, Paris, Albin Michel, 2012, 207 p.; T. Cowen, *The great stagnation. How America ate all the low-hanging fruit of modern history, got sick, and will (eventually) feel better*, New York, Dutton, 2011, 109 p.; T. Jackson, *Prosperity without growth. Economics for a finite planet*, London, Earthscan, 2010, 253 p.; S. Latouche, *Le pari de la décroissance*, Paris, Fayard, 2010, 302 p.; F. Morin, *Le nouveau mur de l'argent. Essai sur la finance globalisée*, Paris, Seuil, 2006, 278 p.; F. Morin, *Un monde sans Wall Street?*, Paris, Seuil, 2011, 184 p.
8. Inter alia Al Gore, *The future*, London, WH Allen, 2013, 533 p.; S. Hessel, *Engagez-vous*, La Tour d'Aigues, Ed. De l'Aube, 2011, 93 p.; P. Larrouturou, *Pour éviter le krach ultime*, Nova éditions, 2011, 255 p.; R. Reich, *Le jour d'après. Sans réduction des inégalités, pas de sortie de crise*, Paris, Vuibert, 2011, 177 p.
9. Inter alia L. Chauvel, *Le destin des générations. Structure sociale et cohortes en France du XXe siècle aux années*, Paris, PUF, 2010, 426 p.; C. Felber, *L'économie citoyenne, un mouvement a vu le jour*, Paris, Actes sud, 2011, 204 p.; R. Skidelsky and E. Skidelsky, *How much is enough? The love of money and the case for good life*, London, Allen Lane, 2012, 243 p.; G. Standing, *The precariat, the new dangerous class*, London, Bloomsbury, 2011, 198 p.; R. Wilkinson and K. Pickett, *The spirit level. Why equality is better for*

everyone, London, Penguin Books, 2010, 375 p. (and trying to affect the importance of the work of R. Wilkinson and K. Pickett and C. Snowdon, *The spirit level delusion*, London, Little Dice, 2010, 167 p.)

10. Inter alia H. Achterhuis, *De utopie van de vrije markt*, Rotterdam, Lemniscaat, 2010, 317 p.; M. Sandel, *supra* note 3; M. Sandel, *Justice. What's the right thing to do?*, New York, Farrar, Straus and Girous, 2010, 308 p.; T. Todorov, *Les ennemis intimes de la démocratie*, Paris, R. Laffont, 2012, 258 p.
11. Inter alia D. Graeber, *Debt. The first 5000 years*, New York, Melville House, 2012, 534 p.; P. Jorion, *Le capitalisme à l'agonie*, Paris, Fayard, 2011, 345 p.; P. Jorion, *Misère de la pensée économique*, Paris, Fayard, 2012, 351 p.
12. Inter alia D. Kahneman, *Thinking, fast and slow*, London, Allen Lane, 2011, 499 p.; R.H. Thaler and C.R. Sunstein, *Nudge. Improving decisions about health, wealth and happiness*, New Haven, Yale University Press, 2008, 293 p.; P. Verhaeghe, *Identiteit*, Amsterdam, De bezige bij, 2012, 271 p.
13. Inter alia N. Baverez, *Après le déluge. La grande crise de la mondialisation*, Paris, Perrin, 2011, 188 p.; T. Judt, *Ill fares the land*, London, Allen Lane, 2010, 237 p.
14. Inter alia O. Berruyer, *Les faits sont têtus*, Paris, Les Arènes, 2013, 327 p.
15. Inter alia C. de Duve, *Genetics of original sin. The impact of natural selection on the future of humanity*, Yale–Paris, University Press–Ed. Odile Jacob, 2010, 223 p.
16. Inter alia A. Admati and M. Hellwig, *The bankers' new clothes. What's wrong with banking and what to do about it?*, Princeton, Princeton University Press, 2013, 398 p.; B. Lietaer, C. Arnsperger, S. Goemer and S. Brunnhuber, *Money and sustainability. The missing link*, Devon, Triarchy Press, 2012, 211 p. (B. Lietaer is a professor and expert in finance; C. Arnsperger is a professor in economics; S. Goemer is an expert in engineering, system physics and psychology; S. Brunnhuber is medical director and chief medical officer at the hospital for integral psychiatry in Saxonia (Germany); R.G. Rajan, *Fault Lines. How hidden fractures still threaten the world economy*, Princeton, Princeton University Press, 2010, 260 p.; G. Ugeux, *La trahison de la finance. Douze réformes pour rétablir la confiance*, Paris, Ed. Odile Jacob, 2010, 255 p. (Mr Ugeux does not tackle the issue of tax avoidance as a remedy to restore confidence and finance).
17. Inter alia C. Bessy, T. Delpeuch and J. Pélisse (eds.), *Droit et régulations des activités économiques: perspectives sociologiques er institutionnalistes*, Paris, L.G.D.J., 2011, 358 p.; R. Houben, *De financiële crisis en privaatrecht*, in *Economische groei in Europa: eerst de crisis dan het recht*, Antwerp, Intersentia, 2011, pp. 1–32; K. Geens and C. Clottens, *Financieel recht: een stand van zaken*, in *Vennootschaps- en financieel recht*, Bruges, Die Keure, 2011, pp. 105–126; C. Williams and P. Zumbansen (eds.), *The embedded firm. Corporate governance, labor and finance capitalism*, Cambridge, Cambridge University Press, 2012, 473 p.
18. Inter alia M. Lewis, *The big short. Inside the doomsday machine*, New York, Norton, 2010, 288 p.; G. Tett, *Fool's gold. How unrestrained greed corrupted a dream, shattered global markets and unleashed a catastrophe*, London, Abacus, 2010, 356 p.
19. In French: '*article 6: On ne peut déroger, par des conventions particulières, aux lois qui intéressent l'ordre public et les bonnes mœurs*'. In Dutch: '*artikel 6: Aan de wetten die de openbare orde en de goede zeden betreffen, kan door bijzondere overeenkomsten geen afbreuk worden gedaan*'.
20. Called *Cour de cassation* (in French); *Hof van Cassatie* (in Dutch).
21. Cass. 9 December 1948, Pas. 1948, I, 699.

22. H. De Page, *Traité élémentaire de droit civil belge*, I., Brussels, Bruylant, 111, no. 91.
23. '*[L]a loi ordre public est celle qui touche aux intérêts essentiels de l'Etat ou de la collectivité, ou qui fixe, dans le droit privé, les bases juridiques fondamentales sur lesquelles repose l'ordre économique ou moral d'une société*' (H. De Page, *supra* note 22, I, 111, no. 91).
24. Inter alia P. Van Ommeslaghe, *Droit des obligations*, I, Brussels, Bruylant, 2010, p. 338, no. 216; see also E. Ekelmans: '*qui d'autre que la juge pourrait d'ailleurs apprécier ce lien avec l'état social de la nation? Si le législateur a recours à des notions telles que l'ordre public et les bonnes mœurs, c'est précisément à cause de leur indétermination pour laisser au juge un pouvoir d'appréciation*'. (E. Ekelmans, intervention in a paper drafted by A.C. Van Gysel and J.F. Romain, 'Conclusions générales: l'ordre public entre hétérogénéité et homogénéité', in *L'ordre public. Concept et applications*, Brussels, Bruylant, 1995, 327 p.).
25. Inter alia R. Dekkers and A. Verbeke, *Handboek burgerlijk recht*, III, Antwerp, Intersentia, 2007, 41, nos. 71 and p. 43, no. 72; S. Stijns, *Verbintenissenrecht*, I, Bruges, Die Keure, 2005, p. 38, no. 49; P. Wery, *Droit des obligations*, I, Brussels, Larcier, 2011, p. 302, no. 310 and p. 305, no. 312; P. Wery, *L'essor du droit impératif et ses rapports avec l'ordre public en matière contractuelle*, in I. Samoy (ed.), *Evolutie van de basisbeginselen van het contractenrecht*, Antwerp, Intersentia, 2010, p. 121, no. 1 and p. 125, no. 6.
26. The same rules apply when the breach relates to the general concept of public order and public decency.
27. With the exception of the statute of limitation, those rules, applicable to absolute invalidity, have been elaborated by the Belgian Courts. See with regard to those rules inter alia P. Van Ommeslaghe, *supra* note 24, pp. 351–352; P. Wery, *supra* note 25, pp. 318–324.
28. See inter alia W. Van Gerven and S. Lierman, *Algemeen deel. Veertig jaar later*, in *Beginselen van Belgisch privaatrecht*, I, Mechelen, Kluwer, 2010, p. 127, no. 46; P. Wery, *supra* note 25, p. 298, no. 307.
29. They do the same thing with statutes dealing with public decency.
30. Inter alia R. Dekkers and A. Verbeke, *supra* note 25, p. 18, no. 30; S. Stijns, *supra* note 25, pp. 38–39, nos. 49–50; P. Wery, *supra* note 25, p. 301, no. 310; see also A. Van Oevelen, B. Cattoir, A. Colpaert, M. Van Loon, R. Vincks and L. Van Valkenborgh, *De nietigheid van overeenkomsten wegens strijdigheid met de openbare orde of de goede zeden: algemene beginselen en een grondslagenonderzoek*, TPR, 2011, p. 1362, nos. 9 and p. 1364, no. 14; J.F. Romain, *L'ordre public (notion générale) et les droits de l'homme*, in *L'ordre public, concept et applications*, Brussels, Bruylant, 1995, pp. 26–26, no. 10.2, 10.3 and 12 and p. 202, no. 91. Contra: a few legal scholars consider that public order (and public decency) can be applied as such: inter alia J. Baeck, *Restitutie na vernietiging of ontbinding van overeenkomsten*, Antwerp, Intersentia, 2012, p. 175, no. 261; J. De Coninck, 'De toetsing van een overeenkomst aan de openbare orde naar Belgisch recht', in J. Smits and S. Stijns (eds.), *Inhoud en werking van de overeenkomst naar Belgisch en Nederlands recht*, Antwerp, Intersentia, 2005, p. 188, no. 1 and p. 190, no. 6; S. Van De Mosselaer, *De begrippen openbare orde en goede zeden in de relatie tot de exploitatie van biotechnologische uitvindingen*, Intellectuele Rechten, 2012, p. 121.
31. The vagueness of the concept 'public order' is often underscored and may explain the restrictive approach: inter alia S. Stijns, *supra* note 25, pp. 38–39; P. Van Ommeslaghe, *supra* note 24, p. 154, no. 80 and p. 338, no. 217; W. Van Gerven and S. Covemaeker, *Verbintenissenrecht*, Bruges, Acco, 2006, p. 78; P. Wery, *supra* note 25, pp. 278–299, nos. 307–308.
32. Inter alia S. Stijns, *supra* note 25, p. 38, no. 49; W. Van Gerven and S. Covemaeker, *supra* note 31, p. 78; P. Van Ommeslaghe, *supra* note 24, pp. 276–277, no. 307.

33. The exceptions are J. Baeck, *supra* note 30, p. 175, no. 261; J. Baeck, *Deugenieten en nietigheden*, in *Liber Amicorum Hubert Bocken*, Bruges, Die Keure, pp. 160–164; J. De Coninck, *supra* note 30, p. 201.
34. See *supra* note 22.
35. See *supra* note 21.
36. See *supra* notes 24 and 30.
37. For example: W. Van Gerven and S. Covemaeker (*supra* note 31, p. 79) and S. Stijns (*supra* note 25, p. 39, no. 50) have different views on the question whether the conditions of validity of a contract relate or not to public order; W. Van Gerven and S. Covemaeker (*supra* note 31, pp. 125–126) consider that the abuse of circumstances (*la lésion qualifiée/de gekwalificeerde benadering*) breaches public order, while other legal scholars dispute this position (R. Dekkers and A. Verbeke, *supra* note 25, p. 36, no 61; P. Van Ommeslaghe, *supra* note 24, p. 273, no. 173; P. Wery, *supra* note 25, p. 258, no. 266); for P. Van Ommeslaghe (*supra* note 24, p. 374, no. 237) the national interdiction of compound interest rates deals with public order; P. Wery (*L'essor du droit imperatif et ses rapports avec l'ordre public, supra* note 25, p. 129, no. 15) ranks this interdiction as mere mandatory (*droit imperative/dwingend recht*). From public order, parties cannot validly deviate with a contract or other legal act; from mere mandatory law a deviation is possible and valid once the party protected by the mandatory rule has acquired the protection the rule is providing.
38. See article 6 of the Belgian Procedural Code.
39. See *supra* note no 25.
40. Portalis, Premier exposé des motifs. Session of 24 November 1801 of the *Corps législatif* (in Locré, *Législation civile, commerciale et criminelle*, I, 236, Brussels, Tarlier, 1836); Portalis, Speech on 14 December 1801 before the *Corps législatif* (in Locré, ibid., I, 263); Portalis, Second exposé des motifs. Session of 23 February 1803 (in Locré, ibid., I, 506). See also Grenier, Report for the Tribunal on 27 February 1803 (in Locré, ibid., I, 313).
41. In French: '*article 1133 Code civil: La cause est illicite, quand elle est prohibée par la loi, quand elle est contraire aux bonnes mœurs ou à l'ordre public*'. In Dutch: '*artikel 1133 BW: De oorzaak is ongeoorloofd, wanneer zij door de wet verboden is, of wanneer zij strijdig is met de geode zeden of met de openbare orde*'.
42. S. Stijns, *supra* note 25, p. 103, no. 142; P. Van Ommeslaghe, *supra* note 24, pp. 306–307, no. 195; P. Wery, *supra* note 25, pp. 283–285.
43. S. Stijns, *supra* note 25, p. 99, no. 136; P. Van Ommeslaghe, *supra* note 24, p. 281, no. 180 and p. 354, no. 228; P. Wery, *supra* note 25, p. 276, no. 289.
44. Articles 36, 45.3, 62 and 65.1 of the Union Treaty.
45. Article 52.1 of the Union Treaty.
46. Articles 2, 4, 5, 15, 16, 17 and 18 of the ECHR.
47. See the review of the decisions of the Court of Justice in H. Gilliams, D. Arts, J. Wouters, P. De Man, P. Wytinck and A. Godfroid, *Kroniek van rechtspraak: Europees ondernemingsrecht* (januari 2008–december 2010), TBH 2001, pp. 620, 622, nos. 53–54; pp. 623–624, nos. 55–60; p. 624, nos. 62–63; pp. 627–680, nos. 77–83; pp. 636–638, nos. 93–98; pp. 647–648, no. 117; pp. 642–645, nos. 108–112.
48. See inter alia GWH 15 July 1993, Judgment no. 62/93; GWH 3 December 1998, Judgment no. 126/98; GWH 8 November 2000, Judgment no. 113/2000.

49. The use in private law of open or vague concepts is in itself open to criticism: inter alia L. Cornelis, 'De achtereenkomst', in R. Feltkamp and F. Vanbossele (eds.), *Wilsautonomie, contractvrijheid en ondernemingscontracten*, Antwerp, Intersentia, 2011, pp. 25–85.
50. See previously nos. 7–8.
51. Larousse (French), Van Dale (Dutch).
52. Still to be determined, see hereafter nos. 38–43; see also J. Cotta, *Qui veut la peau des services publics?*, Paris, JCG, 2011, 345 p.
53. Although the voting right is always linked to membership of the community.
54. Plural or multiple voting rights awarded to a single individual conflicts with democracy. When a voting right is granted to a legal entity, plural or multiple voting rights are the result (see N. Shaxson, *Treasure Islands*, London, Vintage Books, 2011, pp. 245–297, and, more specifically, p. 265).
55. See R. Wilkinson and R. Pickett, *The spirit level. Why equality is better for everyone*, London, Penguin Books, 2010.
56. Those 'things' being described hereafter in nos. 38–43.
57. See inter alia Al Gore, *The Future*, NY, WH Allen, 2013, pp. 104–124; T. Todorov, *Les ennemis intimes de la démocratie*, Paris, R. Laffont, 2012, pp. 137–180 and 227–247.
58. 5–10% of the community members: see Al Gore, *supra* note 57, pp. 8–12; O. Berruyer, *Les faits sont têtus*, Paris, Les arènes, 2013, pp. 145–175.
59. That financial and economic crisis will only end once all its negative effects on public finance will have been lifted.
60. See inter alia A. Admati and M. Hellwig, *supra* note 16.
61. Inter alia C. de Duve, *Genetics of original sin. The impact of natural selection on the future of humanity*, Yale-Paris, Yale University Press-Ed. Odile Jacobs, 2010, pp. 146–158. See also, D. Aricly, *The (honest) truth about dishonesty*, London, Harper Collins, 2012, 284 p.
62. See inter alia T.F. Ruiz, *The terror of history. On the uncertainties of life in western civilization*, Princeton, Princeton University Press, 2011, 178 p.
63. To be controlled by public authorities, not by private interests.
64. About joint liability: see inter alia B. Dubuisson and V. Callewaert, *La responsabilité civile, Chronique de jurisprudence 1996-2007, I, Le fait générateur et le lien causal*, Brussels, Larcier, 2009, pp. 342–348; T. Vansweevelt and B. Weyts, *Handboek buitencontractuele aansprakelijkheidsrecht*, Antwerp, Intersentia, 2009, pp. 835–838.
65. See also the paper of Prof. Dr H. Cousy in this book.
66. See also the paper of Prof. Dr H. Cousy in this book; see also A. Admati and M. Hellwig, *supra* note 16, pp. 66–69.
67. Under circumstances, the statute of limitation can last longer: A. Lenaerts, *Fraus omnia corrumpit: autonome rechtsfiguur of miskend correctiemechanisme?*, Leuven, 2012–2013, pp. 244–265.
68. X. Harel, *La grande evasion, Le vrai scandale des paradis fiscaux*, Babel, LLL, 2010, 316 p.; N. Shaxson, *supra* note 54.
69. Inter alia P. Van Ommeslaghe, *supra* note 24, pp. 442–460.
70. In Belgian law, the reasons are called *la cause/de oorzaak* of the contractual obligation.
71. See *supra* note 68.
72. Inter alia T. Vansweevelt and B. Weyts, *supra* note 64, pp. 3–5 and 125–163.
73. See article 2262*bis* of the Belgian *Code civil*.

GENDER INEQUALITIES AND FAMILY SOLIDARITY IN TIMES OF CRISIS

Alain Laurent Verbeke, Elisabeth Alofs,
Christine Defever and Dimitri Mortelmans

Besides sociological, demographic and cultural determinants, also economic conditions can induce a shift in the social responsibilities of an individual, his family and society. Due to the current poor economic situation of most European countries, public funds are scarcer and the financial sustainability of public safety nets for those in precarious situations is at risk. That is why the financial crisis, topic of this book, has raised questions about which risks should still be covered by society and which risks could be covered via solidarity in private relationships and family law. Focusing on the socio-economic situation of women as one of the vulnerable groups, this chapter tackles the question whether a shift from public to private law protection can provide a solution for the limited public funds in times of economic crisis.

It is without doubt essential to our modern western society and identity, ever since the emancipation movements in the 20th century, that men and women are of equal value. This core value has been embedded in numerous legal documents, national legislation and international treaties.[1] Today's society however demonstrates some hypocrisy on two counts.

First of all, there are *foreign cultures* where women do not enjoy an equal legal position as men do and are not entitled to equal opportunities in education, work, career, leisure time, etc. Nevertheless many European countries have accepted in their midst the existence and flourishing of such cultures that fundamentally and conceptually discriminate against women. The mere fact that we accept such views to co-exist in our society, often for reasons of political correctness, is a denial of the very essence and core values of our culture and identity. Multiculturalism and integration cannot be achieved if we fail to claim respect for essential values such as the equal treatment of men and women. How respectful can the European culture be when it is too shy or cowardly to fight for one of its most fundamental values? Respect for women starts with banning all rules and practices of female discrimination on our territory.

Secondly, although in our own *western culture* legal equality between men and women has been promoted as essential, western societies fail to operationalise that value in everyday life. In the first section of this chapter (1), sociological data are presented that demonstrate that *de facto* equality has not been achieved. For biological, social, psychological, traditional and other reasons, in day-to-day reality women continue to be 'second class citizens'. The 'glass ceiling' is a permanent challenge for women, on the labour market, in boards and in politics. Even more staggering is the weak position of women in their most intimate context: the relationship with their life partner. This precarious situation of women particularly causes problems when the relationship is disrupted by divorce or break-up, which is the case in more than fifty percent of relationships. The data demonstrate that the socio-economic position after a break-up is far more disadvantageous for women compared to their former male partners.

Notwithstanding those data, the law and particularly family law erroneously starts from the premise of equality between the sexes. This dogma of formal equality, together with emancipatory ideas, has led to the de-institutionalisation, individualisation and liberalisation of family law over the past decades. As will be described in the second section of this chapter (2), these trends have led to the abolishment of financial responsibilities within the family and to a lack of solidarity within family law. As mentioned before, this lack of solidarity mainly causes a problem when the family is disrupted by divorce or relationship break-up.

Given the persisting disparities between men and women in everyday life, the absence of responsibilities and solidarity in family law is questionable. Couldn't, or indeed shouldn't, family law pursue a protective role, which aims at compensating the actual differences between men and women which all too often lead to individual poverty, especially for women? As mentioned above, this question is even more urgent in times of economic crisis, as the sustainability of public safety nets is being queried. In the third section of this chapter (3), we therefore argue in favour of a more inclusive and equitable family law which recognises the existing differences between individuals, particularly between men and women. We aim to create a family law that tackles and adjusts the pernicious consequences of these inequalities.

1. GENDERED SOCIO-ECONOMIC INEQUALITY

The increased standard living conditions in nearly all western societies after World War II resulted in an enormous increase of female participation in the labour market. As a consequence, the dominant model of the male breadwinner of the fifties and sixties was slowly replaced by the dual-earner family, which became the standard for contemporary families.[2] Yet the relative dominance of these dual-earner families cannot conceal the fundamental gender disparities in paid labour and care within these households.

This first section starts with an overview of the socio-economic inequalities between men and women on the labour market and in the household (1.1). Next, we will look at the consequences of these inequalities when the family is disrupted by divorce or relationship break-up (1.2). We will see that the socio-economic position before and after a break-up is far more disadvantageous for women compared to the male partners.

1.1. SOCIO-ECONOMIC INEQUALITIES BETWEEN MEN AND WOMEN

In this section an overview of the labour force participation (1.1.1), wage and position (1.1.2) and career (1.1.3) inequalities between men and women will be presented. Subsequently, we will look at their position and responsibilities in the family and tackle imbalances in the division of household tasks and care between men and women (1.1.4).

1.1.1. Inequality in labour force participation

In general, women are less active on the labour market. Table 1 shows the percentage of women and men aged 15–64 years in Belgium who are working. The difference in employment rate between men and women has decreased over the years but still remains substantial. In 2012, almost 67% of men (aged 15–64 years) were working, compared to merely 57% of women.

Table 1. Evolution of employment rate in Belgium, by gender, 2000–2012, in %

	2000	2001	2002	2003	2004	2005	2006	2007	2008	2009	2010	2011	2012
Men	69.3	68.8	68.3	67.3	67.9	68.3	67.9	68.7	68.6	67.2	67.4	67.1	66.9
Women	50.8	51.0	51.4	51.8	52.6	53.8	54.0	55.3	56.2	56.0	56.5	56.7	56.8

Source: ADSEI, Labour Force survey.

More striking are the gender disparities when looking at the part-time employment rate (table 2). Although part-time working has increased considerably over the past decade, there continues to be a major difference between women and men. In 2012, 43.5% of the women who were active on the labour market worked part-time. In the case of men, this was only 9%.

Table 2. Evolution of part-time employment rate in Belgium, by gender, 2000–2012, in %

	2000	2001	2002	2003	2004	2005	2006	2007	2008	2009	2010	2011	2012
Men	4.3	4.7	5.1	5.8	6.3	7.1	7.0	7.1	7.5	8.2	8.4	9.2	9.0
Women	34.9	35.8	36.4	38.0	39.3	40.4	41.0	40.5	40.8	41.4	42.1	43.3	43.5

Source: ADSEI, Labour Force survey.

Apart from the plain percentages, there is also a major difference in the reasons why people work part-time. An analysis of a Belgian sample from the Survey on Income and Living Conditions (SILC) conducted in 2005,[3] shows that only a small minority (1%) of men working less than 30 hours a week, mention household tasks or care as a reason to work part-time. This percentage is considerably higher among part-time working women (30%).

1.1.2. Inequality in wage and position

On average in 2013, a woman earned 10% less than a man per hour worked. Due to a large share of part-time working women, the pay gap rises to 23% on an annual basis. This raw gender pay gap can be attributed to a number of external factors. Only 26% of the gap is due to individual characteristics of the worker such as education, work experience, and years of service in the company. A dominant part of the gap can be brought back to gender segregation on the labour market (52% of the explained part of the gender pay gap).[4] Women turn out to be over-represented in sectors, professions and positions that pay less well. To a large extent, unequal pay is a question of unequal work.

Indeed, within the labour market differences between 'female' and 'male' professions and industries can be observed. So-called 'female' professions are systematically less well-paid in comparison with 'male' professions and industries. A major explanation for this difference lies in the perception society has of certain professions. Being a construction worker, for example, is considered as being a 'tough profession' meriting a higher wage. A geriatric assistant on the other hand is not considered to have a 'heavy profession' and therefore tends to be paid considerably less. Industries with higher-ranked positions are frequently more male-dominated than industries that are perceived to be lower (or 'softer'). Studies have shown that the gender segregation on the labour market already starts when adolescents make subject choices in secondary school. Girls select themselves into lower-ranked sectors with worse payment and status.[5]

In addition, compared to men, the share of women in higher positions on the Flemish labour market is significantly lower than their overall share on the labour market.[6] Not only are there fewer women in executive positions, their relative share according to positions in the labour market also decreases along the corporate ladder. Baerts et al.[7] conclude from a large collection of studies that leading positions and promotions are far less reserved for women than for men. Women face the so-called 'glass ceiling' preventing them from achieving higher positions on the labour market, despite their abilities. Looking at the Belgian figures for 2010, only 34.1% of executive and higher management positions are occupied by women (ADSEI).

Not only are the positions on the labour market gendered, women also face inequalities within a similar position. Within the same profession, women have less extra-legal advantages, cost deductions, daily allowances, bonuses or double holiday allowance. Men also receive more flexible wage arrangements or sickness and hospitalisation insurance.[8]

1.1.3. Inequalities during career

As shown above, women do more part-time work than men. But during their life, they also use career breaks (maternity leave, time credit) more often. More than 66% of people taking a career break are women. This hegemony of women becomes even more apparent for full-time breaks and thematic leaves, such as parental leave, leave for medical assistance or leave for palliative care (respectively 77% and 72%). This percentage is lower for part-time breaks (63%), where part-time options are gradually finding their way to men.[9] The household and specifically the care of (young) children is the predominant motivation for these career decisions among women.[10] For men, ending their career in a part-time schedule is clearly the most dominant reason. Alternatively, more men use their time out to try a new job or to start their own business.[11]

The only reversed gender gap is found in research on the wage penalty of career breaks. In general, wage differentials between men with and without a break are much higher than between women with and without a break.[12] Men experience a larger drop in income after returning from a career break compared to women.[13] In addition, wage growth for men is slower after they return from an interruption. In other words, the penalty for a career break in terms of wages is higher for men.

Apart from career breaks, women show greater variability and less stability in their careers, often resulting in more vulnerable positions. Entry into the labour market is often more difficult for women, causing a longer unemployment period before finding their first full-time position. They also switch more often between part-time and full-time jobs (often between different jobs). Men, on the other hand, have careers that show less variability and that are more stable and traditional, characterised by full-time jobs and easy job market entries.[14]

1.1.4. Inequalities within the household

The inequality on the labour market and in career paths finds its origin in the traditional division of labour in households. Different studies find that even when women work an equal share in the labour market, they still are confronted with a larger share of the responsibilities at home.[15] In addition, part-time working women have a higher chance of being responsible for a dominant share of the household work, while the opposite is not true for households with part-time working men.[16]

The division of household work in families with children is even more unequal compared to childless households.[17] Time-use research shows that, in a week, men spend seven hours more time on paid labour than women. Women spend eight hours and 35 minutes more on household work and an additional one hour and 35 minutes more on parenting and care for the children. In sum, the weekly work load of women in the household is three hours higher than that of men.[18] In general, young, highly educated men with higher professional positions participate more in the household work.

Married men and men who work longer hours in paid labour help less. The most equal division of household work can be found in childless households where both partners work and where the woman has a significant share in the household income, and where both partners have a positive attitude towards equal gender roles.[19]

When families choose to decrease the working hours of one of the parents, women are usually the ones who step forward as it is predominantly women who face the dilemma of combining work and family life.[20] Indeed, the labour market participation of a family with children is 6.4% lower compared to a household without children. This difference is completely due to a reduction in working hours for women. A majority of working women decrease their activity after the birth of their first child. This reduction in working hours is a rarity among new fathers.[21]

This is not a value-free choice. The choice is inspired by traditional gender roles and societal expectations of the position of men and women in a family.[22] Even among women themselves, the idea exists that it is the responsibility of women to take care of (young) children. It is a societal legitimation to reserve the caring role for women. There are signs that the classic breadwinner model is fading or at least revealing its pitfalls[23] but research from the Panel Study of Belgian Households shows that breaking the ruling social conventions is only marginally present among families.[24] Moreover, these decisions are not only value-driven. Another important incentive to tip the balance towards women is the wages of the partners.[25] The one earning less income has less bargaining power in the couple. The loss of income by reducing one's working hours is less for the one with the lowest income. Referring to the discussion of the gendered labour market above, men have higher positions and higher wages than their partners, even though the educational level of women has risen enormously.

1.2. SOCIO-ECONOMIC INEQUALITIES BETWEEN MEN AND WOMEN AFTER A RELATIONSHIP BREAK-UP

The previous section showed huge gender differences in caring for children. As a consequence, women are less active on the labour market. They work more part-time and less in managerial roles. Women are working in less well-paid industries and interrupt their career more often to combine work and family life. The result is that they have less social and economic capital and during the course of their life they accumulate fewer pensions rights than their partners.

The issue of these inequalities becomes apparent when the relationship ends in a divorce or a break-up. In this section, the consequences of relationship and labour market inequalities after the dissolution of the relationship will be analysed. Many findings show that women, again, are most disadvantaged, particularly when they end up as a single mother.

1.2.1. Inequalities in the division of care

A longitudinal study on register data revealed that the odds that women ultimately become the head of a single-parent household are four times higher than the odds for men. Other data shows that 13.1% of fathers head single-father households one year after the break-up while 50.6% of divorced men are single without children one year after. The opposite is true for women: single-mother households are found in 54.8% of cases while only 10.4% of women are single with no children after the break-up. Therefore, women with children prior to divorce have a much higher chance of becoming a single parent.[26]

Not only do women have a higher chance of heading a single-parent household, they also stay longer in this type of household. It is found that 73.1% of the women who were single mothers at the end of the first year after divorce are still in this position one year later. For single fathers, this is only 62.9%. Four years after divorce the single mother percentage drops to 45.9% (31.4% for single fathers).[27]

Moreover, women also have more children in their household compared to single fathers (mean of 1.3 children for women vs. 0.4 children among men). In addition, the age of the children is lower when they live with their mother (mean age of the youngest child is 9.5 years compared to 14 years when living with the father).[28]

1.2.2. Inequalities in the financial consequences

Different longitudinal studies have shown that the financial situation of men is relatively stable or even improves after relationship break-up. For women, the evolution shows a negative trend in all studies. Their situation after a break-up only improves at a slow pace, taking a considerable number of years to overcome the financial consequences of divorce. Based on the Belgian Panel data from 1992 to 2002, men would see their OECD equivalised income (i.e. household income that takes into account the size of the household, and the number and age of children to allow for comparison over different household types) increase by almost 5%. Women, on the other hand, face a decrease in equivalised income of 18.8%. When faced with a loss in income, it takes at least five years for 45% of women to reach their pre-divorce income level.[29]

The evolution of income is determined by many factors. The height of the pre-divorce income determines the drop in income afterwards.[30] In addition, the relative contribution of the partners to the household income before the divorce is important for the post-divorce trajectory. When there are inequalities during the marriage, the financial consequences show one clear winner and one loser. Since men often earn a larger share of the household income, the drop in income for women is usually much greater. Suddenly, women need to run a household without the (higher) income of the partner. For a man, being a single breadwinner in a household, a divorce implies a financial gain. The more hours he works, the bigger the gain.[31]

When children are involved, the custody arrangements determine to a large extent the financial consequences for the parents. The parent residing with the children is financially worse off. In particular, a higher total number of children and more young children increase the financial disadvantage. More children and younger children are factors that will have already influenced pre-divorce income (being lower) but the effect continues to be negative after the break-up. Having children has an effect on the family income of about 9% compared to households without children. Additionally, the wage gap increases by about 50%.

Re-partnering is held out as a successful strategy for women to counterbalance the negative financial consequences. For men, finding a new partner is shown to be less successful. One explanation for this difference is the labour market position of the new partners. The wage gap turns out to be negative for women. When a woman re-partners, the odds are higher that this will be accompanied by an increase in her total household income. For men, the odds are greater that a lower-earning partner will be found, which leads to a decrease in his total income.[32]

The results from panel data were recently confirmed by a large-scale study on register data:[33] the financial drawback is biggest among women heading single-parent households after divorce. This is illustrated in figure 1. Stressing the financial consequences for women, we should not forget that there are also a considerable number of men who undergo a dramatic financial decline after divorce. Moreover, the subjective experience can also differ between divorcees. Transfers from one partner to the other ex-partner can trigger a more negative impression of the actual financial evolution.[34]

One situation where this happens is when one partner is supposed to pay child support for the children or alimony to the ex-partner. The Belgian divorce law of 2007 restricts the duration of alimony payment (maximally to the duration of the broken marriage).[35] As a consequence, the most vulnerable group – mothers with young children from a short marriage – are allowed the least amount of alimony. The child support payments are freed from a time constraint. In literature, there is a disagreement about whether or not alimony and child support payments help people stay out of poverty.[36] A crucial question is also whether or not child support and alimony are actually paid (or can be paid).[37] Paying alimony seems to be closely related to the degree of initiative in breaking up the relationship and the degree of contact with the children afterwards.[38] Therefore, a positive effect of shared co-residence in the correct payment of transfers between former partners could be expected.

Figure 1. Evolution of the total gross yearly household (OECD and inflation corrected) for different family types in the year of the divorce (T, 2004), 2003–2008

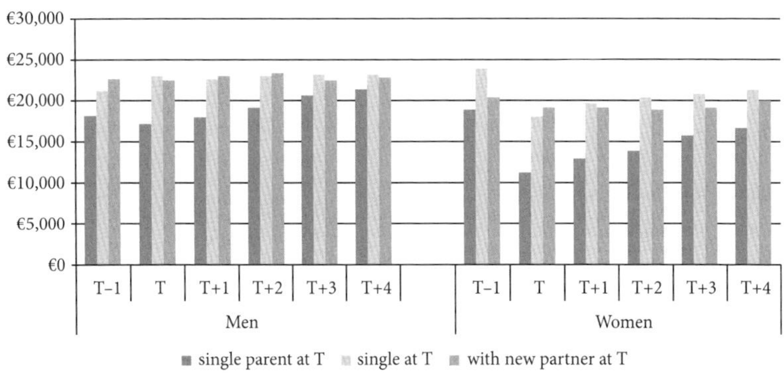

Source: Data warehouse 'Labour market and social protection' – Crossroads Bank Social Security, own calculations.

2. ABSENCE OF SOCIAL RESPONSIBILITIES AND SOLIDARITY IN FAMILY LAW

The law, particularly family law, is dogmatically premised on the equality between men and women despite the existence within today's society of undeniable gender differences. Because of this 'formal' equality, and together with the emancipation of women, family law has been subjected to trends promoting the individual. The disappearance of responsibilities and solidarity in family law is particularly noticeable in the form and content of intimate relationships (2.1), in the limited protection of the weaker spouse, often the wife, after divorce (2.2) and in the limited, almost absent, protection of unmarried partners, in particular when their relationship breaks down (2.3).

2.1. FORMAT OF INTIMATE RELATIONSHIPS

Last century's emancipation of women has radically impacted the form and content of intimate relationships.

First, over the course of the last century, marriage has been transformed from a strategic alliance for family power and property interests into a private bond of love between two individuals who want to share their lives together. Whereas previously emphasis lay on the societal roles that marriage fulfilled – to wit, procreation, raising children, provision of material security to the family, protection of family property[39] – marriage is now seen as a private agreement based on love. And this 'agreement' must be able to be dissolved when such love ends.[40] This concept of marriage seems to return to some of the basic principles of the French Revolution, when the law relating to marriage was also based on affection, love and autonomy rather than on legal obligations and coercion.[41] This change in the concept of marriage is characterised by a strong orientation toward self-determination and by an individual pursuit of satisfaction and inner harmony.[42] This 'de-institutionalisation' of marriage goes hand in hand with a liberalisation and contractualisation of the law of divorce. Those defending marriage as an unassailable institution[43] have had to concede to those defending marriage as a revocable contract.[44]

Secondly, over the course of the last two decades, marriage has rapidly lost its monopoly as the only possible format for a durable relationship. Secularisation brought the acceptance of many other models to organise one's love life. Unmarried cohabitation has become the norm in many societies. At some points legislators intervened and offered a model of legally organised unmarried cohabitation. Often this was an answer to the demands of same-sex couples. Fortunately in many European jurisdictions same-sex couples now enjoy a fully equal treatment and can also choose to marry.[45]

Autonomy and the freedom of choice have become the credo for many couples in organising their intimate relationships. However, this claim for autonomy may come with severe inconveniences in case of break-up, at least for the weaker party, who is usually the woman, as shown in section 1.

2.2. NO EFFECTIVE PROTECTION FOR MARRIED WOMEN UPON DIVORCE

The liberalisation of divorce law has reinforced the fragility of marriage. Love as the binding factor between spouses has led to less sustainable marriages than those based on property and social objectives.[46] The liberalisation of divorce law and the introduction of a 'right to divorce' in many European jurisdictions have increased the instability of marriage. This has led to the arrival of a new social risk, connected with the vulnerable family situation of a person.[47] The freedom to choose – in this case whether or not to remain married – creates today's divorce risk.[48]

In most continental jurisdictions, matrimonial property law does not offer any protection for the weaker party upon divorce. Although the default system (the legal regime) in principle offers some protection and solidarity (e.g. community property or compensation mechanisms), spouses may contract out of this regime. They can do this by concluding a pre- or post-marital contract, such as a contract of separation of property. Here, the title (property) principle rules in its full glory. Each spouse owns the assets in his or her name, or his or her share in the joint assets. An entitlement to maintenance still exists for the weaker party upon divorce, when matrimonial property law fails to create a reasonable protection, but this entitlement was often reduced in time or in extent by the latest divorce reforms (e.g. the Belgian divorce reform in 2007).

Although this freedom of choice, the contractualisation of matrimonial property law and the right to divorce may nicely fit our modern society's need for autonomy of both spouses, acting as independent and free individuals, it does ignore the consequences of day-to-day reality of how many couples and households are organised. Although the freedom of choice argument is gender-neutral and applies to men and women, social reality teaches us that there is a greater risk of women being treated unfairly. Whatever one's moral opinion may be, one cannot deny after considering the data shown in section 1 that many couples do make a choice that allows the husband to fully invest in his professional career and that does not allow the wife, in order to combine with children and household, to realise her full career potential.[49] She rather seeks a balance with family tasks. She then chooses another less demanding career (also less rewarding financially), or a nine-to-five job, a part-time job, a temporary career break, etc. The situation of women nowadays is often much more complex than in the old black and white days of housewives without any activity whatsoever on the job market. Today women juggle to keep all the balls in the air simultaneously. And very often it is the woman who reduces her career ambitions, picking a less demanding job and hence not fully realising her potential. Not surprisingly marriage for a professionally active woman in today's society has been qualified as a *Doppelbelastungsehe*.[50] She bears twice the burden, both at home and at her job.[51] In addition to all of this, it seems to be common for women to spend their income on consumer goods while men tend to invest.[52]

The choices women make in balancing work and family may be perfectly valid and sound during the marriage, in order for the couple and the family unit to find its private equilibrium, optimise their joint venture and realise their common dreams. A family policy that allows partners to agree on the division between income-generating labour on the one hand and care for the household and the children on the other can therefore be approved.[53] If the most necessary or efficient division of tasks would be to allow one type of task to be undertaken solely or mostly by one of the spouses, such a choice must be possible. Although economic independence may be stimulated by government, it need not be. After all, there are limits to the outsourcing of caring activities (the so-called *marketisation* of care) and parents often cherish a deserved desire to provide some of that care themselves.

Such choices may however come with devastating consequences upon divorce, resulting in one of the spouses receiving all of the assets and benefits and the other spouse being sent away with virtually no assets and the loss of a career and earning capacity.[54] In corporate law, regarding the relationship between business partners, many jurisdictions know the forbidden *societas leonina* where one partner takes all the profits and the other one just the losses. However, when the partners are not business partners (corporate law) but lovers (family law), this fundamental principle does not apply.

Given the adverse risks linked to a divorce, the introduction of a 'right to divorce' must not lead to the removal of responsibilities between spouses. On the contrary, it can be argued that the existence of a 'right to divorce' and an efficient and flexible divorce procedure justify a strengthened post-marriage solidarity. Whatever the decision of the spouses about the division of labour during the marriage, the consequences thereof must be borne by both when the marriage ends.[55] After the dissolution of the marriage the economic self-reliance of each spouse will once again be the starting point, but this does not prevent the division of the economic advantages and disadvantages resulting from the division of tasks during marriage. When the income of the former spouses is insufficient, an appeal can be made to communal solidarity in the form of social security or social support. Communal solidarity must nonetheless remain subsidiary to the solidarity between the former spouses within private law to compensate the economic inequalities caused by the relationship break-up.[56]

In Anglo-American jurisdictions this unfair situation is corrected through imperative law. The tradition of strict title (property) principle has been mitigated, as early as in the seventies of last century, by devices of equitable distribution of all sorts.[57] The judge can decide according to equity, as he thinks fit, to reallocate property and ignore title of assets. Moreover the judge must take into account a long list of statutory factors to justify such decision.[58] Although the weaker or poorer spouse does not enjoy a vested or secure entitlement but merely a possibility to participate in the marital wealth, the evolution in most US jurisdictions is towards a presumption of a 50/50 sharing of the marital gains.[59] And in England the recent case law of the House of Lords also points in this direction.[60] Continental legal systems as well seem to need a similar hard core protection through imperative legal provisions.

2.3. NO PROTECTION FOR UNMARRIED COHABITANTS

Another major flaw of traditional family law is that it does not take enough into account the social reality that many people live together unmarried.

In some jurisdictions unmarried cohabitants may register and enjoy a treatment similar to marriage. In other jurisdictions a semi-system exists. This is the case in Belgium with the rather peculiar system of legal cohabitation (articles 1475–1479 of the Belgian Civil Code), offering a limited set of rules.

Quite a number of unmarried partners live together in a de facto cohabitation that is not officially registered (although they may be domiciled at the same address and therefore enjoy several fiscal and social security benefits). For them no solidarity protection whatsoever is available. Matrimonial property law and inheritance law do not apply. All couples who have an intimate conjugal relationship, but decided not to enter into marriage are subject to the common rules of contract and property, and contractual freedom. It is quite easy to picture the situation of the wife in the break-up of a seventeen-year cohabitation with three children. As to the property aspects, the strict separation of property rule applies, with all the consequences as described above. Very often, even a right to maintenance or alimony is not available.

3. CREATING A FAIR FAMILY LAW

Taking into account the established gender inequalities, the question arises whether there is justification to de-institutionalise and remove solidarity from family law as has been done over the past decades. Couldn't, or indeed shouldn't, family law pursue a protective role, based on compensating for the actual socio-economic differences between man and wife which all too often give rise to endangered livelihoods and individual poverty after the break-up of the relationship? As already mentioned, the necessity of private solidarity is a hot topic in times of crisis when public finances are scarce and the financial sustainability of public safety nets is called into question. In the following section, first we debunk the arguments which underlie liberal family law, namely the autonomy of will and the freedom of choice. Then we make a number of suggestions to come to a more solidarity based and fair family law; a family law that takes the existing gender inequalities as its starting point and strives to reduce the pernicious financial consequences that these inequalities lead to.

3.1. FALLACY OF AUTONOMY AND CHOICE[61]

The factual situations of married couples under strict separation of property (in jurisdictions without imperative corrections), and of unmarried cohabitants without a contractual arrangement establishing property solidarity, are very similar in the event of the break-up of the relationship. For many, scholars and courts alike, the situation of spouses under separation of property or unmarried partners does not present a case for discrimination, since they supposedly have opted for this regime and not for the system of marriage or the legal regime in marriage with its focus on solidarity and all its protective rules.[62] It is a free and deliberate choice, so goes the argument.

So please accept the consequences of your choice. Do not claim rules you did not opt for. And certainly do not complain about discrimination.

In the following section, these arguments will be refuted. First we will consider the situation of the unmarried cohabitants (3.1.1) and then expand the analysis to those married under separation of property (3.1.2).

3.1.1. Unfairness for the weaker partner in unmarried cohabitation

The unmarried couple has made a choice not to be bound to each other. The choice was made not to be protected, to remain free. They had the choice to opt into the protective format of marriage. Yet they freely decided not to do so. Therefore, they should not get such protection. The general principles of the common law of contracts and property should be applied. This was their choice. Not applying specific principles of matrimonial property law, alimony law and inheritance law is the evident consequence of that choice. Hence this cannot be discriminative, as it is commonly said.[63]

This emphasis and rather formal focus on marriage may surprise. Indeed, it has been argued that in most international human rights instruments, it is not so much marriage as an institution that is protected but rather the family as the basic unit of society.[64] In Australia the consequences of a relationship are not based on the ceremony of marriage but rather on the relationship of interdependence between the parties[65] (see also the concept of the 'common law marriage'). Both elements invalidate the traditional choice argument: choice for marriage as such is not relevant and choice in itself is not an adequate frame because of the interdependence between the parties. We will formulate some arguments why the autonomy and choice argument in the context of marriage and matrimonial contracts is an inadequate and even erroneous frame.

3.1.1.1. No fully and adequately informed consent

First of all, for a choice to be binding in its legal consequences, it should be made with fully informed consent. It is very doubtful that married people have clear and sound knowledge about most legal regulations that govern the marriage. It is equally doubtful that unmarried couples would have explicit knowledge about the absence of such regulations in their case. It is naïve and unrealistic to assume that unmarried partners and spouses have a decent grasp of all of the legal consequences of living together or marrying.[66]

In a case of the Canadian Supreme Court, Justice L'Heureux Dubé put it elegantly in her dissenting opinion:

> 'Most people are not lawyers. They are often not aware of the state of the law. Worse, many maintain positive misconceptions as to what obligations and rights exist in association with marriage and other relationships.'[67]
>
> 'The fact that marriage gives rise to legal obligations does not, by itself, signal that the source of those obligations is a bargained-for exchange or the product of a consensus. While the price of a haircut is known in advance and can be contracted for (with a higher price for perms than for brushcuts), the same cannot be said about marriage.'[68]
>
> 'If I am incorrect in concluding that the source of the obligations in the MPA (Matrimonial Property Act of Nova Scotia) is not based on the choice of marriage, it does not follow that heterosexual unmarried cohabitants enter into their relationships specifically to avoid those legal obligations. In other words, the choice argument fails from both sides: many unmarried partners do not choose to cohabit or remain unmarried so as to avoid the legal consequences of marriage.'[69]

It therefore remains to be seen and proven that spouses and partners have made one or the other choice with an informed consent that is sufficient to qualify for a binding contract and to be bound by all of its consequences.

3.1.1.2. 'Will-deficiency' in love

Secondly, even with such full and complete information, one can doubt whether in fact a *free and autonomous choice* has been made at all. This is the point of interdependence of the parties as mentioned earlier. Picture the woman who has been informed of all the legal consequences and after four years of living together with a man and having his child, kindly asks him to marry her. The man however does not like the idea. He does not like the formalities. It is an old-fashioned establishment relic. And, 'honey, we don't need this. Our love is all that matters'. What can this woman do? It takes two to marry. So she cannot make the choice for marriage if he does not join her in that choice. Therefore she did not make the choice to avoid marriage, and she cannot be held liable for the choice which she did not make.

The counterargument could be that the woman effectively did make such choice not to marry, because she decided to stay in the relationship. It is her autonomy and decision to stay in the relationship or to leave. It is true that a rational actor could argue that given the wish of the woman to marry, the moment the man refuses to fulfil this wish, she should leave the relationship.

Since she did not decide to do so, one could argue that she has deliberately joined the choice of the man, which was not to marry. Therefore she also made the choice not to marry, and is bound by its legal consequences.

Here the reply might be that the choice to stay in the relationship and therefore not to marry, is not a free and autonomous choice. Given the intimate conjugal relationship and the fact that the woman loves the man, she has not made a free and deliberate choice. Her consent to that particular choice is 'poisoned', 'contaminated' or 'hindered' by her love. Maybe we should introduce a new *will-deficiency in love and romance* in concluding valid contracts.[70]

Furthermore, her choice may also have been influenced by the presence of the child they have together. Would it not be in the interest of the child that its parents stay together as a couple? So the autonomy and will of the woman may have been impacted by the child's interest and fate. Her free will is deficient as is the case when a contract is made by mistake or under duress such as threat or force.[71] Therefore, she did not make the free choice not to marry and cannot be bound by the legal consequences of such choice not made.

3.1.1.3. Not words but behaviour and actions count

How can we reconcile this with the perspective of the man? On his side, one can argue that he did make a free choice not to marry. Suppose he knew very well what he was doing. He was fully informed on all the legal ins and outs and the consequences of marriage, legal cohabitation and de facto cohabitation. Based on this information he made up his mind and with informed consent he decided the best choice was not to marry. He made a choice in favour of freedom, not being bound, being able to escape and getting out whenever he wishes to, with as low and cheap consequences as possible. Therefore his choice should be respected and legal consequences that are not those of his choice should not be imposed on him. This sounds like a strong argument, does it not?

Not really. It is correct that he may have said: 'I want freedom. I do not want to marry. I want to be able to end this relationship whenever I wish with no strings attached and with no responsibilities or liabilities'. And his actions may have been in line with his words in the very first months or even years of the relationship. However, at some point in time, his words have been overruled by his actions and behaviour.[72] The longer he stays in the relationship, the more he commits to the common project, dreams, hopes and lives together, the more his behaviour is inconsistent with his words. At some point, he reaches a tipping point: a point where his behaviour is so clearly and explicitly in contradiction with the words he once pronounced, that he cannot return to the freedom of his words anymore.

3.1.1.4. Point of no return

There is a wide margin of discretion and appreciation to define this tipping point of no return. It can be a multitude of elements, such as three years of living together, or having a child together, or the fact that a substantial contribution is made by one or by both partners to the relationship or in the sole interest of the other partner.[73] The concrete determination or defining criteria of the point of no return must be made in specific legislation. It will depend on the political process and it is an arbitrary choice. Hereafter we refer to unmarried cohabitation that has reached the point of no return according to a set of legal criteria to be agreed upon, as *durable cohabitation* or *conjugal cohabitation.*

What is not arbitrary but certain is that the point of no return is out there. We may debate its conditions, but not the principle itself. And once it is reached, there is no way back. Once the man has said A, but is overwhelmingly doing B, he should not be held to the consequences of A, but to the consequences of B.[74] This does not contradict his choice. For it is his behaviour and his own pattern of actions that constitute his choice. It is the choice of actions, the choice of life, which determines his responsibilities, not the choice pronounced in cheap words, one day, a long time ago.

From this point of no return, a protective format similar to the one of marriage and the legal regime with its focus on solidarity and all its protective rules (namely principles of matrimonial property law, alimony law and inheritance law) must be applied. Consequently the harsh principles of the common law of contracts and property will be corrected through imperative rules with a protective role.

3.1.2. Unfairness of matrimonial contracts of strict separation of property

At the moment of conclusion of the matrimonial contract, often a pre-nuptial agreement, both spouses agree on the words of a contract for full autonomy and independence. Upon divorce, even after fifteen or twenty years of marriage and two or three children, the property relationship between the spouses is governed by these strict words. The inequities and unfairness of the title principle, leaving the vast majority of the assets to the husband, do not seem to overrule, for Belgian and many continental courts, the words of the original contract. The situation is very different from the Anglo-American approach.

The defenders of contractual autonomy and legal certainty produce again the choice argument. Both spouses made a choice for separation of property and they should respect it.

It is striking to observe such vigorous defence of contractual autonomy while in other areas of law, such as labour law or consumer law, numerous imperative rules protecting the weaker parties allow the overruling of contractual arrangements.[75] It is difficult to understand why the development of contract law for consumers into a protective format whereby a signed contract may even be revoked unilaterally within a fixed period, would not be equally applicable in long term contracts between intimate partners. For the advocates of contractual autonomy, apparently employees and consumers deserve more protection than spouses.

3.1.2.1. Fully and adequately informed consent

The choice fallacy claims that the spouses were fully informed, by the notary, about the consequences and risks of the separation of property. With that knowledge they made the choice for that contract and now, upon divorce, they must just live by the consequences of that choice and accept them.

We can challenge this choice dictate with the same arguments as above. Even with full information about the legal rules, did they really understand the concrete consequences of all these rules? Could they imagine the impact of the arrival of children and the ensuing effect on the organisation model, responsibilities and task divisions in the family? As for all long term contracts, it is difficult to predict all events coming up and all surprises of life. People may lose their jobs, a spouse may get sick, children may have social or psychological problems, etc.

The minority opinion of Justice L'Heureux Dubé in the quoted Canadian decision, is again illuminating:

> 'The marital relationship changes over time. Houses and other assets are bought and sold, one of the partners is promoted or loses their job, children are born, accidents occur, or a member of the family becomes ill. These and other events

> are rarely anticipated at the outset and appropriately bargained for. Further, neither spouse can anticipate who will contribute what to the marriage. As a consequence, even the most intelligent of adults lack the capacity to evaluate the commitments involved in any agreement dealing with the consequences of a dissolution that will only come after great change occurs in the relationship.'[76]

Fully informed consent to agree with a contract of strict separation of property requires information.[77]

First of all, the information must be complete and comprise the full picture of the legal rules, including the alternatives. A common reason for spouses under Belgian law to opt for a separation of property is the overkill creditor protection of the community regime in case of professional debts.[78] Offering the strict separation of property as the solution for this creditor risk is not giving full information.[79] The full picture includes explaining that one indeed needs a contract of separation of property to counter that risk, yet not a contract of strict separation. One can perfectly mitigate the creditor risk with a contract of separation with a 50/50 participation clause in the marital gains.

Secondly, the information should not merely be about the legal rules but also explain the very concrete consequences and possible risks of these rules in different scenarios. Therefore it is vital to ask the wife whether she understands that such contract and its principles of autonomy may result in a scenario where she is depending on maintenance upon divorce after twenty years. So the story goes:[80]

> 'A woman, a successful lawyer, quits her job and the junior partner track in her law firm, only after three years of marriage because of the work with their two children. She would work part-time in a notary's office, earning about ten times less. All her time would be devoted to raising the children, organising the household and supporting her husband. He would need that, being an intern at the local hospital with the ambition of becoming head of department. Many evenings of listening to him, reassuring and helping him, hosting dinners for the hospital's Board of Directors. Feeling independent, she would be using her small salary to pay the groceries and the kids' stuff. The house in Brussels and later the house at the beach in Knokke would be bought with the husband's management company. All would go rather well for a couple of years, however she would not be able to continue working at the notary's office because of the youngest son's learning disorder. He would need all the help and assistance of his mother. But she would be happy, knowing that she and her husband would be in it together, for better and for worse. And then she would be so surprised, after twenty years, to learn that her husband needed some space, and that a new

> young and beautiful doctor of 27 at the hospital was helpful in giving him some extra oxygen. And then he would ask her to live by the rules of their contract of autonomy and independence, and apply the title principle. The house and apartment would be his, also the stock portfolio and the Porsche. The VW Golf and one small bank account would be hers. And of course he would pay maintenance for the children and also for her, for a couple of years until she finds a new job.'

If the wife receives this kind of full and realistic information, chances are high that she will not make the choice for the strict separation of property.

This is why we need to stimulate much more open communication and negotiation before the marriage about the possible matrimonial contracts.[81] Such negotiation may and should empower the weaker party, often the woman, helping her to discover and assert her own legitimate interests. She must overcome the romantic idea that, although he insists on strict separation of property, he means so well.

And even if the weaker party does agree with the strict separation of property, the question remains whether it has been a free and autonomous choice, as explained above concerning the choice to marry or not. It also takes two to agree to a marital contract.

3.1.2.2. Not words but behaviour and actions count from the point of no return

The fundamental idea of freedom to act but being held responsible for those acts also counts in the context of matrimonial contracts of strict and pure separation of property. How can a civilised society accept to only look at the words of twenty years ago? Here too, the reasoning should be that both spouses thought and assumed they would organise their partnership in full equality, autonomy and independence and therefore opted for these words. However over the years they may have shaped their joint venture in a totally different way with a role and task division that became much more complicated than ever assumed and often with a huge contribution of one of the partners, mostly the wife, to the household and the children. Thereby, she is sacrificing, at least partially, her own earning capacity and career potential. The couple's behaviour and actions in that case have overruled the words of the contract. Although they agreed to A in words, the choices they have made over the years through their actions were for B, and it is to B they should be held. As long as both spouses have contributed equally to the partnership, in all kinds of relevant ways, they should share equally in the marital gains or partnership assets. Why would one contribution, working on the labour market, be exclusively decisive? Therefore, also for married couples who have chosen for strict separation of property, there should be a point of no return where contractual autonomy is replaced by a protective format of imperative rules with a focus on solidarity.

4. CONCLUSION

A discrepancy exists between the ideal image of an emancipated and individualised society where each individual is financially independent, on the one hand, and the socio-economic reality on the other. Even if complete financial dependence between spouses is no longer the starting point when living together, a certain level of income dependency remains. Upon entry into a relationship, whether or not within a marriage, an economic unit is created which leads to dependency between the partners caused by the division of tasks and income within the couple. Women in particular remain dependent on a degree of 'income sharing' in a relationship, because they – more often than men – work part-time, make use of the system of career breaks or continue to work full-time but curtail their career prospects and choose a so-called nine-to-five job so that they can take on caring tasks. This division of activities and choices within a relationship still leads to inequalities between men and women in the labour market as well as in their respective earning capacities. As a result, divorce or relationship break up continue to go hand in hand with a loss of prosperity and higher risk of poverty, especially for women.

The legal protection of a partner upon the dissolution of a relationship seems to be insufficiently attuned to today's society. Due to the economic crisis, public funds to cover this risk are scarce. We advocate that a shift from public to private law protection is needed.

In most western legal systems, family policy and family law legislators have, with some success, focused on realising the ideals of freedom and equality. In contrast, the ideal of fraternity has been neglected. The role of solidarity in provisions relating to co-habitation has been eroded. Yet a balance between these three revolutionary ideals is essential. The neglect of one of the three principles (in this case fraternity or solidarity) will in the longer term be detrimental to the other two (that is equality and freedom). The legislator too often assumes the economic self-reliance and equality of the partners, and pays too little attention to the financial consequences of the breakdown of a relationship. It is remarkable how little importance the legislator attaches to the economic impact that co-habitation, and marriage in particular, has on some people, primarily women and children.

Moreover, we must emphasise the advantages that the government gets from promoting and supporting relationships, such as marriage, at times of economic crisis. A relationship between partners is the 'cheapest' and most efficient way to guarantee the livelihood of an individual, namely by placing the responsibility for that economic security with another individual, the partner. In a partnership the social and other risks that may befall an individual are dealt with communally. Given the financial limits of the social security system and the welfare state, the benefit of such private partnerships should not be underestimated. At the peak of the welfare state, a reduction of family solidarity was forecasted, but we must now realise, at a time of ever-increasing economic and financial difficulties, that the opposite is true. The family must be once again held responsible for guaranteeing the livelihood of the individual. Family law needs to shape this solidarity and make it a reality.

In this chapter some suggestions have been made to come to a more solidarity-based and fair family law, that takes the existing gender inequalities as its starting point and strives to compensate for the pernicious financial consequences that these inequalities lead to. We had a particular focus on the precarious situation of unmarried cohabitants and spouses married under separation of property.

First, the necessity of more open communication and transparent and informed negotiation about the consequences of the choice to marry or not, and under which regime, was emphasised. Such negotiation should empower the weaker party, often the woman, helping her to discover and assert her own legitimate interests.

Secondly, the idea of freedom to act yet being held responsible for those acts was promoted. On each relationship with a certain degree of interdependence, a protective format with a focus on solidarity should be applied. From the so-called 'point of no return', the autonomy of will and the freedom of choice of the partners not to be in a relationship characterised by solidarity could be overruled by imperative corrections to protect the weakest party. Criteria to define the point of no return can be: three years of living together, or having a child together, or the fact that a substantial contribution is made by one or by both partners to the relationship or in the sole interest of the other partner. An example of such an imperative correction to the autonomy of will and the freedom of choice is the equal division of the marital gains or partnership assets when both spouses have contributed equally to the partnership in any relevant way.

Endnotes

1. See: art. 10, §3 Belgian Constitution; art. 14 European Convention on Human Rights and Protocol 12; art. 2.2. et seq. International Covenant on Economic, Social and Cultural Rights 1966; art. 26 International Covenant on Civil and Political Rights 1966; Convention on the Political Rights of Women 1953; Convention on the Elimination of All Forms of Discrimination Against Women 1979; arts. 10, 19 and 157 Consolidated version of the Treaty on the Functioning of the European Union; Council Directive 75/117/EEC of 10 February 1975 on the approximation of the laws of the Member States relating to the application of the principle of equal pay for men and women; Council Directive 76/207/EEC of 9 February 1976 on the implementation of the principle of equal treatment for men and women as regards access to employment, vocational training and promotion, and working conditions; Council Directive 79/7/EEC of 19 December 1978 on the progressive implementation of the principle of equal treatment for men and women in matters of social security; Council Directive 86/378/EEC of 24 July 1986 on the implementation of the principle of equal treatment for men and women in occupational social security schemes; Council Directive 86/613/EEC of 11 December 1986 on the application of the principle of equal treatment between men and women engaged in an activity, including agriculture, in a self-employed capacity, and on the protection of self-employed women during pregnancy and motherhood; Council Directive 96/97/EC of 20 December 1996 amending Directive 86/378/EEC on the implementation of the principle of equal treatment for men and women in occupational social security schemes; Council Directive 97/80/EC of 15 December 1997 on the burden of proof in cases of discrimination based on sex; Council Directive 2002/73/EC of the European Parliament and of the Council of 23 September 2002 amending Council Directive 76/207/EEC on the implementation of the principle of equal treatment for men and women as regards access to employment, vocational training and promotion, and working conditions; Council Directive 2004/113/EC of 13 December 2004 implementing the principle of equal treatment between men and women in the access to and supply of goods and services; and Directive 2006/54/EC of the European Parliament and of the Council of 5 July 2006 on the implementation of the principle of equal opportunities and equal treatment of men and women in matters of employment and occupation.
2. L. Snoeckx, B. Dehertogh and D. Mortelmans, 'The Distribution of Household Tasks in First-Marriage Families and Stepfamilies across Europe', in J. Pryor (ed.), *The International Handbook of Stepfamilies: Policy and Practice in Legal, Research, and Clinical Environments*, New Jersey, John Wiley & Sons, 2008, pp. 277–298.
3. C. Defever and D. Mortelmans, *De Socio-Economische Positie van Vrouwen en Mannen na de Transities Echtscheiding en Verweduwing. Een Longitudinale Studie op de Kruispuntbank Sociale Zekerheid*, Antwerp-Hasselt, Steunpunt Gelijkekansenbeleid, 2011.

4. H. Van Hove, *The Gender Pay Gap in Belgium. Report 2013*, Brussels, Institute for the Equality of Women and Men, 2013.
5. A. Leyman and N. Steegmans, *Het Vlaamse Onderwijs in Genderstatistieken*, Antwerp-Hasselt: Steunpunt Gelijkekansenbeleid, 2006.
6. A. Van Woensel, *Genderjaarboek 2007 MV United: in Cijfers*, Brussels, ESF-Agentschap-Departement Werk en Sociale Economie, 2007.
7. A. Baerts, N. Deschacht and M.-A. Guerry, *Carrières van Vrouwen en Mannen: een Literatuurstudie*, Brussels, VUB, 2008.
8. A. Baerts, N. Deschacht and M.-A. Guerry, *Carrières van Vrouwen en Mannen: een Literatuurstudie*, Brussels, VUB, 2008.
9. D. Frans, D. Mortelmans and C. Masquillier, *Financial Consequences of Career Breaks: a Latent Growth Model on Register Data*, Antwerp, Steunpunt WSE, 2011.
10. B. Desmet, I. Glorieux and J. Vandeweyer, *Wie zijn de Loopbaanonderbrekers? Sociodemografische Kenmerken, Motivaties en Arbeidsverhouding van Loopbaanonderbrekers*, Brussels, TOR, Vrije Universiteit Brussel, 2007.
11. D. Frans, D. Mortelmans and C. Masquillier, *Financial Consequences of Career Breaks: A Latent Growth Model on Register Data*, Antwerp, Steunpunt WSE, 2011.
12. D. Frans, D. Mortelmans and C. Masquillier, *Financial Consequences of Career Breaks: A Latent Growth Model on Register Data*, Antwerp, Steunpunt WSE, 2011.
13. D. Frans and D. Mortelmans, *Longitudinale Gevolgen van Loopbaanonderbrekingen*, Antwerp, Steunpunt WSE, 2009.
14. N. Soens, A. De Vos, D. Buyens, L. Heylen, A. Kuppens, I. Van Puyvelde and D. Mortelmans, 'Belgische Loopbanen in Kaart: Traditioneel of Transitioneel?', in *Reeks Actuele Problemen met betrekking tot de Sociale Cohesie,* Ghent, Academia Press, 2005.
15. M. Kremer, *How Welfare States Care: Culture, Gender and Parenting in Europe*, Amsterdam, Amsterdam University Press, 2007.
16. K. Vanderweyden, 'Van Huisman tot Carrièrevrouw. Over Minder Werken en Sociale Integratie bij Mannen en Vrouwen', in H.I.V. Gezinswetenschappen (ed.), *Vaders in Soorten,* Tielt, Lannoo, 2002.
17. M. Jansen and A. Liefbroer, 'Samen Kiezen, Samen Delen? De Invloed van Waardenoriëntaties van Levenspartners op de Geboorte van Kinderen en de Taakverdeling', (2002) 1 *Tijdschrift Sociale Wetenschappen*, 2–22; I. Glorieux and J. Minnen, 'Kinderen Maken het Verschil. Over de Invloed van Kinderen op het Tijdsbestedingspatroon van Ouders', (2004) 1 *Tijdschrift van de Gezinsbond – Studiedienst*, 2–10.
18. I. Glorieux, J. Minnen and T.-P. Van Tienoven, *Een Weekje België. Resultaten van het Belgisch Tijdsbestedingsonderzoek 2005*, Brussels, TOR, Vrije Universiteit Brussel, 2008.
19. D. Mortelmans, W. Ottoy and M. Verstreken, 'Een Longitudinale Kijk op de Gender-Verdeling van Huishoudelijke Taken', (2003) 24 *Tijdschrift voor Sociologie*, 2–3.
20. G. Beets, 'De Timing van het Eerste Kind: een Overzicht', (2004) 1 *Bevolking en gezin*, 115–142.
21. D. Mortelmans, S. Van Ourti and M. Verstreken, 'De Transformatie van een Man in een Vader. De Gevolgen van het Eerste Kind op het Leven van een Man', in H.I.V. Gezinswetenschappen (ed.), *Vaders in Soorten,* Tielt, Lanoo, 2002.
22. J. Dirk Vlasblom and J. Schippers, 'Changing Dynamics in Female Employment around Childbirth: Evidence from Germany, the Netherlands and thc UK', (2006) 2 *Work, Employment and Society*, 329–347.

23. K. Vanderweyden, 'Van Huisman tot Carrièrevrouw. Over Minder Werken en Sociale Integratie bij Mannen en Vrouwen', in H.I.V. Gezinswetenschappen (ed.), *Vaders in Soorten,* Tielt, Lannoo, 2002.
24. D. Mortelmans, S. Van Ourti and M. Verstreken, 'De Transformatie van een Man in een Vader. De Gevolgen van het Eerste Kind op het Leven van een Man', in H.I.V. Gezinswetenschappen (ed.), *Vaders in Soorten,* Tielt, Lanoo, 2002.
25. K. Vanderweyden, 'Van Huisman tot Carrièrevrouw. Over Minder Werken en Sociale Integratie bij Mannen en Vrouwen', in H.I.V. Gezinswetenschappen (ed.), *Vaders in Soorten,* Tielt, Lannoo, 2002.
26. C. Defever, W. Van Lancker, T. Hufkens, D. Mortelmans and B. Cantillon, 'De Inkomenspositie en het Armoederisico van Alleenstaande Ouders in Vlaanderen', in J. Noppe, L. Vanderleyden and M. Callens (eds.), *De Sociale Staat van Vlaanderen 2013,* Brussels, Studiedienst Vlaamse Regering, 2013.
27. C. Defever, W. Van Lancker, T. Hufkens, D. Mortelmans and B. Cantillon, 'De Inkomenspositie en het Armoederisico van Alleenstaande Ouders in Vlaanderen', in J. Noppe, L. Vanderleyden and M. Callens (eds.), *De Sociale Staat van Vlaanderen 2013,* Brussels, Studiedienst Vlaamse Regering, 2013.
28. C. Defever and D. Mortelmans, *De Socio-Economische Positie van Vrouwen en Mannen na de Transities Echtscheiding en Verweduwing. Een Longitudinale Studie op de Kruispuntbank Sociale Zekerheid,* Antwerp-Hasselt, Steunpunt Gelijkekansenbeleid, 2011.
29. E. Speltincx and T. Jacobs, *Gezinsontbinding in Vlaanderen. Boek 2: Gevolgen van Echtscheiding,* Antwerp, Panelstudie van de Belgische huishoudens, 2000; D. Mortelmans, M.T. Casman and R. Doutrelepont, *Elf Jaar uit het Leven in België: Socio-Economische Analyses op het Gezinsdemografisch Panel Psbh,* Ghent, Academia Press, 2004); M. Corijn, 'Impact op de Sociaal-Economische Positie van Ex-Partners', in C. Van Peer (ed.), *De Impact van een (Echt)Scheiding op Kinderen en Ex-Partners,* Brussels, Studiedienst van de Vlaamse Gemeenschap, 2007; M. Jansen, 'De Financiële Gevolgen van Relatiebreuken: Terugval en Herstel bij Mannen en Vrouwen', in D. Cuypers, D. Mortelmans and N. Torfs (eds.), *Is Echtscheiding Werkelijk Win for Life?,* Bruges, Die Keure, 2008; D. Mortelmans, L. Snoeckx and P. Raeymaeckers, 'Belgium: Economic Hardship Despite Elaborate Childcar and Leave Time Programmes', in H. Andeb and D. Hummelsheim (eds.), *When Marriage Ends. Economic and Social Consequences of Partnership Dissolution,* Cheltenham, Edward Elgar Publishing Limited, 2009.
30. D. Mortelmans, L. Snoeckx and P. Raeymaeckers, 'Belgium: Economic Hardship Despite Elaborate Childcar and Leave Time Programmes', in H. Andeb and D. Hummelsheim (eds.), *When Marriage Ends. Economic and Social Consequences of Partnership Dissolution,* Cheltenham, Edward Elgar Publishing Limited, 2009.
31. M. Corijn, 'Impact op de Sociaal-Economische Positie van Ex-Partners', in C. Van Peer (ed.), *De Impact van een (Echt)Scheiding op Kinderen en Ex-Partners,* Brussels, Studiedienst van de Vlaamse Gemeenschap, 2007; M. Jansen, 'De Financiële Gevolgen van Relatiebreuken: Terugval en Herstel bij Mannen en Vrouwen', in D. Cuypers, D. Mortelmans and N. Torfs (eds.), *Is Echtscheiding Werkelijk Win for Life?,* Bruges, Die Keure, 2008; T. Jacobs, A. Bauwens and E. Speltincx, *Gezinsontbinding in Vlaanderen. Boek 1: Persoonlijke relaties in beweging,* Antwerp, Panelstudie van de Belgische huishoudens, 2000.

32. M. Jansen, 'De Financiële Gevolgen van Relatiebreuken: Terugval en Herstel bij Mannen en Vrouwen', in D. Cuypers, D. Mortelmans and N. Torfs (eds.), *Is Echtscheiding Werkelijk Win for Life?*, Bruges, Die Keure, 2008.
33. C. Defever and D. Mortelmans, *De Socio-Economische Positie van Vrouwen en Mannen na de Transities Echtscheiding en Verweduwing. Een Longitudinale Studie op de Kruispuntbank Sociale Zekerheid*, Antwerp-Hasselt, Steunpunt Gelijkekansenbeleid, 2011; C. Defever, W. Van Lancker, T. Hufkens, D. Mortelmans and B. Cantillon, 'De Inkomenspositie en het Armoederisico van Alleenstaande Ouders in Vlaanderen', in J. Noppe, L. Vanderleyden and M. Callens (eds.), *De Sociale Staat Van Vlaanderen 2013*, Brussels, Studiedienst Vlaamse Regering, 2013.
34. D. Mortelmans, *Copingstrategieën en Beleving van Sociaal-Economische Gevolgen bij Gescheiden Vaders*, Antwerp, Universiteit Antwerpen, 2007.
35. Art. 301, §4 of the Belgian Civil Code. See also: D. Mortelmans, F. Swennen and E. Alofs, 'De Echtscheiding en haar Gevolgen: een Vervlochten Evolutie van Recht en Samenleving', in D. Cuypers, D. Mortelmans and N. Torfs (eds.), *Is Echtscheiding Werkelijk Win for Life?*, Brugge, Die Keure, 2008.
36. C. Dewilde, 'The Financial Consequences of Relationship Dissolution for Women in Western Europe', in E. Ruspini and A. Dale (eds.), *The Gender Dimension of Social Change. The Contribution of Dynamic Research to the Study of Women's Life Courses*, Bristol, Policy Press, 2002; B. Cantillon, G. Verbist and V. De Maesschalck, *Sociaal-Economische Levensomstandigheden Van Eenoudergezinnen in België*, Antwerp, Centrum voor Sociaal Beleid, 2003.
37. T. Boelaert (ed.), *Alimentatie: tussen Theorie en Praktijk. Enkele Beschouwingen over de Tegemoetkoming van de Dienst voor Alimentatievorderingen*, Bruges, Die Keure, 2008; S. Petit, 'Gebruik Van Psbh-Gegevens om een Beter Beeld te Krijgen van Nieuw Samengestelde Gezinnen in België', in K. Boudewijnstichting (ed.), *Het Kind in een Nieuw Samengesteld Gezin*, Brussels, Konink Boudewijnstichting, 2008.
38. D. Mortelmans, *Copingstrategieën en Beleving van Sociaal-Economische Gevolgen bij Gescheiden Vaders*, Antwerp, Universiteit Antwerpen, 2007; M. Cancian and D. Meyer, 'Who Gets Custody?', (1998) 2 *Demography*, 147–157.
39. H. De Page, *Traité Elémentaire de Droit Civil Belge*, I, Brussels, Bruylant, 1939, nos. 564, 565, 567; G. Baeteman, *Overzicht van het Personen- en Gezinsrecht*, Deurne, Kluwer, 1993, pp. 383–385; B. Poelemans, *Scheiden op Maat. Pleidooi voor een Gematigde Hervorming van het Echtscheidingsrecht*, Ghent, Mys & Breesch, 1994, p. 4; J.-L. Renchon, 'La Nouvelle Réforme (précipitée) du Droit Belge du Divorce: le "Droit" au Divorce', (2007) *RTDF (Revue trimestrielle de droit familial)*, 927 et seq., 934 et seq., 1059 et seq.
40. See also: M. Antokolskaia, 'Objectives and Values of Substantive Family Law', in J. Meeusen, M. Pertegas, G. Straetmans and F. Swennen (eds.), *International Family Law of the European Union*, Antwerp, Intersentia, 2007, pp. 54 et seq.; B. Cantillon, *Nieuwe Behoeften naar Zekerheid. Vrouw, Gezin en Inkomensverdeling*, Leuven, Acco, 1990, p. 340; D. Dandoy, 'Plaidoyer en faveur de mécanismes juridiques plus cohérents pour appréhender au moment de la rupture du couple, la problématique de l'économie conjugale', (2013) *Familie & Recht*, 1 et seq. (available at www.familieenrecht.nl); J.-L. Renchon, 'Le Droit de la Personne et de la Famille: de l'Indisponibilité à l'Autodétermination', in D. Heirbaut and G. Martyn (eds.), *Napoleons Nalatenschap*, Mechelen, Kluwer, 2005, pp. 101 and 132 et seq.

41. E. ALOFS, 'Het Echtscheidingsrecht en -Risico in Historisch Perspectief', in D. DE RUYSSCHER, P. DE HERT and M. DE METSENAERE (eds.), *Een Leven van Inzet. Liber Amicorum Michel Magits*, Mechelen, Kluwer, 2012, pp. 89 et seq.
42. Criticising the new concept of marriage: C. DE WULF, 'Slotbeschouwingen bij de Cyclus "Familiale Vermogensplanning in de 21ste Eeuw"', in X. (eds.), *Familiale Vermogensplanning*, Mechelen, Kluwer, 2004, pp. 757 et seq.; J.-L. RENCHON, 'La Nouvelle Réforme (Précipitée) du Droit Belge du Divorce: le "Droit" au Divorce', (2007) *RTDF (Revue trimestrielle de droit familial)*, 927 et seq., 934 et seq., 1058 et seq.
43. H. DE PAGE, *Traité Elémentaire de Droit Civil Belge*, I, Brussels, Bruylant, 1939, no. 567.
44. See: J. FIERENS, 'La Quadrature de la Faute dans le Cercle du Divorce', (2007) *JT (Journal des tribunaux)*, 336; J. FIERENS, 'La Figure Contractuelle dans la Formation du Lien Matrimonial, le Divorce et l'Etablissement de la Filiation', in Y. POULET, P. WÉRY and P. WYNANTS (eds.), *Liber Amicorum Michel Coipel*, Brussels, Kluwer, 2004, pp. 283, 287–288, 298–299; G.P. HOEFNAGELS, 'Liberalisering, Humanisering en de Echtscheiding door Onderlinge Toestemming', (1984) *FJR*, 52; G.B. HOEFNAGELS, 'Het Huwelijk als Relatie en als Instituut', in X. (eds.), *Het Huwelijk*, Zwolle, Tjeenk Willink, 1984, pp. 15 et seq.; B. POELEMANS, *Scheiden op Maat. Pleidooi voor een Gematigde Hervorming van het Echtscheidingsrecht*, Ghent, Mys & Breesch, 1994, p. 12; J.-L. RENCHON, 'Le Droit de la Personne et de la Famille: de l'Indisponibilité à l'Autodétermination', in D. HEIRBAUT and G. MARTYN (eds.), *Napoleons Nalatenschap*, Mechelen, Kluwer, 2005, pp. 132 et seq.; H.C.F. SCHOORDIJK, 'Lets over het Huwelijk als Overeenkomst. Een Enkele Opmerking over Huwelijk en Vermogensrecht', in X. (eds.), *Het Huwelijk*, Zwolle, Tjeenk Willink, 1984, pp. 94 et seq.
45. See: K. BOELE-WOELKI and A. FUCHS (eds.), *Legal Recognition of Same-Sex Relationships in Europe*, Antwerp, Intersentia, 2012, 312 p.
46. B. POELEMANS, *Scheiden op Maat. Pleidooi voor een Gematigde Hervorming van het Echtscheidingsrecht*, Ghent, Mys & Breesch, 1994, p. 4; A. WYLLEMAN, 'De Ontwikkeling van het Patrimoniaal Familierecht in het Belgisch Burgerlijk Wetboek', in D. HEIRBAUT and G. MARTYN (eds.), *Napoleons Nalatenschap*, Mechelen, Kluwer, 2005, p. 232.
47. See also: E. ALOFS, 'Het echtscheidingsrisico in België', (2013) *T.Fam. (Tijdschrift voor Familierecht)*, 24–29; E. ALOFS, 'Het echtscheidingsrecht en -risico in historisch perspectief', in D. DE RUYSSCHER, P. DE HERT and M. DE METSENAERE (eds.), *Een leven van inzet. Liber amicorum Michel Magits*, Mechelen, Kluwer, 2012, pp. 77–117; G. BONOLI, *Modernising Post-War Welfare States. Explaining Diversity in Patterns of Adaption to New Social Risks*, paper prepared for presentation at the 2nd ESPAnet annual conference, Oxford, 9–11 September 2004, www.spsw.ox.ac.uk/fileadmin/static/Espanet/espanetconference/papers/ppr%5B1%5D.6B.GB.pdf, pp. 11–12.
48. D. GELDOF, *Niet Meer Maar Beter. Over Zelfbeperking in de Risicomaatschappij*, Leuven, Acco, 1999, p. 63.
49. See also: R. HOLTMAAT, *Met Zorg een Recht? Een Analyse van het Politiek-Juridisch Vertoog over Bijstandsrecht*, Zwolle, W.E.J. Tjeenk Willink, 1992, 394 p.
50. A. VERBEKE, *Goederenverdeling bij Echtscheiding (Property Division Upon Divorce)*, Antwerp, Maklu, 1991 and 1994 second unrevised edition, pp. 22–24 (available at http://ssrn.com/abstract=1751574).
51. A. VERBEKE, *Goederenverdeling bij Echtscheiding (Property Division Upon Divorce)*, Antwerp, Maklu, 1991 and 1994 second unrevised edition, pp. 284–287 (available at http://ssrn.com/abstract=1751574).

52. A. Verbeke, 'Gender-Ongelijkheid bij Zuivere Scheiding van Goederen. Pleidooi voor een Gedwongen én Onderhandelde Aanpak', (2010) *TEP (Tijdschrift Estate Planning)*, 104 (available at http://ssrn.com/abstract=1751029).
53. See also: T.L.J. Bod, *Het Pensioenbegrip. Enige Beschouwingen over het Pensioen en zijn Rechtskarakter*, Zwolle, W.E.J. Tjeenk Willink, 1994, p. 34; D.M. Campagne, *Alimentatie, Onderhoudsplicht tussen Voormalige Echtgenoten, Betalingen terzake van Echtscheiding, een Evolutie*, Deventer, Kluwer, 1978, p. 210; L. De Witte and L. Van den Bossche, *Vermits het Recht niet tot Liefde kan Dwingen… Naar een Schuldloze Echtscheiding*, Brussels, SEVI, 1986, pp. 66, 73.
54. See also: D. Dandoy, 'Playdoyer en faveur de mécanismes juridiques plus cohérents pour appréhender au moment de la rupture du couple, la problématique de l'économie conjugale', (2013) *Familie & Recht*, 17 et seq. (available at www.familieenrecht.nl).
55. See also: T.L.J. Bod, *Het Pensioenbegrip. Enige Beschouwingen over het Pensioen en zijn Rechtskarakter*, Zwolle, W.E.J. Tjeenk Willink, 1994, p. 34; L. De Witte and L. Van den Bossche, *Vermits het Recht niet tot Liefde kan Dwingen… Naar een Schuldloze Echtscheiding*, Brussels, SEVI, 1986, pp. 13, 67; M.J.A. Van Mourik, 'Het Huwelijk', in X. (eds), *Het Huwelijk*, Zwolle, Tjeenk Willink, 1984, pp. 10–11; A. Verbeke, 'Weg met huwelijk en echtscheiding', (2004) *TPR (Tijdschrift voor Privaatrecht)*, 969 et seq.
56. L. De Witte and L. Van den Bossche, *Vermits het Recht niet tot Liefde kan Dwingen… Naar een Schuldloze Echtscheiding*, Brussels, SEVI, 1986, p. 73.
57. A. Verbeke, *Goederenverdeling bij Echtscheiding (Property Division Upon Divorce)*, Antwerp, Maklu, 1991 and 1994 second unrevised edition, pp. 240–270 (available at http://ssrn.com/abstract=1751574); A. Verbeke (General Reporter) and S. Cretney, F. Grauers, P. Malaurie, H. Ofner, M. Savolainen, F. Skorini and G. van der Burght (Country Reporters), 'European Marital Property Law. Survey 1988–1994', (1995) *ERPL*, 445–482 (available at http://ssrn.com/abstract=2178521), 467–468.
58. A. Verbeke, 'Judicial Application of Statutory Factors for an Equitable Distribution of Marital Property upon Dissolution of the Marriage on Divorce in New York: An Illustration', (1998) *Zeitschrift für Rechtsvergleichung*, 170–214 (available at http://ssrn.com/abstract=2178522).
59. J. Scherpe, 'Marital Agreements and Private Autonomy in Comparative Perspective', in J. Scherpe (ed.), *Marital Agreements and Private Autonomy in Comparative Perspective*, Oxford, Hart, 2012, pp. 461–472.
60. *Miller v Miller, McFarlane v McFarlane* [2006] UKHL 24, §11 et seq.; §30 et seq. and §138 et seq.: 'needs, compensation of relationship generated economic disadvantage and equal sharing'. See also: J. Eekelaar, 'Property and financial settlement on divorce – sharing and compensating', (2006) *Fam. Law*, 754 et seq.; M. Thorpe, 'Financial Consequences of Divorce: England versus the Rest of Europe', in K. Boele-Woelki, J. Miles and J. Scherpe (eds.), *The Future of Family Property in Europe*, Cambridge, Intersentia, 2011, p. 5.
61. Largely based on A.L. Verbeke, 'A New Deal for Belgian Marital Property Law', in E. Alofs, K. Byttebier, A. Michielsens and A.L. Verbeke (eds.), *Liber amicorum Hélène Casman*, Antwerp-Cambridge, Intersentia, 2013, pp. 479–485.
62. C. Forder and A. Verbeke, 'Geen Woorden maar Daden. Algemene Rechtsvergelijkende Conclusies en Aanbevelingen', in C. Forder and A. Verbeke (eds.), *Gehuwd of niet. Maakt het iets uit?*, Antwerp, Intersentia, 2005, pp. 503–511 (available at http://ssrn.com/abstract=1750883).

63. e.g. Belgian Constitutional Court, no. 28/2013, 7 March 2013, B.6.2. See the analysis of these arguments in C. Forder and A. Verbeke, 'Geen Woorden maar Daden. Algemene Rechtsvergelijkende Conclusies en Aanbevelingen', in C. Forder and A. Verbeke (eds.), *Gehuwd of niet. Maakt het iets uit?,* Antwerp, Intersentia, 2005, pp. 503–538 (available at http://ssrn.com/abstract=1750883).
64. P. Bakker, 'Chaos in Family Law: A Model for the Recognition of Intimate Relationships in South-Africa', (2013) 16/3 *PER/PELJ*, 130.
65. P. Bakker, 'Chaos in Family Law: A Model for the Recognition of Intimate Relationships in South-Africa', (2013) 16/3 *PER/PELJ*, 130, footnote 79.
66. See also: D. Dandoy, 'Playdoyer en faveur de mécanismes juridiques plus cohérents pour appréhender au moment de la rupture du couple, la problématique de l'économie conjugale', (2013) *Familie & Recht,* 34 et seq. (available at www.familieenrecht.nl).
67. §143 in Supreme Court of Canada, *Nova Scotia AG v Walsh*, 2002 *SCC* 83; (2002) 221 *DLR (4th)* 1; 32 *RFL (5th)* 81.
68. §147 in Supreme Court of Canada, *Nova Scotia AG v Walsh*, 2002 *SCC* 83; (2002) 221 *DLR (4th)* 1; 32 *RFL (5th)* 81.
69. §148 in Supreme Court of Canada, *Nova Scotia AG v Walsh*, 2002 *SCC* 83; (2002) 221 *DLR (4th)* 1; 32 *RFL (5th)* 81.
70. See also: D. Dandoy, 'Playdoyer en faveur de mécanismes juridiques plus cohérents pour appréhender au moment de la rupture du couple, la problématique de l'économie conjugale', (2013) *Familie & Recht,* 32 et seq. (available at www.familieenrecht.nl).
71. *Cf.* C. Fried, *Contract as Promise,* Cambridge MA, Harvard University Press, 1981, pp. 58–59 and 92–102.
72. C. Forder and A. Verbeke, 'Geen Woorden maar Daden. Algemene Rechtsvergelijkende Conclusies en Aanbevelingen', in C. Forder and A. Verbeke (eds.), *Gehuwd of niet. Maakt het iets uit?,* Antwerp, Intersentia, 2005, pp. 553–555 (available at http://ssrn.com/abstract=1750883).
73. Article 1.1., 2, a, b and c in I. Schwenzer, *Model Family Code,* Antwerp, Intersentia, 2006, pp. 8–9.
74. Not Words but Actions: 'Geen Woorden maar Daden'. See C. Forder and A. Verbeke, 'Geen Woorden maar Daden. Algemene Rechtsvergelijkende Conclusies en Aanbevelingen', in C. Forder and A. Verbeke (eds.), *Gehuwd of niet. Maakt het iets uit?,* Antwerp, Intersentia, 2005 (available at http://ssrn.com/abstract=1750883).
75. B. Tilleman and A. Verbeke, '(Re-)codification du Droit des Contrats?', in *Droit des contrats. France, Belgique,* Brussels, Paris, L.G.D.J., 2005, pp. 24–30.
76. §147 in Supreme Court of Canada, *Nova Scotia AG v Walsh*, 2002 *SCC* 83; (2002) 221 *DLR (4th)* 1; 32 *RFL (5th)* 81.
77. Belgian Constitutional Court, no. 28/2013, 7 March 2013, B.6.2.
78. A.L. Verbeke, 'A New Deal for Belgian Marital Property Law', in E. Alofs, K. Byttebier, A. Michielsens and A.L. Verbeke (eds.), *Liber amicorum Hélène Casman*, Antwerp-Cambridge, Intersentia, 2013, p. 467.
79. A. Verbeke, 'Huwelijkscontract: de Sky is bijna the Limit', in B. Tilleman and A. Verbeke (eds.), *Liber alumnorum KULAK and Amicorum Macours,* Bruges, Die Keure, 2005, pp. 169–194 (available at http://ssrn.com/abstract=1794023).
80. *Cf.* 'The Story of Hannelore and David', in A. Verbeke, 'Recht is Balans is een Werkwoord', (2000–2001) *RW (Rechtskundig Weekblad)*, 969–978.

81. A. Verbeke, 'Gender-Ongelijkheid bij Zuivere Scheiding van Goederen. Pleidooi voor een Gedwongen én Onderhandelde Aanpak', (2010) *TEP (Tijdschrift Estate Planning)*, 114–116 (available at http://ssrn.com/abstract=1751029).

SPECULATION: THE DEVIL BURNING DOWN THE HOUSE?

On Derivatives, Gambling, and Public Policy

Ignace Claeys*

1. INTRODUCTION: THE 2008 FINANCIAL CRISIS AND THE DERIVATIVES MARKET

The 2008 financial crisis[1] has awakened a recurring debate on speculation, as did the 1929 crisis and many other financial bubbles.[2] The debate now focuses on speculative derivatives, and in particular on over-the-counter or OTC derivatives (as opposed to exchange-traded derivatives).[3] These financial instruments are considered to be at the origin of a systemic risk, in that they are believed to undermine the system organising our society and to diminish our welfare, at least if they are left entirely unregulated. They are concluded on a large scale, since they do not require a substantial up-front investment and they do not presuppose that the parties own the underlying instrument. They also have the benefit of allowing short positions (positions whereby someone expects falling prices) to be taken.

What is known as the worldwide domino or cascading effects was caused by defaults of systemically important international financial institutions[4] due to such institutions being too large or too interconnected to fail.[5] Consider the bailout of AIG in the US, Merrill Lynch being saved by a sale to the Bank of America, and the bankruptcy of Lehman Brothers.[6] In addition, the bailouts of the banks Dexia and Fortis by several EU states may be recalled.[7]

The defaults negatively affected not only the companies on the losing side of derivatives and their shareholders and creditors, but also society in general. Tax money was infused in order to pay out the counterparties to the derivatives transactions, thus backing up the derivatives market.[8] Even though some of the money lost may be recovered in litigation against the winning counterparties or others, the bailouts are considered to decrease societal welfare as, in admittedly simplified terms, less tax money means reduced or lower-quality public services.[9]

The risky nature of derivatives was not unknown in 2008. It had already been experienced before by both public and private institutions (even before the 2000 deregulation in the US), for example in the Orange County crisis in 1994 and the LTCM (Long Term Capital Management) bailout in 1998.[10] Long before the 2008 crisis, legal scholars too were warning of a potential systemic crisis caused by derivatives.[11]

Meanwhile, derivatives losses are not a matter of the past. They continue to receive media coverage, although no longer necessarily as breaking news. For example, at the beginning of 2013, the centuries-old Tuscan bank Monte Paschi di Siena, which allegedly had kept loss-making derivatives hidden from the supervising authorities, had to be bailed out.[12] Derivatives in food commodities are described as 'bets on agricultural commodities' said to cause increased food prices, even though derivatives players[13] allege that the increase in food prices has its origin simply in the laws of (increasing) demand and (decreasing) supply.[14] Just as George Soros became world-famous in 1994 for the huge profits realised by his speculative moves against the British pound, the more recent speculation against the Japanese yen generated huge profits for some hedge funds (and equal losses for the contracting parties) in 2013.[15] These are but three examples which show the ongoing impact of derivative positions on the economy throughout the world in 2013.

The continued media coverage does not come as a surprise. The number of derivative positions grew especially in the years before the 2008 financial crisis, but they continue to be taken in huge quantities. A rough idea of those quantities can be formed by comparing the number of OTC[16] derivatives with the real economy worldwide as expressed in global gross domestic product (GDP), which does not include financial transactions. The GDP in 2012 amounted to a little over USD 70 trillion.[17] OTC derivatives are sometimes said to account for many times more than the world GDP, but this is only true when comparing the GDP with the total of the notional amounts of derivatives (not an accurate measure). According to the ISDA market analysis of OTC derivatives,[18] the notional amount outstanding of OTC derivatives was USD 565.2 trillion at year-end 2012 (almost eight times the world GDP), as compared to USD 529.7 trillion at year-end 2007. The gross market value – defined by the ISDA as the 'aggregate positive values of all outstanding contracts to in-the money counterparties' – amounted to USD 24.7 trillion in 2012 (3.9% of the notional amounts) as compared to USD 15.8 trillion in 2007 (2.7% of the notional amounts). The gross credit exposure amounted to USD 3.6 trillion in 2012 (14.6% of the gross market value) as compared to USD 3.3 trillion in 2007 (20.6% of the gross market value).

2. ON THE ENFORCEABILITY OF SPECULATIVE DERIVATIVES FROM THE PERSPECTIVES OF BETTING AND PUBLIC POLICY

This chapter seeks to identify the relevant considerations determining whether speculative derivatives should be enforceable as a matter of law if, in the end, they have a useful social purpose. It does not aim to answer the question of whether speculative derivatives *actually* are socially harmful or, in fact, useful. That question would require in-depth, well-informed empirical research[19] and an analysis of speculation from economic, historical, sociological, ethical, political and other angles.

Like any other types of contracts, speculative transactions may not be enforceable because one of the contracting parties did not know what transaction it entered into due to lack of information or due to plain fraudulent behaviour by the other party. Individual contracting parties are protected by general rules of contract law such as mistake, deceit, duress, misrepresentation and pre-contractual liability, even though the general rules on the burden of proof may make it difficult for an uninformed party to win its case. They may also avail themselves of specific rules on investor protection as currently enshrined in the EU in the MiFID rules[20] as implemented in national rules of the EU Member States. This chapter does not go into those general contract law rules or specific investor protection rules, which aim at the protection of an *individual* contracting party/investor.[21]

The key question for this chapter is, rather, whether general rules of contract law imply that speculative transactions lack enforceability because they are contrary to the interests of society or the general or public interest. This chapter does not aim to assess whether or not a particular transaction was suitable for a particular investor.[22] Rather, it aims to assess whether or not it is in the interests of society or, better formulated, whether or not it is detrimental to our society to enforce a particular type of transaction (namely derivatives, especially those of a speculative nature).

This key question is analysed from two legal perspectives.[23] The first perspective is whether speculative transactions are – or should be – unenforceable *bets*.[24] Both proponents and opponents of speculative transactions, including legal writers, speak plainly of 'bets' when referring to speculative derivatives.[25] We will analyse whether these derivatives are bets in the legal meaning of the word (gambling or wagering). The second perspective is to determine whether (speculative) derivatives infringe *public policy* or public order, mainly because of their systemic risk and the accompanying disruption to welfare distribution. In both perspectives, we will have to take into account the ramifications of both old and recent regulation on derivatives in this regard.

Many legal systems are (or have been) reluctant to have bets enforced in court, even though some of the best lawyers consider this to be a paternalistic rule.[26] They have also developed a general rule that contracts cannot be enforced if they are contrary to the fundamental social, ethical, economic or political principles of a society or, as lawyers call those principles for short, public policy/order and good morals.[27]

This chapter does not aim to cast doubt on the usefulness of derivatives as such. We wonder whether *speculative* transactions such as speculative derivatives may be held unenforceable on the basis of current general rules of private law or, to the contrary, whether they are unenforceable only if specific regulation so provides. The question is relevant since the market is considering so-called regulatory arbitrage to overcome regulatory measures imposed to downsize systemic risk. By way of illustration, we will just quote one interviewee in *Risk* magazine, October 2012: 'We're comparing the possible risk we will incur by trading a swap future versus the swap, and it looks like it's going to be worth taking that risk in order to avoid the huger margin obligation'.[28] The question whether speculative derivatives may be held unenforceable apart from specific regulation is also important because of possible public choice problems, inasmuch as financial markets may not be efficiently regulated.[29]

The stakes for the question whether speculative derivatives are bets or may infringe public policy are not low, given the remedies involved. Bets or contracts contrary to public policy cannot be enforced in court.[30] Moreover, persons offering these types of contracts may be held liable in tort for placing such contracts on the market, contrary to public policy.

Before being able to tackle the two key questions of whether speculative derivatives are bets (9–10) and whether they infringe public policy (11), we need to sketch some context, first on speculation theory (3), the law's divergent attitude towards speculation in general (4), the vague concept of speculation (5), a short history of so-called "difference contracts" (6), and a differentiation of derivatives contracts (7), in order to arrive at the theory of enforceable and unenforceable aleatory contracts (8). We end with some concluding remarks (12).

The method used in this chapter to analyse the legal treatment of speculative transactions, primarily in some EU states and occasionally in the US, is eclectic in nature and certainly does not aim to replace the need for legal advice on the enforceability of a derivatives transaction under a given legal system. It is simply not possible to cover all possible relevant legal sources in the various states on both sides of the Atlantic Ocean. However, as the editor of this book has rightly emphasised, such methodology problems should not lead lawyers to refrain from participating in the public debate on speculation in general and on speculative derivatives in particular. This chapter will hopefully serve as a stimulus for further research.

3. SPECULATION THEORIES

Given the current statistics on derivatives trading[31] and given the financial crisis in 2008, it is no wonder that speculative derivatives have refuelled speculation theories. Broadly speaking, one can distinguish two general modes of thinking on speculation.

In one category of thinking, speculation is one of the main causes of the financial turmoil and should therefore be forbidden[32] or at least strongly curtailed by regulation because it endangers the financial stability of our societal system and, much like gambling, only moves financial resources from one person to another without merit. This view is also expressed by some key politicians and by part of the *vox populi*. It was already voiced at the end of the 19th century, when reference was made to a 'general principle that human folly cannot be a just means to enrich oneself.'[33]

Another category of thinking is mainly voiced by the financial sector and many economists.[34] They argue that it is impossible to distinguish non-speculative transactions from other transactions[35] and that it is not expedient to forbid all speculative derivatives, because they are socially valuable.[36] However, most of the proponents of speculation meanwhile recognise that some speculative transactions were at the heart of the financial crisis and should therefore, without being forbidden, be regulated in order to decrease the potential for systemic crises (for example by reporting or even public disclosure requirements increasing transparency on OTC derivatives or, if necessary, by requiring OTC derivatives to be cleared through a clearing house that provides guarantees against default by imposing margin requirements on the clearing members – who in turn impose margin requirements on their clients).

The starting point of the second line of thinking remains that speculation is a right[37] and any regulatory restrictions on speculation should not unduly restrict the fundamental freedom to conduct a business, in particular the freedom of contract,[38] and should not infringe the freedoms of the internal market. These established freedoms are fundamental principles which are prerequisites for initiative and entrepreneurship and which therefore propel economic growth and welfare. Restrictions on speculation should therefore respect these fundamental principles, just as restrictions on gambling should.[39]

It comes as no surprise that discussions on speculation are often framed in ideological terms. Anyone who dares to attack speculation, and the enforceability of speculative derivatives in particular, must betray the principles of capitalism. Speculation is situated in the middle of a field of high tension between personal freedom and public interest. While it may satisfy some instinctive needs of speculators who have an interest in asserting their freedom of contract, it harms others. (This is the reason why it is often called a zero-sum game.) According to some, it may even be socially harmful (less than a zero-sum game). Speculators and economists, to the contrary, emphasise the social utility of speculation, as we will explore further.

4. THE DIVERGENT LEGAL TREATMENT OF SPECULATION

In the legal systems analysed, we did not find a general rule either allowing or forbidding speculation (leaving aside for the moment the general rules on bets and public policy).

In particular settings,[40] explicit statutory prohibitions of speculation do exist, most often without a legislative definition of the concept of speculation. Belgian law, for example, forbids real estate investment companies from engaging in speculative transactions,[41] without defining speculation. Some types of speculative transactions may also be subject to stricter regulatory rules than non-speculative ones. For example, the accounting rules for derivatives are stricter for the speculative types than for the risk-hedging types.[42]

On other occasions, the legislator's wish to deter speculative transactions is the underlying reason for a specific rule, even though speculation is not required to be established as such in order for the rule to apply. For example, under French and Belgian law, whenever a claim of €100 is disputed between a creditor and a debtor and the creditor assigns or transfers that claim to another person (the assignee) for (let us say) a price of €50,[43] the debtor can free himself fully by paying the price of €50 agreed for the assignment of the claim. This rule applies regardless of whether or not the assignee has purchased the claim for speculative reasons, but the legislator nevertheless adopted this rule in order to curb speculative assignment of claims.[44] It does not as such forbid an assignment of a disputed receivable, but it certainly deters people from taking over a disputed claim.[45]

It may also be the aim of more or less severe tax rules to limit the number of particular types of speculative transactions rather than to forbid them entirely. For example, taxes on the sale of immovable assets, if sufficiently high, result in fewer transactions made for the sole pursuit of profit on the purchase and subsequent resale of immovable assets. The tax on financial transactions, also known as the Tobin tax, has recently been promoted by eleven EU Member States for the same reason of deterring speculative financial transactions.[46]

The opposite may also be true. The legislator may offer incentives to give a boost to desirable speculation because of the alleged positive effects of particular types of speculative transactions. Economic growth and the stability of the financial system are two explicit reasons why the legislator sought to increase the efficiency of collateral arrangements in the Belgian collateral law of 15 December 2004[47] implementing and broadening the scope of the EU Directive on financial collateral arrangements (Directive 2002/47 of 6 June 2002). The legislator explicitly envisaged increasing the efficiency of collaterals as an incentive for derivatives (as well as credit contracts). It is worth quoting the legislator's considerations: 'Financial collaterals are an absolutely necessary requirement for the conclusion of (1) credit contracts and (2) derivatives contracts. Through credit contracts, companies acquire external resources. Through derivatives contracts, companies cover market, credit, currency, and other risks: the rise of interest rates, the decrease of the USD, the increase of commodities prices, etc. Both are essential for the functioning of industrial and commercial companies. Adequate legislation on collaterals provides companies with access to such agreements, and at a lower price. This has positive effects on economic growth and employment.' The Belgian collateral law extended the scope of the Directive on financial collateral arrangements from the financial sector to the entire economy, including both industrial and commercial companies and natural persons. For industrial and commercial companies, it would imply amongst other things: 'access to derivatives transactions, whereby the industrial and commercial companies act mainly as sellers of risk. This makes the entrepreneurial scene less vulnerable to external economic shocks, with a reduced risk of insolvency, preservation of economic activity and employment as a short-term benefit and increasing economic growth as a long-term benefit.' With regard to natural persons, the legislator describes the perceived positive effects of the increased efficiency of collaterals as follows: 'Access to derivatives operations, whereby the natural persons act mainly as buyers of risk, and this is the framework for the maximisation of the return of their asset management (cf. also the role of the "hedge funds"). By their presence in the market they have a downward impact on the price of risk transfer, having a lower cost for risk hedging for industrial and commercial companies as a consequence.'[48] The legislator clearly encourages derivatives, including when they are speculative at least for the buyer of the risk.

An older example of legislators allowing a particular type of speculative transactions is the annuity contract (*lijfrente, rente viagère*). Society considers it desirable that a person is able to make provision for his old age by selling a good in return for an annuity for the rest of his life.[49]

In the context of general open-textured rules which in essence refer to the criterion of the reasonable person, courts may be reticent in formulating a general ruling for all proposals against or in favour of speculation. The following examples demonstrate how parties have to carefully assess the possible relevance of general rules before engaging in speculative transactions.

A famous example in English law is the much criticised decision in *Hazell v Hammersmith and Fulham LBC* in 1998, in which the House of Lords decided that all interest rate swaps (not only those of a speculative nature) are beyond the powers (ultra vires) of local *public* authorities.[50] In any event, public authorities need to take into account the financial aspects of their decisions in order to act in conformity with the principle of reasonableness.[51]

A *private* person managing another's money may also be confronted with a similar restriction on the basis of general rules of tort law. For example, the custodian of a minor may be expected to refrain from engaging in speculative transactions (whatever that means) with the minor's funds managed by that custodian.[52]

General rules of corporate law may also be relevant. According to a decision by a Belgian commercial court, a director of a company should not conclude forward contracts in foreign currencies which are not linked to transactions on sale/purchase of goods, because such purely speculative transactions are not part of the corporate purpose of the company. The fact that the company has the power to perform all financial transactions which are useful or positive for attaining its corporate purpose does not mean that speculative transactions on foreign currencies may be concluded on behalf of a company, at least according to that judicial decision.[53]

In the context of the rules on unjustified enrichment, a speculative motive may justify someone's impoverishment. For example, when a person makes a great deal of effort (an impoverishment) for an aged person while speculating on being appointed as a beneficiary in that aged person's will but is not in the end appointed as a beneficiary, he will not be able to claim that the deceased's estate has been unjustifiably enriched by his efforts. Thus, one man's speculation is a justification for another's enrichment.[54]

This brief overview of the law's attitude towards speculation is admittedly eclectic and even anecdotal, but it already serves to show that it is simply not helpful to analyse whether speculation in general is or should be allowed or forbidden. In some situations, speculation is desirable and is therefore encouraged; in other situations, it is detrimental and is therefore forbidden or at least deterred. From the perspective of the opponents of particular types of speculative transactions, it would appear to be confusing and unwise to tackle speculation in general, as some instances of speculative transactions may well be considered as being beneficial to society. An arrow needs a clearly-defined target in order to hit home. Speculation is not such a target.

5. SPECULATION: A VAGUE CONCEPT?

Some types of speculation are socially useful. This is one reason why speculation in general should not be forbidden. Proponents of speculation often advance another reason against such general prohibition: it is simply too difficult to distinguish speculative from non-speculative transactions (investments in particular). Fervent opponents of speculation agree that speculation is a vague concept.[55]

Before discussing some possible tests for delineating speculation, we should first note that several criteria sometimes proposed are irrelevant:

- Even though some scholars state that speculation is at the heart of a particular category of contracts (namely aleatory contracts),[56] the *nature of a contract*[57] does not help in distinguishing speculative from non-speculative transactions. An aleatory contract is not necessarily speculative. An insurance contract, for example, is not speculative, although it is an aleatory contract. Non-aleatory contracts may also have a speculative motive. Think of the simple sale of an immovable or a painting.

- The *nature of the goods* sold is not relevant either for distinguishing the area of speculation. Speculation may relate to various types of objects, such as commodities, paintings, immovable assets, stock, bonds, etc.[58]
- The *professional* or *private (retail)* capacity[59] or the *private* or *public* nature of a party is not relevant either in defining speculation: professionals and non-professionals in both the private and public sphere may all have actual speculative goals when concluding a transaction.[60]
- Neither is the existence of *uncertainty* (or the factor of coincidence or luck) relevant for determining whether or not a transaction is speculative.[61] Insurance or risk-hedging contracts are concluded to deal with uncertainty as much as speculative contracts are. A contract for the purchase of a good is also, economically speaking, uncertain as regards its future value. In the end, uncertainty is more or less inherent in every contract, as many writers rightly emphasise.[62]

But how, then, can we define speculation? Speculation is a motive for one or more persons to conclude a transaction. In finance,[63] speculation is often defined by distinguishing it from three other motives for concluding financial transactions. The first motive other than speculation is *risk hedging*. A financial transaction with a speculative motive is characterised by taking an additional risk rather than hedging or minimising a risk. A second motive other than speculation for concluding a financial transaction is *investment*. A financial transaction with a speculative motive is said not to be characterised by contributing capital directly or indirectly to some branch of the real economy with the goal of allocating some resources to their most optimal use. A third motive other than speculation is *arbitrage* (e.g. by high frequency traders), which aims at profiting within a very short time from a price differential at a given moment in time for the same exchange of certain goods. A financial transaction with a speculative motive is not characterised by the observation of a price differential in two markets. Opponents of speculation make this distinction between speculation and the three other motives on the basis that risk hedging, investment and arbitrage are legitimate economic purposes and speculation is not.

Speculation is also defined by three characteristics in terms of *speed* (high-frequency computer trading being the most extreme form), *high risk*,[64] and a *potentially high return*. A speculative transaction, however, is often[65] not a short-term transaction.[66] Moreover, it is also associated with high (more than 'normal') risk, although it is difficult to determine from which risk level onwards a transaction becomes speculative. Finally, a speculator assumes a high (more than 'normal') risk for the potential of a higher return than other (non-speculative) transactions.

The goals of risk hedging, investment and arbitrage as distinguished from speculation[67] all seem to lack, to some degree, one or more of the three characteristics traditionally linked with speculation in terms of speed, risk and return.[68] The high risk factor is said to be lacking in both risk-hedging transactions (at least for the hedger) and in arbitrage transactions. The speed factor is usually lacking for investments[69] and also for some hedging deals. The potentially high return factor is lacking for hedging transactions as well as for many (but not all) investments.

Even if one accepts that speculation may be defined by distinguishing it from other financial transactions by different motives and characteristics, the distinction is in any event not easy in practice. The (ab)normality of risk and return is more subjective than objective and a rather uncertain measure. Moreover, motives for financial transactions, as for many contracts, may be mixed. For example, a party may conclude a transaction partly for risk hedging and partly for speculative reasons. The transaction may be entirely aimed at risk hedging for one party while being purely speculative for the other party, as is true in the case of insurance for example[70] (when one speaks of 'pure speculation', we assume this means that no other motive is present for the transaction envisaged).

Given the difficulties in discerning motives or intentions, the attempt has been made in the past to consider a transaction as speculative if its link with the real economy is weak. This is considered to be the case with the so-called 'difference contract': a contract for the potential or future sale of goods, which however does not end up with the physical delivery of the goods or services but is (intended from the start to be) settled in cash for the difference in value of the two at some given moment in time. A difference contract is potentially dangerous because the number of difference contracts is not restricted by the scarcity of the goods or services in the real economy. It is also dangerous because fewer funds need to be invested initially as compared to other types of contracts that usually have a similar response to market changes. In the event of low collateral, a multitude of high volume transactions may cause substantial systemic risk.[71]

6. DIFFERENCE CONTRACTS

Once upon a time, the idea that transactions should not be enforceable when they increase risk without a sufficient connection to the real economy inspired courts and state legislators to forbid the enforcement of so-called 'difference contracts' (*Differenzgeschäfte, des contrats de différence*).

In several legal systems on both sides of the Atlantic, difference contracts have been challenged before the courts. Contracts to sell and purchase a good at a given price at a future date (*forwards* or, if exchange traded, *futures*) may turn into difference contracts if the good sold is not physically delivered but is settled by the balance between the contractually fixed price and the market price at the time when performance is due. In the event of *option* contracts on the basis of which a party has the power to exercise a right to purchase or sell a good, the sales contract (if the option is exercised) may also be turned into a difference contract. Again, physical delivery is replaced by a settlement in cash of the difference between the price set in the option contract and the market price at the time when the option is exercised.

At the end of the 19th century and the beginning of the 20th century, contracts which ended up with a settlement in cash instead of physical delivery were challenged before various US state courts as being contrary to public policy or otherwise illegal as wagering (gambling).[72]

Gradually, however, courts came to consider that a contract was only unenforceable if it was established that it had been the parties' intention from the start (i.e. as from the conclusion of the contract) that performance would occur by means of a settlement in cash. If a contract left it open whether the contract would be performed by physical delivery or by cash settlement, it was generally enforceable. According to a Supreme Court decision in the 1884 case *Irwin v Williar*, difference contracts were nothing more than wagering 'if, under guise of such a contract [a contract for the sale of goods to be delivered at a future day], the real intent be merely to speculate in the rise or fall of prices, and the goods are not to be delivered, but one party is to pay to the other the difference between the contract price and the market price of the goods at the date fixed for executing the contract'.[73] Subsequently, private futures exchanges were organised in order to privately ensure payment in case of default on such futures contracts.[74]

In the 1905 decision known as *Chicago Board of Trade v Christie Grain*, the Chicago Board of Trade[75] asserted that its quotations of price on sales of grain were trade secrets which should not be furnished by telegraph companies to bucket shops[76] or places where they were used as a basis for bets as illegal contracts. The main defence of the telegraph companies was that the Chicago Board of Trade was the greatest bucket shop of all because it was a place which 'permitted the pretended buying and selling of grain, etc., without any intention of receiving and paying for the property so bought, or of delivering the property so sold.' The authoritative Justice Holmes rejected that defence in three steps. In the first place, he considered:

> 'Of course, in a modern market, contracts are not confined to sales for immediate delivery. People will endeavour to forecast the future, and to make agreements according to their prophecy. Speculation of this kind by competent men is the self-adjustment of society to the probable. Its value is well known as a means of avoiding or mitigating catastrophes, equalising prices, and providing for periods of want. It is true that the success of the story induces imitation by the weak, and that incompetent persons bring themselves to ruin by undertaking to speculate in their turn. But legislatures and courts generally have recognised that the natural evolutions of a complex society are to be touched only with a very cautious hand, and that such coarse attempts at a remedy for the waste incident to every social function as a simple prohibition and laws to stop its being are harmful and vain.'

In other words, the social utility of future trading and speculation in general outweighs its negative impact. In the second step in his reasoning, Justice Holmes referred to hedging risks as a 'serious business purpose' and the 'legitimate and useful purpose that it may be offset before the time of delivery in case delivery should not be needed or desired.' He distinguished such contracts from 'purchases made merely with the expectation that they will be satisfied by set-off', which he considered to be mere wagers forbidden by the Illinois legislation of the day. Finally, Justice Holmes concluded that the proportion of contracts actually ending up with a cash settlement rather than a physical delivery 'throws no light on the question of the proportion of serious dealings for legitimate business purposes to those which fairly can be classified as wagers, or pretended contracts.' In other words, futures as such are not wagers or pretended contracts. In order for futures to be considered as wagers, the initial expectation that the goods promised would not be actually delivered had to be established.

Since the majority of case law referred to the criterion of the initial intention of the contracting parties to settle the contract in cash,[77] it became very hard to establish the existence of a wager. If the contract left both modes of settlement open, it was generally considered to be enforceable (not a bet). Although the theory of difference contracts started with an objective measure delineating speculative from non-speculative transactions, it ended up with a subjective measure which in practice carved out the unenforceability rule (although allegedly a matter of international public policy[78] in the US) for difference contracts almost entirely.[79]

On the other side of the Atlantic, the effect of the possible unenforceability of difference contracts had a remarkable impact on the Dutch Options Exchange of Amsterdam even at the end of the 20th century. Approximately one month after its inception, the decision was made to close it temporarily because of the possible unenforceability of options if the contracts did not result in physical delivery. The Dutch legislator finally intervened with an act of 31 October 1986 adding contracts for difference[80] to the enumeration of enforceable aleatory contracts in article 7A:1811 of the then Dutch Civil Code.[81] No distinction was made between exchange traded and over-the-counter contracts. The Dutch legislator thus came to the same conclusion as US Justice Homes did in 1905: the options market is socially useful and should not be forbidden. It was considered to be in the interest of the Netherlands as a financial centre. However, the new Dutch Civil Code no longer includes that enumeration of aleatory contracts, because the legislator thought that no legal effect was attached to that enumeration. This may renew the same debate as to whether the contracts explicitly named as aleatory contracts apart from bets (insurance and annuities) are the sole aleatory contracts, leaving no room for other types not named in the Civil Code such as contracts for difference.[82] In the authoritative Asser legal series, it is explicitly 'assumed' without further explanation that a difference contract is an enforceable aleatory contract, albeit not named in the Civil Code.[83]

A century before, in French law, an act of 28 March 1885 (after a crash in 1882) already provided that difference contracts on futures markets could not be characterised as unenforceable bets: 'No person can invoke article 1965 of the Civil Code [the legal provision on the unenforceability of bets] in order to escape his obligations, even if they result in the payment of a mere difference.'[84] Legal scholars do not seem to agree on whether this law only applies to transactions concluded on an official market (*marché officiel*),[85] as seems to be argued for Dutch law on a comparative law basis.[86] With this provision, the legislator no longer allows judges to verify the parties' intentions (e.g. speculative intentions) when concluding a difference contract on a *marché officiel*.[87]

In German law, difference contracts (*Differenzgeschäfte*) lacked enforceability, as was enshrined in §764 BGB (the 1896 German Civil Code). This rule (the so-called *Differenzeinwand*) was entirely abolished by a statute of 2002,[88] but futures transactions were apparently already enforceable on the basis of the *Börsengezetz* of 1896. The rule on the unenforceability of bets (§762 BGB), however, still exists, but it is not applicable to derivatives in the meaning of §2 of the German commercial law on securities if they are concluded with a business.[89]

In Belgian law, the rule on unenforceability of betting was once applied in some case law in relation to difference contracts.[90] However, it was excluded for futures contracts on securities and commodities by Royal Decrees of 15 October 1934 and 30 November 1939 in relations with professionals without restriction and with non-professional 'orderers' with the requirement of a minimum margin.[91]

In summary, while US courts gradually limited the unenforceability of difference contracts to those where it was the established intention of the parties from the start to settle the contract in cash, legislators on the other side of the Atlantic explicitly intervened in order to prevent courts refusing to enforce difference contracts for the mere reason that they were considered to be bets.

7. DERIVATIVES: DIFFERENT TYPES, DIFFERENT GOALS

Let us further narrow down the discussion to those speculative instruments which are considered to have been at least one of the causes of the 2008 financial crisis and therefore return to derivatives.

Derivatives exist in *various types*, even though they all have the common characteristic that their value is derived from an underlying financial instrument, index or economic measure. They may be concluded through an exchange or just between two private persons (over the counter, OTC). Exchange traded derivatives are deemed to create less systemic risk because the clearing house requires an initial margin as a security for payment and makes additional margin calls when a particular position so requires.[92] This institutional safety valve is missing in OTC derivatives, unless it is imposed by regulation or by contract.

The main categories of derivatives are forwards (traded over the counter) or futures (traded on an exchange), options, and swaps.[93] These 'plain vanilla' instruments are offered in various more complicated variants (the so-called 'exotic' types of derivatives). Let us keep it simple and briefly consider the 'plain vanilla' forwards or futures, options, and swaps.[94]

Forwards or futures are, in principle, sales contracts that have to be performed at a future time for a price that is already fixed at the time of the conclusion of the forward or future. At that time, the price to be paid and the goods to be transferred are known. It is, however, questionable to characterise these contracts as sales (as some legal scholars do) when they are intended[95] to be settled in cash.[96] Once actual delivery is no longer part of the promises arising out of such a contract, it is no longer a sales contract. This in turn begs the question whether it can be classed as a specific known or nominated type of contract. At the time the parties enter into the contract, they do not know whether or what amount they will have to pay, because that depends on *coincidence* (*alea*), which is a characteristic of aleatory contracts.[97]

While forwards (OTC) and futures (exchange traded) are contracts with an obligation to perform in the future, *options* do not yet create rights or obligations to perform, except for the possible payment of a premium and the right of the option holder (buyer) to exercise his option. In the event of exercise of the option, a sales contract is formed and the seller of the option has the duty to either purchase or sell the underlying asset (depending on whether it is an option to sell or to purchase). *Option* contracts are distinguished from the *sales* contracts that come into existence when the option holder decides to exercise his option right. These contracts are generally considered to be commutative contracts. When the option right is exercised, a sales contract is concluded, unless – again – it was clear from the outset that the option holder would be paid in cash for the difference between the market price at the time of the exercise of the option and the strike (the price set in the option contract).

In the event of a *swap*, as from the start, no delivery of a good is envisaged. While futures may be sales and options may lead to sales, swaps are by their nature difference contracts. Moreover, swaps are usually[98] OTC transactions. They also allow the swapping of a rather large variety of risks, such as currency, interest or default risks.

Let us take two examples: an interest rate swap and a credit default swap.

An interest rate swap,[99] generally considered to be the most frequently concluded swap, is an agreement by which a person promises to pay a fixed rate of interest on a nominal amount on a periodic (e.g. quarterly) basis during a given period (e.g. five years) while his contracting party pays a floating/variable interest rate on the same notional amount for the same periodicity for the same duration. The 'plain vanilla' IRS consists of two payment legs: a leg based on a fixed rate and a leg based on a variable or floating rate such as the LIBOR. The party having to pay the fixed interest on a nominal amount is better off when interest rates are rising (as happened in 1994 after Orange County (California) had taken the wrong side of the bet). The party having to pay the floating interest rate on the nominal amount is better off when interest rates are declining (as occurred from 2009 onwards). Payments (cash flows) are made periodically by the party who owes the balance (by netting the reciprocal debts). When interest rates are high, the floating rate payor will have to cash out. When interest rates are low, the fixed rate payor will have to make quarterly payments. At the time of entering into a swap, a contracting party therefore does not know whether he will have to pay or receive funds, for how long, and for what amounts.

In other words, unlike futures and contracts in the event of the exercise of options, swap contracts are *always* aleatory in nature. Forwards or futures, and contracts arising when an option is exercised, are aleatory if they are settled in cash or at least if settlement in cash is agreed from the start as the sole mode of settlement of the contract to the exclusion of physical delivery.

Another specific type of swap is the credit default swap (CDS): one party to the CDS (the 'buyer' of protection) pays a periodic premium in exchange for a promise by the other party (the 'seller' of protection) to make an agreed payment in the case of a contractually defined credit event such as the bankruptcy of a referenced entity.[100] The characterisation of this kind of swap is hotly debated, as various scholars across national borders consider this contract to be an insurance contract because a periodic premium is paid for the other's promise to cover for an uncertain event in the future. At stake in the debate is whether CDS offerors need to be licensed insurance companies and whether a CDS is only valid to the extent that it is made to cover an insured person against actual exposure to risk (if not, there is no insurable interest and, thus, either there is not a valid insurance contract[101] or there is another type of contract[102] – according to some, a bet).

All these types of derivatives (futures/forwards, options, swaps and CDS) may be used for *different purposes*. They may be speculative in nature, but this is not necessarily the case. An option or future may be concluded by an industrial or commercial company in order to protect itself against increases in prices for the commodities it needs or against the risk of lower prices for the product it brings on the market at a later point in time. Interest rate swaps (IRS), for example, are often made for purposes of risk hedging or minimisation. A debtor having to pay a floating interest rate to his creditor may want to hedge for several reasons against the risk that the floating rate will rise above a particular interest rate level. The creditor of a loan may want to hedge against the risk of default of his debtor by concluding a credit default swap. A company trading internationally may want to minimise currency fluctuations by entering into a currency swap.

However, derivatives may also be used for speculative purposes. This is true, for example, when an interest rate swap is transacted while the parties do not have an existing underlying risk to hedge. One party is willing to pay a fixed rate on a notional amount in return for a variable rate on a notional amount because he expects a rise in the interest rates and therefore netted payments in his favour. He makes a pure profit if the expected interest rate rise occurs. If not, he makes a pure loss. There is no offsetting with an interest rate due under an underlying loan, because none of the parties – by hypothesis – have such a loan or such an interest risk to hedge. The same is true for credit default swaps (CDS): they allow 'investors unrelated to the loan contract to speculate on changing credit quality for profit'.[103] For example, someone may be expecting the default of a bank that is granting mortgages too easily on the market without sufficient collateral. If the bank actually defaults, the party that 'purchased' a credit default swap makes a pure profit. In the reverse situation, he makes a pure loss.

When derivative contracts are concluded by parties without a hedging interest in the underlying assets, the link with the real economy disappears and the market value of these transactions may far outweigh that of the real economy transactions, with the potential of an increased risk for our societal system.

The foregoing shows that, although derivatives have in common the fact that their economic value is derived from the value of some particular underlying asset, their legal characterisation and therefore the legal framework may nonetheless differ from type to type. The derivatives are contracts, but they are not all sales contracts. It is true that, from an *economic* perspective, all these contracts are often called 'sales' contracts and the parties 'sellers' and 'buyers' of risk.[104] For example, the parties to a credit default swap (CDS) are called the buyer and the seller of protection against the default of the referenced entity. However, in *legal* terms,[105] it is advisable not to refer to a 'buyer' or 'seller' of a CDS or to characterise a CDS as a 'sales contract', because this is simply not accurate. This is important, because otherwise it would be tempting to apply the rules applicable to sales contracts without any further thought.

To the extent that derivatives are not sales contracts but aleatory contracts, the question then is whether they are bets in the legal meaning of the word, especially when they are speculative in nature.[106]

8. ENFORCEABLE AND UNENFORCEABLE ALEATORY CONTRACTS: HOW TO DISTINGUISH THEM?

Aleatory contracts (*aleatorische Verträge, des contrats aléatoires*) have always had a difficult struggle for life. Insurance contracts needed the theory of the insurable interest to stay alive (even though Australian law recently abolished that fundamental requirement). Insurance contracts exist to protect an existing interest of the insured against an uncertain future event. For example, you can insure your house against damage or against your liability arising from your house. Your house or estate is your interest thus insured.

If, however, you pay a premium for obtaining a payment when a stranger's house is damaged, you do not have an insurable interest. Such a contract is often considered to be either an invalid insurance contract or an unenforceable bet. From the first point of view (that it is an insurance contract but an invalid one), the insurable interest is seen as a requirement for the *validity* of an insurance contract.[107] From the second point of view (that it is a bet and therefore unenforceable),[108] the insurable interest is, rather, an element essential in order for a contract to be characterised as an insurance contract. In other words, it is required for the *existence* of an insurance contract. If the insurable interest is lacking, the contract is not an insurance contract but another type of contract – specifically a bet. The outcome, again, is that the contract is unenforceable.

Assuming that a contract without an insurable interest for the insured is not an invalid insurance contract, the crucial question is whether it is automatically a bet or whether it could be an aleatory contract of a type other than a bet. It may have been premature to jump to the conclusion that it is a bet.

There is no doubt that insurance contracts and bets are both types of aleatory contracts. At the time of concluding these contracts, the parties do not know whether one or both parties will have to perform, or at least what amount of performance, or when they will have to render. The parties to an insurance contract do not know whether the insurer will have to perform, the scope, or the timing of performance. The parties to a bet are in the same position: they do not know who will win and who will lose the bet.

Although insurance and bets are clearly two types of aleatory contracts, there are also other types of aleatory contracts.

Clearly, the legislator has explicitly categorised a number of contracts as enforceable aleatory contracts to be distinguished from unenforceable bets. In many legal systems, an annuity (*lijfrente*, *rente viagère*), for example, is aleatory because the party purchasing the good against the promise of a payment of an annual sum as long as the seller lives does not know for how many years the seller will still live and therefore how long the purchaser will have to pay annuities. The annuity is neither insurance nor a bet, given the legislator's express intention, but an enforceable category of aleatory contract. Under French and Belgian law, an assignment of a disputed receivable is another example of an enforceable type of aleatory contract.[109]

As to the question to which type of aleatory contracts derivatives belong, two further questions may be raised in many (especially civil law) legal systems. In section 10, we will go into the question whether meanwhile the legislator has not explicitly created derivatives as a specifically named aleatory contract in specific regulation. We now consider the other question – whether there are still other (*sui generis*) types of aleatory contracts than those named in a civil code or other legislation. Naming some types of aleatory contracts in legislation does not necessarily exclude the existence of other, innominate, aleatory contracts. In other words, the list of aleatory contract types expressly named in legislation is not necessarily a finite list of aleatory contracts.[110]

This is important. If a contract that is aleatory in nature is not an insurance contract given the lack of an insurable interest, it may well be a bet (as many assume), or it could be a *sui generis* aleatory contract, if it is accepted that other aleatory contracts exist than those explicitly named by the legislator. In other words, the jump from insurance contracts to bets may have overlooked the existence of a *sui generis* type of aleatory contract.

The legislators have usually not indicated whether or not the named types of aleatory contracts were all-inclusive. When looking at these named types of aleatory contracts, we observe two categories: on the one hand there are the enforceable ones such as insurance contracts and annuities (*lijfrentes*), and on the other hand there are unenforceable bets (gaming or wagering). There is no explanation for the distinction between enforceable and unenforceable aleatory contracts except that the legislator considered enforceable aleatory contracts to be socially useful, in contrast with the unenforceable ones which are mere zero-sum games or even worse. The existence of the category of *sui generis* aleatory contracts presupposes that there is a societal reason to enforce such contracts. In other words, there is a reason not to characterise these useful *sui generis* aleatory contracts as bets which, as a rule, are unenforceable.

The follow-up question then is: what is the criterion to distinguish enforceable from unenforceable contracts? It is difficult to determine whether or not an aleatory contract is a bet, because legislators do not usually define the concept of bets. Inspiration may be drawn from the reasons advanced for why some aleatory contracts are enforceable and bets are unenforceable.

Insurance contracts are nowadays considered to be useful for society. They allow the pooling of resources to spread risks and they allow the minimising of risks. Insurance contracts have a 'cause' other than the mere uncertainty of winning or losing.[111]

In the French and Belgian Civil Codes, games with an outcome that does not merely depend on luck but also on skill and bodily exercise, unlike other bets, are enforceable as a rule.[112] This rule exists because the social utility of those games was explicitly recognised by the legislator back in 1804.[113]

Bets are often said to be unenforceable because they may ruin the debtor and his family and because they are unethical. When analysing the explanatory documents for the French Civil Code, it is clear that the social harm caused by bets is the key reason why they are not enforceable.[114] They are not of economic value to society.[115]

Therefore, an aleatory contract that does not have the structure of a named enforceable aleatory contract should not necessarily be classed as a bet. It could, alternatively, be an enforceable aleatory contract, albeit not of a type named by the legislator, when it is socially valuable or at least, on balance, not socially harmful.

Within the category of aleatory contracts, a distinction needs to be made between contracts which are useful to society and those which are not. The explanatory documents for the French Civil Code on bets word it as follows: 'In order to establish serious causes for obligations between humans, something more solid and real is needed than the bizarre desire to give oneself up to the quirks of fate'.[116]

The core of the matter is expressed in the following sentence of the French explanatory documents on bets: they have no actual utility which could compensate for the vices and abuses inherent in them.[117] In other words, a balancing exercise needs to be conducted in order to determine whether an aleatory contract is a bet: do the benefits outweigh the disadvantages? For annuities, the French legislator conducted that very balancing exercise and concluded that the benefits outweigh the disadvantages (the possible abuses). [118]

This is, in legal terms, what may have happened with derivatives. Derivatives, even though they are (were) not named by the legislator, may still not be bets but *sui generis* aleatory contracts that are enforceable in court, if or to the extent that they are socially useful and not mere zero-sum games (what one wins, the other loses, without any benefit to society).

If a new type of aleatory contract is placed on the market, arguably the threshold question is whether or not it is to be deemed useful to society.[119] This is not the same as the question whether a contract is speculative or not.

This explains why, based on the explanatory documents for the French Civil Code, society does not forbid speculation but rather only excessive,[120] immoral,[121] or shameful speculation.[122]

9. DERIVATIVES: ENFORCEABLE INNOMINATE ALEATORY CONTRACTS?

As explained before, a great deal is at stake with the question of the adequate categorisation of derivatives as bets, insurance contracts, or innominate aleatory contracts. To the extent that derivatives are bets, they would be unenforceable in court. If they are insurance contracts, they would have to satisfy the relevant requirements of insurance regulation – implying, for example, that they could only be placed on the market by licensed insurance companies. However, if they are innominate aleatory contracts, distinguished from bets, they are subject neither to a general unenforceability rule nor to insurance regulation.

Derivatives have a risk sharing or shifting function (as all contracts do in some respects), but they are not insurance contracts by virtue of that fact. One of the essential characteristics of an insurance contract is often lacking in derivatives: the payment of a (periodic) premium for a promise to make whole the insured in case of the realisation of the risk insured. Take, for example, a 'plain vanilla' interest rate swap that is characterised by two periodic cash flows: there is no upfront payment of a premium in return for a promise to cover a risk if that risk is realised. The credit default swap (CDS) is an exception, in that a premium is periodically paid in return for a promise to pay in the event that a default event is realised.[123]

Another characteristic element of insurance contracts is missing in many (though not all) derivative contracts: the insurable interest, i.e. the interest the insured has in the asset covered by the insurance contract (the actual loss). Though subject to possible debate, the insurable interest is not as much a validity requirement as an essential characteristic of an insurance contract. If there is no insurable interest, it is not necessarily an invalid insurance contract, just as a contract is not yet an insurance contract for the mere reason that there is an insurable interest.

The lack of an insurable interest does not imply that an invalid insurance contract has been concluded; rather, the conclusion may be that no insurance contract at all has been concluded. Applying this to the CDS of a speculative nature, the fact that none of the parties have an insurable interest does not yet make the CDS an (invalid) insurance contract. It could, alternatively, be an innominate aleatory contract that is considered to be useful. If not, it is either an invalid insurance contract or an unenforceable bet. The choice is yours.

A number of tests have already been proposed to distinguish (speculative) derivatives from bets, although they do not all share the same degree of persuasiveness.

The rationality of the decisions leading to a speculative derivative is often advanced as a criterion distinguishing it from a bet or gambling. While gambling or bets are the result of pure luck, speculative transactions, it is claimed, are the outcome of rational calculus, based on mathematical models and a scientific probability theory. Nevertheless, each derivative position has a winning side but also a losing side, and in this respect is like casino gambling. The derivative decisions may be rationalised, but it is difficult to accept the argument that they are rational and, for this sole reason, not bets.[124] That being said, several court decisions have cited the argument of rational calculus, which is also accepted by many scholars.[125]

Another classic criterion to exclude speculative derivatives from the category of bets is based on the idea that bets are excluded as soon as a financial institution is involved as a party or derivatives relate to financial markets.[126] The mere fact that financial institutions develop mathematical models and appear to be more professional in taking derivatives positions boils down to the same argument of rationality.

One totally unconvincing argument is that a financial derivative is not gaming or a 'play' activity,[127] as is the case with casino gambling, for example. The financial context as opposed to a casino context is not, however, a sufficient guarantee against excessive bets. The existence of licences and prudential authorities does not as such suffice to exclude the characterisation of speculative derivatives as bets. The 2008 financial crisis (like many prior examples) has demonstrated that supervision – preventive or prudential – does not sufficiently protect society against excessive speculation.

Does this mean that speculative derivatives are bets and no other argument remains to justify their enforceability? In any event, one type of derivative is not considered as a bet even by the most fervent supporters of a ban on derivatives. This is the derivative type that serves a risk-hedging function for both parties to the transaction or even for one of the parties. In other words, the issue as to whether a derivative is a bet is restricted to the situation where the motive of *both* parties is speculative. Many legal scholars have been emphasising this point for a long time with regard to exchange-traded difference contracts: since the bank only executes an order for such difference contracts as a middleman and is not the counterparty, such an order is not speculative.[128]

Further elaborating on the view that derivatives of the risk-hedging type are enforceable, the criterion for distinguishing a bet from another aleatory contract may be whether a sufficient legitimate interest or purpose of a party is served by the contract. A derivative is not a bet if it serves the interest of a party having a risk which is hedged by the derivative.[129] From this point of view, the lack of an interest other than the mere pursuit of profit would imply the existence of a bet.

The question whether derivatives are unenforceable bets or rather enforceable aleatory contracts is clearly too general. No-one seems to doubt that derivatives are socially useful if they serve risk-hedging purposes. A company borrowing at a floating interest rate may want to hedge the risk of interest rate rises above a defined level by concluding an interest rate swap whereby it swaps its floating rate position for a fixed rate position. The company may find a company with the reverse position, willing to hedge a risk of interest rate drops, e.g. a company which has lent money at a floating interest rate and is seeking the certainty of a fixed interest rate.

The chance of these two companies finding each other and of their respective positions perfectly matching each other, however, is rather small. The interest rate may be based on a different reference rate (Libor or Euribor) or the spread in fixed interest rate may be too wide, the notional amount may differ (e.g. €100,000 or €1,000,000), the currency of the underlying loans may differ (euros and yen, for example), etc.

In other words, it is hard to imagine that a market that is limited to purely risk-hedging derivatives would be an efficient market, while the social utility of risk hedging is (assumed to be) beyond doubt. It is legitimate for an entrepreneurial company to hedge or minimise the risk inherent in its economic activity which is – by hypothesis – contributing to the welfare of our society.

This explains why legal scholars like Lynch in the US accept the enforceability of not only purely hedging derivatives but also derivatives between a hedging party and a speculating party. However, Lynch vehemently opposes derivatives when both parties are merely speculating. According to Lynch, those derivatives should be classed as bets and should be contrary to public policy because they are 'less than zero-sum transactions' and 'add artificial risk to the economy'.[130] For Stout, too, they are 'simply bets' because they have no significant useful purpose.[131] Roberts adheres to the view that 'it is hard to see what the wider economic benefits of derivatives are outside the rather special case of hedging' because the losses would most often fall on small and medium enterprises (SMEs), local governments and local commercial banks.[132]

On a practical level, the distinction between so-called 'merely speculative' transactions and others may give rise to many intricate and costly disputes.[133] A transaction may be concluded partly for risk hedging, partly for speculative reasons for one party and entirely speculatively for the other. The question also arises whether a speculator hedging his respective positions would no longer be a risk hedger in the view of these scholars. It may also be true that a person uses a position to give the impression that he wants to hedge it while it may already be hedged by another position, etc.

Fundamentally, the issue boils down to determining whether purely speculative transactions are bets because the parties to those transactions have no interest other than the mere pursuit of profit that depends on luck or, in other words, because both are merely speculating.

There seems to be a *shift* from reasoning based on a legitimate interest other than speculation for at least one of the parties (such as risk hedging)[134] towards the question whether a given type of contract has a *legitimate economic purpose or other societal purpose* (although the argument is most often limited to the economic sphere). The reasoning would imply that an aleatory contract is not a bet if it serves a useful purpose for society.[135] In other words, instead of focusing on the interest of the individual parties, the focus now is on the interest of society in speculative derivatives.

This idea appears to be reflected in US legal literature. Chicago law professor M. Todd Henderson argues: 'we do not want regulating these bets as gambling for the same reason that the secondary market in "stocks" is not regulated as gambling, even though it is. The reason is that gambling is socially useful'.[136] Scott and Gelpern write: 'Speculation may be the dark side of derivatives, but speculators are crucial to the market. They are the risk takers who permit hedgers to lower their risks.'[137] The same idea can be traced back in French legal scholarship, where 'social utility' is the explanation for why difference contracts are not bets.[138]

The idea is essentially one inherent in all *sui generis* contracts: courts accept the existence of a *sui generis* contract because they consider the contract to be socially or economically useful. The effect of such characterisation of a contract as *sui generis* is most often that it is not subject to a particular mandatory law which applies to a particular nominate contract (such as a commercial lease, for example).

Let us assume that a derivative fails to be a bet not only if one of the parties has an interest of its own other than the pursuit of profit, but also if the derivative serves a useful economic or other societal purpose. The crux of the discussion then becomes whether speculative derivatives are still useful to society or whether their utility is smaller than their damaging or potentially damaging effects on society. Do the negative externalities outweigh the benefits?

The positive effects of speculative derivatives are the *efficiencies* they create for the markets. As already illustrated, the more speculative the transactions and the broader the market, the higher the chance that a person looking to hedge his existing risks will find a suitable instrument. For example, speculation on the rise or fall of interest rates makes it easier for risk hedgers to find a hedging tool on the market. The more players there are on the market for interest rate derivatives, the greater the possibility of hedging. The benefit to society is that resulting from the liquidity of the market. Speculative derivatives may also have the beneficial effect of increasing price efficiency.[139] Speculative CDS may give valuable information on the financial situation of debtors (so effectively used in practice) and therefore improve the efficiency of debt markets.

While these positive effects have been emphasised by many for a long time, the negative side of speculative derivatives erupted to the detriment of governments (and taxpayers) in the wake of the financial crisis of 2008. The systemic crisis is often attributed to the existence of speculative derivatives concluded in over-optimism and irrationality,[140] which implies inefficiency rather than increased efficiency.

In summary, a derivative transaction may have several functions, principally risk hedging, speculation and arbitrage (correcting mispricing). All functions appear to be useful for the organisation of our society and our economy in particular. It may therefore not be wise to apply the unenforceability rule on bets to derivative transactions in general. Bets in the legal meaning of the term are by definition transactions which are of no value to society and which are therefore unenforceable. To the extent that derivatives have more positive than negative effects, freedom of contract may regain its territory. M.T. Henderson, for example, arrives at the same end result when stating that derivatives are bets but are not regulated as wagering because they are 'socially useful' gambling, although the choice of the word 'gambling' is unfortunate because it has the connotation of not being socially useful.

An empirical question arises: do the benefits outweigh the negative effects of speculative derivatives? 'Is liquidity of markets just a religion?' as Berruyer asks.[141] The associated question is whether the answer to the empirical question may change if other system characteristics are varied, for example by external or self-imposed regulations setting position limits or transaction limits or by diminishing the interconnectedness in our society.

This is a perfect example of the limits of theoretical research and the necessity of empirical and interdisciplinary research. The legal question of whether speculative derivatives should be characterised as bets depends on the outcome of empirical research, at least if one accepts the legal thesis that an aleatory contract is only an unenforceable bet if, in the end, it is socially harmful. Without proper interdisciplinary research, the debate between proponents and opponents of speculation will be continued without end, or with catastrophic results. Proper empirical and interdisciplinary research requires available and reliable information to be researched; the lack of such information may be an obstacle requiring urgent regulation. Information is knowledge – in this context, knowledge concerning whether or not speculative derivatives are, legally speaking, bets.

If no reliable information is made available, should we then take the risk that speculative derivatives may cause further systemic risk, or should the cautious position be that speculative derivatives are bets until further research results prove the contrary? This question may not need to be resolved if the legislator considers (independently of the basis of such considerations) that derivatives are socially useful and should only be subject to certain regulatory restrictions. We will explore this in the following section.

10. DERIVATIVES: NOT BETS – AND EVEN ENFORCEABLE NOMINATE ALEATORY CONTRACTS? THE REGULATOR'S VOICE IN THE DEBATE

Even if it were the conclusion that speculative derivatives are bets in the legal meaning of the word, this may not matter any longer because of successive legislative interventions in both the EU and the US.

The legislation exempting difference contracts from the unenforceability rule on bets has already been discussed above[142] and its relevance for speculative derivatives remains undisputed. The incorporation of these rules in successive statutes of more recent date somehow obscures their older origins. The French Act of 28 March 1885, for example, is now part of the Monetary and Financial Code (article L-211–35). The relevant Belgian rules of the Royal Decrees of 15 October 1934 on security futures and 30 November 1939 on commodity futures[143] are now excerpted in an Act of 2 August 2002[144] (article 32) and their scope has been extended to currency forwards/futures in an Act of 4 December 1990.[145] In the UK, too, section 36 of the Financial Services Act 1986 played down the rule against wagering in the financial sector for a series of transactions (including options, futures, and differences) concluded 'by way of business' (meanwhile, in section 10 of the Gambling Act 2005,[146] a series of derivatives are excluded from the scope of section 9 on betting by reference to the regulated activities in the meaning of section 22 of the Financial Services and Markets Act 2000 as amended by the Financial Services Act (FSA) 2012).

Those national regulations in the EU do not entirely speak with one voice. Several types of transactions are outside the scope of these regulations. Sometimes, OTC derivatives are not covered. On other occasions, transactions with a private person outside of a business context are out of scope.

In other words, the general rules distinguishing enforceable and unenforceable aleatory contracts, and therefore determining whether a transaction is a bet, might still matter, were it not that the European regulator's recent interventions seem to have fundamentally changed the legal landscape. Regulation No 648/2012 of 4 July 2012 an OTC derivatives, central counterparties and trade repositories has created a general framework for over-the-counter derivatives in the EU. The Regulation on OTC Derivatives, also called EMIR (the European Market Infrastructure Regulation), introduces a duty to clear certain types of standardised OTC derivatives through a CCP, a central counterparty, through which each purchase or sale of such derivatives has to be made.[147] For those types of derivatives that are not subject to such clearing duty, a duty to limit risks is created. Finally, for both cleared and uncleared types of transactions, information has to be provided to 'trade depositories' on the conclusion, modification and termination of each derivatives contract.[148] Risk hedging is explicitly envisaged to exclude non-financial counterparties from duties if the derivatives 'are objectively measurable as reducing risks directly relating to the commercial activity or treasury financing activity of the non-financial counterparty or of that group'.[149]

This framework seems to exclude the possibility for courts to characterise any kind of derivatives (OTC or not, speculative or not) as bets. If a framework is created by the legislator for a particular type of transaction and this framework is complied with, the idea of leaving such transactions unenforceable as bets seems to be a contradiction in terms. The regulation of a type of transaction cannot be reconciled with the idea that, as a rule, such transactions would be unenforceable in court (at least in principle; see below on the public policy defence).[150]

In the US, several scholars, including Cornell professor Lynn Stout and Maryland professor Michael Greenberger, have pointed to the deregulation wave brought in by the Commodity Futures Modernisation Act of 2000 (CFMA) signed by President Clinton. That deregulation wave paved the way for OTC derivatives, since the exchange trading and clearing under the Commodities Exchange Act of 1936 were no longer required 'as long as the counterparties to the swap were "eligible market participants"'.[151] Stout stated that purely speculative OTC derivatives became enforceable for the first time in history with the 2000 Act.[152] Greenberger further summarised:

> 'Recognizing that the deregulation of swaps would remove the Act's bar against excessive speculation in regulated exchange traded futures, the CFMA also expressly preempted state gaming and anti-bucket shop laws, which would have barred the otherwise unregulated speculative activity authorized by the CFMA.

> Finally, to ensure that not even the CFMA itself could be used as a basis to challenge the legality of a swap, the Act provides that no agreement, contract, or transaction between eligible contract participants [...] shall be void, voidable, or unenforceable [...] based solely on the failure [...] to comply with the terms or conditions of an exemption or exclusion from any provision of this chapter or regulation of the Commission:
>
> [...] In sum, what was then estimated to be the multi-trillion dollar OTC derivatives market was removed from almost all pertinent federal and state enforcement to which trading markets had been subject since the New Deal, as well as a central premise of the common law of contracts, i.e., that illegal contracts are subject to a declaration of unenforceability'.[153]

Greenberger concluded:

> 'Had those laws not been preempted, it is almost certain that at least some states would have banned these investments as unlicensed gambling or illegal bucket shops'.[154]

Meanwhile, the Dodd-Frank Act[155] seems to confirm the position that speculative derivatives are enforceable. Title VII of that Act, on Wall Street transparency and accountability, includes a subtitle on the Regulation of Over-the-Counter Swaps Markets. Section 723 provides for a mandatory clearing requirement and limits participation in swaps as a rule to eligible contract participants, but exemptions may be introduced.[156]

11. PUBLIC POLICY: THE JUDICIARY'S VOICE IN THE DEBATE?

If the rules on bets are not applicable to speculative derivatives (as explained in section 9) or if regulation has excluded the possibility to characterise speculative derivatives as unenforceable bets (as explained in section 10), a subsequent legitimate question is whether derivatives, even though enforceable as a rule, may still be unenforceable because they would otherwise infringe public policy.

The starting point of this question is the idea that a society organises itself without having the intention of destroying itself. Self-destruction cannot be assumed for any societal system.

The potential for self-destruction actually exists, given the systemic risks as attributed by many writers, including some legal scholars, to speculative derivatives – especially since the 2008 financial crisis, but also before.[157] Warren Buffet's well-known observation that derivatives are financial weapons of mass destruction captures well the idea of systemic risk. Systemic risk exists because of the size of risky transactions, the lack of adequate margin requirements, the interconnectedness of financial and non-financial entities and the resulting domino effect of the default by a major player. Self-destruction may also be caused by the potential of a fundamental shift of wealth in society that causes a manifest imbalance without any link to the real economy (talent or labour). This idea is ideologically highly sensitive and restricts the idea that money can produce money. However, societal discussions on high salaries for CEOs, for example, show that the idea of manifest imbalances in wealth and the growing inequalities in society may no longer be sustainable or accepted.

Assuming for the purpose of this chapter that redistribution and wealth balances are a political issue within the legislative powers and not within the judiciary powers, it is nevertheless worth briefly exploring the issue of whether the potential of a systemic crisis may not be a sufficient cause for considering speculative transactions (such as derivatives) to be contrary to public policy and therefore unenforceable, not so much as a matter of general principle, but rather only in circumstances where the systemic risk has exceeded a level that society cannot be deemed to accept because it is potentially self-destructive. Phrased differently, the question is whether 'brokerage firms are able to capture the private benefits of idiosyncratic, over-the-counter contracts, while externalising the risk of systemic meltdown of the entire system'.[158]

In legal terms, we wonder whether the potential effect of a proposed contract is taken into account in assessing the legality or illegality of that contract. Even if there is no specific regulation forbidding speculative derivatives, they might still be forbidden in some circumstances on the basis of general concepts of contract law. In particular, we think of the concept of public policy and the generally accepted rule that contracts are not enforceable when they infringe public policy or public order. Public policy or public order is a broad and therefore imprecise concept which denotes the fundamental principles and essential rules in a society from an economic, ethical, social, and political perspective. Tax law, criminal law, and urban planning rules, for example, are often considered to be part of public policy. In private law as well, several principles and rules belong to public policy, although more debate exists as to exactly what constitutes private-law public policy. For example, the binding force of a contract and freedom of contract can be said to be part of public policy,[159] even international public policy.[160]

This reasoning starts from the assumption that public policy, as accepted in many legal systems, can be determined by courts apart from the legislative instances of public policy.[161]

A contract will only be unenforceable for reasons of public policy if there is some recognised link between the contract and the envisaged violation of public policy. If someone promises to murder someone in exchange for a determined price, for example, the contract will not be enforceable because the very *subject matter* of one of the promises (murdering) is contrary to public policy and makes the contract unenforceable, even void. The other contracting party promises to pay in order to invite someone to murder. The *determinant reason* (cause) why that other party is willing to promise the payment of a sum of money is equally contrary to public policy and makes the contract unenforceable, even void.[162]

Although some scholars hold a restrictive view on the playing field of public policy, a contract may not only be unenforceable because the subject matter or the determinant motive for assuming an obligation infringes public policy but also because its *effects* would undermine public policy. The most prominent example is a contract with anti-competitive effects. Article 101 of the Treaty on the Functioning of the European Union explicitly prohibits 'as incompatible with the internal market: all agreements between undertakings, decisions by associations of undertakings and concerted practices which may affect trade between Member States and which have as their object or *effect* the prevention, restriction or distortion of competition within the internal market'.[163]

The broad question is whether such effect-based assessment of contracts under the public policy theory is generally applicable or whether it is limited to certain legislative rules of public policy such as competition law rules. At first sight, there is no reason to restrict the playing field of public policy. Public policy refers to the fundamental principles on which a society is based. No system can be expected to allow transactions that have the potential to make its fundamentals explode, but I agree that this topic is worth further exploration.

When applied to derivatives, there is evidently a considerable degree of legal uncertainty that may be caused by the risk of illegality following a judicial assessment of the (potential) effects of a transaction. The advantage of generality and an inherent degree of legal uncertainty is, however, the preventive function of the general rule, as long as judges do not overestimate the potential negative effects of a particular transaction. The danger of judges over- or under-assessing the potential risk is not small, since judges are not trained to perform such assessment, even though they may be informed by the parties, counsel and technical experts appointed by the parties or the court.

The legislative forum may be more appropriate to adequately assess the pros and cons of a given type of contract. The legislator is able to gather information from various perspectives, and the debate encompasses many more voices than the actors involved in a judicial procedure. Even though it is beyond the scope of this contribution to determine in general precisely when the systemic risk of a speculative transaction could exceed the threshold of legality, we think of aspects such as the interconnectedness of the parties intending to conclude a contract with other key societal players, the size of the transaction, and the number of similar transactions. All of these factors may play an important role for assessing the degree to which a transaction increases systemic risk and the harm it may cause to the system, such as the potential of the domino effect of a default (the threat to the orderly functioning of financial markets) or the destabilisation of prices on markets.

Avoiding overkill is crucial, because speculative transactions such as derivatives also have beneficial effects on our society and because 'systemic risk increases with many *desirable* types of investments'.[164] Derivatives are said to increase liquidity, allowing efficient risk-hedging opportunities and price efficiencies. The excesses on the US housing market revealed in the recent financial crisis, for example, might only have become apparent at a later stage had it not been for speculative derivative positions.

But perhaps the debate on whether courts could hold derivatives unenforceable because of their potential negative impact on the system is much ado about nothing. A legislator may not need to provide a specific rule allowing courts to assess whether or not a speculative derivative is contrary to public policy; the general public policy rule may suffice as a matter of principle. However, an exception exists if the legislator has regulated a transaction in such a way that the public policy rule does not have any role to play.

That is what appears to have occurred recently in the EU with regard to the specific issue of short selling (which includes the use of speculative derivatives).[165] The possibility that a court could decide that public policy would resist short selling in some circumstances seems to be implicitly excluded by the Short Selling Regulation.[166] Article 28 of that regulation authorises the European Securities and Markets Authority, ESMA, (not the judiciary) to take measures, albeit in exceptional circumstances, if the orderly functioning and integrity of financial markets or the whole or part of the financial system in the EU are threatened with cross-border implications and if no competent state authorities have taken measures to address that threat or if the measures taken by one or more competent state authorities do not adequately address that threat. In these circumstances, ESMA has the powers and the duty to require persons having net short positions in some financial instrument or class of financial instruments to notify or make public some information or prohibit or impose certain conditions on entering into a short sale or a transaction creating or relating to an envisaged financial instrument 'where the effect or one of the effects of the transaction is to confer a financial advantage on such person in the event of a decrease in the price or value of another financial instrument'. These measures must satisfy certain requirements such as the proportionality between their benefits and the 'detrimental effect on the efficiency of financial markets, including by reducing liquidity in those markets or creating uncertainty for market participants' (Article 28(3)).

With this Regulation, the EU legislator has empowered ESMA to address systemic risks inherent in short selling. According to the opinion of Advocate General Jääskinen of 12 September 2013,[167] the Regulation and its Article 28 are the result of 'a basic policy choice made by the legislator to the effect that under normal conditions short selling is useful but in defined exceptional circumstances it can pose a threat to the proper functioning of the internal market. The further policy choice has been made that this threat needs to be addressed, if necessary by action taken at the EU level. Hence, the essential value judgements underpinning Article 28 […] have been made by the EU legislature'.[168]

The Advocate General also insists on the complexity of such matters as justifying the fact that those powers are allotted to the ESMA: 'while the application of the criteria and terms of Article 28 […] require complex assessments of facts, ESMA was established for precisely this purpose. ESMA is a compound structure that brings together national expert authorities who are obliged to consult the ESRB. In my opinion, the need to make such technically difficult assessments on an objective and non-political basis is an argument in support of conferral of the powers concerned on an expert agency rather than on the Commission'. The Advocate General adds: 'the possibility of disagreement between experts on a subject matter does not necessarily imply the existence of subjective judgements or untrammelled discretion in any legally relevant sense. It is not uncommon for experts, and indeed judges, to disagree. Objectivity is in fact dependent on procedural guarantees ensuring that decision makers base their assessments on a broad factual basis and sound methodology, after having consulted the relevant actors. These requirements are reflected in Article 28'.

These considerations of the Advocate General reflect well the idea that the judiciary may not be the appropriate forum to decide under the umbrella of public policy whether certain short selling transactions should be forbidden in particular circumstances. However, although this reasoning does not seem to be refutable as far as short selling is concerned because of the existence of specific regulation, does this imply that we would always have to await the decision of a legislator to regulate a matter before it can be addressed, even if there is a serious threat to the financial stability of our society, for example? Freedom of contract exists only within the confines of public policy (amongst other rules) and it is not expedient to await a new crisis and the regulatory response to prevent a similar type of crisis again, without being able to prevent a different type of instrument from causing another type of crisis. That is exactly the preventive function and value of the public policy rule which, admittedly, has to be applied in a prudent manner on the basis of all relevant information. It also has to be acknowledged that a court decision may arrive too late.

12. CONCLUDING REMARKS

Speculation and gambling are concepts that are left undefined in legislation. Gambling and public policy (with imprecise content) are legal concepts, but not everyone agrees that speculation should be considered a legal concept (except in some specific legislation). Rather, speculation is considered to be a term used in economic parlance. Speculation is definitely a state of mind, a motive, a purpose for which a transaction is concluded. Nothing more, nothing less.

The interrelationship between speculation and gambling or bets has been at the heart of many historical debates. It has changed throughout history due to new legislation and case law. Speculative transactions are bets if they do not satisfy any economic or other societal needs. If they do satisfy some needs, they may be distinguished from bets and receive the label of a *sui generis* or innominate aleatory contract or, in the event of regulation, even a nominate derivatives contract. The societal need for speculative derivatives is perceived to be their contribution to the quality of pricing of the underlying assets through better information (e.g. on debt quality) and the increased availability of risk-hedging instruments for industrial and commercial companies (sometimes called the religion of the liquidity of markets).[169]

The multi-million dollar question, however, is: in what circumstances is the satisfaction of those societal needs outweighed by its negative effects – such as the chances of a systemic crisis? Can these negative externalities be internalised by the public policy concept? The complex relationship between law and economics, between broad general rules and specific regulation, and between the judiciary and the legislature, make it difficult for the classic private law instrument of public policy to be utilised efficiently.

Speculation is arguably a false criterion to distinguish enforceable from unenforceable contracts, because speculation may be good for society and because in practice it is difficult to distinguish the speculative motive from non-speculative motives.

Given the fact that the crisis of 2008 is said to be partly due to speculative derivatives, it may be wiser to oblige parties to consider the potentially damaging effects in the context of a liability rule of general prudence and as a matter of unenforceability of transactions when concluded in infringement of public policy (even though difficult to apply), rather than automatically considering all speculative derivatives as bets.

Endnotes

* Ignace Claeys teaches at the Ghent University Centre for the Law of Obligations and is an Attorney in Brussels. This contribution was finalised at the end of December 2014.

1. See, for the USA, the Angelides report (The Financial Crisis Inquiry Commission, *The Financial Crisis Inquiry Report, Final Report of the National Commission on the Causes of the Financial and Economic Crisis in the United States*, January 2011, available at http://fcic-static.law.stanford.edu/cdn_media/fcic-reports/fcic_final_report_full.pdf) and the Levin-Coburn report (US Senate Permanent Subcommittee on Investigations, *Wall Street and The Financial Crisis: Anatomy of a Financial Collapse*, 13 April 2011, Washington, 639 p., available at www.ft.com/cms/fc7d55c8-661a-11e0-9d40-00144feab49a.pdf). For the EU, see the Liikanen report (High-level Expert Group on reforming the structure of the EU banking sector, *Final Report*, 2 October 2012, available at http://ec.europa.eu/commission_2010-2014/barnier/headlines/news/2012/10/20121002_en.htm).
2. See, for a succinct overview of notorious crises, J.K. Galbraith, *A Short History of Financial Euphoria*, 2nd ed., Penguin Books, London, 1993, 113 p.

3. The current context differs substantially from the context of the 1940s, as can be derived from e.g. J. LEBRUN, *Les marchés à terme et l'exception de jeu en Belgique. Les réformes en 1934 et 1939*, Louvain, Nouveaux Publications Universitaires, 1945, p. 399: 'one should not forget that the futures are actually only effected on securities traded on futures exchanges.'
4. This time, the fallacy of *post hoc ergo propter hoc* most probably does not apply.
5. See, on systemic risk and how to measure it, the clear and recommended overview by J.A. CHAN-LAU, *Systemic Risk Assessment and Oversight*, London, Risk Books, 2013, 322 p.
6. See M.T. HENDERSON's succinct and clear account of the 2008 crisis in 'Credit Derivatives Are Not "Insurance"', in University of Chicago Law & Economics. Olin Working Paper No. 476, 2009, available at http://ssrn.com/abstract=1440945, p. 56: 'This counterparty risk was bigger than anyone thought: firms no one thought would fail, like AIG, failed by taking on too much risk. This led to a cascade of failures of brokers, like Lehman Brothers, and other intermediaries, which in turn led to huge collateral calls and a general constriction of credit flows. Quite simply, the mispricing of and realisation of counterparty risk caused the credit crunch.'
7. France, Belgium (and its regional entities) and Luxembourg bailed out Dexia. The Benelux states did the same for Fortis.
8. See M. GREENBERGER, 'Overwhelming a Financial Regulatory Black Hole with Legislative Sunlight: Dodd-Frank's Attack on Systemic Economic Destabilization Caused by an Unregulated Multi-trillion Dollar Derivatives Market', *Journal of Business & Technology Law*, 2011, 150.
9. For further perspectives on social services, see the contribution by Ludo Cornelis in this book.
10. For a short summary of these and other events, see A.M. Chisholm, *Derivatives Demystified. A Step-by-step Guide to Forwards, Futures, Swaps and Options*, 2nd ed., Wiley, Finance Series, 2010, pp. 11–12.
11. L.A. STOUT, 'Why the Law Hates Speculators: Regulation and Private Ordering in the Market for OTC Derivatives', 48 *Duke Law Journal*, 1999, 701–786.
12. 'Italy's Central Bank wins Backing', *Financial Times*, 30 January 2013; 'Italian Bank Sheds Light on Derivatives Loss', *Financial Times*, 29 January 2013.
13. A well-known player is Armajaro founder Anthony Ward, alias 'Chocfinger', who holds positions in the cocoa market.
14. 'Food Price Speculation Taken Off The Menu', *Financial Times*, 4 March 2013.
15. 'Hedge Funds Reap Billions on Yen Bets', *Financial Times*, 13 February 2013.
16. Over-the-counter, as opposed to exchange traded. According to the statistics of the Bank for International Settlements (BIS), in 2012, 83.7 million *futures* contracts were *exchange* traded for a notional amount of US $24.12 trillion in December 2012 and 128.9 million *option* contracts for a notional amount of US $30.31 trillion in December 2012 (see www.bis.org/statistics/r_qa1306_hanx23a.pdf). Swaps are currently quasi-exclusively OTC.
17. US $71,606,350,000,000 according to the World Bank in 2012, see http://en.wikipedia.org/wiki/List_of_countries_by_GDP_(nominal).
18. ISDA, 'OTC Derivatives Market Analysis Year-End 2012', June 2013, available at http://assets.isda.org/media/467fbf64/438d9f0f.pdf/.
19. See section 9.

20. MiFID stands for the Markets in Financial Instruments Directive which entered into force on 1 November 2007 (financial lawyers and regulators love shortcuts that no layman understands and which impede interdisciplinary debate – a typical trick to make the others feel stupid and an incentive for the others not to ask any further questions in order not to look stupid, much like the naked emperor in the tale by Hans Christian Andersen).
21. See, for an example, 'Four banks found guilty of mis-selling derivatives', *Financial Times*, 20 December 2012, on interest rate swaps concluded by Italian local public authorities which swapped their fixed interest rate for a floating interest rate and which were confronted with vast losses due to the later increase in the interest rate.
22. Admittedly, the two questions may be merged into one rule, as seems to have occurred in a Swiss decision of the Swiss *Bundesgericht* of 15 March 1994, *BGE* 120 II, 42: in order to determine whether a transaction is a bet/game, it is relevant whether there is a complete imbalance between the estate and the risk ('*völlige Missverhältnis zwischen der Vermögenslage und dem Verlustrisiko*') and, in the event of exchange traded transactions, a complete lack of knowledge of the exchange ('*das völlige Fehlen von Kenntnissen im Börsenwesen*').
23. Insurance law is another perspective closely related to but not analysed in this contribution. See the contribution by H. Cousy in this book on this perspective.
24. We do not enter into the distinction between games and bets since the unenforceability rule is the same for both.
25. For example A.M. Chisholm, *supra* note 10, pp. 10–11 ('a large speculative bet'); M.T. Henderson, *supra* note 6, pp. 11, 18, 26, and 31; L.A. Stout, 'Uncertainty, Dangerous Optimism, and Speculation: an Inquiry into some Limits of Democratic Governance', 97 *Cornell L. Rev.*, 2012, 1192 ('Derivatives are nothing more or less than bets on financial phenomena. Again, this is not a figure of speech'). Even the German Civil Supreme Court (*Bundesgerichtshof*) speaks of an interest rate bet (*Zinswette*) when referring to interest rate swaps (see the reference in J. Roberts, 'Financial derivatives: investments or bets?', *Butterworths Journal of International Banking and Financial Law,* 2011, 317).
26. For example, R. Zimmermann, *The Law of Obligations. Roman Foundations of the Civilian Tradition*, Oxford, University Press, 1996, p. 8, who asks the question: 'Is it really acceptable to maintain that the law has to prevent people from ruining themselves by indulging in gaming and betting?'
27. The Draft Common Frame of Reference (DCFR), a recently established set of rules on European private law proposed by mainly academics, speaks of fundamental principles or principles 'recognised as fundamental in the laws of the Member States of the European Union' (II.-7:301 DCFR, in C. von Bar and E. Clive, *Principles, Definitions and Model Rules of European Private Law. Draft Common Frame of Reference (DCFR)*, Munich, Sellier, 2009, p. 535).
28. 'RIP OTC: swap futures gain buy-side fans', *Risk*, October 2012 (2), 4.
29. In this direction: L.A. Stout, *supra* note 25, p. 1196.
30. I do not enter into the debate on the precise nature of the possible remedies (voidness, unenforceability, lack of standing, etc.), which may vary from one legal system to another. The activity of betting as such is not necessarily forbidden, but the contracts on bets may be void, even though restitution of bets performed may be excluded. See, for example, section 1965 in the French (and Belgian) Civil Code (CC); section 762 of the German Civil Code (BGH); section 7A:1825 of the Dutch Civil Code (NBW); section

513 of the Swiss Law of Obligations (*Obligationenrecht* – OR). According to the Belgian Court of Cassation, a bet is invalid because of an illicit cause or determinant motive, viz. a cause that infringes public policy (Cass. 19 November 1891, *Pas.* 1892, I, 18).

31. See section 1.
32. See for example O. Berruyer, *Les faits sont têtus*, Paris, Ed. Des Arènes, 2013, pp. 314–315; P. Jorion, *Misère de la pensée économique*, Paris, Fayard, 2012, pp. 147 ff.
33. Public Ministry in an opinion on a Belgian Court of Cassation decision of 19 November 1891, *Pas.* 1892, I, (18) 20 (the original text reads: '*ce principe général que la folie humaine ne peut être un moyen juste de s'enrichir*').
34. Recently compared to the witches of Macbeth by the Belgian fiction writer Tom Lanoye on Flemish Radio 1, 5 September 2013. He also compares polls with these witches (www.standaard.be/int/dmf20121002-062).
35. In an interview, a Dutch high frequency trader said: 'In some sense each transaction is speculation' (I. De Witte, 'Jan Modaal betaalt rekening van de tobintaks', *De Tijd*, 25 January 2013).
36. For example R.A. Posner, *Economic Analysis of Law*, Boston, Little, Brown and Company, 1992, p. 445: 'The speculator is the eager searcher for undervalued and overvalued securities. The information that he uncovers diffuses rapidly throughout the market.'
37. See already, albeit not in the context of bets, the Belgian 'liberal' law professor F. Laurent, *Principes de droit civil*, XXIV, Brussels, Bruylant, 1878, p. 575, no. 581 ('*car spéculer est aussi un droit*'). See also the highly recommended book by Hamburg sociology professor U. Stäheli, *Spectacular Speculation. Thrills, the Economy, and Popular Discourse*, Stanford, University Press, 2013, p. 187 ('The United States differed from Germany in that a "right to speculation" was assumed there') and the quotation on p. 781 ('Speculation is inherent in the human constitution, and men have a legal and moral right to speculate, provided they do so reasonably, intelligently and at their own risks'). See also M. Radin, 'Maintenance by Champerty', 24 *California Law Review* 48, 1935, 70: 'Speculation in the United States never had the continuous history of slight moral obliquity which it retained in England, even after loans on interest were not merely legal but constituted one of the economic bases of society'.
38. The freedom of contract is part of the freedom to conduct a business, as recognised in Article 16 of the Charter of Fundamental Rights of the European Union, and has been a basis to dispute the validity of European legal instruments (see e.g. EU Court of Justice, *Sky Österreich*, 22 January 2013, no. C-283/11, http://eur-lex.europa.eu/LexUriServ/LexUriServ.do?uri=CELEX:62011CJ0283:EN:HTML). See also the case before the German Constitutional Court (*Bundesverfassungsgericht*) of 28 March 2006, *GRUR* 2006, 688 on the conformity of the state law on lotteries (*Staatslotteriegesetz*) of Bavaria with the freedom to choose an occupation or profession in article 121 of the German Constitution (GG).
39. For the freedom of establishment and freedom of services in gaming and betting, see for example the EU Court of Justice case *Gambelli* of 6 November 2003, Case C-243/01, in particular no. 63: 'moral, religious and cultural factors, and the morally and financially harmful consequences for the individual and society associated with gaming and betting, could serve to justify the existence on the part of the national authorities of a margin of appreciation sufficient to enable them to determine what consumer protection and the preservation of public order require' and no. 67: 'whilst in

Schindler, *Läärä* and *Zenatti* the Court accepted that restrictions on gaming activities may be justified by imperative requirements in the general interest, such as consumer protection and the prevention of both fraud and incitement to squander on gaming, restrictions based on such grounds and on the need to preserve public order must also be suitable for achieving those objectives, inasmuch as they must serve to limit betting activities in a consistent and systematic manner.'

40. L.A. Stout also gives some examples in *supra* note 25, p. 1200, at footnote 72.
41. Section 34, §3, of the Royal Decree on real estate investment companies, *Belgian Official Gazette*, 28 December 2010. See also section 31 of the Programme Act of 27 December 2005 on the Agency for the reduction of the total cost of energy; the Agency's investments must be non-speculative.
42. See the International Financial Reporting Standards IFRS 9 on Financial Instruments. For Belgium, see Commissie voor Boekhoudkundige Normen, CBN-advies 2011/18 – De boekhoudkundige verwerking van de renteswap, 5 October 2011, and CBN-advies 2010/12 – De toepassing van de algemene boekhoudprincipes op afgeleide financiële instrumenten, 8 September 2010.
43. Such assignment is considered to be an aleatory contract (see e.g. H. De Page, *Traité élémentaire de droit civil belge*, IV/1, 1972, Brussels, Bruylant, p. 467, no. 463).
44. See H. De Page, *supra* note 43, IV/1, p. 468, no. 464.
45. The French legislator has provided for some exceptions to that rule in article 1701 of the Civil Code because it considered that there is a 'legitimate cause' of a fully enforceable assignment in those exceptional circumstances (see H. De Page, *supra* note 43, IV/1, p. 473, no. 472).
46. 'The whys and wherefores of an EU "Tobin tax"', *Financial Times*, 4 March 2013, p. 14.
47. Act on financial collateral and on various tax provisions relating to real collateral contracts and loans relating to financial instruments, *Belgian Official Gazette*, 21 February 2005.
48. Parliamentary Documents of the Belgian Chamber 2004–05, 51–1407/001, pp. 10–11, also extensively quoted in Constitutional Court decision no. 167/2008 of 27 November 2008 (holding some rules of the act of 15 December 2004 unconstitutional when applicable to natural persons who are not merchants).
49. A person appointed by courts or by operation of law to manage another's assets has to be 'very prudent' when considering entering into a purchase in return for an annuity, a rather vague criterion advanced by T. Wuyts, *Vermogensbeheer door ouder(s), voogd en voorlopige bewindvoerder*, Antwerp, Intersentia, 2005, p. 90, no. 156.
50. [1992] 2 AC 1. For an analysis from different angles, see P. Birks and F. Rose (eds.), *Lessons of the Swaps Litigation*, Mansfield Press, 2000, 402 p. Courts are more reluctant vis-à-vis public authorities in order 'to protect the public fisc for the benefit of tax payers' (H.L. Scott and A. Gelpern, *International Finance, Law and Regulation*, London, Sweet & Maxwell, 2012, p. 904).
51. See also, on the general principle that imposes to be economical as part of the principle of reasonableness (in Dutch *zuinigheidsbeginsel*), C.M. Billiet, 'Beginselen van behoorlijk bestuur en bestuurlijke handhaving. Evenredigheid en zuinigheid in het sanctioneringsproces', *Tijdschrift voor Milieurecht* 2008, 308–309; P. Nicolaï, *Beginselen van behoorlijk bestuur*, Deventer, Kluwer, 1990, pp. 456–458.
52. Justice of the Peace of Zomergem (Belgium), 30 September 2009, *RW* 2010–11, 379.

53. Commercial Court of Kortrijk, 19 February 2003, *TRV* 2003, 417, annotated by J. Vananroye. However, if such transactions have been made for years on behalf of the corporation with the consent and approval of all shareholders and its board of directors, the person performing these transactions should not be held to have acted negligently, according to the court. Once a decision has been made to efficiently make an end to the currency forwards, existing contracts may still be prolonged in order not to take heavy losses immediately and therefore to possibly escape a threatening heavy loss through an extension of the contract, the court ruled. See also the list of cases of negligence of directors under Belgian law, as provided by H. Braeckmans and R. Houben, *Handboek Vennootschapsrecht*, Antwerp, Intersentia, 2012, p. 337, no. 610, as freely translated from Dutch: 'all too speculative transactions or imprudent investments'. The latter seems to suggest a differentiation in degree of speculation and to consider only excessive speculation as imprudent. In other words, there must some degree of speculation before it turns into negligent behaviour, and the degree will depend on the actual circumstances of a case.
54. See J. Baeck, 'Multi-inzetbaar in het Belgische privaatrecht: de vordering uit ongerechtvaardigde verrijking', in Vereniging voor de vergelijkende studie van het recht van België en Nederland, *Preadviezen 2012*, Boom Juridische Uitgevers, 2012, p. 221, no. 34.
55. P. Jorion, *supra* note 32, p. 40.
56. '*La spéculation est l'âme des contrats aléatoires*' (quoted in A.-C. Muller, 'Aléa et marchés financiers', *L'aléa*, Journées nationales Tome XIV/Le mans, Paris, Dalloz, 2011, p. 82, note 35).
57. The fact that speculation does not determine the characterisation of a contract does not mean that speculation would be a mere economic term devoid of legal effect. It may still be important as a motive or *causa* (compare to J.B. Huizinck, 'Overeenkomsten tot verrekening van een prijs- of koersverschil', *WPNR* 1987, no. 5820, p. 131).
58. This is also reflected in history, see J.K. Galbraith, *supra* note 2.
59. The professional or retail nature of a client is relevant, for example, under the rules of MiFID (Directive 2004/39/EC of the European Parliament and of the Council of 21 April 2004 on markets in financial instruments amending Council Directives 85/611/EEC and 93/6/EEC and Directive 2000/12/EC of the European Parliament and of the Council and repealing Council Directive 93/22/EEC).
60. That being said, some persons, such as public authorities, may be forbidden to conclude transactions for speculative reasons (see section 4), but that is a normative issue different from the factual question whether someone actually has a speculative motive.
61. Compare to the definition of the International Food Policy Research Institute, *When Speculation Matters*, February 2009, accessible at www.ifpri.org/publication/when-speculation-matters, p. 2: 'Speculation is the assumption of risk of loss in return for the uncertain possibility of a reward'.
62. See for example M.T. Henderson, *supra* note 6, p. 5 ('In fact, every contract assigns, shares, and apportions some sort of risk') and p. 23 ('Every contract has a degree of insurance embedded in it').
63. See E. Banks, *Finance – the basics*, Routledge, 2011, p. 7.
64. See for example a definition of speculative activities in a Flemish decree (freely translated from Dutch): 'activities which are not in conformity with the goals of this decree, as well as activities whereby financial products and/or contracts are handled

and whereby *irresponsible risk positions* are taken in order to book profit or capital gain' (emphasis added in Decree of 7 May 2004 of the Flemish Community and the Flemish Region on provisions on cash, debt and guarantee management).

65. An IRS (interest rate swap) for ten years, for example, is not exceptional.
66. Compare to the definition of J. Lebrun, *supra* note 3, p. 126, as translated from French: 'transaction aiming at realising a return in a relatively short time'.
67. See the definition of financial speculation by the International Food Policy Research Institute, *When Speculation Matters*, February 2009: 'Financial speculation involves the buying, holding, selling, and short-selling of stocks, bonds, commodities or any valuable financial instrument to profit from fluctuations in its price as opposed to buying it for use or for dividend or interest income'.
68. Much emphasis is sometimes put on return in the process of distinguishing it from risk hedging, see for example G. Schrans and R. Steennot, *Algemeen deel van het financieel recht*, Antwerp, Intersentia, 2003, pp. 126–127, no. 125.
69. See the inspirational view of Daniel Baron Janssen in 'De beurstraders ruïneren de wereldeconomie', *De Tijd*, 12 October 2013: 'Many of the family shareholders will pass the shares received from their parents on to their own children'.
70. Thus, a Belgian scholar explicitly considers that an insurance contract is a sort of bet when analysing it from the perspective of the insurer (P. Colle, *Algemene beginselen van het Belgisch verzekeringsrecht*, Antwerp, Intersentia, 2006, p. 13, no. 4).
71. Compare to the definition of a derivative in International Accounting Standard IAS 39, one of the elements being that it 'requires no initial net investment or an initial net investment that is smaller than would be required for other types of contract that would be expected to have a similar response to changes in market factors'.
72. See American Law Reports, ALR 3rd, 'Law of Forum against wagering transactions as precluding enforcement of claims based on gambling transactions valid under applicable foreign law', §6.
73. Supreme Court 1884, *Irwin v Williar*, 110 US 499.
74. See for more details and further references, L.A. Stout, 'Derivatives and the Legal Origin of the 2008 Credit Crisis', 1 *Harvard Business Law Review*, 2011, 14–17.
75. *Board of Trade of the City of Chicago v Christie Grain & Stock Company*, 8 May 1905, Supreme Court Reporter, 1904, 198 U.S. 236, 637 ff.
76. U. Stäheli, *supra* note 37, p. 245 clearly explains the origin of the term: 'The term "bucket shop" is said to have referred originally to the practice of collecting beer dregs in a bucket to be shared among paupers who could not afford to drink at a bar. Financial bucket shops stood in for conventional brokerages rather than pubs'.
77. See U. Stäheli, *supra* note 37, p. 242.
78. See for example the consideration reported in the *New Jersey Flagg v Baldwin* (1884) case in American Law reports, ALR 3rd, 'Law of Forum against wagering transactions as precluding enforcement of claims based on gambling transactions valid under applicable foreign law', §6: 'the policy evidenced hereby was of such public interest that comity did not require the enforcement of a contract stigmatized by it'. For German law, see *Munchner Kommentar*, §762, no. 1. In Belgian law, the president of the Commercial Court of Brussels decided that the defence of gambling is not part of international public policy (decision of 12 May 1987, *Droit bancaire et financier* 1989, 265, annotated by C. Martin).
79. See U. Stäheli, *supra* note 37, p. 242.
80. In Dutch: '*koersverrekeningsovereenkomsten*'.

81. See ASSER-VAN SCHAICK, *Bijzondere overeenkomsten*, VIII, *Bewaarneming, borgtocht, vaststellingsovereenkomst, bruikleen, verbruikleen, altijddurende rente, spel en weddenschap*, Deventer, Kluwer, 2012, pp. 282–283.
82. See, on all this, H. BAIS and B. JONGMANS, 'Een gokje wagen met een Contract for Difference?', *Tijdschrift voor Financieel Recht* 2010, 194–199. The two Amsterdam attorneys clearly consider the debate as nonsense given the total harmonisation following the MiFID regulation.
83. ASSER-VAN SCHAICK, *supra* note 81, pp. 283.
84. Now article L-211–35 of the *Code monétaire et financier*: '*Nul se peut, pour se soustraire aux obligations qui résultent de contrats financiers, se prévaloir de l'article 1965 du code civil, alors même que ces opérations se résoudraient par le paiement d'une simple différence*.'
85. Against the application of the rule outside 'official markets': A. BÉNABENT, *Droit civil. Les contrats spéciaux civils et commerciaux*, Paris, Montchrestien, 2011, pp. 639–640. Leaving the possibility open, albeit exceptionally: P. MALAURIE, L. AYNÈS and P.Y. GAUTIER, *Les contrats spéciaux*, Paris, Defrénois, 2012, p. 580, no. 984 ('*elles peuvent exceptionnellement être admis, dans les contrats de gré à gré*'), referring to a decision of the French Court of Cassation of 24 November 1909, *DP* 1911, I, 129 that appears to leave more room for OTC difference contracts because of the absolute and general wording of the act of 28 March 1985.
86. See ASSER-VAN SCHAICK, *supra* note 81, p. 284.
87. French Court of Cassation, Civil Chamber, 24 December 1921, *DP* 1922, I, 13 ('*la loi du 28 mars 1885 a entendu, quand les opérations ont pris la forme de marché à terme, interdire aux parties d'opposer l'exception de jeu et aux juges de rechercher l'intention des parties*').
88. See M. HABERSACK (ed.), *Münchner Kommentar zum Bürgerlichen Gesetzbuch*, 5, *Schuldrecht. Besonderer teil III*, Munich, Beck, 2009, §762, p. 901, with reference to a law of 21 June 2002 (Gesetz zur weiteren Fortentwicklung des Finanzplatzes Deutschland).
89. §37 e S. 1 WpHG (*Wertpapierhandelsgesetz* – the commercial law on securities): '*Gegen Ansprüche aus Finanztermingeschäften, bei denen mindestens ein Vertragsteil ein Unternehmen ist, das gewerbsmäßig oder in einem Umfang, der einen in kaufmännischer Weise eingerichteten Geschäftsbetrieb erfordert, Finanztermingeschäfte abschließt oder deren Abschluss vermittelt oder die Anschaffung, Veräußerung oder Vermittlung von Finanztermingeschäften betreibt, kann der Einwand des §762 des Bürgerlichen Gesetzbuchs nicht erhoben werden. Finanztermingeschäfte im Sinne des Satzes 1 und der §§37g und 37h sind die Derivate im Sinne des §2 Abs. 2 und Optionsscheine*.'
90. For example, Court of Appeal of Brussels of 17 November 1904, *Pas.* 1905, II, p. 324.
91. See H. DE PAGE, *Traité élémentaire de droit civil belge*, V, *Les principaux contrats usuels (deuxième partie)*, Brussels, Bruylant, 1975, pp. 308–309; J. LEBRUN, *supra* note 3, p. 16 and pp. 395–398.
92. The clearing house, in turn, may pose another type of systemic risk.
93. In the present analysis, we do not consider other instruments such as caps or floors.
94. For a technical analysis of the exotic ones, see the seminal treatise of S.K. HENDERSON, *Henderson on Derivatives*, Butterworths, 2010, 1281 p.
95. Please note that a sales contract, even though not originally so intended, may end up with a substitute payment on the part of the seller, but this fact does not as such exclude the sales characterisation.

96. Most scholars exclude the sales characterisation (see e.g. ASSER-VAN SCHAICK, *supra* note 81, p. 283; J.B. HUIZINCK, *supra* note 57, p. 131). See also G. SCHRANS and R. STEENNOT, *supra* note 68, p. 139 ff., who distinguish the derivatives from the contracts relating to them and who seem to characterise the contracts creating derivatives as *sui generis* when non-speculative (in particular on pp. 151–152) and as bets when speculative (p. 146). In the context of this chapter, we are mainly interested in the characterisation of derivatives of a speculative nature.
97. See for example L. CORNELIS and J. DELVOIE, 'Contractuele aspecten verbonden aan het bankverzekeren', in K. BYTTEBIER, E. DE BATSELIER and E. JANSSENS, *Bankverzekeren – Bancassurance*, Antwerp, Kluwer, 2002, pp. 299–353, p. 309, no. 15. At p. 310, no. 17, they define an aleatory contract as follows (as translated from Dutch): 'to hedge or run a particular risk, i.e. the chance of a particular future but uncertain event, knowing and accepting that the relation (and the possible equivalence) between the reciprocal obligations will be determined by fate during the performance phase of the contract, each therefore running a contractualised chance of profit or loss'.
98. See H. SCOTT and A. GELPERN, *supra* note 50, pp. 843 and 848.
99. This instrument allows the interest risk to be separated from the other risks of a loan.
100. This instrument allows the credit risk to be separated from the other risks of a loan (see e.g. M.T. HENDERSON, *supra* note 6, p. 8).
101. See the contribution of H. Cousy in this book on this specific issue of CDS and insurance.
102. On pp. 16 and 31 in *supra* note 6, M.T. HENDERSON emphasises that there is no risk pooling for CDS while this is an important feature for insurance contracts. For CDOs (collateralised debt obligations), he contests the insurance language because of the lack of an insurable interest (pp. 17 and 31–32).
103. M.T. HENDERSON, *supra* note 6, p. 8.
104. See for example M.T. HENDERSON, *supra* note 6, p. 3. See also the explanatory documents for the Belgian collateral law quoted in section 4.
105. From an economic perspective as well, see J. ROBERTS, *supra* note 25, (315) 317: 'A better is not a buyer ("emptor"). In a bet, putting the client at a disadvantage is not [...] the same thing as including a "profit margin" in the price for a purchase.' And he continues as follows: 'Typical market transactions are all contracts of sale. With contracts of sale, conflicts of interest are only incidental, because normally both sides increase their "utility" as a result of the exchange [...]. With zero-sum games, however, this does not apply: the loser's purely negative utility cancels out the positive utility on the side of the winner. There is no overall gain in utility' (p. 317). 'A bet is a zero-sum game, not a purchase. There is no reason of policy to shift all the price risk on to one of the parties as in caveat emptor.'
106. As indicated, the particular question whether a CDS is an insurance contract is dealt with in the contribution by H. Cousy in this book.
107. This seems to be the position of the Belgian Court of Cassation in a judgment of 23 April 1992, docket number 9236, *Pas.* 1992, I, 740 (freely translated): 'that, according to article 4 [of the act of 11 June 1874] the validity of the agreement depends on the insurable interest, this means on the condition that the insured has an interest in the damaging event not occurring'. However, the existence of a possible risk is a requirement for the *existence* of an insurance contract according to the summary (full text not available) of an earlier decision of the Belgian Court of Cassation of 19 April 1977 (*Arr. Cass.* 1977, I, 857).

108. See, for Belgian law, the explanatory documents for the Act of 25 June 1992 on land insurance contracts (Belgian Chamber, 1990/91 (47), no. 1586/1, p. 11, freely translated from Dutch: 'One can therefore state that there is no damage insurance without an insurable interest' – 'Without it, there would be no good reason and the agreement would be no more than a bet'. This point of view builds upon previous scholarly work, such as the French scholar J. Hémard, *Théorie et pratique des assurances terrestres*, Sirey, 1924, II, p. 659, no. 747 ('while the insured aims to reduce its risks, the player creates new risks'). This has been repeated in the major treatises on Belgian insurance law: L. Schuermans, *Grondslagen van het Belgisch verzekeringsrecht*, Antwerp, Intersentia, 2008, p. 260, no. 351 ('the insurable interest as validity requirement for the formation of the insurance contract' although at the same page he also refers to the insurable interest as a requirement for the '*existence* of an insurance contract'); M. Fontaine, *Droit des assurances*, Brussels, Larcier, 2010, p. 113, no. 145 ('*l'intérêt d'assurance est une condition essentielle de tout contrat d'assurance; sans lui, l'assurance ne se distingue pas du jeu*'); P. Colle, *Algemene beginselen van het Belgisch verzekeringsrecht*, Antwerp, Intersentia, 2006, p. 15, no. 6, for whom the rationale of the insurable interest is to 'avoid the insurance becoming a bet'.
109. It is however discouraged by the legislator because the debtor may entirely free himself by paying the assignment price to the assignee (see section 4).
110. See, as to Dutch law, J.B. Huizinck, *supra* note 57, p. 130 (considering that the enumeration of aleatory contracts is not exhaustive).
111. P.A. Fénet, *Recueil complet des travaux préparatoires du Code Civil*, XIV, Paris, 1827, p. 539 (freely translated from French: 'the possibility that the insurers give to the insured to make substantial transactions in large numbers, while the obligations arising out of a game are not based on a useful or reasonable motive').
112. Under article 1966 of the French and Belgian Civil Codes, those games may however be unenforceable when a judge considers the sums due excessive.
113. P. Malaurie, L. Aynès and P.-Y. Gautier, *supra* note 85, p. 579, no. 984.
114. See J. Lebrun, *supra* note 3, p. 70 ('*aucune utilité sociale*'). A link between short selling and betting is quickly made when reading the phrase: 'each player only hopes for his own fortune and rests only on the bad luck of the other' ('*Chaque joueur n'espère que de sa fortune, et ne se repose que sur le malheur d'autrui*' (P.A. Fénet, *supra* note 111, p. 533)).
115. See for example J. Roberts, 'Finanzderivate als Glücksspiel? Aufklärungspflichten der Emittenten', *DSTR* 2010, 1082, who considers that the legislator is suspicious of bets because they are '*wirtschaftlich gesehen nutzlos*'.
116. '*Il faut quelque chose de plus solide et de plus réel que le désir bizarre de s'abandonner aux caprices de la fortune pour fonder des causes sérieuses d'obligation entre les hommes*' (P.A. Fénet, *supra* note 111, p. 538). If '*le désir et l'espoir du gain*' are the sole motives of the contract, no action is available (p. 539). A clear moral reason for this rule is at stake: '*tout lien social est rompu*' because each gamer '*ne se repose que sur le malheur d'autrui*' (p. 539). Profit is separated from work, it leads to egoism (p. 540). It is a '*monstre anti-social*' (p. 558). '*Lorsqu'il (le jeu) dégénère en spéculation où l'on cherche à s'enrichir par la ruine de l'autre, il devient immoral, enfante le désespoir et le crime, bouleverse les familles, trouble l'ordre public*' (J.L. Locré, *Législation civile, commerciale et criminelle, ou commentaire et complément des codes français*, VII, Brussels, Librairie de jurisprudence de H. Tarlier, 1836, p. 165). Gaming is not undesirable as much by

its nature as because of its effects. Therefore bets are '*proscrites par la considération des abus et des dangers qu'elles peuvent entraîner*' (P.A. Fénet, *supra* note 111, p. 540; J.L. Locré, *supra* note 116, p. 173).

117. '*N'offrent aucun objet réel d'utilité qui puisse compenser les vices et les abus dont ils sont susceptibles*' (P.A. Fénet, *supra* note 111, p. 544).
118. '*L'avantage de procurer à l'homme isolé, infirme, avancé en âge, le moyen d'assurer la subsistance que ces capitaux ne pourraient pas lui fournir s'il ne les connaît point*' (J.L. Locré, *supra* note 116, p. 166).
119. Given the principle of freedom of contracts, contracts other than aleatory ones are only unenforceable if they do not harm society (if they did, they would be invalid for illicit cause under French law). Aleatory contracts, however, need to be socially useful; otherwise they are bets.
120. '*Spéculation exorbitante*' (P.A. Fénet, *supra* note 111, p. 558, J.L. Locré, *supra* note 116, p. 198).
121. '*Spéculation immorale*' (J.L. Locré, *supra* note 116, p. 166), which as a rule is not the case for games of 'skill and bodily exercise'.
122. '*Spéculation honteuse*' (J.L. Locré, *supra* note 116, p. 188), as in the case of the sale of a '*succession d'une personne vivante*'.
123. Whether or not a CDS is an insurance contract, see the contribution of H. Cousy in this book and M.T. Henderson, *supra* note 6.
124. See P. Jorion, *supra* note 32, p. 169 who speaks of '*la rationalité à la sauce du jour*'.
125. See for example already J. Lebrun, *supra* note 3, p. 296; C. Deneus, 'Des conditions de recevabilité de l'exception de jeu en matière d'opérations de bourse', *Rev. prat. soc.* 1925, p. 50 (versus the adventurous player); G. Schrans and R. Steennnot, *supra* note 68, p. 124, no. 121 (more reserved language on pp. 159–160, no. 146); Commercial Court of Ghent of 27 November 1920, *Pas.* 1922, III, (6) 8, freely translated from French: 'the gambler acts in an adventure influenced by news information, occasional relations or unverified impressions and in the impossibility of making a rational forecast […]; the speculator, to the contrary, only decides after study of the possible transaction, on calculations and projections leaving only a small part to the aleatory element of the transactions'.
126. P. Malaurie, L. Aynès and P.-Y. Gautier, *supra* note 85, p. 580, no. 984 ('*tous ces actes sont valables parce qu'ils constituent des spéculations relatives au marché régulier*'). Compare to J.B. Huizinck, *supra* note 57, pp. 129–132.
127. K. Andries, N. Carette and N. Hoekx, *Les jeux et les paris*, Brussels, Larcier, 2008, pp. 100–102, nos. 154–156.
128. See H. De Page, *Traité élémentaire de droit civil belge*, V, Brussels, Bruylant, 1975, p. 285, no. 296; W. Kupers, 'Termijncontracten in deviezen en artikel 1965 BW' (annotation), *TRV* 1989, p. 558, no. 5 and 6. J. Lebrun, *supra* note 3, p. 58 ('*pour chaque partie les seuls mobiles du contrat*') and p. 127 ('*Pour jouer, il faut être deux*'). Compare the German *Münchener Kommentar*, §762, no. 6 (both parties need to have a '*Spielabsicht*'). Compare the 1881 US Supreme Court case *Irwin v Williar*, 110 US 499: 'A transaction which on its face is legitimate cannot be held void as a wagering contract by showing that one party only so understood and meant it to be. The proof must go further, and show that this understanding was mutual.'
129. This closely resembles the definition of a bet or a gamble as 'an agreement or stipulation to the effect that the parties shall gain or lose upon the happening of an uncertain

event in which they have no interest except that arising from the possibility of such gain or loss' (see American Law Reports, ALR 3rd, 'Law of Forum against wagering transactions as precluding enforcement of claim based on gambling transactions under applicable foreign law', §6).

130. T. Lynch, 'Gambling by Another Name; the Challenge of Purely Speculative Derivatives', 17 *Stanford Journal of Law, Business & Finance*, 2011, pp. 73–74 as well as footnote 115 and the conclusion on p. 130. On p. 96, he states that they are bets 'disguised in the cloak of "derivatives" respectability'.
131. L.A. Stout, *supra* note 25, pp. 1177 ff.
132. J. Roberts, *supra* note 25, (315) 317.
133. L.A. Stout, *supra* note 25, p. 1193 says that the practical effect is an empirical question.
134. See, for example, the Court of Appeal's decision *Earl of Ellesmere v Wallace* of 5 February 1929 [1929] 2 Ch. 1: 'if there is no other purpose in the contract than that of gaming or wagering, it is void – the interest of the parties being evidence of the purpose for which it is entered into' (Lord Hanworth). For German law, see Palandt, Bürgerliches Gesetzbuch, Munich, Beck, 2006, §762, no. 4: *'Der spekulative oder gewagte Charakter macht ein Rechtsgeschäft noch nicht zu Spiel oder Wette, sofern die Parteien darüberhinaus noch wirtschaftliche oder sonst anerkennenswerte Zwecke verfolgen.'* See also P.O. Mülbert and J. Böhmer, 'Ereignisbezogene Finanzprodukte – Zivil-, Kapitalmarkt, Wertpapier-, Straf- und Öffentliches Recht – Teil I', *Zeitschrift für Wirtschafts- und Bankrecht*, 2006, p. 948: *'Die [herrschende Meinung] stellt also nur deswegen auf das wirtschaftlich berechtigte Interesse der Parteien an einem Vertrag ab, um die andernfalls eintretende Unverbindlichkeit selbst wirtschaftlich sinnhafter Geschäfte zu vermeiden'.*
135. The idea that legitimate economic need may suffice to avoid the characterisation of bets is not always accepted. See for example L. Cornelis and J. Delvoie, *supra* note 97, pp. 299–353 p. 301, no. 2, as freely translated from Dutch: 'Neither the emphasis on "the big picture" nor the (legitimate) economic needs which the new products seem to satisfy can undo the private law anchorage thereof, on the risk of creating a colossus on shaky foundations.'
136. See M.T. Henderson, *supra* note 6, p. 11 and also p. 16 ('socially beneficial transactions').
137. H.S. Scott and A. Gelpern, *supra* note 50, p. 846.
138. P. Malaurie, L. Aynès and P.-Y. Gautier, *supra* note 85, p. 580, no. 984 (*'une utilité sociale'*).
139. See e.g. R.A. Posner, *supra* note 36, pp. 47–48 and p. 126.
140. See on various types of irrationality, N.N. Taleb, *The Black Swan. The Impact of the Highly Improbable*, London, Penguin Books, 2010, 444 p.
141. O. Berruyer, *supra* note 32, pp. 303 and 306.
142. See section 6.
143. Summarised in H. De Page, *supra* note 91, V, pp. 308–309.
144. Act of 2 August 2002 on the supervision on the financial sector and financial services. The prior rule was article 42 of the Act of 6 April 1995 on the status and the supervision of investment companies and, before that, article 72 of the Act of 4 December 1990 on financial transactions and the financial markets.
145. Article 218 of the Act of 4 December 1990 on financial transactions and the financial markets.
146. Note that sections 334 and 335 of the Gambling Act 2005 abolished the rule of unenforceability of gaming or wagering contracts in section 18 of the Gaming Act

1845 ('All contracts or agreements [...] by way of gaming or wagering shall be null and void' – see also section 1 of the Gaming Act 1892: 'Any promise, express or implied, to pay any person any sum of money paid by him under or in respect of any contract or agreement rendered null and void by the Gaming Act 1845 or to pay any sum of money by way of commission, fee, reward, or otherwise in respect of any such contract, or of any services in relation thereto or in connexion therewith, shall be null and void, and no action shall be brought or maintained to recover any sum of money').

147. Article 4.
148. See Articles 9 and 11 and Recital 43.
149. See, for example, Article 10(3). See also Recital 19–21 and Article 10 the Regulation. See also the Commission Delegated Regulation (EU) No 149/2013 of 9 December 2012 supplementing Regulation (EU) No 648/2012 of the European Parliament and of the Council with regard to regulatory technical standards on indirect clearing arrangements, the clearing obligation, the public register, access to a trading venue, non-financial counterparties, and risk mitigation techniques for OTC derivatives contracts not cleared by a CCP: 'the clearing thresholds allow an exception to the principle of the clearing obligation for those OTC derivative contracts which may be considered as not concluded for hedging purposes' (Recital 21).
150. An 'enhanced framework for derivatives markets' is also one of the main goals envisaged in the current proposals of MiFID II and MiFIR (Proposal for a Directive of the European Parliament and of the Council on markets in financial instruments repealing Directive 2004/39/EC of the European Parliament and of the Council (Recast) – General approach, 18 June 2013, 2011/0298(COD), 11006/13; Proposal for a Regulation of the European Parliament and of the Council on markets in financial instruments and amending Regulation (EMIR) on OTC derivatives, central counterparties and trade repositories – General approach, 18 June 2013, 2011/0296 (COD), 11007/13).
151. M. Greenberger, *supra* note 8, p. 127, especially pp. 141–142.
152. L.A. Stout, *supra* note 74, pp. 18–22.
153. M. Greenberger, *supra* note 8, pp. 142–143.
154. M. Greenberger, *supra* note 8, p. 147.
155. Dodd-Frank Wall Street Reform and Consumer Protection Act (signed by President Obama on 21 July 2010).
156. See L.A. Stout, *supra* note 74, pp. 35–36.
157. See e.g. L.A. Stout, *supra* note 11, p. 701.
158. M.T. Henderson, *supra* note 6, p. 58.
159. The binding force of contracts has been recognised as a fundamental principle in e.g. EU Court of Justice, 16 June 1998, C-162/96, *Racke*, www.curia.eu; the then EC Court of First Instance, 25 May 2004, T-154/01, *Destilleria v Palma*, www.curia.eu. Freedom of contract has also been recognised as part of the freedom to conduct a business as enshrined in Article 16 of the Charter of Fundamental Rights of the EU.
160. As to the binding force of contracts, see P. Mayer, 'La sentence contraire à l'ordre public au fond', *Revue de l'arbitrage* 1994, 632, no. 20 and 633, no. 22.
161. On 'virtual public policy' in France, see: N. Borga, *L'ordre public et les sûretés conventionnelles. Contribution à l'étude de la diversité des sûretés*, Paris, Dalloz, 2009, p. 1; J. Ghestin, *Traité de droit civil. Les obligations. Le contrat: formation*, 2nd ed., Paris, LGDJ, 1988, pp. 92–94, with reference to a decision of the French court of cassation of

4 December 1929 (freely translated from French: 'the cause is unlawful if it is contrary to public policy without the need for it being prohibited by legislation').

162. Please note that the concepts used of subject matter and cause are (French) civil law concepts. In particular, the concept of cause is subject to much debate.
163. See, on this effect-based reasoning in the context of competition law, J. Bourgeois and D. Waelbroeck, *Ten years of effects-based approach in EU competition law. State of play and perspectives*, GCLC Annual Conference Series, Brussels, Bruylant, 2013, 302 p.
164. T. Lynch, *supra* note 130, p. 104.
165. See Recitals 10 and 12 as well as the scope as defined in article 1 of the Short Selling Regulation cited in the following footnote.
166. Regulation (EU) No 236/2012 of the European Parliament of the Council of 14 March 2012 on short selling and certain aspects of credit default swaps.
167. Opinion delivered on 12 September 2013 in Case C-270/12, *United Kingdom v Council and European Parliament*, nos. 97, 99 and 100.
168. On the usefulness of short trading, see e.g. F. Bogaert, 'Het verbod op short selling. Belgische reglementering en Europese ontwikkelingen', *Financieel Forum* 2010–11, 50–51.
169. See note 141.

CDS, SWAP OR INSURANCE?
What's in a name!

Herman Cousy*

What this chapter is concerned with is the somewhat problematic relationship between the esoteric, fast-developing and highly globalised world of the financial industry on the one hand and the way in which the law (in the general sense of the apparatus of legislation, regulation and sanctioning) can or should react toward such developments on the other hand.

Our quest is to discover how the law seizes onto these fast developments of financial instruments, transactions and techniques. The issue is illustrated by reference to the discussion about the exact nature of one of the most notorious financial derivatives, namely credit default swaps (CDS) and about their relation to the legally heavily regulated activity of insurance. There is a lot to be said about the comparison between CDS and insurance, all the more because the discussion has seldom been treated in depth[1] and because the issue has been, to the best of our knowledge, rarely if at all challenged in court.

The origins of the insurance transaction offer an historic example of the way in which the law has acquired a grip on what was originally considered to be a speculative and even suspicious operation,[2] and of the difficult and long process of the legal embedding or 'juridification'[3] of the activity of insurance.

Although the origins of modern insurance go back to the 14th century, it has taken several centuries before the insurance activity and industry have finally obtained the status of a recognised legal transaction and of a fully regulated industry. In civil law countries this process by which insurance has acquired full legal acceptance and dignity is illustrated by the fact that in some recent codifications, the insurance contract is being dealt with in the Civil Code (as is the case in the new Dutch Civil Code), instead of the Commercial Code, or of a separate legislation. In the continental European legal system, such evolution must be considered as a true 'upgrading' of the insurance activity. In the Napoleonic *Code Civil* of 1804, insurance was still dealt with in one single article (namely in Article 1964), in which insurance was ranked in the (generally suspicious looking) category of the 'aleatory contracts' (such as betting and gambling) and was further simply expelled toward the most distant outer regions of the law, i.e. the law of the sea. Over the past two decennia, almost all EU Member States have upgraded, modernised or simply renewed their insurance contract legislation.[4] The process of regulating the insurance industry has thus been slow and only recently been completed (under the impulse of the EU internal market directives) by acquiring the status of a fully regulated sector and industry. The process of 'juridification' has been long but the successive phases of this process are similar or at least comparable to the legal processes to which certain new financial derivatives are presently subjected.

In the very first phase, the challenge was to find a criterion to distinguish between the legally valid contract of insurance on the one hand, and the game of betting and gambling on the other, the latter being excluded from a right of action in court in the wording of Article 1965 of the Napoleonic (and presently in the Belgian) Civil Code. The criterion was sought in the doctrine of the illicit cause, but found largely to be present in a newly created specific insurance law concept, namely the requirement of the existence of an insurable interest (*l'intérêt d'assurance, die Versicherungsinteresse, het verzekerbaar belang*). The doctrine was gradually refined and a distinction was made between two different sorts of insurance, according to whether or not the principle of indemnity (*le principe indemnitaire, het indemnitair beginsel*) applies: indemnity insurance and fixed-sum insurance. Whereas over the centuries, the rights and obligations of the parties to the contract were (almost exclusively) governed by the contractual policy conditions, the insurance contract would later become the object of legislation, first by way of default legislation (*droit supplétif, aanvullend recht*), through mandatory law.[5] So far legislation has remained at the level of national law, which may be replaced in the near future by a more uniform law, at least at the EU level.[6]

The inversion of the production cycle combined with the problematic asymmetry of information, both characteristic of the insurance transaction, led to the creation of a public law prudential regulation of the supervision of the financial soundness of the insurance undertaking. In many EU Member States this was to last until the 1970s before a generalised supervisory legislation and regulation was introduced.

Quite recently the process of shaping a legal framework for insurance has entered a new phase, in which quite remarkably the usual relationship between financial law and insurance law is reversed. Whereas in the past, insurance law appeared to play the leading role, at present it is the other way around, and insurance law follows the example that was first developed in another area of financial law, namely in the law on securities and investment. Along the lines of what had been proposed by the IOSCO,[7] the EU legislation has introduced, first in the Investment Services Directive (ISD)[8] and later in the Markets in Financial Instruments Directive (MiFID),[9] the concept of 'rules of conduct (of business)', which is mostly considered to be a novum in the scala of types of legal rules.[10] As is to be expected,[11] the concept is now being introduced in the other financial sectors such as credit institutions especially concerning insurance undertakings and more specifically insurance intermediaries.[12]

With a bit of goodwill it is possible to recognise and identify comparable steps or phases in the ongoing process of juridification of financial derivatives in general and of credit default swaps in particular.

However there are differences. The first difference is that the process of transformation of a speculative and unregulated financial transaction into a duly legally framed transaction and defined contract, through the successive steps of correctly defining the transaction, the legal organisation of the protection against the counterparty risk, and a balanced treatment of the rights and obligations of the parties, is moving forward at a much faster pace than what happened with insurance. A second difference comes from the particularity of CDSs, and more specifically from the possible similarity of this financial technique with the (meanwhile) heavily regulated operation of insurance. Therefore there is a preliminary question to clarify here, namely whether a CDS is not merely an insurance in disguise, governed by existing insurance law.

This question is debatable and there are at least two camps. According to one view, supported by traditional insurance lawyers, there is no need to conceive a new legal framework for this so-called 'new' financial operation since it is at least in some of its applications apparently an insurance activity for which a fully-fledged legal apparatus is available, both in private law and public law.

Many professionals of the financial industry however take a different, albeit paradoxical, stand.[13] Whilst admitting that at least in some cases the CDS transactions are economically equivalent to insurance, they do not attach much attention to the question as to whether from a legal perspective CDS should be considered as insurance contracts, claiming that a CDS is a (new) credit derivative, for which a framework is presently being created through the voluntary development at industry level of standard contract clauses.[14] The truth is that because of the enormous size of the CDS market and the nature of the participants (banks, investment banks, hedge funds, commercial undertakings and insurance companies) few people in the financial industry appear to be very much worried about the legal qualification problem.[15]

The qualification discussion therefore offers an illustration of the delicate relationship between law and finance, and, as will be demonstrated, of the way in which the legal discussion is somewhat set aside by the weight of the worldwide financial transactions.[16]

1. CREDIT DEFAULT SWAP: AN INSTRUMENT OF CREDIT RISK MANAGEMENT

For the reader who is less familiar with financial jargon, a very few concepts and terms are hereafter described in a simplified way. In the world of finance, the CDS is to be situated in the sphere of risk management techniques, more specifically, in so-called credit risk management. A credit risk is present in all contracts that give one party a future obligation to the other, the risk being that the first party, the debtor, will fail to meet its obligations toward his creditor. The so-called credit risk refers to insolvency (default risk) but also to many other situations like any waiver, deferral, rescheduling or unfavourable adjustment of terms,[17] and to other circumstances that diminish the creditworthiness of the other party.

In the sphere of risk management, credit risk management occupies an important place. The insurance industry has developed techniques to manage and reduce credit risk, the best known of these being credit insurance, either private or public. But besides credit insurance, and partially because of the limitations and restrictions that are linked to credit insurance,[18] credit derivatives were developed. After having developed high-tech methods for hedging and diversifying interest rate and currency risks, the financial industry has looked for comparable techniques to cope with credit risks and developed them.

A derivative instrument (*produit dérivé*) is at the most basic level a contract, the value of which derives from another asset (bond, stock, commodity, etc.). The key idea on which derivatives are built is that those who buy and those who sell them are each making a bet on the future value of the underlying asset.[19] Financial derivatives have in common that they are agreements that shift risk from one party to another, and that their value is 'derived' from the value of an underlying financial instrument, or an index or another financial key figure like a currency rate or an interest rate.[20] After having created the more traditional futures and forward rate agreements and swaps (swaps of interest rates, currency rates and commodities rates), the financial industry has added so-called credit derivatives. A credit derivative is an agreement designed to shift credit risk between parties[21] with the purpose of allowing this credit risk to be hedged, traded or transferred. In a credit derivative a party sells to the other party protection against the occurrence of an event which has an adverse or negative effect on the credit, the so-called credit event. One usually distinguishes between three sorts of credit derivatives: the total return swap,[22] the credit default option and the credit default swap, the latter having attained the highest volume of contracts outstanding, in the period before the financial crisis of 2008.

The oldest derivatives are those on commodities, the trading of which began in the middle of the 19th century. Financial derivatives have been developed since the late 1970s when at the outset the technique of swaps was used.[23] In the early 1990s a new sort of derivative that would protect lenders (bankers and others) against defaults by their debtors was created: the credit derivative. Whereas the booming swap business did not seem to overly worry the mind of the regulators, swaps and derivatives became the object of self-regulation when a group of bankers set up in 1985 an industry body that by way of self-regulation would be issuing standards for swap deals: the International Swaps and Derivatives Association (ISDA). Whereas commodities derivatives were the object of a regulation by the law, the financial industry (and ISDA) on the other hand took a firm stand against any such public regulation of the financial derivatives. They proved to be remarkably successful in fending it off.[24]

The idea of using the derivative technique to shift credit risks arose in the early 1990s. In the beginning the banks used the risk shifting credit derivatives for purposes of their own.[25] At a later stage the banks would make the product available to corporate and public-sector clients by advising and assisting clients in the making of such deals.

The credit derivative market has swiftly grown to enormous proportions. In particular the amounts outstanding on credit default swaps have increased constantly and indeed grown dramatically up to the year 2008.[26] Since the crisis these amounts have substantially decreased, although they still represent sizable amounts of money.[27]

A credit default swap (CDS) in its simple form can be defined as a contract between two parties, (the buyer and the seller of protection), in which the buyer acquires the right to a payment when a 'credit event' occurs as regards the 'reference obligation' of 'the reference entity'. The reference obligation (or more generally the 'reference asset') is often a 'bond obligation', but can also be another debt instrument. The reference obligation can be a single instrument or can consist of a portfolio of instruments (like loans), that are often backed by collateral, like a mortgage (mortgage backed securities, MBS) or by another asset (asset backed securities, ABS). The reference asset can even be a more complex (securitised) product like the (in)famous collateral debt obligations (CDO)[28] or one layer thereof. This reference entity can be an individual corporation, financial or non-financial, or a public law entity such as a central or local government or public body. Where there is more than one entity, the contracts are called 'multi-named' instead of 'single-named'. The reference entity is not a party to the contract. The seller of protection is a bank, or an insurance undertaking, a hedge fund or another financial entity. During the term of the contract (five to ten years) a premium is paid, mostly periodically, and the premium is called 'the spread' (credit default spread premium). When the credit event occurs (e.g. a non-payment or default, or a credit-rating deterioration, a bankruptcy or restructuring of the reference entity) the credit event payment falls due, and the CDS comes to an end. The occurrence of the credit event leads to settlement or liquidation. One distinguishes between the cash settlement (the seller of protection pays a sum of money, which is either a fixed sum or for an amount which corresponds with the depreciation of the reference asset) or a physical settlement (the seller pays the nominal value of the reference asset to the buyer in exchange of the delivery of the reference asset by the buyer).[29]

To give a more lively picture of one of the contexts in which the CDS have appeared, let us have a succinct look at the story of the financial guarantee insurance in the US.[30] Before the outbreak of the 2008 financial crisis, a small number of insurers practised financial guarantee insurance, by assuming the unconditional obligation to take the place of the issuer of debt instruments, whenever this issuer may fail in the correct performance of his obligations outside the instrument. Since these insurers were obliged to limit their activity to these sorts of operations, they were called 'monoline insurers' or 'monoliners'. In the beginning monoliners limited themselves to ensuring guarantees for securities that were issued by public entities, like municipalities or local hospitals and the like, and they did so, not so much to cover insolvency risks (public entities not being or to a very less extent subject to that kind of risk), but to 'enhance' the credit rating of those issuing entities while being covered by insurers with excellent reputation and rating. The goal here was 'credit enhancement' but in a further phase the protection was extended to other instruments (like mortgage-backed securities, or more generally asset-backed securities), and still later they trod a highly dangerous path when they started guaranteeing the reimbursement of certain layers of the so-called structured financial products, more precisely the collateral debt obligations (CDO). In the process of issuing those guarantees, use was increasingly made of the technique of credit derivatives, and more particularly of credit default swaps. The use of the technique of credit default swaps to guarantee the performance of these complexly structured financial products proved to be a dangerous path. When the special purpose vehicles (SPVs) that issue the CDS ('transformer SPVs') are covered by guarantee insurance, it is ultimately the insurer who will bear the cost of the credit event payment.[31]

2. CDS: BETWEEN SCYLLA AND CHARYBDIS – INSURANCE OR SOMETHING NEW?

One cannot but admit that at first sight a CDS looks very much like an insurance contract, in which the policyholder pays a premium to buy coverage against the risk that the debtor of a given monetary debt is subject to failure. More specifically the transaction looks like a credit insurance contract, although there are several differences such as the fact that this insurance is limited to covering the risk of the non-reimbursement of the credit, whereas under a CDS, protection is also given against a broader defined risk, also including for example the decline of the creditworthiness arising from events like restructuring, rating decline, etc.

If the insurance qualification is correct, a CDS can be compared more specifically to a property insurance (*assurance dommage*) and thus to an indemnity insurance (as opposed to a fixed sum insurance).[32]

However the insurance qualification has always been contested by the financial industry. In their view a CDS is an operation closely linked to a credit transaction, i.e. credit derivative, which therefore can be offered and sold by a credit institution and not only by insurers. The derivative in question is called a 'swap'. One can see the likeness indeed insofar as in a CDS the buyer of protection is, in accordance with the specifications and terms, transferring the counterparty risk from the original debtor to the entity which sells protection.

The qualification debate is not irrelevant.[33] If indeed we are in reality dealing with an insurance contract, the basic principles of insurance law, amongst which the principle of insurable interest, are applicable, and insofar as the operation is one of indemnity, the indemnity principle must be respected. In addition, if the operation is one of insurance, the entity which professionally produces and sells this product must be considered as an insurance undertaking which is subject to the supervisory legislation and, inter alia, due to obtain the proper authorisation. Contracts that are concluded in violation of these mandatory rules of public (supervisory law) and private law (law of insurance contract) risk to be sanctioned by nullity! If CDSs are insurance contracts, banks would not be authorised to make and market these products.

In what follows, attention is concentrated on two issues. The first issue is the question whether credit default swaps are insurance, and therefore possibly void, contracts in those cases where the insurable interest requirement is not satisfied. The second question concerns the fate of a CDS that is concluded with a counterparty who is not an authorised insurer. In this connection brief attention will be given to the way in which ISDA and recent EU regulation try to protect the protection buyer by requiring the centralisation of the counterparty risks that are involved in the operation.

An important element in the discussion about the exact nature of the CDS operation is the fact that CDSs can also be (and, as would appear, mostly are) bought or acquired by protection buyers who do not have ownership of (or a comparable insurable interest in) the positive or negative evolution in the value of the reference asset. In such a hypothesis the protection buyer pays a premium in view of obtaining the agreed payment when the reference asset is subject to a credit event, although he does not own the asset in question and although his estate does not suffer damage because of the credit event. In such a constellation, the CDS is called a non-covered CDS or, in more plastic language, a 'naked CDS'.

This leads us to a striking observation. It has taken legal thinking and rule making centuries of development and refinement to come to the axiom that an aleatory operation like the insurance contract can only be valid if the requirement of an insurable interest is fulfilled. The same requirement is totally abandoned when it comes to appraise the legal status of a CDS, which is indeed a credit derivative, but which is highly comparable, if not similar to an insurance contract.

The question arises as to why a buyer should be prepared to pay a premium to cope with the situation where a credit event threatens an asset in which he (the buyer) has no interest. A possible answer is of course 'speculation', although members of the financial industry would rather answer that this is a technique of pro-active risk management, combined with the pursuit of profit. The buyer of a naked CDS is taking a not-covered 'short position', i.e. he is betting on a bear market, in which the value of the reference obligation goes down. If such credit event actually occurs, the buyer makes a net profit.

However the naked CDS can also serve more than purely speculative purposes. One possibility is that the buyer, although not keeping himself the reference asset in question, possesses other assets that are subject to developments similar or comparable to the reference asset. In such cases the transaction is a hedging operation: the buyer of the CDS intends to compensate the losses suffered on his own balance sheet assets with the profit that he makes out of the depreciation of the reference asset which he does not own.[34] More generally it is claimed that (naked) CDSs play a useful (and legitimate) role in the risk management policy and particularly in the risk diversification policy of an entity.

Let us go back to confronting the figure of the naked CDS with the requirements of insurance contract law. If this transaction should be considered as one of insurance, then the policyholder or insured should possess an insurable interest in the non-occurrence of the insured (credit) event. In the old and classical definition of Ehrenberg[35] an insurable interest is the link between a person and whatever is subject to the insured risk because of which such person suffers a (financial) loss when a given fact occurs. If the policyholder or insured does not have such an interest, a validity requirement of the insurance contract is lacking. It is generally recognised that insurable interest is a necessary requirement of a valid insurance contract, also in English law.[36] Under Belgian law, there is a longstanding and generally accepted view that the concept of insurable interest distinguishes a valid contract of insurance from gaming and betting, in the sense of article 1965 *Code civil.*

Here we come to the essence of our account, which relates to the manner in which the debate about the nature of a CDS is usually held in the financial industry, and to the way of reasoning that is thereby followed. According to a traditional logic, the reasoning should be that a (naked) CDS must be considered as a game of chance because of the absence of an insurable interest, with all the consequences thereof (cf. above: non-enforceability and even nullity). However in the financial industry the generally accepted view would rather appear to be that CDSs, at least some of them like the naked CDSs, are not insurance because they require that the buyer has an insurable interest in the subject matter. This is for instance the approach that is voiced in a well-known opinion that was made by a Robin Potts QC on behalf of ISDA (the so-called 'Potts Opinion'). In the version of this opinion that is reproduced in a report of the English Law Commission on insurance law,[37] the theory is upheld that credit default options plainly differ from contracts of insurance in the following critical respects:

1. the payment obligation is not conditional on the payee's sustaining a loss or having a risk of loss; and
2. the contract is thus not one which seeks to protect an insurable interest on the part of the payee. His rights do not depend on the existence of any insurable interest.[38]

The Potts Opinion appears to have had a convincing influence in the UK. In the US a serious debate has raged about the exact legal qualification of CDSs even among those in public authority.[39] No lesser body than the New York State Insurance Department (NYSID) has hesitatingly taken various positions about the qualification issue. In the course of the financial crisis, the NYSID adopted the view that a CDS is (only) an insurance contract if the buyer of protection is effectively holding an interest in the reference obligation.[40] It may be true that the NYSID seemed to consider that naked CDS could be marketed, be it under the conditions imposed by the federal authorities (SEC and Commodity Futures Trading Commission). But drawing the logical conclusions, the National Conference of Insurance Legislators (NCOIL) issued in its 'credit default insurance model legislation' a prohibition on so-called naked credit default insurance.[41] The federal legislator would however decide the other way by prescribing, in the Dodd-Frank Act 2010 that 'security based swaps' and 'swaps' are not insurance and that they cannot be considered as such by state legislators.[42]

In the logic of Belgian insurance law, a CDS and certainly a naked or uncovered CDS cannot be considered to be a valid insurance contract because of the absence of an insurable interest. Such a transaction must therefore be considered to be a game of chance, in the sense of article 1965 of the Civil Code. According this article, which originated in the *Code Napoléon* of 1804, the law does not allow a legal claim for payment for debts arising from such transactions of gaming and betting.

Whereas article 1965 Civil Code only appears to bar an action in court to obtain payment, the case law of the highest courts both in Belgium and in France have gone further, by considering betting and gaming contracts to be null and void, not so much because of the said article 1965, but because such contract is void because of its illicit cause.[43] Unless legalised in specific cases by legislation, bets and games are considered to be contrary to the *ordre public*.[44] The sanction is therefore the 'absolute' nullity of the contracts, which means that the judge must *ex officio* declare the contracts null and void, even if the parties do not ask for it.[45]

In recent times, however, legislators have withdrawn some games from the field of application of the general provision (in Belgium article 1965).[46] They did likewise in the context of a changing specific legislation on casino games. They did so in a totally different context, namely that of the financial legislation concerning financial instruments.

And so did the Belgian legislator, in a bold legislative move in article 2 of the Act of 2 August 2002 on the supervision of the financial sector and the financial services (Financial Supervision Act) which contains a list of financial instruments, mentioning inter alia 'derivative instruments for the transfer of credit risk'. According to article 32 of the same Financial Supervision Act, transactions of financial instruments are withdrawn from the application of article 1965 Civil Code, if they are carried out on a regulated market[47] or an equivalent market, with a qualified intermediary as intervening person or as counterparty, and also in the case that these transactions are liquidated by payment of the differences in prices. A credit default swap can indeed be considered as a transaction for the payment of a price difference, since there is no delivery of securities or of goods, and payment is measured by a difference in the price of the reference asset.

If they fail to meet these conditions, transactions that are concluded outside such regulated markets remain exposed to the risk of being declared void. However in this last case, the application of the sanction under article 1965 Civil Code can be avoided by virtue of the unwritten interpretation rule according to which the exception of betting and gaming requires that both parties have the intention to engage in games of chance, and that the proof of this speculative intention is given by the claimant. To identify such intention, delicate concepts are used (like 'legitimate economic motivation'), and nuanced distinctions are made like the difference between '*le jeu de hazard*' and '*la speculation raisonnée*'.[48]

One is inclined to express amazement in the face of such a succinct and brief reaction of the legislator to financial instruments, like credit default swaps, against the dangers of which several authoritative commentators have warned by remarking that 'as with all derivatives, these tools [...] offer a way of controlling risk, but they could also amplify it'.[49] At the very least one might expect lawmakers to impose certain prudential requirements to make sure that those who sell 'protection' are capable of living up to their obligations. A first step toward such a legal embedding is taken by the EU Regulation No 468/2012 that will be briefly discussed below.

3. CENTRAL COUNTERPARTY

One of the arguments that is used in the qualification debate is that credit default swaps are not insurance because the seller is not required to maintain any reserves to pay off buyers and because the seller does not need to be a regulated entity. Again, we think that this sort of argument turns matters upside down. It is because a transaction is insurance, that the insurer is obliged to make technical provisions that are covered by matching assets, and it does not follow that a (non-legally regulated) transaction which is very similar to an insurance transaction is not insurance because fundamental rule of insurance law is not respected, rather than the other way around.

As regards insurance, the supervisory legislation indeed requires insurers to provide for technical reserves because of the inversion of the production cycle, and on top of that, to provide for an extra safety cushion, in the form of a so-called solvency margin, because the operation is an aleatory one, and the statistical evaluation of future debts may prove to be inadequate and the reserves insufficient. It is generally accepted that it is the task, even the duty, of the public authorities to enact such a regulation and to install a competent authority with the task of authorising and supervising the insurance business. Since individual buyers of insurance have no means of evaluating the adequacy of the measures taken by the insurer (because of the asymmetry of information), they have to count on the regulatory apparatus of the state. In addition, as was pointed out in the 1986 landmark decision of the Court of Justice of the EU in the *Commission v Germany* case,[50] insurance is a mass phenomenon making the insolvency of an insurer into an issue of general interest to society. In the EU a generalised control of the access to and carrying out of the insurance activity was introduced by the so-called 'Internal Market Directives' (1988–1992), further elaborated later alongside the Financial Services Action Plan, and recently fundamentally reformed by the so-called Solvency II Directive.[51]

Protecting the buyer of 'over-the-counter' (OTC) derivatives cannot be done by copying the model of prudential control of banks and insurance companies. OTC derivative contracts are privately negotiated contracts that lack transparency and that create a complex web of interdependence, which can make it difficult to identify the nature and the level of the risk involved. To enhance transparency and to mitigate the counterparty credit risk, the solution is presently sought in other techniques, like the clearing of all OTC derivatives through a central counterparty (CCP) and the requirement that all OTC derivatives are reported to trade repositories.

The construction of a central counterparty implies that the bilateral relationship between the protection buyer and the protection seller is replaced by two different relationships: one between the seller and the central counterparty, and one between the buyer and the central counterparty.[52] The two parties do not acquire rights and duties towards each other but towards the CCP, and they end up running a counterparty risk against this CCP. To have access to the services of the CCP, the parties have to satisfy certain conditions (like minimal creditworthiness and capital requirements). The intervention of the CCP makes it possible to operate compensation of the rights and obligations of the parties on a multilateral basis, which results in a better risk reduction than in the case of bilateral compensation. Multilateral netting is done by summing up each participant's bilateral net positions with those of the other participants. The result is a multilateral net position, which represents the bilateral net position between each participant and the central counterparty.[53] The risks (credit risk but also the market risk) are spread among the participants and thus 'mutualised'. However the ultimate absorption of risk must come from the equity capital that is injected by the participants. Traditionally such injection is achieved by the posting for each transaction and amount of collateral, the amount of which can change in the course of the transaction with the value of the contracts (the amount of the initial 'margin' is marked to market and can thus be adapted in the course of the contract). However capital requirements have been far below those that are prevalent in insurance contracts. Here again the CCP system tries to remedy the situation. To cope with the need for equity, some CCPs provide for a guarantee fund that is financed by the participants, and that can be used to cover losses that exceed the available amounts of 'margins' that have been posted.

Before the financial crisis, the move to greater transparency in OTC derivatives markets, and toward the creation and use of CCPs, had found its origin in private initiative. As one might expect, public authorities have now taken steps to provide for a legal framework that should contribute to a better management of the derivatives markets and to a better protection of participants and markets against the consequences of crashes and system risks.

As regards credit default swaps, there has been hesitation about the choice of the regulatory approach: either treating CDSs as insurance and submitting them to some model of prudential insurance supervision,[54] or submitting them to an autonomous model, consisting in withdrawing the CDS operations from the exception of gaming and gambling, and organising central counterparties and better registration. The latter approach would prevail, and was chosen by the US federal legislator[55] and by the EU Commission in its Regulation No 648/2012 of 4 July 2012 on OTC derivatives, central counterparties and trade repositories. The Regulation imposes a clearing obligation on a large category of OTC derivative contracts, and provides for risk mitigating techniques for uncleared OTC derivative contracts. It further installs the authorisation (including capital requirements) and the supervision of CCPs, including their duty to inform competent authorities, their conduct of business rules toward clearing members and their duty to collect margins and to maintain a default fund. The Regulation also installs a system of 'trade repositories' (that centrally collect and maintain the records of derivatives).

Both the American and European legislations are based on the paradigm that the public interest is best served by a 'regulated private initiative'.[56] So far this choice has not been heavily challenged. It has been argued that a possible conflict may arise between the private interest of the commercial entities that are authorised as CCP and their public interest tasks. Arguments were also made in favour of public control on the (standardised) contract documents that are used in the transactions.[57]

4. TENTATIVE FINAL CONSIDERATIONS

A first conclusion to be drawn from this short discovery trip into the world of credit default swaps is that the qualification issue is a delicate one, in which simple and hasty conclusions are loathsome. The point that was made in this chapter concerns less the outcome of the discussion than the way in which, in much of the financial literature, the discussion has been held. The thesis that CDSs are not insurance is to a large degree based on the (never seriously challenged) Pott's Opinion, which in our view is based on an invalid argument (and *petitio principii*) that CDS are not insurance, because CDS contracts are concluded in the absence of any insurable interest.

The fact that in most of the literature the discussion about the legal qualification has not been exhaustively covered is in itself symptomatic of the (relative) importance of the legal issue. The qualification issue is simply considered as one of the risks that must be addressed by those that engage this business, like the credit risk itself, or the market risk, or the operational risk.[58] Thinking in terms of risks has become a predominant pragmatic approach, especially in the handling of finance, as appears from the recent legislative monuments like Basel II (and III) and Solvency II. In the genesis of new financial techniques and products, the law is one of those tools or instruments that are used insofar as they serve the goals or set aside when they do not. A popular method to set aside a legal obstacle is to circumvent the rule by giving the product in question another qualification, even another name ('what's in a name?'). One speaks of the technique of 'wrapping' whereby for example products that are essentially the same are wrapped in different coverings or casings, with their respective (and different) legal consequences.

While observing those processes, one is equally struck by the sophistication, speed, creativity and audacity of those who develop and market the new products. This is at odds with the slow, prudent and post factum reactions of the legal apparatus and the law-making process. It appears that law and law makers have no choice but to yield to the sheer magnitude of the financial operations that are developed ahead of receiving a legal blessing. Another recent and interesting example of a debate that was settled by the sheer speed and size of the factual developments in the market is the one concerning the qualification of the new life insurance products, and more specifically life insurance products that are linked to investment funds. One knows now the insurance character of those operations was discussed because of the absence of an aleatory character of the operation and of a sufficient degree of risk taking by the insurer. The French *Cour de cassation* has confirmed this insurance qualification[59] at a moment where the unit linked life insurance had become an unstoppable business that in addition brought salvation to a (at the time) languishing life insurance business.

It has been no different as regards credit default swaps. They escape from legal qualification risks by calling themselves 'swaps' or 'derivatives'. What's in a name!

Endnotes

* Herman Cousy is an Emeritus Professor at the University of Leuven. The author owes warm thanks to Dr L.G. Beckers, former banker and lecturer at KU Leuven University for his invaluable help and advice. However it must be clear that all errors and inadequacies are solely mine.

1. With the exception however of (at least) two recent papers, one that has initiated me in the complexity of the subject matter: the doctoral dissertation of F. Bogaert recently defended at Ghent University and now published as a book (*De overdracht van kredietrisico: de kredietderivaten en de effectisering*, Antwerp, Intersentia, 2013) and the paper by Oskari Juurikkala, 'Credit Default Swaps and Insurance against the Potts Opinion', 26 *Journal of International Banking Law and Regulation*, 128–135 that deals directly with the issue that is covered in this chapter.
2. The slow and difficult process of creating a legal framework for insurance has always fascinated me: see my contribution 'Les différents cadres juridiques de l'assurance', in *L'Encyclopédie de l'Assurance*, Paris, Economica, 1998, pp. 207–234. See also, in Dutch, my contribution 'Over verzekering, juridisering en deregulering', in *Liber Amicorum Lionel Tricot*, Kluwer Rechtswetenschappen, 1988, pp. 141–153.
3. 'Juridification' is probably a neologism, by which we wish to translate the generally acknowledged Dutch term of '*juridisering*'.
4. For more details see my contribution 'Le Spleen de Paris and the Art of Harmonisation and Restatement', in *Essays on Tort, Insurance Law and Society in honour of Bill Dufwa*, Stockholm, 2006, pp. 355–365.
5. For more details see my report on 'Insurance law between business law and business law', in the *Belgian Reports at the Congress of Washington of the International Academy of Comparative Law*, Larcier, 2011, pp. 515–554; also published in H. Heiss (ed.), *Insurance Contract Law between Business Law and Consumer Protection*, Dike, 2012, pp. 81–117.
6. Cf. the *Principles of European Insurance Contract Law (PEICL),* prepared by the Project Group Restatement of European Insurance Contract Law and edited by Sellier, European Law Publishers, 2009, p. 667.
7. International Organisation of Securities Commissions, created in 1983, issued inter alea the 'Objectives and Principles of Securities Regulations'.
8. Directive 93/22/EEC of 10 May 1993, *OJ* L 141, 11 June 1993.
9. Directive 2004/39/EC of 24 April 2004, *OJ* L 145, 30 April 2004.
10. H. Cousy, 'Les règles de conduite et le droit des assurances', in X., *Synthèses du droit bancaire et financier. Liber Amicorum André Bruyneel*, Brussels, Bruylant, 2008, pp. 495–508.
11. Compare: H. Cousy, 'Le secteur des assurances sera-t-il "mifidisé"?', *Bull. Ass.*, 2009, pp. 245–254.
12. As laid down in the Directive 2002/92/EC on insurance mediation (IMD1) and in the proposal for a Directive on insurance mediation (IMD2).
13. O. Juurikkala, *supra* note 1.
14. J.P. Braithwaite, 'The Inherent Limits of "Legal Devices": Lessons for the Public Sector's Central Counterparty Prescription for the OTC Derivative Markets', *European Business Organization Law Review*, 2011, pp. 87–119.

15. O. Juurikkala, *supra* note 1, p. 130. For an occasional in-depth discussion, see W. Beniter, 'Should you be able to sell what you do not own?', *Financial Times*, 16 March 2009, where the author examines the motivations (economical ones, but also traditionally religious ones) for opposing against trading risk in the absence of an insurable risk. This author writes that the non-insurance character of CDSs is based on economically inspired market observations rather than on legal considerations.
16. Compare F. Longfils, 'Le climat c'est de l'argent! Quand le produit dérivé flirte avec la finance et l'assurance', *Forum de l'Assurance*, 2011, p. 46.
17. F. Taylor, *Mastering Derivative Markets. A step by step guide to the products, applications and risks*, 3rd ed., FT Prentice Hall, 2007, p. 145.
18. F. Bogaert, *De Overdracht van Kredietrisico, Kredietderivaten en effectisering*, Antwerp-Cambridge, Intersentia, 2013, nos. 117–120. See (among an abundant literature) in the Belgian legal literature: G. Nejman, 'Les contrats de produits dérivés', *Dossiers du Journal des Tribunaux* 1999 (no. 21), p. 191; Y. Hendrickx, 'Les dérivés de crédit', in *Produits dérivés. Afgeleide producten*, Cahiers AEDBF EVBFR, Brussels, Bruylant, 1999, p. 9.
19. G. Tett, *Fool's Gold*, Little Brown, 2009, p. 10: 'Key to derivatives is that those who buy and sell them are each making a bet on the future value of that asset'.
20. D. Mengle, 'Credit Derivatives: An Overview', *Economic Review of the Federal Reserve Bank of Atlanta*, 2007, p. 1.
21. Ibid.
22. In the 'total return swap' (TRS) the total return of an asset (obligation or other credit entity) equating to the sum of the capital growth of the asset plus incoming cash streams is paid by the protection buyer (the risk seller) to the protection seller (the risk buyer) in exchange for regular payments of a LIBOR-based floating rate plus spread. (F. Bogaert, *supra* note 1, p. 79). The reference obligation remains with (and on the balance sheet) of the buyer to whom the TRS guarantees a specified economic value of the reference obligation (or other credit entity) (F. Taylor, *supra* note 17, p. 158). Credit spread options give a party the right to buy a (credit risk sensitive) obligation with a contractually fixed spread (call option) or to sell it (put option) (F. Bogaert, *supra* note 1, p. 86).
23. A sort of derivative that has been highly successful is the 'swap', i.e. deals in which two parties in the financial market are brought together, who have different needs and different expectations about the future evolution of the market.
24. For a lively description of the situation in America and the UK, see G. Tett, *supra* note 19, p. 47.
25. The goal of getting the outstanding loans and the related credit risk out of the books is particularly important for banks who faced the Basel I rules, requiring them to adapt their spare funds to the amount of their exposure to (inter alia) outstanding loans. Securitisation of those loans is one mechanism to reduce the need for capital reserves. Transferring the credit risk to another counterparty by way of the use of derivatives is another method.
26. Whereas in the *annus horribilis* 2008, the amount outstanding of CDS had risen to around US $38 trillion, the gross market values have steadily declined since the financial crisis. According to the data of the Bank for International Settlements, the CDS outstanding amounts had declined to US $25 trillion by the end of 2012 (BIS, *Statistical release: OTC derivatives statistics at end December 2012*, Monetary and Economic Department, May 2013). At the time of publication of this chapter, the

financial press reports a steep decline of the amounts of swaps outstanding. Single-name CDSs (protecting against the default of companies, banks and governments) have come under pressure of regulators and have shriveled to half of what they once were. On the other hand no hedging through CDSs is needed any more for synthetic CDOs, since these are practically extinct ('Credit default swaps run out of road', *Financial Times*, 13 October 2013).

27. A trillion equals a million times a million, or a thousand billion. It should be borne in mind that in Dutch translation a billion is *een miljard*, and a trillion is *een biljoen*.
28. Collateral Debt Obligations (CDO) are products that originate in credit transactions that are covered by collateral (like mortgages). When portfolios of such collateralised debt instruments are packaged, these packages can be securitised (transfer to investors in the form of bond issues). The securitised package of instruments can be traded as a whole or be traded in tranches ('slicing' or splitting the package up in tranches: super senior, senior mezzanine or junior) which have different risk and return characteristics. These are the Collateral Loan Obligations (CLO) or Collateral Bond Obligation (CBO), or, more generally Collateral Debt Obligations (CDO). In the original 'cash CDOs' the original debt instruments are transferred to the SPV (Special Purpose Vehicles) that are doing the repackaging and selling of the tranches. In a more sophisticated 'synthetic CDO', only the credit risk of the reference entities (the original debt instruments) is transferred to the SPV by using derivatives such as total return swaps or a credit default swap.
29. F. Taylor, *supra* note 17, p. 156.
30. F. Bogaert, *supra* note 18, no. 504.
31. The dramatic situation of America's biggest insurance company AIG was partially due to this type of operation.
32. See however the differing view of the English and Scottish Law Commission, which thinks that credit derivatives most resemble non-indemnity insurance (*English and Scottish Law Commission*), Insurance Contract Law: Issues Paper nr. 4, Insurable interest, 14 January 2008; compare A. Hudson (ed.), *Credit Derivatives Law: Regulation and Accounting Issues,* London, Sweet & Maxwell, 2000, pp. 47 and 55; also cited by O. Juurikkala, *supra* note 1, p. 10.
33. On the qualification debate, see inter alia D. Benton, P. Devine and P. Jarvis, 'Credit derivatives are not insurance products', 16 *International Financial Law Review*, 1997, 29; A. Kimball-Stanley, 'Insurance and Credit Default Swaps: Should Like Things Be Treated Alike?', 15 *Connecticut Insurance Law Journal*, 2008, (241) 243; O. Juurikkala, *supra* note 1, p. 128.
34. O. Juurikkala, *supra* note 1, p. 4: 'Broadly speaking, the uses can be divided into *hedging* (managing and reducing risks) and *speculating* (profit from risk taking)'.
35. Ehrenberg, *Versicherungsrecht*, Leipzig, 1893, p. 8 (cited by M. Fontaine, *Droit des Assurances*, Brussels, Larcier, 2006, no.135, p. 135).
36. Compare M. Clarke, *Policies and Perceptions of Insurance: An Introduction to Insurance Law*, Oxford, 1997, p. 20. It is true that it is sometimes stressed that insurable interest is not a defining feature of the insurance contract, but it is equally acknowledged that insurable interest is a requirement for a valid contract of insurance. Financial Services Authority, *The identification of contracts of insurance*, Policy Statement, July 2004, §2.10. Compare O. Juurikkala, *supra* note 1, p. 12. However one should be aware that the need for a legal requirement of an insurable interest (as opposed to a possible

contractual one) is presently the object of doubt. For instance in English law, see J. BIRDS, 'Insurability: Does insurance contract law need a concept of insurable interest?', in *Over grenzen. Liber Amicorum Herman Cousy*, Antwerp, Intersentia, 2011, pp. 57–64.

37. Law Commission, Insurance Contract Law, www.justice.govt.uk/lawcommission/ docs/ICL4 Insurable Interest.pdf. 2008, 92 p. The original version of the Potts Opinion appears to be not available any more.
38. A comparable approach or kind of reasoning is found in other widespread sources, like the lemma Credit Default Swaps in Wikipedia: 'However, the most important difference between CDS and insurance is simply that an insurance contract provides an indemnity against losses actually suffered by the policyholder, whereas the CDS provides an equal payout to all holders, calculated using an agreed market-wide method'.
39. F. BOGAERT, *supra* note 18, no. 506.
40. NYSID, 'Best practices for financial guarantee insurers', Circular letter, no. 19. And (critical) comments: S. VENOKUR, M. MAGIDSON and A.A. SINGER, 'Comparing credit default swaps to insurance contract: did the New York State Insurance Department get it right?', 28 *The Journal on the Law of Investment & Risk Management Products*, 2008, no. 11, 5; A.S. KRAMER, A.B. HARRIS and R.A. ANSEHL, 'The New York State Insurance Department and Credit Default Swaps: good intentions, bad idea', 22 *Journal of Taxation and Regulation of Financial Institutions*, 2009, no. 3, 22 (also cited by F. BOGAERT, *supra* note 18, no. 504).
41. Further references are found in F. BOGAERT's doctoral dissertation, *supra* note 1, p. 188.
42. The Dodd-Frank Act (also called the Dodd-Frank Wall Street Reform and Consumer Protection Act) invested two federal regulatory agencies with competence over derivatives, according to the nature of the asset: the Securities and Exchange Commission (SEC) over security-based swaps, and the Commodity Futures Trading Commission (CFTC) over other swaps.
43. Cass. 4 June 1903, *Pas.* 1903, I, 276.
44. Cass. 19 November 1891, *Pas.* 1892, I, 18; Cass. 11 juli 1957, *R.W.* 1958–59, 1263. Compare the comments in N. HOEKX, *Kansspelen op het internet*, Larcier, 2011, p. 133, no. 205.
45. e.g. Cass. 30 January 2006, *R.W.* 2007–08, note C. CAUFFMAN, N. HOEKX, *supra* note 44, and the references.
46. Although this legislative approach is not really appropriate, since a prescription like that article 1965 Civil Code is not applicable does not really solve the problem, at least not in Belgian law, since according to the case law of the highest court, the nullity of gaming contracts does not find its basis in this article of the Civil Code, but in those articles (6, 1131 and 1133) of the Civil Code that sanction contracts with an illicit object or cause with (absolute) nullity.
47. In short terms, a regulated market (*un marché réglementé*) is a market enterprise that is authorised by the competent (Belgian or other Member State) authority, and which manages or exploits a so-called multilateral system which confronts or facilitates the confrontation of obligations concerning financial instruments.
48. Compare G. SCHRANS and R. STEENOT, *Algemeen Deel van het financieel recht*, Antwerp, Intersentia, 2003, p. 161, no. 147.
49. G. TETT, "The dream machine: invention of credit derivatives", *Financial Times*, 24 March 2006.
50. ECJ C-205/84, *Commission v Germany*, 1986.

51. Directive 2009/138/EC of the European Parliament and of the Council of 25 November 2009 on the taking-up and pursuit of the business of Insurance and Reinsurance (Solvency II), *OJ* L 17 December 2009, 335, p. 1.
52. About this and the short description that follows, see F. Bogaert, *supra* note 18, p. 142, no. 328 ff; compare G. Schrans and R. Steenot, *Algemeen Deel van het financieel recht*, Antwerp, Intersentia, 2003, p. 385.
53. S. Cechetti, J. Gyntelberg and M. Hollanders, 'Central counterparties for over-the-counter derivatives', *BIS Quarterly Review*, September 2009, pp. 45, 49 and 57.
54. Cf. the initial approach by the New York State Insurance Department (see here above, no. 13). The National Conference of Insurance Legislators (NCOIL) issued in 2000 a 'credit default insurance model legislation', whereby the sale of credit default insurance was submitted to a prior authorisation. In the New York State Assembly proposals were introduced forbidding uncovered credit default swaps and submitting covered ones to the insurance authorisation.
55. Cf. the American Dodd-Frank Wall Street Reform and Consumer Protection Act (July 2010) would allocate regulatory jurisdiction to two different authorities, the Securities and Exchange Commission (security based swaps) and the Commodity Futures Trading Commission (for other swaps).
56. F. Bogaert, *supra* note 18, p. 188, no. 435.
57. Ibid. Compare J.P. Braithhwaite, 'The inherent limits of legal devices: lessons for the public sector's central counterparty prescription for the OTC derivative markets', 12 *European Business Organization Law*, 2011, 107.
58. In F. Bogaert's doctoral dissertation, the relevant chapter (nos 438) has the title: '*Kwalificatie en juridisch risico van de credit default swap*' (qualification and legal risk in CDS).
59. Cass. fr. 23 November 2004, *RGDA* 2005, 110, note L. Mayaux; see also the comments and references in *Lamy Assurances*, 2011, no. 161.

THE INTEREST RATE RESTRICTIONS IN THE FINANCIAL CRISIS

Can we Draw Lessons from Private Law?

Vincent SAGAERT*

1. INTRODUCTION: INTEREST RATES ON THE EDGE OF LAW, RELIGION AND SOCIETY

In the summer of 2013, there was considerable media hype in the British press generated by the proposals of the Archbishop of Canterbury Justin Welby and the Church of England with regard to an alternative to the traditional solutions for consumer credit: they launched the idea that people invested in credit unions, which lend money to people at a reasonable rate. The Church would offer their facilities (churches) and human resources to facilitate the operations of these credit unions. The Archbishop challenged some traditional financiers (especially payday lenders) by vowing that the Church would 'compete them out of existence'. The payday loan companies had attracted a huge amount of criticism because of the excessive interest rates they charge and their aggressive marketing. The Archbishop considered these payday loans against high interest rates as modern forms of slavery.

A few days after this announcement, the Archbishop himself was subject to severe criticism, as he had to admit that the Church of England itself holds a huge stake in one of the financial institutions, Wonga, which he directly promised to 'compete' out of existence. These revelations evidently overshadowed the reform of the money lending proposed by the Archbishop, although this participation violated the proper ethical rules of the Church.

This story – which has been denominated as the '*Jesus v Wonga debate*' – indicates the ethically charged relationship between religion and interest rates. The people criticising the initiative of Welby by saying that the Church should not become involved in this purely financial matter have insufficient memory of the history of both financial markets and the Church. Moreover, the attention it has drawn demonstrates the huge sociological impact of the debate on interest rates.

It is the intention of this contribution to approach this issue from the perspective of private law. However, it is not possible to deal with the subject without taking into account the economic and religious influence underlying the debate. In the second part of this chapter, the results will be applied to the sovereign debt crisis, necessitating countries to obtain credit against very high, and at the very least extremely volatile, interest rates.

2. INTEREST AND CREDIT IN A DIFFICULT INTERPLAY BETWEEN THE PRIVATE AND PUBLIC CONTEXT

Credit agreements can arise from two frameworks. The first scheme is that the borrower enters into the credit agreement because he aims to make profitable investments with the borrowed capital sum. This would be beneficial if the return on the investment exceeds the interest sum agreed upon for the credit agreement. This is the so-called 'investment credit'. However, credit agreements can also come into existence if one contracting party has an excess of money and another contracting party is contingently in shortage of money.[1] These are the credit agreements agreed upon for consumption purposes. We will, for the purposes of this book, focus on this second type of credit agreements (credit for consumption purposes).

In periods of economic stagnation or even recession, obtaining credit is often considered to be necessary for economic survival. However, consumer credit has the feature that it usually further enhances the inequality between both contracting parties, as the debtor has to pay interest on the capital sum in favour of the creditor. Therefore, credit agreements for consumption purposes – and more specifically the interest rate due on the capital sum – leads to a further economic dualism in society.[2] Economic analysis suggests that this money transfer from the poor to the wealthy mainly affects the middle class, which tends to disappear in an economic model in which credit for consumption purposes, flourishes. The effects of this model on a worldwide level are clear: in 2006 more than three quarters of the income is created in the hands of less than 100,000 people. So the gain of money out of money creates, if the loan is made for consumption purposes, an aristocracy and leads to growing dualism in society.[3]

This analysis is intriguing, especially in eras of financial crisis. It has exactly been the reason for the initiative taken by Justin Welby and the Church of England in the summer of 2013 (cf. *supra*). On a legal level, numerous legislators and regimes have imposed restrictions on interest rates, in order to prevent this dichotomy becoming harmful for society. This contribution is not intended to study the ethics of this phenomenon, for which we can refer to other legal literature.[4]

However, the starting point of this contribution is that, apparently, a dichotomy emerges between private national law – where strict interest rate restrictions come into play – and the international lending context – where party autonomy prevails in the field of interest rate determination. We learned that during the sovereign debt crisis, some countries were obliged to borrow money at apparently excessive rates which would not be possible in many private law systems.

Before going into the analysis, we must first determine the concept of *usury*. Usury in the 21st century usually denotes the practice of lending money at an excessive interest rate. Historically, however, there have been long periods of time in which the common definition of 'usury' was much stricter: it prohibited any amount of interest charged on a loan, not just an excessive amount. The Scholastics differentiated between a *legitimate* payment for lending money, which they called 'true interest' (*verum interesse*), and an *excessive* payment as cost for lending money, which they called usury. This historical development will be described below. Interest rate restrictions are therefore all regulations restricting party autonomy in the field, on the level of the validity of an enforcement of the agreement.

3. THE RESTRICTIVE PERSPECTIVE OF NATIONAL LEGISLATORS WITH REGARD TO INTEREST RATES IN PRIVATE LEGAL RELATIONSHIPS

The Belgian legislator is, according to national law, reluctant in the matter of contractual freedom in the field of interest rates. Interest rate restrictions are imposed at different levels. This reluctance comes into play with regard to the different types of interests e.g. (1) conventional interests and (2) default interest. It is not the purpose of this contribution to go into the technical details of specific Belgian regulations which only apply in a private law context, but it is important to see the general framework of interest rate restrictions in Belgian (and foreign) law.

As the following paragraphs will reveal, the legislator has imposed these restrictions with the sole purpose of protecting the borrower against exponential growth of his money obligations. When analysing the sovereign debt crisis, it will appear that another dimension and rationale can be given to these interest rate restrictions, creating a multi-level approach.

3.1. STATUTORY PRIVATE LAW RESTRICTIONS WITH REGARD TO CONVENTIONAL INTEREST RATES

With regard to conventional interests, the starting point laid down in article 1907 of the Belgian Civil Code is, at first sight, reassuring on the level of contractual freedom: the conventional interest may exceed the statutory interest, in all cases which the legislator does not prohibit (art. 1907 Civil Code). This basic principle was introduced in 1865.[5] However, the suspicious nature of interest rates already comes into play in the second paragraph of that same provision, containing a formal restriction to interest provisions in loan agreements: interest rates should always be mentioned in a separate provision of the loan agreement, drawing the attention of the borrower to the duty to pay interests. The remedy is, in order to protect the debtor, strict: if the interest rate is not mentioned in a specific provision, the statutory interest rates will be applied.

However, the most prominent restriction on the contractual freedom with regard to conventional interest rates is to be found in article 1907*ter* Civil Code. This provision imposes restrictions upon conventional interest rates in agreements for the lending of money. If the lender agrees with the borrower upon interest rates or other advantages which exceed the normal interest and risk coverage by abusing the weaknesses, passions or ignorance of the borrower, the judge can, at the request of the borrower, reduce his payment obligations to the payment of the capital amount and the statutory interest rate. This provision allows for a judicial interference with the agreement legally binding between the parties, and can thus be considered as an infringement on the contractual freedom of parties. It is the legal embedding of the so-called '*usury prohibition*', which can be found in different legal systems.

This provision is, according to Belgian law, largely considered to be a statutory application of the doctrine of 'qualified prejudice', as it grants a remedy against the imbalance between the obligations of the contracting parties in a lending agreement. It protects the borrower who is in a position of dependence and thus weakness vis-à-vis the creditor.[6] This provision would not be of public order.[7] However, if the lending agreement tends to abuse the borrower and exploit him, the agreement could be void.[8]

Given its impact, being a statutory exception to the contractual freedom of parties, the case law tends to give a narrow scope of interpretation to this provision. Thus, it would only apply in cases of loan agreements, and not in agreements for credit facilities.[9] Moreover, most legal scholars assume that the provision does not apply to agreements which are governed by specific regulations.[10] For instance, for consumer credit agreements, specific protection applies. Article 21 of the Belgian Consumer Credit Act[11] provides for interest rate restrictions on consumer credit, in providing for maximum expenses for credit agreement to be decreed annually. However, even in that case, article 1907*ter* should apply, as the specific regulation should not deprive the consumer of the protection of this provision. If consumer credit is granted with a large scale of security, for instance with a mortgage, a financial institution accounting for the maximum expenses could abuse such a situation.[12]

Two elements are taken into account in order to assess the excessiveness of the conventional interest rate:

(1) normal market conditions in relation to the risk of insolvency of the debtor/borrower.[13] The personal or property security rights which have been granted in order to secure the payment of the loan agreement must be taken into account in order to assess this risk taken by the lender;
(2) the deviation of normal market conditions is grounded in an abuse of needs, weaknesses, passions or ignorance of the borrower.

The aversion of the Belgian legislator to the concept of usury is sharper than it appears from the mere analysis of civil law. The prohibition of usury is even sanctioned at a criminal level. If a person lends money against interest rates which exceed the statutory interest rates, he can be condemned to a prison sentence (in theory up to one year) and/or with a fine (up to €10,000) if he made a custom of abusing the borrower's weaknesses or passions.[14] However, case law demonstrates even more reluctance in awarding criminal sentences for usury than for applying the prohibition on a private law level. Moreover, it is a debated issue whether these criminal penalties also apply to credit agreements governed by specific legislation, such as the Consumer Credit Act.[15]

3.2. STATUTORY RESTRICTIONS WITH REGARD TO DEFAULT INTEREST RATES

We can analyse the same statutory reluctance with regard to party autonomy for default interest rates. Default interest is due on the ground of contractual default by the debtor to comply with his obligations. According to article 1153, para. 5 of the Belgian Civil Code, the penalty for non-compliance with monetary obligations cannot consist of something other than the default interest, except for the statutory exceptions.

Parties can, in the agreement itself, agree upon a contractual interest rate for the default interest. However, and without prejudice to article 1907 Civil Code, the judge can reduce the contractual default interest rate if the latter manifestly exceed the incurred damage. The downside limit of the revision is that the revised default interest rate may not be lower than the statutory interest rate. This provision grounds the basic idea that contractual default provisions cannot provide for a private penalty with regard to the contractual default. Penalties have, in the eyes of the Belgian legislator, to be imposed by intermediation of a judge.

These restrictions have been the object of critical observations by legal scholars. Looking at it from a comparative perspective, it emerges that Belgian law – together with English law[16] – takes a particular and isolated position in European private law. Most national legal systems do allow for large party autonomy of penalty clauses applying in case of default by the debtor, even if they amount to a private penalty charged to the debtor.[17] As contractual performance should be encouraged, there is no reason why contractual provisions giving an incentive for performance should be censured. Therefore, the choice of the Belgian legislator only to admit contractual indemnities and not to admit contractual penalties is disapproved of by most Belgian scholars.[18]

Another restriction on party autonomy for default interest is the so-called prohibition of anatocism (or 'prohibition of compound interest') (article 1154 Civil Code).[19] This rule entails, as a starting point, that interest on money cannot generate further interest *per se*. In other words, it is not possible to claim interest on the default of paying interest. Again, this interest rate restriction protects the borrower against an exponential increase of his loan payments. In the case law of the Belgian Supreme Court, this strict provision aims at '*prémunir le débiteur contre le fléau de l'usure, et de le protéger efficacement contre son impéritie et son imprévoyance.*'[20] Lietaer et al. give the striking example of Julius Caesar borrowing one cent at an interest rate of 4% in 50 BC; he would – on the basis of compound interest – have to pay *anno* 2012 the value of 2,000 gold spheres with the weight of the planet earth.[21] Compound interest definitely leads to an exponential growth of the interest component, to the detriment of the borrower. In prohibiting principally anatocism, the legislator aims to prevent the debt from increasing exponentially. Moreover, we will analyse that this restriction has also another dimension: it can be necessary in order to keep up in relation to the sustainability of the economic growth (cf. *infra*). This prohibition is traditionally assumed to be of public order,[22] although this is contested in more recent legal scholarship.[23]

However, the statutory restriction of compound interest is not absolute. It is valid, in Belgian law, to generate interest out of interest under the triple condition that (1) the basic interest is already due, (2) the due interest covers at least one full year and (3) the debtor has agreed to do so in a separate agreement or if it has been notified by bailiff to the debtor.

Moreover, banking practice demonstrates that – from an economic point of view – compound interests can factually come into existence in spite of the statutory restrictions. This is notably the case if a borrower has to make a loan in order to make payments under a previous loan or if several successive short-term loans are agreed between the same parties, the later one being used to reimburse the previous one. We could conceptualise this phenomenon as '*factual anatocism*', which economically amounts up to the payment of compound interest. As we will observe in relation to the Greek situation, this situation has occurred with regard to some countries in difficulties during the sovereign debt crisis (cf. *infra*).

3.3. STATUTORY INTEREST RATE RESTRICTIONS IN COMPARATIVE AND EUROPEAN PERSPECTIVE

Belgian law is not isolated in the systems of European private law. The European Union has paid attention to interest rate restrictions in the different Member States. In 2009, a study on interest rate restrictions in the EU was undertaken at the request of the European Commission and gives a clear overview of the large differences between the Member States.[24] It emerges from a comparative analysis that there is a lot of variety in the way Member States cope with interest rates and their legal restrictions.

With regard to direct interest rate restrictions, the Report analyses the existence of a large difference between the historical concept of usury and some forms of interest rate ceilings applied in the Member States.

- All Member States subscribe to the principle of 'good morals' or 'fairness', which explicitly forbids usury, under criminal as well as private law, or implicitly incriminates the intentional exploitation of the weakness of another person at an individual level through extortionate pricing, especially in relation to credit.
- With the exception of two Member States (Ireland and Romania), all have interest rate restrictions in relation to default interest.
- Member States have either some form of an absolute ceiling (Greece, Ireland, Malta) or a relative ceiling based on a reference rate (Belgium, Estonia, France, Germany, Italy, the Netherlands, Poland, Portugal, Slovakia, Spain, Slovenia).[25]

According to the analysis of the economic impact of the interest rate restrictions, Belgium belongs to nine Member States with most significant interest rate restrictions. However, and in spite of the differences existing between the Member States, it emerges from the study that the concept of 'usury' is common to most of the European legal systems.[26] The legal-economic results of the EC Study will be discussed *infra*.

With regard to *default interest*, it is not as common as with regard to conventional interest to encounter strict limitations on the contractual freedom throughout European legal systems. Belgian and English law are two of the few legal systems in Europe imposing restrictions on damage clauses with regard to default interest. In Belgian and English law, conventional default interest may not have a punitive purpose, meaning that conventional default interest can only have as object the compensation for the damage incurred through the late payment by the debtor. It may not provide for a penalty of the debtor for his late payment. This strict view distinctly contrasts with the regulation in most of the European countries (cf. *supra*).

4. THE DEVELOPMENT AND CURRENT RATIONALE OF THE INTEREST RATE RESTRICTIONS

The background for the interest rate restrictions in Belgian statute is grossly reminiscent to religious and historical developments. Without going into detail in these developments,[27] it is important to mention the historical landmarks for the current regulation. It will appear that clear connections exist between the economic development in a certain society at a certain moment and the legal perspective on interest rate restrictions.

Rules with regard to interest rate restrictions are amongst the oldest and most prevalent forms of financial and economic regulation. Plato and Aristotle considered the lending of money against interest as incompatible with human ethics.[28] However, the political view of interest rate restrictions is ethically, and even religiously pre-determined. This appears to be a universal phenomenon. In Islamic financial law, interest on capital is often considered a sin, to the extent that the lender does not take part in the risk of the lending.[29] Hinduism and Buddhism also impose prohibitions against usury, so that it emerges as being a universal rule transcending religious differences.[30]

The same goes, to a certain extent, for the Christian tradition. It is often said that interest rate restrictions in the Western European legal systems are deeply rooted in the Christian tradition. In this tradition, it was held to be 'unsain' to gain money out of money.[31] Even if there are some traces of interest rate restrictions before the birth of Christianity,[32] it emerges that these restrictions have been enhanced under Christian influence. This tradition goes back to the Bible,[33] and was also implemented by Justinianus in the *Corpus Iuris Civilis*.[34] Several concilies explicitly included a general prohibition on usury. However, the ground for this usury prohibition remained uncertain: some took into consideration the growing antagonism between the rich and the poor in society; others founded the prohibition in the objections to slavery or in the similarity of usury to theft or even murder.

Having been re-instated by several leaders, such as Charlemagne, it lasted until the 12th century before the usury prohibition was ethically and economically founded. In that century, Thomas Aquinas made a major contribution to the restrictions on interest rates. He launched the famous proverb *nummus non parit nummos*,[35] which was very strict as it prohibits each form of conventional interest in lending agreements. The underlying rationale was that the natural essence of money is that money merely constitutes a measure of value or intermediary in exchange. The idea, deduced from the Scriptures, is that only human labour should enable people to gain money. The mere fact of having property should not serve as sufficient ground for obtaining other economic values. The increase of money through usury violated this essence. It would amount to 'double charging', which means charging for both the object and the use of the object.[36] Moreover, an equitable transaction was one characterised by an equality of exchange, one where each side received exactly his due. The interest on a loan, in excess of the principal amount, would violate the balance of an exchange between debtor and creditor and was therefore considered to be unjust.

Thus, the argument gained importance in Christian tradition that usury laws constitute a type of social insurance, protecting individuals against contingent disappearance or fall of income.[37] This has to be framed in the contemporary societal model. The feudal lords themselves did not normally need to obtain loans in order to make investments, as they had sufficient money to finance their own investments. Hence, loans were mainly needed for consumer purposes by economically weaker people, in a period of distress, and it was considered to be a kind of social insurance. Credit agreements had to give relief against contiguous fall in wealth or income. Lending money in such situation was considered to be an act of charity, which should not be a source of financial gain.[38]

However, other legal-economic studies contest this idea of social insurance. These scholars suggest that the reluctant attitude of the Church for interest clauses was inspired by self-interest: the Church was a prominent borrower and thus benefited in maintaining as low an interest rate as possible.[39] This view is probably too radical, even if the Catholic Church itself has been benefiting from these laws in obtaining credit.

The development of international trade and commerce in the 15th and 16th centuries gave rise to an increase in the credit needs for economic development. In other words, the pure credits for consumption purposes give way to investment credit. The Church gradually opened up the rules and accepted that money was borrowed against a 'reasonable interest rate'. The first use of interest was through default interests, in other words compensation for delaying the payment of loan obligations, which opened the door for charging penalties (e.g. late fees). The Lombard merchants, the principal moneylenders of medieval times, had established a practice of charging a penalty on default, and the custom spread to other regions.

The shift in the views on usury prohibitions are mainly due to protestant antagonists. Luther still opposed 'fruits for money', but Calvin proposed in his '*Letter about interest*' that money enhanced production and that the results of production are indirectly due to the money which is being lent.[40] King Charles V firstly regulated the loan agreement and made it subject to a maximum interest rate of 12%, in his Perpetual Edict. Finally, the Catholic Church conceded during the 17th and 18th century that lending with a legal interest rate should be acceptable. However, the reluctance of legal scholars towards usury rates remained. For instance, Pothier takes in the late 18th century the view that lending against interest is against public order: '*C'est une règle d'équité, qui doit régner dans tous les contrats, que l'une des parties, qui n'a pas intention de faire une donation à l'autre, ne peut être obligé de lui donner que l'équivalent de ce que l'autre, de son côté, lui a donné ou s'est obligé de lui donner. Si on l'oblige à donner plus, l'équité, qui consiste dans l'égalité, est blessé, et le contrat est inique.*'[41]

The Statute of 3 and 12 October 1789 liberalised the possibility of granting credit against interest, emphasising party autonomy in the contractual field. The Civil Code contained the principle that conventional interest may exceed the statutory interest in all cases, which the legislator does not prohibit. At that stage, no statutory interest restrictions existed. However, an Act of 3 September 1807 readily introduced such statutory restriction. A maximum interest rate of 5% (6% in commercial case) was introduced, imposing a heavy burden on contractual freedom in loan agreements.

These restrictions were criticised because additional expenses were often concealed under alternative headings, such as expenses and suchlike. For that reason, an Act of 5 May 1865 re-introduced the principle of contractual freedom with regard to interest rates. In a second stage, the Criminal Code of 1867 abolished the criminal punishment of usury. This abolishment was grounded in a threefold reasoning: (1) there is no reason why one should impose more restrictions upon the use of capital than upon the use of a house or movable good, (2) parties must maintain their contractual freedom and (3) the increase of the interest rate is an insurance premium against insolvency of the borrower.[42]

This situation lasted until the aftermath of the economic crisis of 1929. Thereafter Article 3 of the Royal Decree no 148 of 18 March 1935 (re-)introduced the restrictions which were analysed above, more notably article 1907*ter* Civil Code and article 494 Criminal Code (cf. *supra*). It is within the ambit of this contribution revealing to analyse how the previous worldwide economic crisis has led to a restriction on interest rates. The 1929 crisis was not only the trigger for the re-introduction of the usury prohibition in Belgian law. Similarly, in France, a decree of 30 October 1935 re-criminalised usury in the law, as reaction against the financial crisis. These foreign restrictions inspired the Belgian legislator to further strengthen the usury laws.

5. LEGAL-ECONOMIC ARGUMENTS IN FAVOUR OF INTEREST RATE RESTRICTIONS

The debates on the legal-economic and social-economic effects of usury laws have been intense and confusing. We limit ourselves to the key elements of these developments. Adam Smith and Jeremy Bentham are often presented as the two protagonists in the beginning of the modern economy. Smith expressed his opinion in favour of a limit on the interest rate in '*order to prevent the extortion of usury*',[43] but was heavily criticised by Bentham in his *Defense of usury* (1787). The usury debate surfaced again in the 1930s with the publications of John Keynes, who contributed to the debate in arguing that 'the payment of interest to the saver [...] is a burden which, if it accumulates with time, may become insupportable.'[44]

The main economic rationale put forward in defence of usury laws, is the protection of the borrower. In the words of the most famous Lord Mansfield, usury laws are put in place 'to protect men who act with their eyes open against themselves.' All usury laws are grounded in the fundamental premise that the bargaining power of the two parties to a loan transaction is seriously unequal.[45] Usury laws prevent financial institutions that control credit from exploiting borrowers who need fresh money.

This underlying reason is, from an economic point of view, solely valid if a loan is made for consumer purposes, because the borrower has a deficit in its consumption pattern. If a loan is made for investment purposes, the borrower could have the free choice between the financial institutions granting him the loan, which scenario would envisage that financial institutions would discount interest rates in order to be competitive. In eras of financial crisis, however, consumer credit tends to prevail on investment credit, making usury laws more accommodating.

Opponents of usury laws generally argue that if a loan is properly secured and the borrower voluntarily agrees to pay a high interest rate, there is no right to deprive the lender of a higher return by imposing a ceiling on the parties. Such interest rate ceiling would contravene the very essence of a free market: enabling parties to negotiate the contractual conditions. This argument, legally translated, amounts to awarding an absolute scope to party autonomy in lending agreements.

Moreover, opponents argue that usury laws are socially disruptive. Instead of protecting borrowers, they exclude borrowers from obtaining a loan. The ones whose risk is so high that it is economically unjustified to grant them a loan at the highest allowed interest rate are exempted from obtaining a loan. Thus, usury laws arbitrarily exclude high-risk borrowers from obtaining loan facilities, even if they could make use of money that is socially or economically beneficial.[46] If interest rates were high, the borrower would take more care to use the money in a profitable manner. This is not only valid for consumer credit, but also for investment credit. In investment financing, the most innovative investments are always the highest-risk investments. Hence, usury laws not only lead to social exclusion, but also to hampering innovation as a key to economic progression.

Moreover, when the interest rate is lower than the market rate for a particular loan, it discourages legitimate lenders from making that loan, which negatively affects potential borrowers, especially less creditworthy borrowers. This would restrain economic development.

Finally, it is alleged that usury laws can easily be circumvented. 'Loan sharks' would gain by the imposition of usury laws. Indeed, if it is prohibited to gain interest on money capital, other techniques are used to turn around this prohibition. It suffices to add the risk of legal prosecution to their loan cost. And other forms of credit, such as sale and leaseback constructions make it easy to evade usury law.

The Study of the European Commission on usury laws, which has already been mentioned, also encompasses the economic effects of interest rate restrictions. We confine ourselves to the main results of this economic dimension of the Study. It emerges from this study that it is best to avoid considering the economic impact of usury laws in absolute terms: 'the impact of interest rate restrictions may be less obvious than postulated by theory.'[47] Some hypotheses are checked after an economic analysis of their probability. In some Member States strict interest rate caps are imposed with regard to conventional interest, because credit at a high price may increase consumer insolvency and reflects the bad functioning of financial markets, especially for small amounts of credit. In other Member States, the absence of such regulations is justified primarily on the basis that caps would reduce access to credit, especially for people with moderate means.[48] Legal interest rate restrictions reduce the lender's opportunity to charge risk-adjusted costs. Obviously, and depending on the level at which the restriction is set; this decreases his willingness to lend money. As a consequence, high-risk borrowers may be denied credit access in the presence of legal interest rate restrictions.[49] High-risk borrowers requesting small amounts of credit can only be served when a certain threshold interest rate is exceeded. Hence, they may not be served credit in the presence of interest rate restrictions. As will be observed, this could have an accessory effect that innovative (high-risk) projects would be exempted from financial resources.

It is sometimes argued that the existence of high-cost credit helps households to avoid obtaining credit from (potentially expensive) non-bank sources, such as utility providers. However, the EC Study demonstrates that it does not appear that there are systematic differences in lending from non-bank sources between countries with and without interest rate restrictions.

The question arises as to whether the historical development of usury laws can give some indications about the economic need and impact of these laws. The historical development suggests that a connection exists between the economic development and usury rules. The increase of economic development apparently opens up the legal regulation of interest. This interaction can be observed in the developments of the 15th and 16th centuries and in the flexibilisation of the rules in the second half of the 19th century. However, times of financial and economic distress can entail a stricter view on the statutory rules in this regard. As a reaction to the 1929 crisis, Belgian and French legislators re-introduced a sharp usury prohibition.

On a purely intuitive basis, this connection could have a rationale. In periods of economic wellbeing, investment loans can prevail over consumer loans. Strict usury prohibitions risk curtailing innovative projects, requiring financial resources at high risk, and thus to burden the economic increase. By contrast, in times of economic crisis, more loans are obtained in order to give a remedy to financial deficits.[50] Consumer loans gain importance and high interest rates run the risk of completely ruining households in financial distress.

6. TOWARDS A MORE COMPLEX CONCEPT OF USURY IN ERAS OF FINANCIAL CRISIS?

An interesting question raised during the financial crisis is whether the usury laws are not too narrow in respect of the criteria at stake. The criteria to determine whether an interest rate is excessive is often less linear, and more complicated, than is often perceived. We can take, as a starting point, a chart from the Financial Stability Report 2009 of the International Monetary Fund.[51]

Figure 1. Composite real private borrowing rate and short-term interest rates (in %)

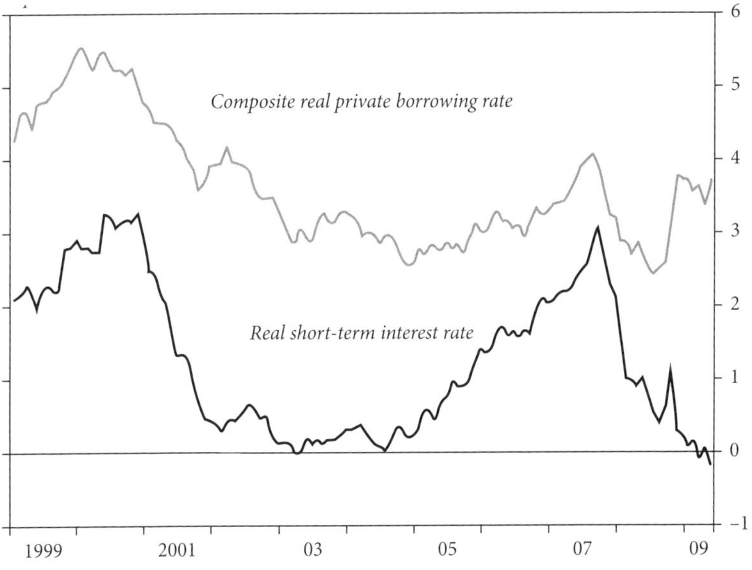

It is remarkable that the development of the private borrowing rate runs parallel to the development of the short-term interest rate for almost a decade. This parallelism gets lost in late 2007, exactly in the period that the financial distress came into its realm. The International Monetary Fund itself declared in its Report 'the gap between short term interest rates and private borrowing rates is now at its widest level since the beginning of the crisis.' Ann Pettifor appreciates this in a clear manner: 'These rates are not just unfair. They are usurious. In the middle of the gravest financial crisis since the war, banks are – effortlessly and immensely profitably – extracting assets from distressed companies, households and individuals.'[52] When comparing the lines of the chart, the net gain of the lenders would reach its maximum margin right at the moment where the financial distress reaches its highest point.

If we take a scholastic approach, such analysis would amount to an attitude of usury. The rate of interest should, from a scholastic perspective, be equal to the normal rate of profit in the community, which the lender could earn if he invested his money himself. If the prevailing rate of profit is high, then the lender should be paid a high interest rate, and if there were few profitable alternatives in the community, then the rate of interest paid to the lender would likewise be low. In an era of financial and economic distress, the alternatives to invest are scarce, but this does – in the current crisis – not result in a decrease of the borrowing interest rate.

From the perspective of a financial risk assessment, this analysis could be attributed to the institutional risks inherent in current credit grants, not only because of the decrease of the real estate market, but also because of the risk of being drawn into the system crisis of financial institutions. However, it is not to be excluded that financial institutions aim in this manner to remedy the downfall of the financial situations of financial institutions. The gain for financial intermediaries could therefore increase in order to cope with their own financial problems.

From a legal perspective, this analysis should make reflect lawyers upon the usury concept and the criteria used to determine whether the interest rate is excessive. At this moment, the criteria for usury are in Belgian law merely determined on the basis of the position of the borrower. As we have been observing in analysing article 1907*ter* of the Civil Code, the Belgian legislator only takes into account circumstances at the borrowing side, e.g. the weaknesses, passions and other grounds for inequality on behalf of the borrower. The position of the borrower is however only one side of the contractual relationship. The position of the lender, and more notably the cost of his own financing on the market, should also be taken into account.[53] The question thus arises as to whether the usurious nature of interest rates should not only be determined according to the debtor's perspective and situation, but also according to the creditor's perspective and situation and the total expense of the loan. If he has been able to borrow money himself at decreasing interest rates, what could then justify the increase of the lending interest rates?

Pettifor raises the question especially in a context where most private banks operate in the grace of State guarantee and should therefore be aware of their social responsibility. It is – from an economic point of view – not self-evident that the profit margins increase on a short-term perspective, if the very borrowing rates of the financial institutions decrease.

7. PARTY AUTONOMY IN PUBLIC LENDING SCHEMES

7.1. THE DEVELOPMENT OF INTEREST RATES IN SOVEREIGN DEBT CRISIS: SOME LEGAL-ECONOMIC PERSPECTIVES

Sovereign debts are a rather recent phenomenon, which did not exist in its current form in ancient times.[54] An issue which has hardly been debated is the application of the aforementioned principles on sovereign debts.

In its study on the influence of interest rate restrictions (cf. *supra*), the European Commission tested the effect of interest rate restrictions on the *level* of over-indebtedness and on its *growth rate* after an economic shock. After thorough analysis, the Report concludes that a direct influence of interest rate restrictions on the level of over-indebtedness is *unlikely*.[55] However, the same Study demonstrates that the protective effect of interest rate restrictions are neutralised, as statutory interest rate restrictions *lead to increased charges as providers will try to compensate the reduced interest revenues by increased charges*. There are examples from different legal systems which illustrate that providers react to regulation by charging fees for which the regulation does not apply.[56]

In sum, the Report concludes that the economic impact of statutory interest rate restrictions is more limited than is often contemplated. It mainly involves three categories of economic effects: (1) firstly, it is likely that the existence of interest rate restrictions excludes some customer groups from credit access; (2) secondly, there might be a reduced set of credit types, as some credit types with very high interest rates are not offered in the presence of interest rate restrictions; and (3) thirdly, one has to keep in mind that suppliers can (to some extent) structure their credit product in such way that the existing interest rate regulation does not apply.[57]

In the very first paragraph of this contribution, we argued that interest in a credit agreement risks, especially in eras of economic stagnation or crisis, to have perverse effects. If the credit agreement is necessary to solve a consumption deficit, the difference in financial position between the lender, who already has a money excess, and the borrower, who already is confronted with a money shortage, will even increase. This undoubtedly becomes clear when analysing the development of interest rates in sovereign debts during the last decades. In doing so, it must be taken into account that the total amount of sovereign debts is considerable: €41,000 billion in

2010. For industrialised countries, this amount has doubled in less than two decades.[58] The interest rates increased and, combined with other factors, even exploded, enhancing dualism between the financial positions of the lending States and borrowing States.

Mostly, countries pay interest rates on their debts through export earnings. These export earnings should thus constitute the counterpart in the balance with the interest rate of sovereign debts. Until the late 1970s, most sovereign debt schemes were characterised by a negative interest rate, meaning that the inflation rate exceeded the interest rate. Taking up credit in this context does not make a country poorer and does not lead towards a downgrading of the creditworthiness of a country.

The financial stability was, since the Second World War, guaranteed by the Bretton Woods doctrine. This doctrine held that the United States would uphold the gold standard, in order to make from the dollar the international reference currency for trade. The countervalue of the dollar was kept in gold in the American Central Bank Service, while the currency of other countries had a fixed exchange rate in relation to the dollar. As all countries were in a fixed relation to the United States as the reference country, their internal position did not change immensely. This also entailed that the variety of interest rates in public lending was quite limited. Other currencies kept in pace with the value increases and decreases of the dollar, guarding the financial stability of the international financial market. This system was possible due to the large gold reserves accumulated during the First World War.

However, the Bretton Woods system declined in the beginning of the seventies. The coverage of the dollar by gold came about in the aftermath of the Vietnam disaster and had to be abandoned by President Nixon right before the oil crisis of the early 1970s. This caused the considerable increase in a variety of interest.

The fluctuations on the international market of sovereign bonds came readily after the abandonment of the Bretton Woods system, especially in low- and middle-income countries. The floating interest rates increased up to 12% in the early 1980s.[59] This created huge transfers of wealth from low- and middle-income countries (mostly borrowing countries) to the high-income countries (lending countries).

If the increase of the interest rate is combined with the devaluation of the local currency in relation to the US dollar (in which most of the loans are determined), this leads to an exponential increase of the interest rate during this period. Hanlon gives the Argentinean example, where interest rates increased from 12% of export earnings up to 43% of export earnings.[60] The pursuant loss of value in the borrowing countries speaks for itself.

This development, which in the 1980s mainly affected low- and middle-income countries, was transposed in the build-up to the financial crisis to high-income countries (or countries which were deemed to be so). High-income countries, and even eurozone countries have seen their interest rates increase, and this increase was exponential in some of the problematic eurozone countries.

For example, the volatile nature of conventional interest rates was a key issue during the second stage of the financial crisis. The Greek example is striking, as it appears from the data disclosed by Eurostat. The interest rates applying to Greece, agreed upon between the eurozone countries, played a major role in the deterioration of the financial situation in Greece. The interest rates increased in the period March-April 2010, pushing the interest on Greek debt papers up to almost 25%. The following chart is revealing, as it demonstrates what the effect of State default on the applied interest rates can be.

Figure 2. Interest rate of Greek two-year government bonds

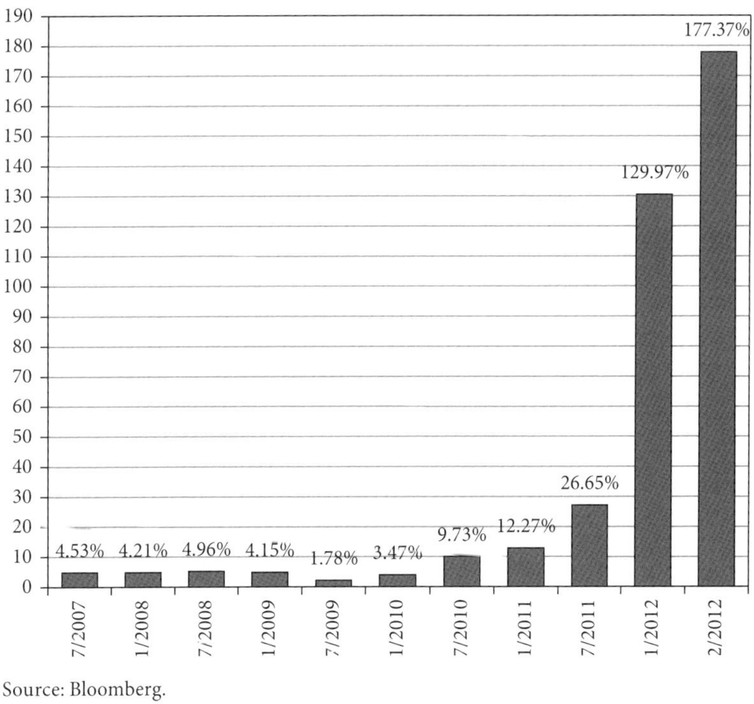

Source: Bloomberg.

The interest rate increase resulted in the incapacity of the Greek state to pay the first shift of loan agreement, on its turn giving rise to a request by the Greek government to the IMF and the European Community to obtain less expensive credit facilities. The IMF board approved a €30 billion three-year loan for Greece in early May 2010, which added to €80 billion being lent to Greece from eurozone countries, as a counterpart to serious cutbacks in expenditure. In November 2010, the term for repayment was extended from 2015 to 2021, increasing the interest rate of the credit facilities. If Greece had taken up all credit facilities in November 2010, the interest rate would have been 5.8%, exceeding the credit costs in the spring of 2010. In March 2011 European leaders awarded a 1% discount as a reward for the retrenchments, subject to the condition that €50 billion would be privatised. The decrease of the interest rates was further sealed in July 2011, when the EFSF agreed to give additional credit facilities for a lower cost of 3.5–4%.

It is clear that private law interest restrictions are not capable of controlling and stabilising public interest rates in eras of sovereign debt. Public debts escape to private law considerations and the cost thereof is more volatile than the cost of private obligations. Although the empirical evidence on the relation between the level of debt and the level on interest rates is unclear, it is mostly considered that the increase of the debt level since 2008 crisis enforced the rise of the interest rates, and vice versa.[61] The effect of the foregoing is re-enforced through the private monopoly position of the lending countries. As Greece does not have any other possibility than to deal with its natural monetary partners, e.g. eurozone countries, there is a quasi-monopoly position on the lender's side. The reason why Greece was unable to obtain a loan from private credit institutions at affordable interest rates is due to fears over an unsustainable debt and deficit burden and further enhanced the monopoly aspect. It is striking to observe that the European Union, on the one hand, aims to bring the usury regulation into the European level in order to improve the competition and free market,[62] but on the other hand creates itself a monopoly towards the countries which are confronting financial difficulties.

The effects of interest on the division of wealth are, from a Greek perspective, obvious: a debtor pays money on the money he needs, and acquires from somebody who has an excess of money. Thus, interest creates a money transfer from those who do not have enough money to those who have a money surplus. It enhances the financial inequalities between people or, as in this case, between countries.[63] This is the rationale behind the historical restrictions on the making of money out of the lending of money. It divides society, from a financial perspective.

Transposed to public lending, the application of a free interest rate system in relation to countries with a financial deficit entails that the poor countries even become poorer, while the rich countries become wealthier.[64] However, the central question is whether the obtaining of credit by Greece, Ireland, Italy and others would have been possible if the contractual freedom in public credit facilities would be more restricted. Leading economists are discussing the topic in general terms, in such a way that no clear message can be deduced.

However, there are some clear conclusions which can be drawn. The volatility and exponential growth of the interest rates in public lending schemes leads to an emphasis on the short-term perspective. The crisis and subsequent exponential growth risk inducing the country to opt for a survival policy on the basis of current economic factors, instead of instigating the long-term viability of the country's finances. The result is that the credit agreements entered into are unbalanced and relate to short-termism. As Nobel Prize Winner Frederick Soddy pointed out a long time ago, 'you cannot permanently pit an absurd human convention, such as the spontaneous increment of debt [compound interest] against the natural law of the spontaneous decrement of wealth [entropy]'.[65] We should have learned lessons from examples in the past – an extreme example was the outcome of the repair payments to be effected by Germany after the First World War – but these risk being repeated nowadays.

Secondly, it is difficult to restrict the discussion to just one interest rate, as interest rates depend upon a complexity of factors. A short-term debt generally leads to lower interest rates than a long-term debt. The risk for insolvency during the period of debt is lower, and thus the cost of the credit is also lower.[66] This leads, according to an economic analysis, in turn to an emphasis on the short-term perspective. The value of a loan agreement with a duration of five years against a 5% interest rate is much higher than the value of a loan agreement with a duration of twenty years. As Lietaer observes: 'If the currency one uses has positive interest rates – as do all our conventional bank debt moneys, then short term priorities will logically prevail.'[67] According to this reasoning, if a currency were used with negative interest rates, a more long-term perspective could be taken into account and would favour world economy. In the words of Lietaer et al., the economic system would gain more sustainability.

Thirdly, the prohibition of compound interest comes into play (cf. *supra*). As the Greek authorities had to obtain new credit in order to pay the previous credit, it accumulated interest payment. The idea of interest on interest automatically creates exponential growth. However, this is not by definition considered to be positive. Compound interests only take into account a short-term perspective. Exponential growth of the due amount is opposed to, and incompatible with, sustainability.[68] As the chart and pursuant debt development of Greece demonstrates, the country was factually captured in a compound interest situation, in which it had to obtain (more expensive) credits in order to pay former loans. The growth of the debt due to compound interest is in a context of financial crisis always higher than the level of growth of the real economy.

In sum, long-term viability is at stake when looking at the volatility of credit costs in the public lending sector. Posner adds another view to the approaches which were presented. According to this author, the provision of welfare in a free market, which does not provide for interest rate restrictions, produces perverse incentives to take excessive credit risks, which both drive up the cost of the welfare system and undermine its goal of poverty reduction. There is, in his view, a tension between freedom of contract on the one hand and the maintenance of minimum welfare rules on the other: 'Because welfare opportunism and welfare circumvention take the form of high-risk credit activity, the State should enact laws that restrict such activity. Restrictive contract doctrines, such as usury laws, perform this function.'[69] The laws against usurious or unconscionable contracts are desirable because they deter this risky, socially costly behaviour.

Transposed to public loans, that would mean that interest rate restrictions would enable to bring a more long term perspective into the debate. Given that States cannot disappear, it is useful to take into account the long-term viability of a State instead.

7.2. PRIVATE INTERNATIONAL LAW AS MODERATOR FOR THE INTEREST RATE

The choice of law clauses is often essential in assessing the risk for bonds, which are issued by national authorities. If the bonds are issued by a national authority under its own domestic law, the risk connected to the bond is, in general terms, higher than if the bond is subject to foreign law. This analysis is normal, as in the first case the debtor would have the sovereign power to unilaterally amend the rules applicable to its own obligations.[70] This considerably enhances the risk of non-payment of these bonds.

This risk is of course mitigated by some legal principles which have been sealed on an international or supranational level, such as the prohibition to expropriate the claim of the lender[71] and by economic constraints, e.g. that the concerned country must be able to go the market again in the future without having broken all confidence of investors. The question was raised whether a mandatory alteration of the payment terms of a domestic sovereign bond in the context of a generalised debt restructuring would contravene the constitutional and international provisions protecting ownership against – amongst others – expropriation. This question however was never raised in domestic law with regard to private loan agreements for which the interest rate was mitigated on the ground of one of the mandatory provisions.

In spite of these protective measures, the prospect of favourable treatment for debt governed by English law *ex ante* would lead an investor to demand a lower interest rate when purchasing foreign debt papers. Lender countries require a so-called 'yield premium' when granting a sovereign issuing debt governed by local law (which the sovereign controls and can change when conditions demand) versus debt governed by foreign law (which the sovereign cannot control).[72]

Applying the previous findings to the Greek debacle, we see that a rough 90% of the Greek sovereign debt was issued under domestic Greek law, which naturally increased the interest rate of the sovereign debt. The reverse side is that the restructuring of debts is more complicated when dealing with foreign bonds than with bonds which are subject to domestic law. For instance for debts governed by English law, the sovereign debtor must seek for an agreement with almost all its creditors. For the bonds issued under foreign law, qualified majorities were required in order to approve the debt restructuring. Bonds governed by Greek law provide creditors with a significantly lower possibility to hold out from any proposed restructuring than bonds governed by English law.[73] This second element might be – at first sight – favourable to the debtor, but it also increases the risk of a carve-out of the obligation. Another element, in the same direction, is that English governed bonds often contain *pari passu* clauses, which the Greek bonds lack.

The result is clear: as Choi, Gulati and Posner point out in their analysis, the interest yield between domestic bonds and English governed bonds increased at the realm of the sovereign debt crisis.

8. CONCLUSION

We have seen in the preceding analysis that there seems to be some dichotomy between the interest regulation in private relations and in public relations. The volatility of interest rates in public lending schemes is not reflected in private relations, given numerous statutory interest rate restrictions in the national legal systems. Even if there is no reason why national interest rate restrictions would not apply to public lending schemes, they cannot give a framework for the volatility of interest rates since the late 1970s, especially when debt default risks coming into play.

It is debated whether interest rate restrictions have a major economic impact. The development of interest rate restrictions in legal history demonstrates that economic arguments were only one factor interplaying with sociological, religious and contiguous elements. The interconnection between these elements often blurs the real justification for interest rate restrictions.

However, this doubt does not prevent us from drawing some clear lines. Interest rates have a pernicious economic effect. In times of economic downfall, interests even increase the differences in financial position between the States. The 'richer' States lend money to 'poorer' States in order to enable the latter to reduce their consumption deficit. The money excess of the formers even increase through the interest payments, while the money deficit of the latter will even deteriorate through the money payment. This mechanism is auto-enforcing in times of financial crisis and deflation: deflation is favourable to creditors, because it increases the value of the outstanding debts.

Moreover, the volatility of the interest rates raises major concerns with regard to the sustainability of the financial growth. Compound interest, leading towards exponential increases of interest payments, is harmful for sustainability. Moreover the term of the credit agreements is shortened in periods of increasing interest rates, stressing again the short-term perspective. This observation is important: while it is often observed that short-termism is one of the main causes of the financial crisis, we have argued that the crisis leads to an even further short-term perspective. Short-termism can thus be seen as both one of the causes and one of the consequences of the crisis.

Endnotes

* Vincent Sagaert is a Professor of Private Law at the Catholic University of Leuven (KULAK Campus) and University of Antwerp, and an Attorney at the Brussels Bar. The author gratefully thanks Professor André Watteyne (Professor Economics KULAK) for his critical and necessary observations on an earlier draft of this article. I am grateful to Benjamin Verheye for his precious gathering of documentation for this contribution. Of course, all mistakes and positions are my sole responsibility.

1. If the income and wealth inequality is permanent, then lending and interest rates will gradually disappear. Only contingent inequalities can give rise to credit agreements (E.L. GLAESER and J. SCHEINKMAN, 'Neither a Borrower nor a Lender Be: An Economic Analysis of Interest Restrictions and Usury Laws', *Journal of Law and Economics* 1998, (1) 9). The fact that interest in itself contributes to the inequality makes this situation purely hypothetical.
2. In economic terms, this statement is only valid if the interest rate of the loan exceeds the inflation margin (as is normally the case).
3. F. MORIN, *Un monde sans Wall Street?*, Paris, Editions du Seuil, 2011, pp. 72–73. Of course, investment loans can decrease the dualism in society: if the use of the money obtained gives a profitability which exceeds the interest rate, the borrower – who was in shortage of money – improves his financial position.
4. We can refer for this dimension to K. BYTTEBIER and M. FLAMMÉE, 'Het vraagstuk van ethisch financieren toegepast op de interestheffing mede vanuit een elementair rechtshistorisch perspectief. Stof voor een morele uitweg uit een wereld in (financiële) crisis?', in *Liber amicorum Michel Magits*, Mechelen, Kluwer, 2013, pp. 2–40.
5. We refer for the historical development of this provision to *infra*, nos. 0-0.
6. *APR*, tw. *Interest*, no. 24; C. BIQUET-MATHIEU, *Le sort des intérêts dans le droit du crédit. Actualité ou désuétude du Code civil*, Liège, 1998, no. 303; P. WERY, *Droit des obligations*, Brussels, Larcier, 2010, no. 265; E. SWAENEPOEL, *Toetsing van het contractuele evenwicht*, Antwerp, Intersentia, 2011, no. 254.
7. H. DE PAGE, *Traité*, V, no. 163.
8. R. DEKKERS and A. VERBEKE, *Handboek Burgerlijk Recht*, Antwerp, Kluwer, 2007, no. 1306.
9. C. BIQUET-MATHIEU, *supra* note 6, no. 291 (this author justifiedly criticises this restriction); R. DEKKERS and A. VERBEKE, *Handboek Burgerlijk Recht*, Antwerp, Kluwer, 2007, no. 1307; Court of Appeal Brussels 15 September 2009, *NJW* 2010, 285.
10. E. SWAENEPOEL, *supra* note 6, no. 255
11. Act of 12 June 1991, *Belgian Official Gazette* 9 July 1991.
12. C. BIQUET-MATHIEU, *supra* note 6, p. 525, no. 306.
13. For instance: Trib. Namur 22 June 1989, *JLMB* 1989, 1320.
14. Article 494 Belgian Criminal Code. This criminal penalty already dates from the Act of 3 September 1807 and was taken over in article 406 of the Napoleonic Criminal Code of 1810.
15. Comp. R. DEKKERS and A. VERBEKE, *Handboek Burgerlijk Recht*, Antwerp, Kluwer, 2007, no. 1307.
16. H. DE PAGE, *Traité*, III, no. 149; P. MALAURIE, L. AYNES and P. STOFFEL-MUNCK, *Les obligations*, Paris, Defrénois, 2003, no. 972.

17. H. SCHELHAAS, *Het boetebeding in het Europese contractenrecht*, Deventer, Kluwer, 2004, 567 p.
18. L. CORNELIS, *Algemene theorie van de verbintenis*, Antwerp, Intersentia, 2000, no. 494. Also: A. GOEGEBUUR, 'Schade- en strafbedingen in rechtshistorisch en rechtsvergelijkend perspectief', *RW* 2001–02, (401) no. 30; I. SAMOY, 'De geoorloofdheid van schadebedingen na de wet van 23 november 1998: de figurantenrol van de werkelijk geleden schade en van de nietigheidssanctie', *R. Cass.* 2001, (342) no. 4.
19. For an excellent and extensive analysis: C. BIQUET-MATHIEU, *supra* note 6, pp. 113–287.
20. Belgian Supreme Court 22 December 1938, *Pas.* 1938, 405.
21. B. LIETAER, C. ARNSPERGER, S. GOERNER and S. BRUNNHUBER, *Money and sustainability. The missing link*, Triarchy Press, 2009, 100.
22. Cass. 22 December 1938, *Pas.* 1938, I, 405; H. DE PAGE, *Traité*, III, no. 150.
23. See P. WERY, *supra* note 6, no. 616 and the references cited.
24. Study on interest rate restrictions in the EU Final Report for the EU Commission DG Internal Market and Services, Project No. ETD/2009/IM/H3/87.
25. Study on interest rate restrictions in the EU, V.
26. Study on interest rate restrictions in the EU, 50–52. With the exception of the United Kingdom, Cyprus and Austria.
27. We refer to E.L. GLAESER and J. SCHEINKMAN, *supra* note 1, pp. 19–25; K. BYTTEBIER and M. FLAMMÉE, *supra* note 4. For a historical overview: J.B. KELLY, *A summary of the history and law of usury*, London, 1835, 275 p.
28. Cf. T. VANDEVELDE, 'Een interestverbod bij Aristoteles', in L. BOUCKAERT (ed.), *Interest en cultuur. Een ethiek van het geld*, Leuven, Acco, 1994, pp. 37–58.
29. See for a more extensive recent analysis: I. MOHAMMAD KHAZAR, 'Prohibition of Interest and Economic Rationality', Arab Law Quarterly 2010, 293–308 (who conclusively argues that there is no justification for States to prohibit the use of interest); L. VAN DEN STEEN, 'Interest als zonde: het islamitisch financieel recht in vogelvlucht', *Tijdschrift voor Privaatrecht* 2011, 781-849.
30. For a comprehensive analysis of the similarities transcending the religions: C. CARDAHI, 'Le prêt à intérêt et l'usure, au regard des législation antiques, de la morale catholique, du droit moderne et de la loi islamique', *Revue internationale de droit comparé*, 1955, 491–544.
31. The Bible already contained 'rules' in this regard: 'If you lend to those from whom you hope to receive, what credit is that to you? Even sinners lend to sinners, to receive back as much. But love your enemies, and do good, and lend, expecting nothing back; and your reward will be great, and you will be children of the Most High; for he is kind toward the unthankful and evil' (Luke, 6, 34–35).
32. See e.g. K. BYTTEBIER and M. FLAMMÉE, *supra* note 4, no. 19.
33. The Bible was however not entirely consistent, as for instance the Parable of the Talents criticises the lazy servant by stating that if he had put his money on deposit with a bank, he would have received it back with interest.
34. Justinianus created a sliding scale of maximum interest rates with 12% only applying to the *foenus nauticum*, 8% to business loans, 6% to those not in business, and 4% to distinguished persons and farmers.
35. T. AQUINAS, *Summa Theologica*, 'De usuris'.

36. According to Thomas van Aquino, this would be morally wrong in the same way as if one sold a bottle of wine, charged for the bottle of wine, and then charged for the person using the wine to actually drink it.
37. E.L. Glaeser and J. Scheinkman, *supra* note 1, pp. 2–33 ff.
38. D. Debrata, *Lending, Interest Rate and Usury – Dilemma Persists*, available at: http://ssrn.com/abstract=1447411.
39. R. Ekelund, R. Hebert and R. Tollison, 'An economic model of the medieval church: Usury as a form of rent-seeking', *Journal of Law, Economics and Organisation,* 1989, 307. For a critical approach of this view: E.L. Glaeser and J. Scheinkman, *supra* note 4, pp. 2–3.
40. Cf. *APR*, tw. *Interest*, no. 8.
41. R.J. Pothier, *Œuvres de Pothier contenant les Traités de droit français*, Tastu, Paris, 1824, IV, *De l'usure*, no. 55.
42. J. Nypels, *Législation criminelle de la Belgique ou commentaire et complément du code pénal belge*, II, Brussels, Bruylant, 1870, p. 658.
43. A. Smith, *An Inquiry into the Nature and Causes of the Wealth of Nations*, Oxford, Oxford University Press, 1776, pp. 356 ff.
44. J. Keynes, 'Saving and Usury', *The Economic Journal,* 1932, 136.
45. Lord Mansfield in *Low v. Walter* (Doug., 735). See further T.A. Westen, 'Usury in the Conflict of Laws: The Doctrine of the Lex Debitoris', *California Law Review,* 1967, 136–137. Comp. B.J. Clary, 'Institutional Usury and the Banks', *Review of Social Economy,* 2011, 436: 'The community valuation is distorted by lenders putting pressure on borrowers to pay too high a rate due to the borrowers' need, by borrowers who borrow for speculative reasons, caring not whether they re-pay the debt, and promising excessive interest, and by financial institutions more interested in fee income than in the repayment of the loan, which might very well be sold to other parties.'
46. Cf. argument made by C. Biquet-Mathieu, *supra* note 6, no. 309. This argument was also raised by the European Commission in an extensive report in 1995: 'A number of criticism have been levelled at usury regulation, notably the argument that the credit market is thereby restricted. Sceptics contend that the credit market will be shut to those who need it most, to groups who need credit to survive, to persons who could not set themselves up without taking out a credit at a very high rate of interest. Regulating maximum rates would be tantamount to outlawing credit for risk individuals' (European Commission, report on the operation of Directive 87/102/EEC, COM(95)117, no. 295). This criticism raises the question of credit function in society: in certain situations credit may compensate for a lack of purchasing power but it can never make good structural lack of resources: Connecting this argument to a more sociological issue, it is argued by Marxist doctrine that wealth should be created and re-distributed by the government; private individuals should not be allowed to decide upon the obtaining of credit by X, Y or Z. Private individuals should only be allowed to gain money on the basis of their labour, not on the basis of their wealth.
47. Study on interest rate restrictions in the EU, 325.
48. Study on interest rate restrictions in the EU, III.
49. Study on interest rate restrictions in the EU, X.
50. Compare however for analysis of the medieval developments: B. Schnapper, 'Repression de l'Usure et l'Evolution Economique (XIIIe-XVIe Siecles)', *Legal History Review,* 1969, 47–76.

51. The chart is from the October 2009 Global Financial Stability Report of the International Monetary Fund. The composite real private borrowing rate (RPBR) is a GDP-weighted average of the US, Japan, eurozone, and the UK RPBRs.
52. A. Pettifor, 'Credit, usury and political power: chasing the moneylenders from the temple that is our democracy', EBOR Lecture delivered at York St. John University, York, 25 November, 2009, available at www.debtonation.org
53. C. Biquet-Mathieu, *supra* note 6, no. 307: '*Comme le taux qui doit être comparé au plafond légal est un taux tout compris, ce plafond légal doit être déterminé en tenant compte tout à la fois du coût des ressources des prêteurs, de leur marge, du risque d'insolvabilité des emprunteurs ainsi que des frais et autres coûts, fixes et variables, afférents au crédit.*'
54. E.J. Hamilton, 'The Origin and Growth of the National Debt in Western Europe', *American Economic Review*, 1947, 118–130; J.H. Munro, 'The medieval origins of the financial revolution: usury, "rentes", and negotiability', *International History Review*, 2003, 505–562.
55. Study on interest rate restrictions in the EU, XIII.
56. Study on interest rate restrictions in the EU, XIV.
57. Study on interest rate restrictions in the EU, XV.
58. F. Morin, *supra* note 3, pp. 78–79.
59. J. Hanlon, 'Defining "illegitimate debts". When creditors should be liable for improper loans', in C. Jochnick and F.A. Preston, *Sovereign debt at the crossroads. Challenges and proposals for resolving the third world debt crisis*, Oxford, Oxford University Press, 2006, p. 115.
60. J. Hanlon, *supra* note 59, p. 115. With regard to low- and middle-income countries, the increase of the interest rates and the devaluation of the local currency was even reinforced by the fall of the prices of non-energy commodity prices. Hanlon describes that in 2001, these prices had decreased by 76% in relation to the 1990s prices. For a description: J.T. Cuddington, 'The extent and causes of the debt crisis in the 1980s', in I. Hushain and I. Iwan (eds.), *Dealing with the debt crisis*, Washington, World Bank, 1989, pp. 15–44.
61. See H.J. Blommestein, 'Public debt management and sovereign risk during the worst financial crisis on record: experiences and lessons from the OECD area', in C.A. Primo Braga and A. Vincelette (eds.), *Sovereign debt and the financial crisis. Will this time be different?*, Washington, World Bank, 2011, pp. 453–455.
62. Report on the operation of Directive 87/102/EEC for the approximation of the laws, regulations and administrative provisions of the Member States concerning consumer credit. COM (95) 117 final, 11 May 1995: 'The Commission would like usury to be debated at Community level. In the framework of monetary union, i.e. when creditors will be dealing in ECU, it follows logically that any rules on usury, should they be necessary, must apply at Community level'.
63. We repeat that this conclusion only applies for credits granted in relation to borrowers with a financial deficit. If a country borrows money to make investments with a (potential) high benefit.
64. B. Lietaer, C. Arnsperger, S. Goerner and S. Brunnhuber, *supra* note 22, p. 106.
65. F. Soddy, *Cartesian Economics: The Bearing of Physical Science Upon State Stewardship*, Hendersons, 1922, p. 30.
66. C. Yew, *Sovereign debt crisis and international financial architecture*, Grin Verlag, 2006, p. 6.

67. B. Lietaer, C. Arnsperger, S. Goerner and S. Brunnhuber, *supra* note 22, p. 98
68. B. Lietaer, C. Arnsperger, S. Goerner and S. Brunnhuber, *supra* note 22, p. 100.
69. E. Posner, 'Contract Law in the Welfare State: A Defense of the Unconscionability Doctrine, Usury Laws, and Related Limitations on the Freedom to Contract', *Journal of Legal Studies,* 1995, 286.
70. S.J. Choi, M. Gulati and E. Posner, *Pricing Terms in Sovereign Debt Contracts: A Greek Case Study with Implications for the European Crisis Resolution Mechanism,* John M. Olin Law & Economics Working Paper No. 541. See also for this question: A. Gelpern and B. Setser, 'Domestic and External Debt: The Doomed Quest for Equal Treatment', *Georgetown Journal of International Law,* 2004, 795–814.
71. This prohibition is imposed by several international treaties. We can refer in the European framework to Article 1 of the First Protocol of the European Convention on Human Rights and Fundamental Freedoms. This provision is entirely part of the fundamental principles underlying the European Union.
72. S.J. Choi, M. Gulati and E. Posner, *supra* note 70, p. 2.
73. S.J. Choi, M. Gulati and E. Posner, *supra* note 70, p. 13.

POLITICAL, ECONOMIC AND LEGAL FOUNDATIONS OF THE CONCEPT OF ENTERPRISE

Matthias Gesquière*

'We are all prisoners of a rigid conception of what is important and what is not. We anxiously follow what we suppose to be important, while what we suppose to be unimportant wages guerrilla warfare behind our backs, transforming the world without our knowledge and eventually mounting a surprise attack on us.'

M. Kundera

1. INTRODUCTION

At the end of the Middle Ages, which is the historical point of departure of the analysis further on in this chapter, what is identified as 'perspective' was embodied in the arts.[1]

Perspective allows one to incorporate in one's vision, elements which the observed person himself does not observe,[2] and is therefore an ambitious enterprise. The application of perspective however compels modesty, as it necessarily excludes from its vision an infinite number of other elements.

The purpose of this chapter is to elaborate the author's personal perspective upon the political, economic and legal foundations of the concept of enterprise, triggered by the most recent financial and economic crisis which began in 2008 and which preoccupies the hearts and minds of the citizens of our civilisation even today.

This enterprise is both modest and ambitious.

It is modest, because this chapter's author is a lawyer, trained to analyse and to interpret legal texts, but not necessarily equipped with the methodological tools to examine economic, sociological, philosophical and political features of our society.

It is also ambitious, as lawyers must step out of their comfortingly enclosed technical field into the open field of society whose dynamics lead to the formulation of legal texts in the first place. Limiting one's vision to the sole study of legal texts convicts the lawyer to remain in a vacuum lost in time.[3] Worse still, it may transform the lawyer into the (often unknowing and unwilling) accomplice of certain forces in society that press forward against the interests of other members of our society. I refer to the chapter of Ludo Cornelis earlier in this book, of which the point of departure is the sad diagnosis of lawyers' silence in the face of the crisis of 2008 (some exceptions notwithstanding), although instruments causing this crisis were engineered with the active collaboration of these lawyers (credit default swaps for example).

Acting upon Ludo Cornelis' inspirational call, the best result this chapter may achieve is that it inspires other lawyers as well to develop their own insights into the workings and foundations of our society, improving and correcting the author's personal views expressed in this chapter.

2. SYSTEM ANALYSIS AS A POINT OF DEPARTURE

The current financial and economic crisis is considered to be a systemic crisis.[4] The point of departure of our analysis of enterprise should therefore be the system in which economic agents are functioning. Luhmann's system theory shows that society does not contain a centre, but consists of several social subsystems (such as inter alia the economic system, the political system and the legal system).[5] Systems are operationally closed. In Luhmann's own words:

> '[K]nowledge is possible only because there are no operational relations between system and environment. [...] With its cognitive operations, it cannot intervene in the environment but must always search within the system for a connection, a deduction, a further insight, or recourse to the system memory'.[6]

This implies that no point of reference independent from the system itself exists to evaluate the system, and that it is useless to evaluate the system on the basis of norms borrowed from other systems.

The preceding observations raise the question of whether the actual economic system, which tradition considers to have been built upon the principles of rationality and efficiency, may be subject to scrutiny, assuming principles arising out of moral or political systems. In what way is the concept of justice able to hold the economic system to account?

One of the traditional solutions to this dilemma is to postulate the following division: the economic system aims at efficient production of means, whereby the political system aims at equitable distribution of these means between the members of the community.[7] This chapter's scope does not allow us to look deeper into the actual merits of this approach, which are in fact rather limited.[8] For one thing, the members of the community are also the members of the economic system. Functioning in an economic system ruled by principles of rationality and efficiency may even cause psychological disorder, as recent work from a Belgian psychologist seems to point out.[9]

Raising the question of how to hold the actual economic system to account, should also not blind us to the fact that the economic system itself does not hesitate to impose its principles of rationality and efficiency upon the whole functioning of society. André Gorz's passionate and eloquent analysis of this problem deserves full quotation:

> 'Growth of the economy as a system, growth of consumption, growth of individual incomes, of the nation's wealth, of national power, of milk yields, of airspeed or the speeds of runners, swimmers or skiers, the same quantifying undifferentiated value judgement applies on all levels and excludes in principle all idea of limitation or self – limitation. Quantitative measurement as a substitute for rational value judgement confers supreme moral security and intellectual comfort [...]. The "irresistible dynamic" with which the "economic sub-system" swallows up all areas of social activity and life shows up now in a new light: it is not inherent in *this* economic system; it is inherent in economic rationality itself'.[10]

Later in this chapter, we shall briefly return to the post-war consensus leaving production to the economic system, and distribution to the political realm.

That systems are operationally closed does not revoke the basic assumption of most actual system theories that they are dealing with 'open systems', which are, in one way or another, related to the environment in which these systems operate.[11]

The economic system is therefore also an open system, which, in contrast to the teachings of classic economic theory, does not obey laws of its own in splendid isolation. Classic economic theory's focus on equilibrium for instance disregards the law of entropy, stating that through the course of time, order leads to disorder. The focus on efficiency goes against the findings of research into complex flow networks, which has shown that, in order to slow down entropy, systems need an optimal balance between efficiency and resilience.[12]

Later in this chapter, the preceding insights shall allow us to defend a proposal for a renewed synthesis between the economic and the political system.

First we must proceed with a more detailed analysis of the capitalist system in relation to the political system.

3. MACRO-ANALYSIS OF THE CAPITALIST SYSTEM

3.1. THE BUILDING BLOCKS OF THE CAPITALIST SYSTEM

Traditionally the following elements are considered to be the building blocks of the capitalist system: the search for profit, the accumulation of profits (meaning that profits are not consumed but re-invested), private property and production aimed at the market.[13]

To these elements, the transformation of labour into a fictitious commodity may be added as one of the building blocks of the capitalist system, whereby labour power may even be considered as the 'sole source of real added value (and hence profit) for capital taken as a whole'.[14] This feature of capitalism has always been the most sensitive one. Although today workers have obtained the freedom to sell their labour-power by means of contract, one still tends to perceive and to react against the antagonism between workers and capitalists. Recent Belgian legal scholarship for instance identified the 'entrepreneur' as a risk manager, being able to transfer the risk of his business to other persons, including his employees.[15]

Using this antagonism as the point of departure for recent research[16] may be praiseworthy, as it consists of scholarship from the heart, aimed at the protection of a group of members of our community perceived as the weaker party.

This chapter shall not further elaborate upon this antagonism, for several reasons.

As both the entrepreneur and the employee are bearing risks, the main difference between both may well be that the entrepreneur is willing to invest in a production process which shall bear fruit at the end, while the worker prefers to sell his labour in exchange for immediate present satisfaction.[17] Therefore the risks borne by the entrepreneur may be higher than those borne by the employees.

On a more general level, Sloterdijk, one of the leading philosophers of our time, proposes to eliminate the division between capitalists and employees altogether, and to replace it with the division between debtors and creditors.[18]

The capitalist system is perceived to be a global system. The classic story of the emergence of globalisation starts with the nationalistic economic model of mercantilism (for instance existing in 17th-century France), which has been steadily overcome with passing time and has now transformed into a global economy.[19]

Such analysis is understandable as it is based upon one of the building blocks of the capitalist system, the market economy, which tends to be linked with (local, national) government protecting the market and its agents. For a market economy to flourish within a secure environment, contracts and property rights need to be enforceable primarily and preferably by government intervention.[20] According to Polanyi, government even enforced the market economy upon the members of local communities, instead of the market economy being the result of a free and spontaneous design of the citizens.[21]

Another approach is being offered by the great French historian of capitalism, Braudel, claiming that the following division is in place:

> '[T]he distinction of sectors between what I have called the "economy" (or the market economy) and "capitalism" does not seem to me to be anything new, but rather a constant in Europe since the Middle Ages. There is another difference too: I would argue that a third sector should be added to the pre-industrial model – that lowest stratum of the non-economy, the soil into which capitalism thrusts its roots but which it can never really penetrate. This lowest layer remains an enormous one. Above it, comes the favoured terrain of the market economy, with its many horizontal communications between the different markets: here a degree of automatic coordination usually links supply, demand and prices. Then alongside, or rather above this layer, comes the zone of the anti-market, where the great predators roam and the law of the jungle operates. This – today as in the past, before and after the industrial revolution – is the real home of capitalism'.[22]

One of the consequences of this theory is that capitalism has never been under the control of any government, but has always swept above local communities, market economies and governments, upon which capitalism was nevertheless dependent, and with whom it cooperated but also entered into conflict.

3.2. ARRIGHI'S ACCUMULATION CYCLES THEORY AND ITS BROADER CONTEXT

A profound analysis of the mutual dependence of capitalism and governments, and the resulting systemic accumulation cycles as from the heydays of the Genoese City State (1557–1627) through the current final days of the US regime, has been carried through by Giovanni Arrighi, former Professor at Johns Hopkins University.[23]

Arrighi's analysis is extremely interesting, as it shows that crises have always been part of the capitalist system since the end of the Middle Ages, and may enlighten an inquiry into the way in which enterprise is organised, such organisation depending on the specific accumulation cycle of which the enterprise is being a part.

The thesis that cycles and crises are inherent to the capitalist system due to the tendency of the rate of profit to fall, is one of the cornerstones of Marxist teaching.[24] Other economists have also enquired into the causes of 'business cycles' – Schumpeter is famous for having identified the process of 'creative destruction' as the mechanism causing subsequent crises of the capitalist system.[25]

Wallerstein developed a world-system theory, which may be compared with Arrighi's as to its historical and geographical range.[26] As an orthodox exponent of Marxism, Wallerstein's theory however considers sovereign states as being primarily subject to the capitalist engine driving the all-encompassing world economy. Postulating that all governments are essentially controlled by, at least subject to the capitalist system may well be one of the essential flaws of orthodox Marxism.

Arrighi's theory is more nuanced than Wallerstein's, as it clearly separates the drive for power, inherent in governmental structures such as states, from the drive for profit, inherent in agents of the capitalist system such as corporations.

The division between these two human enterprises, and their mutual dependence (leading to cooperation and conflict), has already been theorised by Lane, according to whom there are 'two kinds of enterprises: (1) those that produce protection and are called governments and (2) those that produce goods or other services and pay governments for protection'.[27]

One may link this division with the study pursued by Hirschman and which shows that the drive for profit (or 'personal interest') has been able to cool down the violent passion for power inherent in human nature. Systems driven by the urge for profit may therefore be less damaging to human survival on this planet, than systems driven by the urge for power.[28] This leads us to the position defended by Sloterdijk that the modern state, using its power to force citizens to pay their taxes, has sapped all energy from their citizens who remain entrenched in their own private interests, deprived from their 'thymotic' drive (or passion if you will) to contribute to the community's well-being in a voluntary way. Sloterdijk therefore proposes that freely donated contributions to society would gradually replace enforced taxation.[29]

Considering the economic system as a separate sphere, to be distinguished from the sphere of 'power', and even the whole of society, may have its roots in the religious crisis of the sixteenth century, ending the spiritual unity of the western world. The Concordat of Worms (1122) already divided the spiritual realm from the temporal realm, allowing the subsequent development of the secular state.[30] The spiritual unity was subsequently broken by Protestantism, which favoured an approach to the economy differing from the traditional medieval economic system. In the words of Tawney, one of the main defenders of this thesis:

> 'The theory of a hierarchy of values, embracing all human interests and activities in a system of which the apex is religion, is replaced by the conception of separate and parallel compartments, between which a due balance should be maintained, but which have no vital connection with each other'.[31]

Weber's research confirms that the Protestant spirit was highly favourable to the development of modern capitalism,[32] although Tawney rightly points out that Protestantism initially tried to contain the urge for profit within the moral boundaries of the religious sphere:

> 'The emergence of the idea that "business is business", and that the world of commercial transactions is a closed compartment with laws of its own, if more ancient than is often supposed, did not win so painless a triumph as is sometimes suggested. Puritan as well as Catholic accepted without demur the view which set all human interests and activities within the compass of religion. Puritans, as well as Catholics, essayed the formidable task of formulating a Christian casuistry of economic conduct'.[33]

The fact that capitalism has outgrown the protestant religion may have wounded capitalism in its core. As Bell has argued, the protestant spirit of restraint (or industrialism), which forms the incentive for the capitalist not to consume but to postpone satisfaction by re-investment of profits, has been gradually eclipsed by modern culture's pleas for instant and instinctual gratification. Bell also identified the paradox that capitalism itself may have intensified the urge to consume, as it is the engine of consumption which kick-starts the current economy into action in the first place.[34]

Briefly returning to the division between the sphere of power and the sphere of profit, emerging out of the spiritual unity of the Middle Ages, one may link this division with the broader cultural phenomenon of the erosion of the unity of sense which encompasses all of nature in the world view of the Middle Ages to the finally remaining sense-giving unit of the individual subject in modern times, standing naked in the senseless world[35] and even the senseless universe.[36]

Apart from the separation of the realm of power and the realm of profit, the other basic element of Arrighi's analysis consists of the essential formula of capitalist logic identified by Marx: 'MCM'.

This brief formula may be interpreted as follows: the initial stage of an accumulation cycle consists of the transformation of monetary assets into (fixed) capital. This transformation takes place within 'input–output' units (business entities such as industrial corporations). As these units function in the 'real' world (full of risk and hazards), they are the preferred tools of the capitalist when profit opportunities are plenty. When profit opportunities are decreasing, typically at the end of an accumulation cycle, (fixed) capital is turned into monetary assets through the process of 'financialisation'.

Arrighi's own words may enlighten the preceding passage:

> 'Marx's formula tells us that capitalist agencies do not invest money in particular input–output combinations, with all the attendant loss of flexibility and freedom of choice, as an end in itself. Rather, they do so as a means towards the end of securing an even greater flexibility and freedom of choice at some future point. Marx's formula also tells us that if there is no expectation on the part of capitalist agencies that their freedom of choice will increase, of if this expectation is systematically unfulfilled, capital tends to revert to more flexible forms of investment – above all, to its money form. In other words, capitalist agencies "prefer" liquidity, and an unusually large share of their cash flow tends to remain in liquid form'.[37]

Arrighi's thesis is rooted in Nobel Prize-winning economist John Hicks' findings that capitalist agencies tend to divert their future investments away from further expansion of their commerce in the material everyday world (which would increase risks of conflict through competition with other agencies willing to expand their commerce as well), into 'immaterial' investments in the 'higher' world of finance (and patronage of arts, an evolution which may have spurred the renaissance).[38]

The interplay between capitalist agencies and government agencies (empires, nation states, etc.) has led to Arrighi's identification of several succeeding accumulation cycles of capital, whereby the financial expansion (into crisis) of one regime of capital accumulation has led to the emergence of a new regime, which in its revolution initially focused on investment in material input–output unities and later evolved into a new wave of financialisation.

This chapter is not the place to analyse in depth Arrighi's theory, the texture of which is very richly woven. Even a rather extensive summary may not include all the nuances of this author's reasoning, and therefore weakens the persuasive power of its discourse.

It may suffice to state that Arrighi has identified the following cycles of capital accumulation, each having a specific design of consensus between the sphere of power and the sphere of profit, enabling capitalist accumulation but eventually leading to a 'regime crisis': the Genoese, the Dutch, the British and the US-dominated cycles. The current economic and financial crisis may be considered as the closure of the financial expansion phase of the US cycle of capital accumulation, which may lead to a new global accumulation cycle dominated by Asian values.

Specifically as to the tendency of each cycle to end in a systemic crisis leading to a subsequent cycle, Arrighi states the following:

> 'Each swing in the pendulum originated in the dysfunctions of whatever organizational thrust – formal or informal – happened to be dominant at the beginning of the swing. The "regulatory" thrust of the US regime developed in response to the dysfunctions of the "deregulatory" thrust of the British regime. And so today's "deregulatory" thrust may well be indicative of a new swing of the capitalist world-economy towards "economic freedom"'.[39]

The merits of Arrighi's theory cannot be underestimated. Firstly it allows us to minimise the perceived 'uniqueness' and 'apocalyptic character' of the current economic and financial crisis. It calls for expansion of and engagement in a comparative analysis (currently limited to the Great Depression of the 1930s) from the vantage point of a bird's eye view of the entire development phase of the capitalist system. Furthermore it allows us to grasp more fully the features of the current phase of the capitalist system's development which consists of a consensus model between the sphere of profit and the sphere of power typical for the US-dominated phase of accumulation. We shall return to this in the next sections of this chapter. It also allows us to situate specific models of input–output units (as 'paradigms of company designs') into the accumulation cycle in which they find their origins. We shall come back to this in the next section.

3.3. THE MOST RECENT CONSENSUS MODEL

The most recent fully developed consensus model between the sphere of power and the sphere of profit (as part of the US-dominated cycle of accumulation) may be identified from the perspective of the capitalist agents as 'Fordism'. The large corporation is perceived to be the cornerstone of the system and the engine of the system's progress, whereby mass production is connected with mass consumption. The point of departure in this system was Taylor's theory of scientific management, teaching 'the increase of labour productivity by breaking down each labour process into component motions and organizing fragmented work tasks according to rigorous standards of time and motion study'.[40]

According to Professor David Harvey, one of the most influential researchers of the system of post-modernity:

> 'What was special about Ford (and what ultimately separates Fordism from Taylorism), was his vision, his explicit recognition that mass production meant mass consumption, a new system of the reproduction of labour power, a new politics of labour control and management, a new aesthetics and psychology, in short, a new kind of rationalized, modernist, and populist democratic society'.[41]

From the perspective of government, the consensus model may be described as the Keynesian welfare state. The essence of this type of 'state' is the focus upon full employment of the members of its community, whereby this community typically consists of citizens belonging to the confines of the nation state.[42] The nation state has indeed been the post-war vehicle that has moulded citizens in a form of collective identity strong enough to accept responsibility for each other's welfare.[43]

Even if one may consider himself as a member of the European Community, it may well be argued that the European Community is mainly a design to rescue the nation state, as Milward and others have explained.[44]

The mould of citizenship confined to the borders of the nation state may in itself prevent citizens from being willing to bear responsibility for citizens belonging to other nation states, even within the European Community. Already in the 1990s, Habermas identified this issue, which has become acute in today's European sovereign crisis demanding solidarity between the members of different nation states. This solidarity is however reluctantly underwritten and in some cases even bluntly refused – which should not surprise us bearing in mind the words of Habermas:

> 'At the same time, however, it is also true that the national basis for civic solidarity has become second nature, and this national foundation is shaken by the policies and regulations that are required for the construction of a "multicultural civil society"'.[45]

From the perspective of the citizen, one may even speak of 'divided citizenship'.[46] One is at the same time a member of the political system (confined to the borders of the nation state), performing his rights and duties within a parliamentary democracy and a member of the techno-economic system 'defending his private interests in the fields of work and business'.

3.4. THE MOST RECENT CONSENSUS MODEL UNDER PRESSURE

The aforementioned features of the most recently fully accomplished consensus model between government and capitalist agencies (Fordism, Keynesian welfare state and divided citizenship) are currently under pressure.

The business unit model of Fordism is evolving to a system of 'flexible accumulation', with 'new forms of labour organization and new locational principles'.[47]

Instead of organising mass labour within the confines of the command-and-control-oriented corporation, employers exploit 'much more flexible work regimes and labour contracts'. Today's corporations not seldom consist of a core of employees enjoying job security but nevertheless obliged to show flexibility and mobility, and a periphery encompassing inter alia readily dispensable employees.[48]

Instead of organising mass production, today's corporations more often have to prove more adaptable to the ever-shifting demands of consumers in order to survive. For instance, consider the ever-improving technique of 3D printing, enabling the fabrication of products adapted to a range of customised consumer preference as opposed to mass production, may be one of the main signals of a 'third industrial revolution'.[49]

The contradictions inherent in the Keynesian welfare state have also become apparent. From an economic perspective there is a contradiction between wages paid to employees, and profits. For the system as a whole, wages guarantee purchase power of consumers, increasing the potentiality of increasing profits. For an individual firm, wages correspond with costs, limiting the actual profits.[50] An increasing focus on wages as a problem of profit-squeeze, undermines one of the basis foundations of the Keynesian welfare state aiming at full employment.[51] There is a further economic contradiction between taxation and profits, equally undermining the Keynesian welfare state's foundations. Capitalist agents enjoy the fruits of public services and government intervention, but consider taxes as a cost, which squeezes profits.[52]

Political problems of the Keynesian welfare state are clearly perceivable as well. As mentioned above, the Keynesian welfare state has been confined to the borders of the nation state. As a unit of organisation, the nation state has come under pressure due to globalisation and its corresponding mobility of capital, for instance enabling large corporations to evade taxation.[53]

The welfare state also seems to have turned into the victim of its own success. The benefits accrued through state intervention are considered by the receiving citizens as a 'given'. In the words of Beck, 'in establishing itself, the welfare state has sacrificed its utopian energies'.[54] This is a dangerous situation, as considering the institutions of the welfare state and its benefits to the community as 'given by nature' in a situation where certain powers in society tend to undermine these institutions and question the opportunity and even the rightfulness of further investments in public services, may give free rein to these powers to the detriment of the whole of society.[55] One may nevertheless observe that it may well be a form of 'rational ignorance' of citizens not to invest their time and devotion into the exercise of their democratic rights to influence their government's policy, thereby giving way to government's influence by special-interest groups which do have the resources to invest in these matters, such as different lobbying groups for (sectors of) corporations.[56]

This last issue brings us to the fact that the citizen is being confronted with a phenomenon Beck coined as the 'unbinding of politics'.[57] On the one hand, traditional politics seems powerless to tackle the major problems of our times. On the other hand, the techno-economic subsystem has acquired a political dimension surpassing traditional political structures and decision-making mechanisms. Citizens find themselves in a hybrid and confusing atmosphere, with a political system that has largely lost its legitimacy, and a techno-economic system that has not yet required any legitimacy to act in society's best interest. As Beck put it, 'one might say that the devil of the economy must sprinkle himself with the holy water of public morality and put on a halo of concern for society and nature'.[58]

3.5. TOWARDS A NEW CONSENSUS MODEL?

In the long run, the current crisis needs to lead to a new consensus model. One of the basic principles of such a new consensus model should be that the economic system is once and for all considered as a part of the larger social system, which is in turn considered as belonging to the all-encompassing bio-system.

Such a consensus model should restore the primacy of citizens as members of the social system, equally sharing their place in dependency of the larger bio-system, having an equally shared interest in the economic system as a means to an end, with the most fundamental end being the survival of the human race.

In such a system, the two basic conditions of a valid theory of political obligation (meaning that each citizen accepts the legitimacy of the system and is willing to take up his political duties and obligations, instead of focusing upon the exercise of individual rights) may be met: (i) citizens seeing themselves as equal in some respects which resonate as being more fundamental than all the other respects in which they are unequal, and (ii) a cohesion of interests among those having a voice in influencing government.[59]

A consensus model of this kind may be the secular equivalent to the protestant religion morally encompassing the capitalist system in a bygone era.[60]

A new consensus model requires that one proceeds with a renewed evaluation of the building blocks of the capitalist system, of which the most important are the focus on profits, the market economy and private property.

The drive for profit has been identified as one of the major flaws of humankind, and hence one of the main reasons for continuous defaults of the manmade economic system, including the current financial and economic crisis.

To plead for an economic system without recognising the drive for profits may be praiseworthy, but nevertheless completely out of touch with the reality of the human essence. Coming after Machiavelli, it is no longer defendable to start any theory from man as he should be, instead of man as he actually is. There are plenty of theories pointing out and explaining man's possessiveness, from Keynes' 'animal spirits' and Girard's '*désir mimétique*'[61] through Fukuyama's argument of the biological foundations of politics.[62]

In the following section, this chapter pleads for a balanced 'wealth creation' as point of departure of a more ethical economic system.

The market economy conceptualised as a free and open field into which all capitalist production flows, also needs revisiting.

For one thing, explaining the gap between the corporation as a tight organisation of command and control prior to and during production on the one hand, and the necessity of 'free' market – exchange post-production, needs more elaborate rethinking and research. This research needs to take into account the capitalist agents' own drive to control, suspend and even supersede the market as shown by J.K. Galbraith,[63] as well as the fact that imposing a market economy upon communities which were held together by solidarity and a sense of mutual obligation, wrecked and destroyed these economies as Polanyi has showed.[64]

In his brilliant study *Seeing like a State*, Professor Scott of Yale University states the following, by itself summing up the major issues identified in this chapter:

> 'The market is itself an instituted, formal system of coordination, despite the elbow room that it provides to its participants, and it is therefore similarly dependent on a larger system of social relations which its own calculus does not acknowledge and which it can neither create nor maintain. Here I have in mind not only the obvious elements of contract and property law, as well as the state's coercive power to enforce them, but antecedent patterns and norms of social trust, community, and cooperation, without which market exchange is inconceivable. Finally, and most important, the economy is "a subsystem of a finite and nongrowing eco-system", whose carrying capacity and interactions it must respect as a condition of its persistence'.[65]

Private property as one of the founding principles of the capitalist system needs rethinking as well. In his authoritative study of the history of natural law, Leo Strauss stressed the difference between classic natural right theories (such as those defended by Plato and Cicero) and modern natural right theories, propagated by the pioneering philosophers Hobbes and Locke.[66]

The primal focus of classic natural right theories was on civil society, in which every citizen had its place, and which was held together by trust and the sense that man's 'natural sociality' obliged one to uphold the principles of justice in relation to one's fellow citizens who had a right to expect such way of behaviour.

In modern natural right theories the focus shifted to the individual subject instead of the whole of society as the source of right. The basis individual right of the subject is the right of self-preservation. In the words of Strauss:

> 'If then, natural law must be deduced from the desire for self-preservation, if, in other words, the desire for self-preservation is the sole root of all justice and morality, the fundamental moral fact is not a duty but a right; all duties are derivative from the *fundamental* and inalienable right of self-preservation [...] If we may call liberalism that political doctrine which regards as the fundamental political fact the rights, as distinguished from the duties, of man and which identifies the function of the state with the protection or the safeguarding of those rights, we must say that the founder of liberalism was Hobbes'.[67]

Further elaborating upon Hobbes' point of departure that the right of self-preservation is the foundation of society, Locke isolated property rights as one of the fundamental natural rights, which consist, more precisely, of the right to appropriate and accumulate property:

> '[S]ince self-preservation and happiness require property, so much so that the end of civil society can be said to be the preservation of property, the protection of the propertied members of society against the demands of the indigent – or the protection of the industrious and rational against the lazy and quarrelsome – is essential to public happiness or the common good'.[68]

Harvard economist Marglin confirmed the historical shift from the medieval concept of property as a social construct enabling several mutually dependent members of a community (bound together by a sense of duty and obligation), each claiming its own rights upon a (common) good (such as land held in common by lords and serfs), to the modern concept of property as a right excluding all others from the benefits derived from a specific good. The Enclosure Movement in England (which started in the 15th century) was one of the transforming processes in that respect.[69] Property as an obligation has been transformed into property as an individual right to exclude.

This modern concept of property rights is no longer appropriate in a society that needs a renewed focus on the public (communal) good. However, the concept of an individual (property) right may not be redundant altogether, as several studies have shown that formal property rights may be indispensable for progress and wealth creation.[70]

C.B. Macpherson is one of the most profound re-thinkers of the concept of property, whereby society's individuals' rights are not being abandoned altogether, but are instead being conceived as an individual's right to revenue. Property as a right to exclude is being transformed to a 'right not to be excluded from the use or benefit of the accumulated productive resources of the whole society'.[71] We shall return to this issue in this paper's next chapter.

4. MICRO-ANALYSIS: TOWARDS A 'NEW THEORY OF THE FIRM'?

Legal scholars embarking upon a venture to analyse the concept of the firm from a larger perspective than the one confined to strictly legal principles, traditionally limit their voyage to the fields of 'law and economics'.

These fields are not the 'Elysian' ones, as their roads all lead to the concepts of rationality and efficiency, hardly encompassing the whole of human nature, as argued above.

This paper argues that the approach offered by 'law and economics' is not the sole approach to analyse the nature of the firm.

Firstly, the type of firm which is the object of the study depends on the accumulation cycle of the encompassing system as a whole. The following basic types of firms may be distinguished, based upon the aforementioned research by Arrighi: (i) the VOC (*Verenigde Oost-Indische Compagnie*), belonging to the accumulation cycle dominated by the Dutch regime, of which the basic feature is its patronage by the government enabling the internalisation of protection costs within the capitalist system; (ii) the classic industrial production firm (mostly in family hands), belonging to the British accumulation cycle, allowing the internalisation of production costs within the capitalist system; (iii) the 'vertically integrated firm', product of the US led accumulation cycle, allowing the internalisation of transaction costs within the capitalist system; and (iv) the 'network firm', belonging to the current accumulation cycle succeeding the cycle dominated by the US.

The theory of the firm proposed by Coase, stating in its essence that the main reason to incorporate a firm consists of replacing market transactions based upon the price mechanism (and the transaction costs these entail) by transactions integrated within a structure coordinated by the entrepreneur,[72] may be considered as an exponent of the US-led accumulation cycle focused on eliminating external transaction costs.

Theories of the 'trust firm' (hinted at below) may be the most appropriate way to approach modern enterprises functioning as 'network firms' within the current accumulation cycle.

Secondly, mainstream economic theory still argues that the creation and the survival of the classic capitalist firm (with its organisational command and control structure) can be explained by reasons of efficiency. However, alternative theories, such as the one defended by Harvard economist Marglin, explain that capitalist enterprise has been created to 'make the capitalist indispensable', by 'enhancing the control of the boss over the workers – indeed, as a means of ensuring a place for the boss in the enterprise'.[73] These alternative theories question the reality of the concept of efficiency to explain the creation of the modern firm.

One may also question the feasibility of limiting one's analysis to the concept of efficiency. It may come as a surprise that Berle and Means, founding fathers of the economic analysis of property relations connected to the firm out of which the 'agency theory' has been developed, argued for an ethical control of enterprise to the benefit of the whole of society, since the shareholders as formal property owners of the firm were no longer in control anyway. In their own words,

> '[T]he "control" of the great corporations should develop into a purely neutral technocracy, balancing a variety of claims by various groups in the community and assigning to each a portion of the income stream on the basis of public policy rather than private cupidity'.[74]

It is a pity that the ethical dimensions of the research pioneered by Berle and Means have been overshadowed by the increasing importance attached to efficiency, illustrated by the more 'mature' agency theory developed by Fama and Jensen who argued that the basic separation between ownership and control (or more precisely between 'risk bearing' and 'decisions power') is the most efficient solution to govern a certain type of corporation.[75]

As mentioned in the first section, Lietaer and others also pleaded against a one-sided attention on the concept of efficiency, arguing for a combination between efficiency and resilience as the recipe for any micro- or macro-system's survival.

This chapter argues that a valid theory of the firm should consider the firm as an integral part of society aiming at wealth creation, as one may suppose that the creation of wealth shall continue to be one of the basic features of mankind for some time to come.

The concept of wealth creation is nevertheless larger than the narrow concept of 'profit', as Blair showed in her definition of wealth creation encompassing all interests of the members of society involved:

> 'In general, a business enterprise can generate wealth in three ways. First, it can provide products and services that are worth more to the customer than the customer pays for them. Customers capture the benefits of this activity in the form of "consumer surplus". Second, it can provide opportunities for workers to be more productive at their jobs than they could be in other available employment. To the extent that they earn higher incomes than they could elsewhere, the employees of such a company capture some of the wealth created by the enterprise. Third, the enterprise can provide a flow of profits to its investors that is greater than those investors could get by investing in alternative activities. If the wealth captured by consumers, employees, and suppliers of capital (the sum of consumer surplus, labour surplus, and capital surplus) exceeds any external costs (such as air pollution) imposed on the surrounding community or on others who are not direct participants in the enterprise, the enterprise is creating wealth'.[76]

The creation of wealth should therefore be a public enterprise endorsed by all members of the community.

As economists and political scientists in recent studies have shown, communities may only achieve their goals if there is a sufficient degree of trust between the members of the community.[77]

The corporation is one of the devices which facilitates this trust – in the words of Seabright:

> 'The formal and informal institutions underpinning modern firms (everything from company law and accounting systems to dress codes, safety procedures, and management-speak) can be understood as ways of making trust achievable between strangers'.[78]

Further elaborating upon these positive aspects of the corporation's institutional framework, Mayer defends the concept of the 'trust firm', based upon the two-faced features of the corporation as a commitment device on the one hand, and as a control device on the other hand.[79]

Investing in a corporation's capital allows shareholders to commit themselves to the corporation's goal in a relatively permanent and therefore credible way. Commitment by shareholders allows the corporation to successfully convince its employees and other collaborators of the seriousness of the corporation's enterprise, thereby allowing employees and other collaborators to offer their own commitment in turn.

A corporation is also a control device, allowing control over persons (such as employees) who are not able to commit themselves through investment, and at the same time allowing a corporation to control its own destiny, for instance through the concept of the corporation's own legal personality combined with affirmative asset partitioning and defensive asset partitioning (limited liability).[80] A corporation able to control its own destiny enhances the credibility of capital's commitment to the corporation's enterprise, in sharp contrast with a corporation that is being controlled by shareholders maximising short-term value.

The right balance between commitment and control is necessary for the corporation to function in the best interest of society. Recently capitalist agents' attention focused too much on the corporation as a control device, whereby shareholders wished to regain more control over the corporation in order to direct the corporation's activities towards maximising shareholder value, more often than not with a short-term perspective.[81]

In order to enhance the commitment functions of corporations, Mayer proposes to enable corporations to develop the following features: (i) the corporation should uphold strong values, (ii) it should allow a body of 'trustees' to oversee the corporation's own endorsement of these values, and (iii) it should apply mechanisms that work as an incentive to enhance shareholder's long-term commitment (such as loyalty dividends).

Mayer's proposal resonates well with recent developments in our economic system.

The French legislator for instance introduced the possibility to grant additional voting rights and more substantial dividend rights to shares which were retained by shareholders for at least two years, enabling corporations to reward the loyalty (and long-term capital commitment) of its shareholders.[82]

Proposing that corporations enhance values as the core of their personality, thus replacing the naked profit motive as the corporation's drive for existence (and survival), may also allow the 'fluent' network firm being the corporation's archetype of the current accumulation cycle (see above), to obtain a fixed anchor point. It is to this anchor point that members of the network firm who are not legally bound to each other within a formal group entity may communally attach themselves.

The concept of the 'trust firm' fits nicely into the Anglo-Saxon legal system familiar with the concept of the trust. The essence of this concept consists of executing one's formal property rights to the benefit of another person.[83]

Our continental legal system has more difficulties with the introduction of mechanisms of trusts. According to Belgian law, trusts may not be created without explicit intervention from the legislator.[84]

Several legal scholars nevertheless plead for the introduction of a more coherent trust system into our Belgian civil law, but even these scholars would not go so far as to state that a corporation should be considered as a trust device.[85]

Nevertheless, already in the 1970s Walter Van Gerven proposed that the shareholder's property rights over a corporation should be exercised in the corporation's interest, to be distinguished from the shareholders' own interests.[86] In that respect, the corporation's interest encompasses interests that are larger than the shareholder's interests, including for instance the interests of the corporation's employees.

Van Gerven's vision may be situated in the historical development of subsequent perspectives upon property rights, evolving from viewing property as an exclusive and absolute right in the wake of its incorporation in the Civil Code of 1804[87] to the vision of incorporating property into the larger public order, emphasising the 'social function' of property and pleading for legal limitations upon the exercise of property rights, for instance through the medium of the prohibition to abuse one's rights to the detriment of others.[88]

However, not the shareholders but the corporation (with legal personality and limited liability) itself is owner of the corporation's assets. What shareholders have lost on the level of formal property rights, they may try to regain through the means of their instruments to control the corporation. Even if one desires to control the corporation, one cannot altogether refute the idea that the corporation, as a separate legal entity, has to pursue its own interests. A debate between defenders of the thesis that the corporation's interest is limited to the shareholder's own interests anyway, and defenders of the argument that the corporation's interest should also encompass the interests of a larger group of stakeholders (and even the whole of society), is still going on in Belgian (and European) law.

It is not the purpose of this chapter to take a position in this debate. This chapter argues instead that the essence of the debate should not be the definition of 'corporate interest', but a more fundamental discussion of the definition of 'property', which was also the focus of Van Gerven in his ground-breaking paper of 1976.

The entity finally owning and controlling the enterprise – albeit the shareholders or the corporation as such – should in any case exercise its property rights in a way which also encompasses the interests of the whole of society.

The 'social function' of property should thereby be restored, whereby the owner's duties are as integrally a part of property as the owner's rights. This stance is being defended by recent scholarship, such as David Lametti's, who stated that, 'in addition to being considered as an institution with limitations, [property] will have to be seen as an institution where positive duties of stewardship and proper use may also be required'.[89]

Linking the enterprise with the broader concept of property in its social context, may revitalise discussions on 'corporate social responsibility', a concept which has, due to the vagueness and confusion over its meaning and implications, apparently sterilised the debate.

Two recent legal developments in Belgium may illustrate and enlighten the issue of reconceptualising the concept of property in the context of the corporation and the business enterprise it is running.

Technically, shareholders do not own the assets of a corporation with legal personality and limited liability. These assets, forming the company or 'enterprise' of the corporation, are owned by the corporation itself.

The Act on the Continuity of Companies of 31 January 2009 introduced a split between the corporation as the legal entity and the 'enterprise' as the valuable contents of this entity. In the event that the continuity of the 'enterprise' may have come under threat, the assets of the 'enterprise' may be transferred to another entity through the legal proceedings of 'transfer under judicial authority'. The Belgian legislator thereby acknowledged the value of the 'enterprise' for society, and allowed a mechanism to safeguard the further existence of the 'enterprise' to the benefit of the members of society involved (such as employees).

The Act of 27 May 2013[90] amending several provisions of the Act on the Continuity of Companies of 31 January 2009 reinforced this idea, as it introduced a new provision to article 62 of this Act which obliges the persons controlling (or having controlled) the corporation and who control certain rights necessary for the continuation of the enterprise, and who are offering to take over the enterprise, to share these rights with other entities interested in taking over the enterprise as well.

The Act of 11 July 2013,[91] which shall enter into effect no later than on 1 December 2014, introduced an overhaul of the classical system of pledge rights, enabling all creditors to obtain a pledge upon the whole business of the debtor through mere registration.

Although the debtor may still be considered as the formal owner of his business' assets, his ownership rights, and more precisely his right to dispose of the assets, are to a great extent exercised in the pledge-owning creditor's interest.[92]

This Act creates the possibility to obtain a registered pledge of the whole business to all creditors, whereas the current legislation regarding business pledges limits its application to credit institutions.

This chapter argues that our legal concept of property may be evolving towards Macpherson's idea that property consists of a 'right of revenue'. The corporation may in that respect be considered as a public device allowing a right of revenue to workers, creditors and shareholders.

The gradation of these rights may differ, depending on the perspective on the interests at stake.

For instance, the shareholders' right of ultimate control of the corporation, entrenched in classical company law, is traditionally being defended on the argument that shareholders are the 'sole' residual claimants. This argument may no longer hold, as several other categories of entities may be considered as residual claimants (such as employees of whom the remuneration is connected to the company's results).[93]

Insolvency law is the legal field by excellence that seeks to strike a balance between the interests of government (as creditor of tax and social security contributions), private creditors, employees and shareholders. The Act of 31 January 2009, as recently amended, may be perceived as a 'cocktail' of rights and duties, balancing the aforementioned interests in a masterly but not always successful way.

In general, our legal system requires an all-encompassing and coherent approach of the 'firm' as a legal concept separate from its formal wrapping of the 'corporation':

> '[T]here are legal aspects of the "firm" as a productive entity which are not captured by company law, but which are to be found in complementary and related fields such as employment law, insolvency law and tax law. Although employees and creditors do not feature much if at all in core company law, they

are inescapably present in the economic or organizational entity the "firm". Employment law, insolvency law and tax law may be defined separately from the field of company law, but they interface with company law at numerous points, and the law of the business enterprise cannot be viewed in the round unless the interactions between these areas of law are taken into account'.[94]

This chapter argues that the corner stone of such a synthesising system should consist of the 'property rights' of the enterprise, developed along the lines of an interpretation of property as a social function.

Macpherson himself had the concept of the corporation in view in developing his plea for a renewed interpretation of property:

'Investors, to the extent that they are pure *rentiers*, have of course always seen their property as a right to a revenue. But with the rise of the modern corporation, and the predominance of corporate property, more individual investors of all sorts become *rentiers* and become aware that this is what they are. Their property consists less of their ownership of some part of the corporation's physical plant and stock of materials and products than of their right to a revenue from the ability of the corporation to manoeuvre profitably in a very imperfect market'.[95]

Abandoning the focal point upon property rights as an exclusive individual right, but not abandoning individual rights altogether, may lead to a general re-introduction into the legal system of the essence of the medieval concept of property, whereby several persons may exercise several rights upon one and the same asset.[96] The rights of one person may hold the exercise of another person's rights in check, with duties as integrally a part of the institution of property as individual rights.

The current economic and financial crisis strengthens the plea for a renewed interest in public order. Authors attacking the corporation, and mainly the corporation's drive for profit to the detriment of other members of society's interest, rightly claim that the corporation in itself, as a separate legal entity enabling limited liability for its shareholders, is created by government. It should therefore be a small step for governments to enforce new legislation upon the corporation which may accrue to the broader community's interest.[97]

This chapter defends the thesis that the positive aspects of the corporation, as a trust enhancing unit, should be the point of departure of any government intervention into the inner functioning of the company.

It is comforting that recent proposals to reform corporations, introduced in the wake of the current crisis, tend to focus on the trust enhancing features of the corporation, even if these proposals classically focus upon workers' rights and taxation.

For instance, it has been proposed to strengthen the ties between employees and the firm by distributing 'free' shares in the corporation's statutory capital.[98] This proposal may enforce the possibility for employees to control the credibility of the shareholders' commitment to the corporation's longer-term interests.

Another proposal consists of a more severe taxation of profits that are not being re-invested by shareholders.[99] One way to look at this proposal is to consider it as an incentive for shareholders to uphold their commitment to the corporation's capital.

5. CONCLUSIONS

It may not be appropriate to end this chapter with a conclusion, as its only intention is to testify to its author's concern at the current state of affairs, and to raise some questions needing further research and development.

One conclusion may nevertheless arise. It is the observation that all serious scholarship by political scientists, economists and lawyers concurs that the current state of affairs shall not endure, and needs to lead to a 'new synthesis'.

The role and purpose of the state in this 'new synthesis' is open to debate, as well as fairly all other issues heating the discussions between left and right since the French Revolution.

As long as there is an open and intellectually honest debate going on, things may not be lost.

One may however fear the worst if the majority of our citizens would no longer be interested in participating in these discussions, because they have become too cynical, or worse, merely interested in earning their own living blissfully unaware of the broader picture.

Our universities should therefore not only prepare their students to master their trade or technique allowing them a decent living in society, and deliver finished products to the market place, but endow their students with a lifelong propensity for critical reflection on society, and the courage to act upon this reflection.[100]

Endnotes

* Matthias Gesquière is a Researcher at the Free University of Brussels and an Attorney at the Ghent Bar.

1. This invention is traditionally ascribed to Brunelleschi (1377–1446): see E.H. GOMBRICH, *The Story of Art*, London, Phaidon, 2006, p. 170.
2. N. LUHMANN, *Introduction to systems theory*, Cambridge, Polity Press, 2013, pp. 112–113: 'Being interested in seeing what others do not see is a fascinating and, it seems to me, specifically European or "modern" achievement that actually reaches back all the way to the Middle Ages. […] In a space that is painted from the viewpoint of central perspective, it is possible to represent how certain people, due to their specific position in space, cannot see certain things'.
3. Reference to Gilmore's *dictum* is appropriate: 'The law reflects what was, sometimes what is, never what will be'.
4. R. SKIDELSKY, *Keynes, The return of the master*, London, Penguin Books, 2010, p. 165. A. KLIMAN, *The failure of capitalist production*, London, Pluto Press, 2012, argues that all government intervention since the New Deal policies tackling economic and financial crises, has been aimed at saving the capitalist system as such (see esp. p. 181 ff).
5. This chapter's synopsis of Luhmann's views is based upon F. MORTIER and K. RAES, *Een kwestie van behoren, stromingen in de hedendaagse ethiek*, Ghent, Mys & Breesch, 1997, pp. 236–248. See also: N. LUHMANN, *supra* note 2.
6. N. LUHMANN, *supra* note 2, p. 64.
7. See S. MARGLIN, *The dismal science: How thinking like an economist undermines community*, Cambridge, Harvard University Press, 2008, pp. 173 ff.
8. See the poignant statement from D. STRAUSS-KAHN, former head of the IMF, quoted by T. JUDT, *Ill fares the land*, London, Penguin, 2010, 189: 'The success of postwar democracy rests on the equilibrium between production and redistribution, regulated by the state. With globalization, this equilibrium is broken. Capital has become mobile: production has moved beyond national borders, and thus outside the remit of state redistribution […] Growth would oppose redistribution; the virtuous circle would become the vicious circle'.
9. P. VERHAEGHE, *Identiteit*, Amsterdam, De Bezige Bij, 2012. For the negative effects of a 'rationally' conceived system of division of labour upon the personal pride one could derive from one's work, see R. SENNET, *The Craftsman*, London, Penguin, 2008.
10. A. GORZ, *Critique of economic reason*, London, Verso, 1988, p. 121.
11. In N. Luhmann's system theory, an operationally closed system is connected with its environment through 'structural coupling' – see N. LUHMANN, *supra* note 2, pp. 85–101.
12. See B. LIETAER, C. ARNSPERGER, S. GOERNER and S. BRUNNHUBER, *Geld en duurzaamheid, Van een falend geldsysteem naar een monetair ecosysteem*, Utrecht, Uitgevrij Jan van Arkel, 2012, pp. 104–124.
13. See for instance F.C. LANE, *Profits from power, Readings in protection rent and violence-controlling enterprises*, Albany, State University of New York Press, 1978, pp. 66–71.
14. B. JESSOP, *The Future of the Capitalist State*, Cambridge, Polity Press, 2002, 13.
15. K. NEVENS, *De arbeidsrelatie, de zelfstandige en de ondernemer*, Bruges, Die Keure, 2011, p. 592, no. 933.

16. See also for instance M. Rigaux, *Tussen burgerschap en sociale concurrentie*, Antwerp, Intersentia, 2004; M. Van Putten, *Het arbeidsrecht en de onderneming*, Antwerp, Intersentia, 2009.
17. See for instance J. Huerta de Soto, *Money, Bank Credit and Economic Cycles*, Auburn, Ludwig von Mises Institute, 2009, pp. 286–287.
18. P. Sloterdijk, *Repenser l'impôt, Pour une éthique du don démocratique*, Paris, Libella, 2012, p. 179: '*le grand moteur du mode moderne de l'économie ne doit en aucun cas être recherché dans l'opposition entre le capital (industriel) et le travail. Il se dissimule plutôt dans la liaison antagoniste entre créanciers et débiteurs. Il s'agit de l'inquiétude que l'on nourrit pour le remboursement de crédits qui fait, depuis le début, fonctionner la gestion moderne – et face à cette inquiétude, capital et travail sont du même côté*'. See for a profound study of the relationship between debtor and creditor D. Graeber, *Debt, The First 5,000 Years*, New York, Melville House, 2012.
19. See for instance R.B. Reich, *The work of nations*, New York, Vintage Books, 1992.
20. See J. Hicks, *A theory of economic history*, Oxford, Oxford University Press, 2011, pp. 36–38, for an exploration of the conditions which have lead to local government enabling market economy to flourish, for the first time in an efficient way by city states: 'Both the protection of property and the protection of contract must be established, at least to some extent, if the mercantile economy is to flourish [...] The need is therefore for a small community, with good opportunities for trading outside it; but it must be an independent community, independent enough to be able to mould its institutions to meet its own needs. These are stringent conditions, but there is a well-known case in which they are met. They are met in the City State'. See also M. Olson, *Power and Prosperity, Outgrowing communist and capitalist dictatorships*, New York, Basic Books, 2000.
21. K. Polanyi, *The Great Transformation, The political and economic origins of our time*, Boston, Beacon Press, 2001. See for recent reappraisal of the work of K. Polanyi: H. Achterhuis, *De utopie van de vrije markt*, Rotterdam, Lemniscaat, 2011, esp. pp. 141 ff.
22. F. Braudel, *Civilization and Capitalism, II, The Wheels of Commerce*, Berkeley, University of California Press, 1992, pp. 229–230.
23. G. Arrighi, *The Long Twentieth Century, Money, Power and the Origins of our Times*, London, Verso, 2010.
24. See for instance M. Desai, *Marx's revenge. The resurgence of capitalism and the death of statist socialism*, London, Verso, 2004, p. 78. It is noteworthy that Adam Smith was one of the first defenders of the thesis of the tendency of falling profits – see G. Arrighi, *supra* note 23, p. 228.
25. See J.A. Schumpeter, *Capitalism, Socialism and Democracy*, New York, Harper, 1950, pp. 81 ff.
26. See for an excellent concise summary of Wallerstein's views: I. Wallerstein, *Utopistics, or, Historical Choices of the Twenty-first Century*, New York, The New Press, 1998.
27. F.C. Lane, *Profits from power, Readings in protection rent and violence-controlling enterprises*, Albany, State University of New York Press, 1978, p. 2.
28. A.O. Hirschman, *The Passions and the Interests, Political arguments for capitalism before its triumph*, Princeton, Princeton University Press, 1997.
29. P. Sloterdijk, *supra* note 18, p. 7–92.
30. F. Fukuyama, *The origins of political order, From prehuman times to the French Revolution*, London, Profile Books, 2012, pp. 266–267

31. R. TAWNEY, *Religion and the rise of capitalism*, London, John Murray, 1944, p. 8. See also R. TAWNEY, *The Acquisitive Society*, New York, Harcourt, 1920. See for a confirmation (and elaboration) of TAWNEY's thesis (albeit that it is being argued that the origins of modern capitalism in Great Britain are not to be found in Tawney's century (1540–1640), but in the ensuing century 1640–1740): J. MUNRO, 'Tawney's Century, 1540–1640: The roots of modern capitalist entrepreneurship', in D.S. LANDES, J. MOKYER and W.J. BAUMOL (eds.), *The Invention of Enterprise, Entrepreneurship from ancient Mesopotamia to Modern Times*, Princeton, Princeton University Press, 2010, pp. 107–155.
32. See M. WEBER, *L'éthique protestante et l'esprit du capitalisme*, Paris, Plon 1964. See however J. HICKS, *supra* note 20, pp. 78–79: 'Thus the appearance of banking, as a regular activity, is an indication that the bar against interest, at least in appropriate fields, is breaking down. This began to happen, it should perhaps be emphasized, long before the Reformation, in so far as the "Protestant Ethic" had anything to do with it, it was practice that made the Ethic, not the other way round'. The ethos of the (protestant) capitalist class has been captured in a magnificent way by Pierre Ryckmans, a Belgian scholar of classical Chinese art and literature, writing under the pen name of Simon Leys, as follows: 'The members of this closed society had a haughty awareness of the privileges they had inherited at birth, but these in turn were matched by a demanding notion of their duties and responsibilities. Always under the eye of a stern God, they were permanently subject to the scrutiny of their individual conscience. This austere high bourgeoisie knew how to marry mysticism with realism and audacity with common sense. Their prosperity and their power, fruits of their courage and industry, were to them signs of God's favour' – S. LEYS, *The Hall of Uselessness, Collected Essays*, New York, New York Review of Books, 2013, p. 453.
33. R. TAWNEY, *supra* note 31, p. 226.
34. D. BELL, *The cultural contradictions of capitalism*, Basic Books, New York, 1976.
35. See for instance the profound study of L. DUPRÉ, *Passage to Modernity, An essay in the hermeneutics of nature and culture*, New Haven, Yale University Press, 1993 – for instance p. 143: 'It is difficult to avoid the conclusion that modern culture failed in morally justifying itself. Few of its representative thinkers succeeded in construing a coherent theory of responsible action. Bacon promised a moral system but never produced one. The same is true of Descartes [...] The problem directly followed from the disintegration of that all-comprehensive synthesis against which humans had been wont to measure their actions and choices. Once the bond with the whole was broken, the self became sundered from the source of moral content. The loss of content turned ethics into a subjective – through not necessarily a private – concern'. Compare with WEBER's enquiry quoted by C. COLLIOT-THÉLÈNE, *Le désenchantement de l'État, De Hegel à Max Weber*, Paris, Les Éditions de Minuit, 1992, p. 32: '*On peut se demander s'il existe au monde une éthique capable d'imposer des obligations identiques, quant à son contenu, à la fois aux relations sexuelles, commerciales, privées et publiques, aux relations d'un homme avec son épouse, sa marchande de légumes, son fils, son concurrent, son ami et son ennemi*'.
36. See A. KOYRE, *From the Closed World to the Infinite Universe*, Baltimore, The Johns Hopkins Press, 1957.
37. G. ARRIGHI, *supra* note 23, p. 5.
38. J. HICKS, *supra* note 20, pp. 57–59.
39. G. ARRIGHI, *supra* note 23, p. 340.

40. D. Harvey, *The Condition of Postmodernity*, Oxford, Blackwell Publishing, 1990, p. 125.
41. D. Harvey, *supra* note 40, pp. 125–126.
42. B. Jessop, *The Future of the Capitalist State*, Cambridge, Polity Press, 2002, p. 59.
43. See J. Habermas, *The Postnational Constellation, Political Essays*, Cambridge, Polity Press, 2001, pp. 64–65.
44. A. Milward, *The European Rescue of the Nation-State*, London, Routledge, 2000.
45. J. Habermas, *supra* note 43, p. 74.
46. U. Beck, *Risk Society, Towards a New Modernity*, London, Sage Publications, 1992, p. 183.
47. D. Harvey, *supra* note 40, p. 190.
48. D. Harvey, *supra* note 40, pp. 150–151.
49. See for instance the issue of *The Economist* of 21–27 April 2012, discussing the eventual '3d Industrial Revolution', specifically referring to 3D printing. See also the works authored by Jeremy Rifkin, one of the prophets of this 3d Industrial Revolution.
50. I. Wallerstein, *supra* note 26, p. 38.
51. In the words of Marglin and Bhaduri: 'high employment encouraged the growth of wages and inhibited the growth of productivity; this put pressure on profits, and the resulting pressure on profits led to a crisis of accumulation. Basically, the Keynesian objection to this view of profit squeeze is that a higher wage should increase aggregate demand, at least under the assumption that the propensity to save out of wages is less than the propensity to save out of profits. Although higher wages may diminish the profit per unit of output, business will make up the difference by an increased volume of production and sales. If investment demand increases with the rate of capacity utilization, there will be even greater aggregate demand, and both aggregate profits and the profit rate will be higher even as the profit share is lower. In this view there is no trade-off between growth and distribution. High-wage policies promote income equality, output, and growth. Policies which increase the workers' share of the pie also increase the size of the pie' (S.A. Marglin and A. Bhaduri, 'Profit Squeeze and Keynesian Theory', in S.A. Marglin and J.B. Schor (eds.), *The Golden Age of Capitalism, Reinterpreting the Postwar Experience*, Oxford, Clarendon Press, 1990, p. 154). It is this argument, forming 'a cornerstone of the "cooperative capitalism" incorporated to a greater or lesser extent in post-World War II regimes of all the industrialized countries', which has come under increasing pressure eroding the economical underpinnings and legitimacy of the Keynesian welfare state.
52. I. Wallerstein, *supra* note 26, p. 39.
53. See for Apple's recent tax evasion schemes, playing out the US and Irish tax systems against each other: 'Cook lightly grilled', *The Economist*, 25 May–31 May 2013, pp. 63–64. See also the paper of Ludo Cornelis published in this book.
54. U. Beck, *supra* note 46, p. 185.
55. See for instance the plea for collective action in view of this situation from T. Judt, *supra* note 8. See also the plea from the heart from Ludo Cornelis in his chapter in this book.
56. For an analysis of this 'rational ignorance' of the ordinary citizen in democratic society (vis-à-vis the influence of government action by special – interest groups which have a very narrow rather than an encompassing interest in the result of government action, to the detriment of the whole of society): M. Olson, *supra* note 20, p. 92 and following. For the influence of lobbying, see: B. Balanya, A. Doherty, O. Hoedeman, A. Ma'anit and

E. Wesselius, *Europe Inc., Regional & Global Restructuring & the Rise of Corporate Power*, London, Pluto Press, 2003. See also the paper of Ludo Cornelis published in this book.
57. U. Beck, *supra* note 46, p. 185.
58. U. Beck, *supra* note 46, p. 186.
59. C.B. Macpherson, *The Political Theory of Possessive Individualism, Hobbes to Locke*, Oxford, Oxford University Press, 2011, pp. 272–273.
60. See for instance H. Jonas, *Le Principe Responsabilité*, Paris, Flammarion, 1995, for a tentative theory of moral obligation encompassing the interests of future generations of the human race.
61. See R. Girard, *Des choses cachées depuis la fondation du monde*, Paris, Editions Grasset, 1978, especially pp. 14 ff.
62. See F. Fukuyama, *supra* note 30, pp. 438 ff.
63. J.K. Galbraith, *The New Industrial Sate*, London, Hamish Hamilton, 1968, pp. 27–31.
64. See the reference in footnote 21. For recent scholarship in that context, see E. Mingione, *Fragmented Societies, A Sociology of Economic Life beyond the Market Paradigm*, Oxford, Basil Blackwell, 1991.
65. J.C. Scott, *Seeing Like a State, How Certain Schemes to Improve the Human Condition Have Failed*, New Haven, Yale University Press, 1998, p. 351.
66. L. Strauss, *Natural right and history*, Chicago, University of Chicago Press, 1965.
67. L. Strauss, *supra* note 66, pp. 181–182.
68. L. Strauss, *supra* note 66, p. 234.
69. S. Marglin, *supra* note 7, pp. 80 ff.
70. See for instance H. De Soto, *Het Mysterie van het Kapitaal*, Utrecht, Het Spectrum, 2000; T. Bethell, *The Noblest Triumph, Property and Prosperity through the Ages*, New York, S. Martin's Griffin, 1998. One should not be blind to the fact that one of the aims of incorporating individual property rights in the Code civil of 1804 in the first place was to put an end to the multi-layered property concept of the *Ancien Régime* which was percieved as an exponent of a rigid hierarchical (feudal) society (see V. Sagaert, 'Het goederenrecht als open system van verbintenissen? Poging tot een nieuwe kwalificatie van de vermogensrechten', *T.P.R.*, 2005, (983) 1016–1017).
71. C.B. Macpherson, *supra* note 59, p. 133.
72. R. Coase, 'The nature of the firm', *Economica*, 1937, 4:16, 386–405.
73. S. Marglin, *supra* note 7, p. 155.
74. A. Berle and G. Means, *The Modern Corporation and Private Property*, New York, Commerce Clearing House Inc., 1932.
75. See H. De Wulf, *Taak en loyauteitsplicht van het bestuur in de naamloze vennootschap*, Antwerp, Intersentia, 2002, pp. 25 ff.
76. M.M. Blair, *Ownership and Control, Rethinking corporate governance for the Twenty-first Century*, Washington, The Brookings Institution, 1995, pp. 240–241.
77. See for instance F. Fukuyama, *Trust, The Social Virtues and the Making of Prosperity*, London, Hamish Hamilton, 1995.
78. P. Seabright, *The Company of Strangers. A natural history of economic life*, Princeton, Princeton University Press, 2004, p. 164.
79. C. Mayer, *Firm Commitment*, Oxford, Oxford University Press, 2013, pp. 141 ff.
80. C. Mayer, *supra* note 79, p. 184: 'Affirmative asset partitioning protects the assets of the corporation from the creditors of the shareholders of the corporation. It prevents shareholders from using the assets of the corporation to settle their personal liabilities.

Defensive asset partitioning is limited liability, which protects the shareholders from the creditors of the corporation. [...] They enable corporations to establish contractual arrangements distinct from those of their owners'.

81. See for instance P. Zumbansen, 'The new embeddedness of the corporation', in C.A. Williams and P. Zumbansen (eds.), *The Embedded Firm, Corporate Governance, Labour, and Finance Capitalism*, Cambridge, Cambridge University Press, 2011, p. 37: 'financial decisions in the recent past have been driven by an increasingly short-term orientation in mind, as regards the maximization of shareholder value in response to highly volatile investor constituencies who, at any time, could "take their money elsewhere". The consequences for corporate law and policy of this shareholder orientation have been occupying scholars and practitioners in a truly global debate over corporate governance'.
82. See resp. arts. L 225–123 and L232–14 of the French Commercial Code.
83. W. Van Gerven, *Algemeen Deel* in *Beginselen van Belgisch Privaatrecht*, I, Brussels, Story, 1987, pp. 465–466.
84. See K. Byttebier and M. Gesquiere, *Algemene Beginselen Insolventierecht*, Ghent, Story Publishers, 2013, pp. 46 ff.
85. See for instance M.E. Storme, 'Van trust gespeend? Trusts en fiduciaire figuren in het Belgisch privaatrecht', *T.P.R.*, 1998, (703) 750 ff.
86. W. Van Gerven, 'Bedrijfsbezetting en verkoop in eigen beheer door werknemers van de onderneming', *RW*, 1976–77, pp. 65 ff.
87. It should be observed that even in the Civil Code of 1804, the 'absoluteness' of property rights is subject to strong limitations, as it is stated that legislation may prohibit certain ways of exercising one's property rights – the original text of article 544 of the Civil Code reads as follows: '*La propriété est le droit de déjouir et de dispoer des biens de la manière la plus absolue, pourvu qu'on n'en fasse pas un usage prohibé par les lois et par les règlements*' – see J.P. Levy, *Histoire de la propriété,* Paris, Presses Universitaires de France, 1972, p. 84. See also for an overview of the different phases of the evolution of the concept of 'property': V. Sagaert, 'Nieuwe perspectieven op het eigendomsrecht na twee eeuwen Burgerlijk Wetboek', in P. Lecocq, B. Tilleman and A. Verbeke (eds.), *Zakenrecht*, Bruges, Die Keure, 2005, pp. 43–85.
88. See for an overview of this evolution: J.P. Levy, *Histoire de la propriété,* Paris, Presses Universitaires de France, 1972.
89. D. Lametti, 'The (virtue) ethics of private property', in A. Hudson (ed.), *New Perspectives on Property Law, Obligations and Restitution*, London, Cavendish Publishing, 2004, p. 66.
90. Belgian Official Gazette 22 July 2013.
91. Belgian Official Gazette 11 July 2013.
92. See R. Jansen, *Beschikkings(on)bevoegdheid*, PhD thesis 2008–2009, Antwerp University, p. 88, who states explicitly, with respect to the current legislation regarding business pledges and therefore, *a fortiori*, applicable to the new Act of 11 July 2013, that the central principle of 'floating' pledge rights consist of the obligation of the debtor not to perform any act which may jeopardise the creditor's security rights ('*Centraal bij alle vlottende pandrechten staat het principe dat de schuldenaar niets mag doen waardoor de zekerheid ten voordele van de pandhouder in het gedrang zou komen*'). Jansen concludes that this principle affects the *ius abutendi* (or the right to dispose of the assets) as one of the main features of the property rights of the owner of the assets.

93. See C. Clottens, *Proportionaliteit van stemrecht en risico in kapitaalvennootschappen*, Antwerp, Biblo, 2012, pp. 220 ff.
94. S. Deakin, 'Corporate governance and financial crisis', in C.A. Williams and P. Zumbansen (eds.), *The Embedded Firm, Corporate Governance, Labour, and Finance Capitalism*, Cambridge, Cambridge University Press, 2011, p. 21.
95. C.B. Macpherson, *supra* note 59, p. 131.
96. See for instance J.P. Levy, *Histoire de la propriété*, Paris, Presses Universitaires de France, 1972, p. 47: '*La conception médiévale de la propriété foncière était beaucoup moins individualiste que la nôtre. En outre du propriétaire, la collectivité villageoise et les voisins exerçaient aussi des droits sur les immeubles*'.
97. See for instance J. Bakan, *The Corporation. The pathological pursuit of profit and power*, London, Constable, 2005, especially pp. 153 ff.
98. G. Giraud and C. Renouard (eds.), *Vingt propositions pour reformer le capitalisme*, Paris, Flammarion, 2009, pp. 105–106.
99. P. Askenazy et al. (eds.), *Les économistes atterés, Changer d'économie!, Nos propositions pour 2012*, Les liens qui libèrent, 2011, p. 171.
100. Compare with M. Nussbaum, *Not for profit*, Princeton, Princeton University Press, 2010.

FOR-PROFIT OR NOT-FOR-PROFIT? THAT'S THE QUESTION

Profit Maximisation in Company Law: Myth or (Legal) Reality?

Alain François and Koen Byttebier*

1. INTRODUCTION

There are probably many causes of the global financial and economic crisis, which has had us in a stranglehold for over half a decade now. Greed, expressed in an unbridled pursuit of profit is undoubtedly one of these causes.[1]

Let's say profit motive is a basic feature, even a constitutive requirement of a company. Then, at the least, the impression may exist that company law constitutes a solid metaphorical fig leaf that justifies an at times pathological and ruthless pursuit of profit.

Better still, company law would *impose* (boards of) directors and executives to always strive for profit or value maximisation for shareholders, expressed – as far as listed companies are concerned – in a constant rise in the share price. This is one of the reasons that led the Canadian law professor Joël Bakan to qualify the (public) company as a 'psychopathic creature'.[2]

In a contribution to a legal conference and subsequent book where lawyers demand the *right to law*, we must ask the question whether company law really is a Frankenstein, creating companies as ruthless – and ultimately self-destructive – money machines.[3]

Or perhaps the obligation to maximise profit or value for the sole benefit of shareholders, simply referred to here as 'shareholder primacy', is just a myth,[4] or at least not the conclusive alibi for psychopathic corporate actions?

The starting point for our mental exercise is in the United States, being the cradle of shareholder primacy on the one hand, and on the other hand increasingly a source of its criticism. Then, we return to Belgium to determine whether Belgian company law, at incorporation and over the life of the company, contains a (similar?) legal obligation for corporate bodies, or from a broader perspective, for the executors of the company agreement, to always seek profit maximisation for shareholders, *despite the consequences.*

2. THE RISE (AND FALL?) OF SHAREHOLDER PRIMACY IN THE US

2.1. THE RISE

While Belgian company lawyers typically debate the broad or narrow definition of corporate interest (see below), in the American context, the discussion primarily revolves around the following question: 'for whom are directors of (public) corporations trustees?' Initially, this involved a predominantly legal debate, partly driven by a landmark decision often cited in legal doctrine – much less in case law – of the Supreme Court of Michigan in *Dodge v Ford* (1919).[5]

Legendary in that context is also the so-called Great Debate between company law professors Adolph Berle (Columbia) and Merrick Dodd (Harvard), the first defending the view of shareholder primacy (1931), and the other a stakeholder-oriented vision (1932).[6] Two decades after World War II, the debate ended in favour of the latter view (which Berle eventually joined in 1954).[7, 8]

In the seventies the debate was revived and ideologised by economists of the Chicago School, starting with Nobel Prize-winning economist Milton Friedman in 1970 who stated in the New York Times Sunday Magazine that because the shareholders are the owners of the public corporation, 'the only social responsibility of business is to increase its profits'.[9]

That thought won academic support in the highly influential *principal-agent theory* founded by Jensen and Meckling.[10]

As agents of the shareholders, who as principals are the owners of the public company, the managers/directors should maximise the interests of the shareholders, which are purely financial. That is the best guarantee that the so-called *agency costs* are kept within reasonable limits. The fear that this will encourage managers to enter into value-destroying short-term decisions is unfounded according to this theory: the so-called *efficient capital market hypothesis* ensures that share prices are a correct measure of value for both the short and long-term prospects of the company.[11]

Although the theory of the firm despite its undeniable merits can be criticised severely from a purely legal perspective (managers/directors are not agents of the shareholders, but are agents of the corporate legal entity; shareholders are not the owners of the company's business),[12] yet feels more like a metaphor, it has become mainstream thinking in the US among company law academics of the Chicago School and far beyond.

Even the influential corporate law professors Hansmann (Yale) and Kraakman (Harvard) went so far as to establish in 2001 in an article in the Georgetown Law Journal (with some overestimation) that 'the triumph of the shareholder-oriented model of the corporation over its principal competitors is now assured', while ascribing ideological hegemony to the model and predicting that the model would also conquer Europe and lead to global 'convergence in most aspects of the law and practice of corporate governance'.[13]

2.2. THE FALL?

Partly as a result of the financial and economic crisis,[14] several separate excesses[15] and growing ecological awareness (that the earth's resources are finite),[16] the *shareholder primacy* model has recently come under pressure, even in its home State, the US. That happened in two ways, the first confirming, the second contesting.

2.2.1. Creation of new legal entities with a softened profit objective

Responding to a growing 'green'[17] market of consumers, employees and investors who put sustainability and corporate social responsibility first,[18] several States have creatively positioned themselves with new *for-profit* legal entities, such as the *low-profit limited liability company* (L3C), the *flexible purpose corporation* (FPC) and above all the *benefit corporation*.[19] In each of these cases, the States seem to have accepted that the 'regular limited liability company' is governed by shareholder primacy, but try to escape this through the creation of new for-profit legal entities with a softened profit objective. At the same time they confirm that shareholder primacy, at least in some form,[20] rules outside those entities.

The *low-profit limited liability company*, or L3C is similar to the Belgian VSO[21] at first sight, given that it is a variant of the *limited liability company* (LLC) that 'expressly recognises that its social mission takes priority over its profit objective'.[22] It was introduced in eight US states, but only enjoys a moderate level of success (again similar to the Belgian VSO).[23]

The *flexible purpose corporation* or FPC is only available in California, where it is a variation on the *corporation*. As with the benefit corporation and unlike the L3C, its objective to create (and distribute) profits does not need to be subordinate to its social purpose. It distinguishes itself from both legal entities because it is given legal grounds to pursue at least one other object (a 'special purpose') besides the maximisation of shareholder value. That special purpose can be specified in a general sense in the articles of association (like in the *benefit corporation*, 'to create material positive impact on society and the environment'), but also in a (very) narrow and time-limited sense.[24] This latter possibility, as well as the lack of a particular right of action in respect of the shareholders if management would fail to pursue the special purpose, exposes the FPC more easily (compared to the *benefit corporation*) to 'greenwashing' abuse, whereby objectives such as sustainability, social, green, charity, etc. are not much more than expensive, hollow words.[25]

The *benefit corporation* finally is enjoying a boom. It was introduced since 2011 in twenty US states (including some large states, such as California and New York, and, foremost, since June 2013, including the corporate giant state of Delaware) and is planned to be implemented in fourteen other states.[26] It aims to offer a credible, reliable and legally secure vehicle to consumers, employees, investors and executives for whom social responsibility is more than an empty slogan or a clever marketing ploy. It arose from the observation that the existing legal framework is inadequate for companies (and hence for *for-profit* vehicles) that place a high priority on responsible entrepreneurship (and thus respond to an increasing demand for products or services, employment in, or investment in such companies). In particular the fiduciary duty of directors to (ultimately) act with a view to maximising the profit of shareholders is regarded as an obstacle.[27]

The benefit corporation is a variant of the *'regular' corporation*, and is characterised by the following:

(1) it shall, in addition to having the normal objectives of a corporation, have '*a purpose of creating a general public benefit*', without prejudice to the possibility to specify one or more '*specific public benefits*' in the statutes; the creation of such general and specific public benefits is in the best interests of the benefit corporation;[28]

(2) an extension of the fiduciary duties of its (board of) directors so they *must*[29] not only take the financial interests of shareholders into account, but also the interests of other *stakeholders*;[30]

(3) the benefit corporation must report annually on the manner in which it has pursued its general and specific public benefit purpose or the extent to which it has created its public purpose by using an independent and transparent 'third-party standard'.[31] It does not come as a surprise that such standard is not set, nor controlled by a government agency, but by private third-party setters (like for example B Lab).[32] The benefit corporation differs in this respect from its British counterpart, the Community Interest Company (CIC), which is under the control of the Regulator, who is appointed by the Secretary of State for Trade and Industry.[33] Another major point of difference is that the benefit corporation has no restrictions in terms of the distribution of profits; so there is no question of a dividend cap or any other form of asset lock, in contrast to the CIC (and the Belgian VSO).[34]

That the benefit corporation is not a stillborn child, but rather seems to be an attractive legal form with a future, is especially evident from the fact that Delaware, which is the home state for 50% of all US publicly traded companies and 64% of the Fortune 500 companies, now offers the benefit corporation too. It does so with legislation that differs in certain areas from that in other jurisdictions (usually involving a relaxation). Particularly striking is the so-called 'tripartite balancing requirement': indeed, Sections 362 (a) and 365 (a) of the Delaware General Corporation Law require directors of public benefit corporations to manage the corporation in a manner that balances (1) the stockholders' pecuniary interests, (2) the interests of those materially affected by the corporation's conduct, and (3) the public benefit(s) identified in the corporation's certificate of incorporation.[35] Delaware seems thereby to be demarcating its extended fiduciary duty to a greater extent than the other jurisdictions, as well as prioritising among the interests to be balanced (and it is notable that the pecuniary interests of the shareholders still continue to play an important role). It is also striking that the Delaware benefit corporations are not required to use a third party standard in connection with the benefit report (which here takes the form of a biennial statement to stockholders).[36]

The criticism of the benefit corporation comes from two angles. Although they welcome the fact that the benefit corporation provides directors and managers with a more certain legal framework to perform a dual mission, i.e. to produce profits and social goods, the partisans of the so-called social enterprise are concerned that the control on the actual enforcement of such dual mission is too weak.[37] This fact, as well as the absence of any asset lock or dividend cap, surely increases the risk that the benefit corporation might in certain cases be not much more than a marketing trick to win over gullible enthusiasts for the green economy and corporate social responsibility (with a primary goal to make profits for the shareholders). Others criticise the extended fiduciary duty of the directors of the benefit corporation for giving too much of an impression that in the regular corporation this duty solely and exclusively applies to shareholders and their pecuniary interests. Ironically the benefit corporation thus (unintentionally) threatens to give to shareholder primacy the (indirect) legal basis that it previously lacked.[38]

2.2.2. Shareholder primacy under attack

While advocates of the new for-profit legal forms and particularly the benefit corporation, try to justify these forms by pointing out that current company law in the US prevents, or at least hinders, directors and managers to pursue a public benefit purpose, which seems to confirm the shareholder primacy model in the regular corporation, one witnesses on the other hand that writings by reputable company lawyers are currently demonstrating that *de lege lata* no legal obligation exists for directors of (regular) companies to exclusively seek profit maximisation for shareholders; and what's more, that *shareholder primacy* would be harmful to shareholders, the company itself and the general public. For example, corporate law professor Lynn Stout of Cornell Law School, is not afraid to declare that: 'The notion that corporate law requires directors, executives, and employees to maximize shareholder wealth simply isn't true'.[39]

In a real page-turner that sometimes resembles a manifesto (albeit on a thorough scientific basis), Stout settles scores with shareholder primacy in a colourful exposé, demonstrating that shareholder primacy gets corporate law and corporate economics, as well as empirical evidence, wrong.[40] For the purpose of this contribution, we limit ourselves to her argument that shareholder primacy is not good law.

Stout calls the notion that under company law, directors or executives of public corporations would have an enforceable legal obligation to maximise the profit of shareholders, a fable, largely arising from the ruling issued by the Supreme Court of Michigan as far back as in 1919 in the case of *Dodge v Ford Motor Company*. Although the Court considered in its ruling '[t]here should be no confusion [...] a business corporation is organized and carried out primarily for the profit of the stockholders. The powers of the directors are to be employed for that end',[41] these are mere *dicta,* which consequently have no precedent value.[42] It is therefore not surprising that the ruling, which was moreover issued by the Supreme Court of a state that is hardly known for its company law, was only referred to once by the chancellors of Delaware, the corporate law state par excellence. Furthermore, it happened in a case relating to controlling shareholders' duties to minority shareholders. After all – and this is another weak point in *Dodge v Ford Motor Company* – the case did not relate to the corporate purpose of a public corporation, rather to the duty of a controlling shareholder in relation to the minority shareholders in a closely held corporation, which Stout calls 'a different legal animal'.[43]

Nor is there any other solid legal basis for shareholder primacy: companies rarely record in their articles of incorporation that the purpose of the company is the profit of the shareholders. Company law of the states does not stipulate this either; on the contrary, in several states, other constituencies' statutes exist providing that directors may serve the interests not only of shareholders but of other constituencies as well. As far as case law is concerned, Stout establishes that 'courts refuse to hold directors of public corporations legally accountable for failing to maximize shareholder wealth'; a finding that is primarily due to a technique used by the courts known as the 'business judgement rule'.[44] Only when public corporations are about to lose their status as a public corporation will the business judgment rule not apply and directors shall have to maximise shareholder value.[45] However, as long as a corporation wishes to remain a public corporation,[46] the directors have considerable autonomy to determine what they will do with the income and assets of the corporation, even if their decisions do not lead to a maximisation of profit.[47]

More fundamentally, Stout reproaches that shareholder value thinking as a concept unrealistically perceives shareholders solely as a homogeneous category of people merely out to achieve the short-term maximisation of profit, thus reducing them to their lowest possible common human denominator: 'impatient, opportunistic, self-destructive and psychopathically indifferent to others' welfare'.[48] Although it cannot be ignored that the role of short-term investors has burgeoned in the capital markets,[49] Stout advocates relinquishing the notion that directors can only aim for the short term profit interests of the shareholders. 'If executives and especially boards of directors want to truly promote "shareholder value", they need to embrace the discretion that corporate law grants them to use their power and authority over the firm as a means to address [...] "the need for mediating the various and often conflicting interests of the shareholders themselves".'[50] After all, the board is charged with serving the best interest of 'the corporation and its shareholders'. This includes long-term shareholders, shareholders eager to make *ex ante* commitments to stakeholders, diversified shareholders, and pro-social shareholders.[51] As we will see below, Stout, who otherwise advocates terminating the tyranny of shareholder value thinking that damages corporations, the public and the shareholders themselves,[52] nevertheless verges on what is known in Belgian law as the modern narrow interpretation of corporate interest.

3. SHAREHOLDER PRIMACY IN BELGIUM?

3.1. INTRODUCTION

What's the deal with shareholder primacy in Belgium? Does an obligation to establish companies with the exclusive aim of maximising profits of shareholders exist, and must companies then only be directed by the compass of shareholder value maximisation? And if that is the case, does this constitute a license to the ruthless pursuit of profits for the benefit of shareholders and for 'psychopathic behaviour'? Or perhaps barking dogs never bite, and shareholder primacy in our region is not the bogeyman that some critics make of it?

3.2. PROFIT (DISTRIBUTION) OBJECTIVE WHEN ESTABLISHING THE COMPANY

The functionalists of the Rennes School have rightly emphasised that the finality of the company as a legal entity is to provide a legal framework for an enterprise.[53] However, the company does not have a monopoly in this area. In the legal landscape, especially in relation to associations, it stands out due to its profit distribution objective (and regarding non-profit associations,[54] that the latter may not have any commercial activity as their main objective).[55]

The profit distribution objective has clear legal grounds in Article 1 of the Belgian Companies Code (BCC), which defines the company and determines that 'a company is established [...] with the purpose of providing its shareholders with a direct or indirect patrimonial advantage'. It is immediately apparent that the law does not expressly mention profit (any more), but a 'direct or indirect patrimonial advantage'. The explicit reference to the notion of profit disappeared in 1995 after a decades-long debate in legal doctrine of the narrow (profit = financial or material enrichment of the shareholders), *versus* the broad interpretation of that term (which includes both an enrichment and costs savings or avoiding any loss to the shareholders), and which was settled in favour of the latter.[56] This already provides evidence that the company does not only exist to enrich its shareholders financially or materially, let alone maximise their wealth (albeit that costs savings and the avoidance of loss also contribute to the shareholders' wealth).

The profit-making objective (in the broad sense of the word) must exist on the one hand in respect of each individual shareholder (where in terms of contract law, it qualifies as the *cause* of his commitment to participate in the company). However, on the other hand, it should also exist as a *cause* of the company itself, which, after all, *de lege lata* still qualifies as a contract.[57] In the first case this involves an individual profit distribution objective and at company level, this involves the collective profit distribution objective.[58]

In the latter sense it coincides with the notion of 'common interest' (section 19, first paragraph BCC, former section 1883, first paragraph Civil Code). Although all kinds of motives may lie at the basis of their participation in the company, one is legally relevant, specifically the motive that converges the interests of individual shareholders, or in other words, is their greatest common denominator: the common or collective profit interest.[59] To put it differently, companies are set up in order to create wealth benefits through the entrepreneurial venture being pursued, benefits that (sooner or later) are to be attributed to individual shareholders. Here lies the germ of what we will call the narrow corporate interest, while the founding fathers of the (Belgian) Civil Code saw this as a manifestation of good faith, which moreover, is strengthened in company matters.[60] Viewed from the 21st century, it would at least be peculiar, or even contradictory, to interpret the profit distribution objective (through the common interest) on the one hand as a manifestation of good faith and on the other hand as accommodating an obligation that induces a ruthless profit maximisation. Therefore, based on the (historical) connection with good faith, it could be inferred that the obligation to set up the company for the benefit of common interest, despite the equation of common interest with the collective profit distribution objective, does not contain any such (even blind) obligation for profit maximisation. On the eve of the industrial revolution and the concomitant *laissez-faire* capitalism, thoughts on the matter were probably otherwise, so that we may not attach decisive importance to the connection with good faith stated in the preparatory works of the Civil Code (1804) for purposes of our mental exercise.[61]

In companies with legal personality the profit distribution objective also immediately determines the legal speciality, but more on that later.

However essential it may be (the profit-distribution object is indeed a constitutive requirement of the company), there is hardly a penalty for any lack of profit distribution purpose in the establishment of the most common types of companies in Belgium, namely the public limited liability company (NV), the private limited liability company (BVBA) and the cooperative company with limited liability (CVBA). Under the influence of European law, the grounds for nullity of these types of companies have been exhaustively defined in the law, whereby breach of the profit objective does not constitute such a ground. This leads to the conclusion that the said companies can be established without any penalty to have ideological (or other lawful) objectives.[62] Individual actions that are taken without a profit distribution objective, however, will potentially encounter the rule of legal speciality (see below).

However, Belgian company law provides a legally cleaner solution for parties wishing to run their venture under a legal entity without (only) being driven by a profit objective. They can choose to establish a commercial company with legal personality as a company with a social purpose (VSO). Similar to the aforementioned American low-profit companies, a softened profit objective applies to the VSO. After all, the aim of the shareholders of the VSO consists of making profits (in the broad sense of the word) through the entrepreneurial venture run by the company, but not to distribute these profits among the shareholders (although a limited profit distribution is allowed (dividend cap)), and rather to allocate it to an (internal or external) social purpose. Stated differently, the VSO and its shareholders are characterised by a collective and individual profit *allocation objective*, respectively. With the creation of this type of company, the Belgian company legislator *intended to serve the social economy*, in its own words. Companies operating in this sector are characterised after all, by (1) their focus on a service to its members or the community, rather than the pursuit of profit and (2) a democratic decision-making process (read: employee participation).[63] The VSO company type aimed to fulfil this need.

It is striking that although no penalties exist for the failure to observe the profit-making requirement in setting up a 'regular limited liability company' (NV, BVBA or CVBA), the BCC does closely watch if companies unfairly claim to be a VSO.[64]

Just like the American low-profit vehicles, to some extent the Belgian VSO confirms that regular companies must be created (and subsequently managed) with a view to delivering profits to shareholders.

Our conclusion is nevertheless that (i) the broad description of the profit objective (whereby the definition of the company in the BCC no longer refers to any notion of profit), (ii) the lack of sanction if, when setting up a regular limited liability company, the requirement of profit objective is not met, and (iii) the relationship with (currently objective) good faith, all already show that the profit objective is not about any hard requirement that may exist and is not a conclusive alibi for ruthless profit maximisation for the benefit of the shareholders.

3.3. PROFIT (DISTRIBUTION) OBJECTIVE DURING THE LIFE OF THE COMPANY: LEGAL SPECIALITY AND (NARROW) CORPORATE INTEREST

The pursuit of profit for the benefit of shareholders during the life of the company having legal personality is tied to two rules that are closely related to each other: the legal speciality and the obligation of the executors of the corporate contract (especially the corporate bodies and individual directors and shareholders) to pursue the corporate interest.

3.3.1. Legal speciality

The principle of speciality traditionally refers to the limits of the legal capacity of the legal person.[65] This deals with one of the limitations of legal capacity to which legal persons are subject, despite the principle of equal treatment with physical (natural) persons.

The speciality principle traditionally links the restriction of legal entities' legal capacity to the legislator's intended purpose for that category of legal persons: the legal person can only be the holder of rights and obligations within the sphere of activity assigned to it by its legal purpose.

In addition, typically the distinction is made between the legal and 'statutory' speciality of the legal person. The legal speciality refers to the legal purpose postulated for a specific type of legal entity. The 'statutory' speciality refers to the particular purpose of the legal person, as is defined by the parties in the articles of association, within the limits of the law (and the legal purpose).

There is no doubt that the speciality principle also applies to companies with a legal personality. It is remarkable, but then again, given the contractual nature of the company, not surprising, that the principle of speciality of the company is attached to the special validity requirements of the corporate contract.

Concerning the *legal speciality*[66] of the regular (or 'capitalist') company,[67] it can be established that this is associated with the profit (distribution) objective by a large majority of legal literature:[68] as opposed to an association, a company can only take civil or commercial actions with a view to the realisation of direct or indirect wealth benefits (profits), that will subsequently be distributed (delivered) to the shareholders. The Belgian Court of Cassation also deduces the legal speciality from the definition of the company that in principle is founded with 'the purpose of providing the shareholders with a direct or indirect patrimonial advantage' (article 1, para. 1 BCC).[69]

Although the legal speciality limits the legal competence of the company and thus the operational and representative capacity of its corporate bodies and, more broadly, its representatives, and although this affects public order (by which actions that repudiate it are absolutely null and void), it still cannot be overlooked that the principle has lost a lot of importance.[70]

This is mainly due to the fact that the notion of profit increasingly is interpreted in a broader sense: as said, it not only entails direct but also indirect patrimonial advantages;[71] in addition, it is conceived as dynamic and forward-looking, by which actions that may not immediately have profit in mind, but which are involved in a wider operation with a profit objective, or more, that give rise to any possible counterpart, correspond with the legal speciality.

This is partly the reason why legal doctrine and case-law are becoming increasingly flexible[72] towards liberalities by the company; what is more, liberalities are just about the only area where the legal speciality can give rise to application cases in company law.[73] Finally, the denial of legal speciality is not among the grounds for annulment of the company, listed exhaustively in the BCC for the main types of companies.[74]

Our conclusion is plain and simple. Although based on the principle of legal speciality, which is counted under public order, companies, their corporate bodies and representatives may be required to always act with the intention of generating profits for the benefit of (ultimately) the shareholders, the threshold to meet this obligation is so low that only pure liberalities (i.e. legal acts without any possible counterpart) can be sanctioned. Consequently, the legal speciality can objectionably provide legal grounds to require companies and their directors to pursue (blind) profit maximisation for shareholders.

3.3.2. The corporate interest

If Belgian company law were to honour shareholder primacy in the admittedly somewhat extreme meaning attributed to it in this chapter, i.e. as a legal obligation for companies, their representatives and – in a broader sense – the executors of the corporate contract to only pursue (even if ruthlessly) value maximisation for the benefit of the shareholders, then this would occur, given the previous negatory partial conclusions, via the obligation to defend the corporate interests.

Corporate interest has been a legal concept since the (Napoleonic) Civil Code,[75] but has entered corporate legislation and, more generally, Belgian company law, as a Trojan horse in particular in recent decades, where it performs a variety of functions (legal touchstone for validity of decisions of corporate bodies or the validity of voting agreements or inalienability clauses, criterion for judicial intervention, etc.).

In other words, the corporate interest and the (mandatory law) duty of the executors of the corporate contract (such as corporate directors and executives) to act in such interest undoubtedly belong to the essentials of Belgian corporate law.

Surprisingly, there is no statutory definition of the corporate interest and no direct and general article in the Companies Code that *indisputably* hosts the rule that imposes the furtherance of such interest.[76] As a result, the definition of the corporate interest as well as its foundations are highly debated. By and large two (main) views can be distinguished.

First there is a so-called 'narrow' view, defining the corporate interest as the (dynamic and future-oriented) collective profit interest of the shareholders.

According to a second 'broad' view, the corporate interest is the product of the partial interests of all stakeholders in and around the company, in one way or the other.

While it is true that the voice of the partisans of the broad view has perhaps sounded louder recently, possibly due to the fact that an enlarged interest has been shown for stakeholders interests in the more recent debates on corporate governance, corporate social responsibility and the financial and economic crisis,[77] it would be wrong to deny the narrow view, which, at least in our opinion and *de lege lata*, finds a much sounder basis in the law. Moreover, in a decision of 28 November 2013, the Belgian Court of Cassation has defined the corporate interest for the very first time, thereby clearly adhering to the narrow view.[78] Therefore, we cannot simply classify the Belgian corporate governance model under the continental European 'stakeholder-oriented' model. On the contrary, we believe our model – at least as far as the subject under discussion is concerned – stands closer to the 'shareholder-oriented' Anglo-American corporate governance model.

This finding makes the debate all the more interesting. In the mental exercise conducted in this chapter examining whether there is room for shareholder primacy in Belgian corporate law, we are not making it easy on ourselves by choosing precisely that perspective on corporate interest, which at least is closest to, or, at first sight coincides with, shareholder primacy. However, in what follows, we shall indicate that this is only an impression, and that the narrow corporate interest, at least in its modern sense, does not allow companies to be driven solely by (potentially ruthless) profit maximisation for the benefit of shareholders.

The concept of 'collective profit interest' is central to the above-mentioned narrow definition of corporate interest.[79] Partly due to the criticism of the adherents of the broad interpretation of corporate interest, this concept has been the object of significant fine-tuning in legal doctrine.

In response to the (from an academic point of view undeserved)[80] reproach that the narrow interpretation of corporate interest *per se* is aimed at short-term profit realisation and maximisation, it was emphasised first and foremost that collective profit interest essentially has a *dynamic and future-oriented character*.[81] This fine-tuned concept of collective profit interest is commonly referred to as 'shareholder long-term interest', which is less precise, however.

After all, the nature of the corporate contract itself, generally creating a durable co-operation between parties, infers that the profit expectations, in principle and insofar as the company has a going-concern status, must be considered in the more or less long term. Pretending otherwise could jeopardise the realisation of the company's object (*maatschappelijk doel/ objet social*), generally referring to a continuous activity.

The future-oriented nature of collective profit interest is further enhanced in commercial companies by the fact that they are a legal subject (the corporate legal person), distinct from the shareholders, with its own interest (e.g. its interest to continue to exist). This interest is recognised by the law and, certainly regarding the most regulated forms of companies, extensively protected. As long as shareholders choose to have the corporate legal person continue to exist as a continuity, they will have to take into consideration this legal protection, which often takes the form of imperative legal provisions. Several of these provisions stimulate a long-term policy.[82]

This does not alter the fact that short-term profit objectives will also need to be pursued under certain circumstances. In addition, the shareholders remain entitled, excepting abuse, to dissolve the company (prematurely), thus deciding on discontinuity. In other words, the executors of the corporate contract retain a policy margin within which they can determine how to spread the profit sharing over time, depending on the factual circumstances (past, present and future).[83]

Recognition is therefore implicit from the above that to a certain extent there is room for a more independent corporate interest, in the sense that it will distinguish itself from the existing shareholders' collective profit interest, considered overly in the short-term, under certain circumstances.[84] This is probably one of the reasons why the corporate interest does not necessarily correspond with the assessment and interpretation thereof by the (even unanimous)[85] shareholders. Another explanation is that the corporate interest is in any case subjected to (a marginal) judicial supervision as a legal term.[86]

Although it cannot be denied that the shareholders may have several individual interests which may converge or conflict, only one of these interests is legally taken into account to determine the common interest (upon incorporation, see *supra*) and the corporate interest (later on), in principle: the profit interest.[87] Still, the corporate interest must not necessarily consist of an immediate and direct acquisition and distribution of profit. Nevertheless, it will always have an at least indirect bearing on the company's profit capacity (and, through the company, the shareholders).

Of course, the company – and, more broadly – the enterprise involve numerous other interests, apart from the shareholders' collective profit interest.

Without a doubt, the relationship between the corporate interest and these so-called partial, category or stakeholders' interests is one of the central topics of the corporate interest debate. It is not so much a question of whether these partial interests must be protected. After all, both inside and outside company law, the legislator has formulated regulations to protect these partial interests. These regulations restrict the company's freedom of policy. Such regulations differ in time and space and are more (limited liability companies) or less (unlimited liability companies) extended, depending on the type of company or enterprise. A relevant question is whether the partial interests must also be protected by means of (the obligation to look after) the corporate interest. It is mainly the answer to this question, which results in the various interpretations of the corporate interest. The mere asking of the question already reveals that the duty to act in the corporate interest, regardless of the broad or narrow view thereon, will most probably not invite companies and their representatives to maximise shareholder wealth to the extreme.

The aforementioned French functionalists of the Rennes school[88] have properly mapped the partial interests of companies or enterprises (better known now as 'stakeholders'). They have rightly pointed out that the partial interests differ depending on the nature of the activity and the extent of the company/enterprise and that they also vary in time and space. Furthermore, the partial interests may converge, diverge and conflict both mutually and within one and the same category. The French functionalists are also responsible for the observation that the legislator, as the sole party competent to determine which partial interests are eligible for protection, has created various company types (and subtypes), allowing for a proper, continuously moving balance of interests in each case.

By far, the Belgian (company) legislator (and, more broadly, company law) focused most on the interests of the *corporate legal person itself*, mainly protecting the existence, assets and moral interests thereof, as well as the shareholders' interests.[89] Consequently, it must be noted that, although looking after the corporate legal person's interests will generally correspond with the corporate interest, both concepts are not synonymous. The corporate interest is broader, more dynamic and more abstract than its etymological relative. In addition, it refers entirely to the protection of human interests.

The category of *shareholders*, which may be very heterogeneous, has shown that it still has a dominant position in the company (including the listed company),[90] although the powers (or rather, competences) have shifted to a large extent from the general meeting to the board of directors (albeit that a certain re-shift has been practised recently).[91, 92] To compensate for the ensuing strengthening of the position of majority shareholders, a greater protection of minority shareholders was aimed for in most of recent legislation.

For the protection of their corporate partial interest, *employees* mainly have to rely on 'external' legislation. The BCC mainly pursues this protection through the traditional channels of information provision and the liability of directors. There is no participation in corporate powers. Staff members' participation in capital is encouraged, confirming that the exercise of corporate power is connected with shareholdership. Nevertheless, a part of case law is willing to provide protection of a greater scope.[93]

The company legislator has also organised the protection of corporate *creditors* through a broad information provision and the liability of directors. In addition, the Belgian Companies Code contains various rules to guarantee the reality and preservation of the share capital. Again, however, there is case law that is willing to provide further protection.[94]

The socioeconomic, social and legal landscape in which the company exists and operates also holds *other interested parties* than the target groups already discussed. With the exception of the so-called group interest regarding companies belonging to a group of companies, they usually have only an indirect relationship with the company.[95]

The stakeholders can also differ depending on the nature and scope of the operations pursued by the company. For instance, chemical companies or other companies burdening the environment inevitably come into contact with the interests of (or rather, defended by) environmentalists. Companies producing goods or providing services need to take into account the needs (regarding safety, user-friendliness, etc.) of consumers and their organisations. Companies operating in a political-cultural environment (for instance, newspaper publishers) will have to take into account these political-cultural interests. Companies having a key role in a local, regional or national community cannot overlook the interests of this community. Companies relying on public savings for their financing must ensure that they do not betray the confidence of financial market investors, etc.

Because a great deal of these interests are actually a part of the *general interest*, various governments have taken actions at various levels, through special and generally imperative regulations. For instance, the still-expanding regulations in the relatively new legal branches of environmental, consumer and financial law, the special regulations for companies operating a certain type of business (such as credit institutions, insurance companies, pension funds, etc.). However, this raises the question whether companies must take into account these derived (private) interests or even the general interest,[96] outside the ever-tightening straightjacket of economic, financial, social and fiscal regulations.[97]

If it cannot be denied that this is the case, under certain circumstances, a second question is immediately raised, i.e. whether the obligation of corporate bodies to look after the corporate interest is the most appropriate means. It is especially the answer to this second question which makes the adherents of the broad and (nuanced) narrow interpretation oppose each other.

Although the narrow interpretation to determine the corporate interest only takes into account the shareholders' collective profit interest, this does not mean that it does not pay any attention to the interests of the other stakeholders, let alone that it would provide corporate bodies with an alibi to strive only at maximisation of shareholder wealth, regardless of the consequences for the stakeholders.

On the one hand, it recognises that these partial interests may indirectly influence the meaning given to collective profit interest. Particularly, it is assumed that the concrete interpretation of the corporate interest takes into account the reaction of the partial interests (stakeholders) and the incidence thereof on the collective profit interest.[98]

On the other hand, it must be underlined that the obligation to look after the corporate interest is limited by other (statutory or common law) provisions which may protect other partial interests.[99]

In both instances, the fact that modern company law has fine-tuned the collective profit interest giving it a dynamic and future-oriented character (see above) and making it more independent, has indeed provided the corporate bodies (including company directors and executives) with more leeway to take into account stakeholders' interests.

Consequently, the narrow interpretation does allow corporate bodies to look after, at least to a certain extent, stakeholders' interests.[100] Simply by doing so, and despite the fact that the principle remains that they should primarily look after the collective profit interest of the shareholders, it is clear that such principle does no (longer) have a justification, let alone a waterproof alibi for harsh shareholder primacy behaviour.

From a technical point of view, and apart from the indirect influence of these interests on the concrete interpretation of the collective profit interest itself, the protection of stakeholders' interests will need to be organised outside (the obligation to look after) the corporate interest. This will need to be done preferably by means of special legislation, inside or outside company law, and, failing this, pursuant to common law and particularly the general legal principle which prohibits the abuse of rights and articles 1382–1383 of the Civil Code (tortious liability). As a result of this legislation or rules of common law, the executors of the company contract will need to weigh the corporate interest against other stakeholders' interests. The corporate interest at certain times, under certain circumstances and in specific legal relations will need to give way. Perhaps more than the fine-tuned collective profit interest, these rules of common law may act as a (in view of the crisis, welcome) Trojan horse to bring stakeholders' interests into the boardroom. Indeed, the greater the application of (soft) rules promoting the protection of partial interests, the greater chance that they will at some point influence the abstract standard of care used by the courts when applying common law.[101]

Apart from the fact that it is supported by various legal grounds, the above-mentioned viewpoint has the advantage that it provides those who must assess the corporate interest (primarily the corporate bodies, but also the courts and even third parties dealing with the company) with a reference which is clearer and more certain than the broad interpretations regarding the corporate interest.[102, 103] In addition, it is an invitation to the public authorities to take action themselves if they find it advisable to provide a greater protection of other parties (or values) involved in the company operations.[104] After all, the authorities cannot (only) rely on the executors of the company contract (particularly the company's management) and possibly the courts to govern society, as implied by the broad interpretations regarding the corporate interest.[105] *De lege lata* and in the existing Belgian corporate governance landscape, this would probably not only imply a lack of realism and even naivety, but would also conflict with the just and democratic viewpoint that the choice of the interests which must be taken into consideration, the determination of their weight and their mutual weighing is primarily a political process.

In summary, it can be established that the debate on narrow *versus* broad corporate interests, at least among lawyers in Belgium, cannot be reduced to a right *versus* left, capitalist or not, neo-liberal *versus* socialist, contradiction. The supporters of the so-called narrow view do not advocate blind profit-maximisation and 'freedom means happiness'. The admittedly growing group of supporters of the broad view generally do not plead for any fundamental reform of corporate law according to the Rhenan or stakeholder-oriented model (entailing co-management for employees, direct rights of claim concerning company matters for stakeholders, etc.).

The central question in the Belgian debate is not whether stakeholders deserve protection (and thus whether they must always be defeated when their interests are weighed against the collective profit interests of the shareholders), but whether they should receive it through the boardroom (where they usually do not have a seat), and thus through the corporate interest.

This leads *a fortiori* to the conclusion that in Belgium, there is *de lege lata* no legal ground, nor any support in legal doctrine or case law, to justify blind profit maximisation, let alone that this would be imposed.

4. CONCLUSION: IT IS THE PEOPLE THAT MAY BE PSYCHOPATHS, NOT COMPANIES

Our concluding remarks can be plain and simple. If greed, materialising amongst other ways via an over-focus on short-term profit making and an obsession with ever rising stock prices, is one of the causes of the worldwide financial and economic crisis we are enduring, this is not because companies are psychopathic creatures that are compelled by corporate law to further just one goal: making their shareholders as rich as possible, no matter what the consequences may be. There seems to be no such rule of corporate law in the US and there certainly is none in Belgium (although shareholder primacy seems to be more strongly embedded in Belgian statutory law). Indeed, even if companies and their corporate bodies are under a duty to always act in the best interests of the company, and even if the corporate interest is *de lege lata* (as was very recently endorsed by the Belgian Court of Cassation) still to be defined in a narrow sense, this duty leaves enough leeway and discretion to take into account other interests than the (dynamic and future-oriented) collective profit interests of the shareholders. And where such other (stakeholders') interests threaten to be insufficiently protected (and be outweighed in their balancing against the collective profit interest), either common law or the (corporate) legislator may come to rescue and actually impose the furtherance of these stakeholders' interests.

Hence, if some corporations, corporate directors or executives and shareholders have given proof of psychopathic behaviour, they cannot hide themselves behind the rule of shareholders' primacy as a justification. The only persons responsible for such behaviour are human beings.

Endnotes

* Alain François is a Professor at the Free University of Brussels and an Attorney at the Brussels Bar. Koen Byttebier is a Professor at the Free University of Brussels and an Attorney at the Brussels and Ghent Bars.

1. e.g. J.G. Taft, *Stewardship. Lessons learned from the lost culture of Wall Street*, Hoboken NJ, Wiley, 2012, pp. 32–34.
2. J. Bakan, *The corporation. The pathological pursuit of profit and power*, New York, Free Press, 2005, pp. 56–59.
3. See also for this metaphor *Louis K. Liggett Co. et al. v Lee, Comptroller et al.*, 288 U.S. 517 (1933) 548, 567, where US Supreme Court justice Louis Brandeis called the public corporation a 'Frankenstein monster which states have created by their corporation law'.
4. Cf. the title (and the argument of) the remarkable book by L. Stout, *The Shareholder Value Myth. How putting shareholders first harms investors, corporations, and the public*, San Francisco, BK, 2012, 134 p.
5. *Dodge v Ford Motor Co.*, 170 *N.W.* 668 (Mich. 1919) ('There should be no confusion [...] a business corporation is organised and carried on primarily for the profit of the stockholders. The powers of the directors are to be employed for that end').
6. See A.A. Berle, 'Corporate powers as powers in trust', 44 *Harvard Law Review* 1049 (1931); E.M. Dodd, 'For whom are corporate managers trustees?', 45 *Harvard Law Review* 1145 (1932); A.A. Berle, 'For whom corporate managers are trustees: a note', 45 *Harvard Law Review* 1365 (1932).
7. A.A. Berle, *The 20th century capitalist revolution*, New York, Harcourt Brace, 1954, p. 169.
8. See L. Stout, *supra* note 4, pp. 16–18; S. Rousseau, 'La *Stakeholder Theory*: émergence et réception dans la gouvernance d'entreprise en Amérique du Nord', in C. Champaud (ed.), *L'entreprise dans la société du 21e siècle*, Brussels, Larcier, 2013, (111) 113–114.
9. M. Friedman, 'The social responsibility of business is to increase its profits', *New York Times Magazine*, 13 September 1970, p. 32, cited by L. Stout, *supra* note 4, p. 18.
10. M.C. Jensen and W.H. Meckling, 'Theory of the firm: managerial behaviour, agency costs and ownership structure', 3(4) *Journal of Financial Economics* 305 (1976). For a short (and critical) overview of this theory, see K. Byttebier, *Het vijandige overnamebod*, Antwerp, Maklu, 1993, pp. 92 ff and 661 ff; see also A. François, *Het vennootschapsbelang in het Belgische vennootschapsrecht. Inhoud & grondslagen*, Antwerp, Intersentia, 1999, nos. 68–69.
11. Although this hypothesis – which holds that as capital markets are efficient, all relevant information to determine the value of a listed company can be assumed to be reflected in the price of its shares – has at some point even been embraced by the US Supreme Court (see *Basic Incorporated v Levinson*, 108 S. Ct. 978; L.Ed.2d 194 (1988)), several corporate scandals have proven that stock prices do not always reflect the company's true value. This has brought Lynn Stout to (colourfully) state that 'if the efficient capital market hypothesis is not dead, it is at least seriously wounded' (L. Stout, *supra* note 4, p. 65).
12. See L. Stout, *supra* note 4, pp. 33–46; see also L.L. Lan and L. Heracleous, 'Rethinking agency theory: the view from law', 35 *Academy of Management Review* 294, 301–302; A. François, *Het vennootschapsbelang in het Belgische vennootschapsrecht*, nos. 69 and 398.

13. H. Hansmann and R. Kraakman, 'The end of history for corporate law', 89 *Georgetown Law Journal* 439 (2001).
14. Entailing the demise of some giant public corporations such as Enron and Worldcom, as well as the collapse of Premier League (investment) banks such as Lehman Brothers.
15. Like the Deepwater Horizon disaster (oil well blowout in the Gulf of Mexico) causing enormous ecological and economical damage mainly as a result of BP's short-sighted ignoring of safety procedures in an attempt to cut costs (see L. Stout, *supra* note 4, pp. 1–2), or the 'psychopathic' behaviour of General Motors causing one of its customers and her children horrible and disfiguring second- and third-degree burns (GM had calculated that it could save $6.19 per automobile if it did *not* alter the design of one of its automobile models to avoid the risk of explosion of the fuel tank in case of crashes; see J. Bakan, *supra* note 2, pp. 61–65).
16. See also the captivating work by T. Jackson, *Prosperity without growth. Economics for a finite planet*, Earthscan, London, 2009, 264 p.
17. Even the so-called green economy is already being called a myth. See A. Kenis and M. Lievens, *De mythe van de groene economie. Valstrik, verzet, alternatieven*, Berchem-Antwerp, EPO, 2012, 336 p.
18. See W. Clark Jr. and E. Babson, 'How benefit corporations are redefining the purpose of business corporations', 38 *Wm Mitchell Law Review* 817, 819 ff (2012).
19. W. Clark Jr., L. Vranka et al., *White Paper. The need and rationale for the benefit corporation: why it is the legal form that best addresses the needs of social entrepreneurs, investors, and, ultimately, the public*, http://benefitcorp.net/for-attorneys/benefit-corp-white-paper (18 January 2013), especially Appendix C; D. Brakman Reiser, 'Benefit corporations – A sustainable form of organization', 46 *Wake Forest Law Review* 591.
20. Indeed, there seems to be debate about the degree of shareholder primacy; according to some authors, the duty to maximise shareholders' profits leaves considerable discretion to pursue other purposes or even the public interest. See E. Elhauge, 'Sacrificing corporate profits in the public interest', 80(3) *New York University Law Review* 733 (2005). According to Brakman Reiser, this debate creates legal uncertainty, as well as practical obstacles for those who want to pursue a dual mission (production of profits and social good). The benefit corporation statutes form a remedy by not only permitting, but also requiring the articulation of a dual mission. D. Brakman Reiser, *supra* note 19, pp. 608–610.
21. Company with a social purpose (*vennootschap met een sociaal oogmerk/société à finalité social*), as governed by sections 661–669 of the Belgian Companies Code.
22. W. Clark Jr., L. Vranka et al., *supra* note 19, Appendix C, II, 2.
23. Ibid., Appendix C, II, 2–4.
24. Ibid., Appendix C, III, 6.
25. Ibid., pp. 2–3 and Appendix C, III, 8–9.
26. See the handy map on http://benefitcorp.net/.
27. For a critique of this – according to some, false – premise that underlies the *benefit corporations* legislation, see M. Underberg, 'Benefit Corporations vs. "Regular" Corporations. A Harmful Dichotomy', http://blogs.law.harvard.edu/corpgov/2012/05/13/benefit-corporations-vs-regular-corporations (see also hereinafter).
28. See §201 'Corporate purposes' of the Model Benefit Corporation Legislation, which can be found on http://benefitcorp.net/for-attorneys/model-legislation.

29. Compare with the so-called *other constituency statutes,* existing in more than half of the states (but not in Delaware, for example), that merely permit (but do not impose) corporate directors to consider the interests of constituencies other than shareholders when making decisions (whereby some of these laws are limited to a take-over context). See W. CLARK JR., L. VRANKA et al., *supra* note 19, pp. 9–10.
30. See §301 (a) 'Standard of conduct for directors' of the Model Benefit Corporation Legislation, which reads as follows:
'(a) Consideration of interests. – In discharging the duties of their respective positions and in considering the best interests of the benefit corporation, the board of directors, committees of the board, and individual directors of a benefit corporation:
(1) shall consider the effects of any action or inaction upon:
  (i) the shareholders of the benefit corporation;
  (ii) the employees and work force of the benefit corporation, its subsidiaries, and its suppliers;
  (iii) the interests of customers as beneficiaries of the general public benefit or specific public benefit purposes of the benefit corporation;
  (iv) community and societal factors, including those of each community in which offices or facilities of the benefit corporation, its subsidiaries, or its suppliers are located;
  (v) the local and global environment;
  (vi) the short-term and long-term interests of the benefit corporation, including benefits that may accrue to the benefit corporation from its long-term plans and the possibility that these interests may be best served by the continued independence of the benefit corporation; and
  (vii) the ability of the benefit corporation to accomplish its general public benefit purpose and any specific public benefit purpose; and
(2) may consider:
  [(i) the interests referred to in [cite constituencies provision of the business corporation law if it refers to constituencies not listed above]; and
  (ii)] other pertinent factors or the interests of any other group that they deem appropriate; but
(3) need not give priority to a particular interest or factor referred to in paragraph (1) or (2) over any other interest or factor unless the benefit corporation has stated in its articles of incorporation its intention to give priority to certain interests or factors related to its accomplishment of its general public benefit purpose or of a specific public benefit purpose identified in its articles.'
At the same time, however, directors receive protection against claims by any other persons than the company itself (acting directly or derivatively) (§305. Right of action); the benefit corporation at its turn cannot be held liable for monetary damages for any failure of the benefit corporation to pursue or create general public benefit or a specific public benefit (§305, (b)). Those are reasons why proponents of the Stakeholder Theory still categorise the benefit corporation as shareholder-centred. See S. ROUSSEAU, *supra* note 8, p. 130.
31. See §401 'Preparation of an annual benefit report' of the Model Benefit Corporation Legislation.
32. See D. BRAKMAN REISER, *supra* note 19, pp. 599–603. See as far as B Lab is concerned: www.bcorporation.net.

33. See Office of the Regulator of Community Interest Companies: information and guidance notes, Chapter 11. See also S.P. Kamerbeek, 'De maatschappelijke onderneming naar Amerikaans model. De Benefit Corporation onder de loep', 7 *Tijdschrift Ondernemingsrecht* 300, 303–304 (2012).
34. See Office of the Regulator of Community Interest Companies: information and guidance notes, Chapter 6; for example: on dissolution of the CIC any surplus assets must be transferred to another asset locked body once all liabilities have been met. Article 661, first paragraph, 9° BCC provides in a similar rule for the Belgian VSO.
35. At the same time, however, such directors receive significant protections against claims by shareholders that challenge disinterested decisions, as well as broad protection against claims based on interests other than those of shareholders. See Sections 365 (b) and (c) of the Delaware General Corporation Law.
36. Sections 366 (b) and (c) of the Delaware General Corporation Law.
37. D. Brakman Reiser, *supra* note 19, pp. 624–625 ('Leaving all content to unregulated standard-setters and providing little guidance or enforcement apparatus for midstream decision-making, however, does not do enough to ensure benefit corporations can enforce a dual mission over time').
38. M. Underberg, *supra* note 27 ('The broader interests of responsible corporate governance are ill-served by creating a false dichotomy between "good" and "bad" companies based on the law that governs their conduct rather than on the choices made by those who run them. There is no legal reason that all companies can't consider a wide range of interests in order to make responsible corporate decisions. Nor is there reason B Corp advocates should provide them with excuses not to do so by overstating the limitations placed on directorial discretion by existing law. It is also unfortunate that this rationale is now enshrined in the legislative histories of the B Corp laws, which could have unintended consequences in future court rulings further defining directors' fiduciary obligations').
39. L. Stout, *supra* note 4, p. 25.
40. See besides L. Stout, *supra* note 4, p. 134, also from the same author: L. Stout, 'Bad and Not-so-Bad Arguments for Shareholder Primacy', Cornell Law Faculty Publications Paper, 2002, 448 (http://scholarship.law.cornell.edu/facpub/448); L. Stout, 'The toxic side effects of shareholder primacy', 161 *University of Pennsylvania Law Review* (2003), and L. Stout, 'Why we should stop teaching *Dodge v. Ford*', 3 *Virginia Law & Business Review* 163 (2008). See also the most interesting work of Leeds corporate law professor Andrew Keay, which deserves our full attention on a next occasion (inter alia: A. Keay, 'Shareholder Primacy in Corporate Law: Can it Survive? Should it Survive?', *European Company and Financial Law Review* 369 (2010) and A. Keay, *The corporate objective. Corporations, globalisation and the law series*, Edward Elgar Publishing Limited, Cheltenham, 2011, 360 p.).
41. *Dodge v Ford Motor Co.*, 170 N.W. 668 (Mich. 1919).
42. Stout even speaks of 'mealy mouthed dicta', in the light of the use of the disqualifier 'primarily'. L. Stout, *supra* note 4, p. 26. See also E. Elhauge, *supra* note 20, pp. 772–775.
43. The focus of Stout's critical research indeed lies on the public corporation (or what we would call the listed companies here). She seems to have fewer problems with shareholder primacy in 'closely held companies' (L. Stout, *supra* note 4, p. 110), probably because she (quite rightly) assumes that by definition, the controlling shareholders of those companies do not succumb so easily to the pressure of aiming for short-term profit-making.

Furthermore, it appears that the rights of shareholders are less sharply defined in American public corporations than in closely held corporations: for example, they have no legal power to demand dividends. This allows Stout to establish that even in that respect, shareholder primacy (currently defined as the power of the shareholders) is less pronounced in public corporations. Note that the shareholders in listed companies under Belgian law certainly have no fewer and, if anything, even more rights than those in non-listed companies.

44. L. Stout, *supra* note 4, p. 29. Stout defines the business judgment rule as follows: 'in brief, the business judgment rule holds that, so long as a board of directors is not tainted by personal conflicts of interest and makes a reasonable effort to become informed, courts will not second-guess the board's decisions about what is best for the company – even when those decisions seem to harm shareholder value'. See also H. De Wulf, *Taak en loyauteitsplicht van het bestuur in de naamloze vennootschap*, Antwerp, Intersentia, pp. 476 ff. Although the business judgment rule resembles the technique used by Belgian courts known as 'marginal control', there are considerable differences between both. Ibid., pp. 478–479.
45. This is known as the Revlon-duty referring at the Delaware case of *Revlon, Inc. v MacAndrews & Forbes Holdings, Inc.*, 506 A.2d 173 (Del. 1986).
46. And as long as the directors do not use the corporate assets and earnings for themselves (duty of loyalty).
47. L. Stout, *supra* note 4, p. 31; E. Elhauge, *supra* note 20, p. 733.
48. L. Stout, *supra* note 4, pp. 9–10 and 101–102; E. Elhauge, *supra* note 20, pp. 800–801. See also J. Bakan, *supra* note 1, p. 60 ('As a psychopathic creature, the corporation can neither recognize nor act upon moral reasons to refrain from harming others').
49. Whereas in 1960, shares were still retained for an average of eight years, the average in 2010 would only be approximately four months. L. Stout, *supra* note 4, p. 66.
50. L. Stout, *supra* note 4, p. 111, citing Iman Anabtawi.
51. Ibid., p. 115.
52. Ibid., p. 113. Stout also levels sharp criticism at initiatives of employers, the SEC, or corporations themselves for granting more power to the shareholders (for example, through staggered boards or dual classes of shares).
53. See J.-P. Paillusseau, 'Les fondements du droit modern des societies', J.C.P. 1984, Ed. G., I, no. 3148, no. 10. See for a summary of the theory of functionalism A. François, *Het vennootschapsbelang in het Belgische vennootschapsrecht,* nos. 74–82.
54. Vereniging zonder winstoogmerk (VZW)/association sans but lucratif (ASBL).
55. K. Geens and M. Wyckaert, *Beginselen van Belgisch Privaatrecht IV, Verenigingen en vennootschappen, Deel II, De Vennootschap, A. Algemeen Deel*, Mechelen, Kluwer, 2011, pp. 222 ff, esp. no. 127.
56. A. François, *Het vennootschapsbelang in het Belgische vennootschapsrecht,* nos. 149–151, esp. footnote 784.
57. While there is considerable debate on the contractual, institutional, functional or structural character of the company, we believe the contractual view still rests on solid statutory grounds. See for example the (general) definition of a company in article 1, first paragraph BCC: 'A company is established by means of a *contract* based on which two or more persons agree to contribute something with the object of exercising one or more accurately described activities and with the purpose to provide the shareholders with a direct or indirect patrimonial advantage' and article 3, §1 BCC: 'The companies

are governed by the *agreements* between parties, civil law and, as far as commercial companies are concerned, by the special law of commerce' (free translations; emphasis added). See on this debate, A. François, *Het vennootschapsbelang in het Belgische vennootschapsrecht,* nos. 41–88. See for a critique, arguing that the statutory definition of the 'company', and more generally, the unique (contractual) model of the company no longer fits, especially for listed companies: X. Dieux, 'Les structures élémentaires de la société: "la trahison des images" (à l'occasion du 10ième anniversaire du Code des societies', in *10 jaar Wetboek van Vennootschappen*, Mechelen, Kluwer, 2011, p. 53; *contra* K. Geens and M. Wyckaert, *Beginselen van Belgisch Privaatrecht IV, Verenigingen en vennootschappen, Deel II, De Vennootschap, A. Algemeen Deel,* pp. 38–39, no. 15.

58. A. François, 'De grondvoorwaarden van het vennootschapscontract', in *De oprichting van vennootschappen en de opstartfase van ondernemingen* (Recht en Onderneming, deel 8), B. Tilleman, A. Benoit-Moury, O. Caprasse and M. Thirion (eds.), *De oprichting van vennootschappen en de opstartfase van ondernemingen*, Bruges, Die Keure, 2003, (153) 192–194.
59. Comp. Professor Stout's criticism on the shareholders' profit interest, that she calls 'the lowest possible common human denominator' (L. Stout, *supra* note 4, pp. 9–10 and 101–102). Besides the fact that the common interest is an explicit statutory term, it does not need to lead to the kind of selfish and ruthless money-driven behaviour that Stout rightfully disapproves (see below).
60. A. François, *Vennootschapsbelang*, nos. 183–189. As the doctrine of objective good faith garnered a following, the duty to participate in (and execute) a company (contract) in the common interest, would degenerate to being simply one of the many standards of conduct for parties, driven by good faith. Ibid., nos. 190 et seq.
61. Although the duty of defending the common interest (narrow corporate interest) has become dissociated from (meanwhile objective) good faith, the relationship between the two, however, has remained. See A. François, *Vennootschapsbelang*, no. 556.
62. K. Geens and M. Wyckaert, *De vennootschap. A. Algemeen deel*, p. 234.
63. See the useful 'Werkstuk ingediend door de minister (van justitie)', *Parl. St.*, Senate, 1993–94, 1086/4, 149.
64. See Article 663 BCC, providing amongst others in a cause for judicial dissolution. Note that there is no such requirement as a third-party standard as is the case in the US benefit corporation.
65. See for a general description A. François, *Vennootschapsbelang*, nos. 431–439.
66. The '*statutory speciality*' of the company is associated with the corporate purpose described in the Articles of Association; in principle, the company can only be legally represented within the limits of the corporate purpose. This determines the (civil or commercial) activities that can be developed by the company and by which the legal purpose (profit distribution objective) will be pursued.
67. The legal speciality of the VSO is associated with the profit allocation objective.
68. See very recently: P.A. Foriers and A. François, 'Een nieuwe kijk op enkele klassieke dichotomieën in het vennootschapsrecht/Un nouveau regard sur quelques dichotomies classiques en droit des sociétés', *De modernisering van het vennootschapsrecht/La modernisation du droit des sociétés*, Larcier, Brussels, 2014, no. 6, 29.
69. See Cass. 30 September 2005, *Arr. Cass.* 2005, p. 1777; *Pas.* 2005, no. 470; *T.B.H.* 2006, p. 1028, note P.A. Foriers; *R.P.S.* 2010, 213, note A. François.

70. P.A. Foriers and A. François, *supra* note 68, no. 7, 30–32. The importance of the '*statutory speciality*' has also reduced greatly, especially for companies with limited liability. Ibid., nos. 6 and 7.
71. That has, as stated, been made clear in the definition of the company in article1 BCC.
72. See for a plea concerning further easing, in the name of legal certainty, P.A. Foriers and A. François, *supra* note 68, no. 7, 30–32.
73. Like for example the provision of security (caution, mortgage, etc.) by the company to the benefit of the creditors of another company. See for other examples, B. Tilleman, *Bestuur van vennootschappen*, Bruges, Die Keure, 2005, pp. 597 ff.
74. See for example article 454 BCC, as far as the public limited company (NV) is concerned.
75. See former article 1859 Civil Code, now article 46 BCC.
76. In his PhD dissertation, one of the authors of this chapter has argued that such statutory base may be found in article 19, first § of the Companies Code (former article 1833, first § of the Civil Code), which reads as follows: 'Each company requires a lawful object and must be concluded in the common interest of the parties' (translation). This article is mandatory law. See A. François, *Het vennootschapsbelang in het Belgische vennootschapsrecht. Inhoud en grondslagen*, Antwerp, Intersentia, 1999, 795 p. Parliamentary proposals, introduced in the wake of the financial crisis, to provide in a (broad) statutory definition of the concept of corporate interest have not been successful (yet?). See Proposal of 25 March 2009 by Mr Philippe Mahoux and others, *Senate*, Session 2008–2009, no. 4-1247/1 and Proposal of 11 February 2009 by Mrs Valérie Déom and others, *Chamber of Representatives*, Session 2008–2009, Doc. 52, no. 1805/001 (corporate interest is 'the interest of the enterprise which is organized as a legal person with its own legal autonomy to sustainably pursue its corporate object, in the common interest of its shareholders and its other stakeholders' (free translation)). See also Report of the Reflection Group on the Future of EU Company Law, Brussels, 5 April 2011, pp. 36–38, proposing an EU Directive or Recommendation with the aim to require (or recommend) that national legislators allow companies in the EU to amend their Articles of Association to reflect that the overall goal of the company is the long term viability and continuity of the enterprise. This proposal has not been implemented in the latest Action Plan of the European Commission, though; see Communication COM/2012/0740 of 12 December 2012 (Action Plan: European company law and corporate governance – a modern legal framework for more engaged shareholders and sustainable companies).
77. See for example Y. De Cordt, 'Les stakeholders dans les Codes de Corporate Governance', *R.P.S.* 2005, p. 54 and Y. De Cordt, *L'intérêt social comme vecteur de la responsabilité sociétale*, Academia-Bruylant, Louvain-la-Neuve, 2008, 156 p.; see also the inspiring work of X. Dieux, 'Shareholdership v. stakeholdership: what else?', in *Tendensen in het bedrijfsrecht. Corporate governance: keurslijf of sleutel tot success?*, Antwerp, Kluwer, 2010, p. 107; X. Dieux, 'Droits, pouvoirs et responsabilités des actionnaires et des autres 'parties prenantes', in X. Dieux and D. Willermain (eds.), *Droit des sociétés*, Bruylant, Brussels, 2012, p. 7; J.-M. Gollier, 'Corporate social responsibility through the prism of company law', in *Company Law and CSR: New Legal and Economic Challenges (analysed from a Comparative Perspective)*, Bruylant, Brussels (forthcoming).
78. Cass. 28 November 2013, *TRV* 2014, 286–288, where the Court held that: 'the interest of the company is determined by the collective profit interest of its current and future

shareholders' (free translation). While this definition was given in the specific context of an inalienability clause (article 510 BCC indeed provides that such clauses are valid insofar as, besides being limited in time, they are always justified on the basis of the interest of the company), there seems to be no reason why it should be limited to this context.

79. The Court of Cassation has made that very clear in its definition. See previous footnote.

80. See A. François, *Het vennootschapsbelang in het Belgische vennootschapsrecht*, no. 361. It is true, however, that the classic narrow view on the corporate interest left very little room to take the interests of the stakeholders into consideration. Ibid., 364.

81. See A. François, *Het vennootschapsbelang in het Belgische vennootschapsrecht*, nos. 366–382.

82. See for example article 616 BCC obliging companies to set up a legal reserve fund with part of their net profit; the articles 636–644 BCC (proceedings of exclusion and withdrawal of shareholders in case of conflict) equally pursue continuity.

83. This representation must be preferred to another representation, which has a significant number of adherents in modern legal doctrine and which extends the definition of the narrow corporate interest to the *profit interests of future shareholders*. See A. François, *Het vennootschapsbelang in het Belgische vennootschapsrecht*, nos. 366 et seq. The latter representation has been used in the definition of the corporate interest by the Court of Cassation in its opinion of 28 November 2013, though: 'the interest of the company is determined by the collective profit interest of its current and future shareholders' (translation). The referral to both the current and future shareholders' profit interests nevertheless gives the corporate bodies and other executors of the corporate contract sufficient leeway to determine how to best spread the profit sharing over time (thereby possibly taking into consideration the interests of different types of shareholders as well as other stakeholders, as we shall see hereafter).

84. The risk of short termism has certainly not diminished (Report of the Reflection Group on the Future of EU Company Law, Brussels, 5 April 2011, pp. 36–37, for a finding of the contrary), especially in companies listed on a stock exchange that are increasingly confronted with shareholders showing little or no loyalty towards the company, which is considered as a mere financial investment opportunity. That is why voices are raised to introduce legal mechanisms to reward loyalty. See C. Clottens, 'Can't buy me love? – Over de beloning van trouwe aandeelhouders', *T.R.V.* 2013, 5. See also Report of the Reflection Group on the Future of EU Company Law, Brussels, 5 April 2011, p. 46 ('In order to favour long term share ownership and shareholder commitment companies' articles should be allowed to provide for long term shareholders' preferential treatment. These benefits might consist of (a) enhanced voting rights, (b) higher dividends'). The overly focus on (and obsession with) stock prices has been pointed out as one of the causes of the financial crisis; see X. Dieux, 'Droits, pouvoirs et responsabilités des actionnaires et des autres "parties prenantes"', pp. 16–17.

85. Or in a single-person company, the interpretation thereof by the sole shareholder.

86. This 'marginal' control leaves the companies, their directors and executives (as well as the other executors of the corporate contract) with considerable room for appreciation when considering the corporate interest in a given case. This is at least reminiscent of the business judgment rule, applied by US courts (see *supra*).

87. The individual interests of the shareholders not discounted in the corporate interest will be weighed against the corporate interest, as the case may be (also see below). As some authors like Lynn Stout (US) and Xavier Dieux (Belgium) have rightly pointed out,

even the profit interests of the shareholders may differ, notably in time. The modern narrow vision of the corporate interest as well as the marginal control practised by the courts leave room for the executors of the company contract (especially the company acting via its corporate bodies) to weigh these profit interests while determining the collective profit interest.

88. See J. Paillusseau, 'Les fondements du droit moderne des sociétés', J.C.P., 1984, Ed. G., I, no. 3148 and the summary of the theory of the Rennes School with A. François, *Het vennootschapsbelang in het Belgische vennootschapsrecht,* nos. 74–82; see also no. 320 et seq. (typology of the different partial interests).
89. A. François, *Het vennootschapsbelang in het Belgische vennootschapsrecht,* nos. 332–338.
90. Compare this with the US, where shareholders' rights and powers are more limited in public corporations, *supra* note 43. Relevant in this respect is also that in Belgium, even listed companies are in almost all cases in so-called firm hands, meaning that they are controlled by one or more controlling (often also majority) shareholders.
91. This led Xavier Dieux to speak of a 'retour à l'actionnaire', thereby referring to several initiatives of the European Commission to (re)strengthen the rights of the shareholders (especially in listed companies; see for example Directive 2007/36 of 11 July 2007 on the exercise of certain rights of shareholders in listed companies, *Official Journal of the European Union*, 14 July 2007, L 184/17; this Directive was implemented into Belgian company law by the Act of 20 December 2010 on the exercise of certain rights of shareholders in listed companies, Belgian State Gazette, 18 April 2011, 24068, whereby certain rights were extended to closely held corporations). X. Dieux, 'Droits, pouvoirs et responsabilités des actionnaires et des autres "parties prenantes"', p. 17.
92. A. François, *Het vennootschapsbelang in het Belgische vennootschapsrecht,* nos. 339–340.
93. A. François, *Het vennootschapsbelang in het Belgische vennootschapsrecht,* nos. 341–346.
94. A. François, *Het vennootschapsbelang in het Belgische vennootschapsrecht,* nos. 347–350.
95. Also see the list of so-called external interests of P. Van Schilfgaarde, *Van de B.V. en de N.V.*, Arnhem, Gouda Quint, 1992, pp. 28–29, no. 6 ('Apart from the concern interest, the interests of creditors, suppliers, consumers, possibly the region's or country's interests, more abstract interests such as housing under certain conditions, the environment, the desired social development, employment, preservation of national identity, etc., come to mind' (translation)).
96. For a specific case, see the so-called *General* sentence of the Brussels Court of Appeals, Brussels (summary proceedings), 1 March 1988, *T.R.V.* 1988, 125 and particularly the note of K. Geens, where the Court judged that the Board of Directors of Société Générale could legally take into account '*les intérêts de la Belgique et* [...] *sa politique industrielle*', when assessing whether a planned capital increase was in keeping with the corporate interest. More generally, the Court believed that '*une sociéte de droit belge peut légitimement, dans l'élaboration de sa stratégie tenir compte des intérêts nationaux, notamment quant à l'emploi et au développement de l'industrie.*' According to the Court, it must only be verified whether such an appreciation is not unreasonable and whether it transcends the private interest of directors. More recently, the same court was a lot more shareholders-minded when assessing the case of the rescue and dismantling of the Fortis group; see Brussels' Court of Appeals, 12 December 2008, *J.T.* 2009, 62; J.-M. Gollier, 'Corporate social responsibility through the prism of company law', in *Company Law and CSR: New Legal and Economic Challenges (analysed from a Comparative Perspective)*, Bruylant, Brussels (forthcoming).

97. It essentially concerns the question whether companies have a 'corporate social responsibility'. See e.g. the remarkable book of J.E. Parkinson, *Corporate Power and Responsibility. Issues in the theory of company law*, Oxford, Clarendon Press, 1993, pp. 260 ff.
98. A. François, *Het vennootschapsbelang in het Belgische vennootschapsrecht,* nos. 384–385.
99. A. François, *Het vennootschapsbelang in het Belgische vennootschapsrecht,* nos. 386–391 (arguing that both the BCC and other statutory law protect stakeholders' interests; furthermore, showing that the corporate interests can only be strived at within the boundaries of mandatory law and that common law rules like for example the general principle that forbids the abuse of rights also bring about protection of stakeholders and hence put constraints on the discretion of the companies and the corporate bodies to further the collective profit interest of the shareholders).
100. Note that this view therefore comes close to the UK concept of the 'enlightened shareholder'. See A. Keay, 'Shareholder Primacy in Corporate Law: Can it Survive? Should it Survive?', *European Company and Financial Law Review*, 2010, 369 et seq.; see also X. Dieux, 'Shareholdership v. stakeholdership: what else?', p. 120.
101. A similar evolution is taking place with the (soft law) rules and recommendations of corporate governance, which are also expected to slowly invade the (hard) law. This process will probably be fastened due to the fact that the rule of *comply or explain* has been endorsed in the BCC. See A. François and W. Van Rie, '*Pro*-actief vennootschapsrecht. *Cre*atief met statuten', in J. Vananroye, J.-J. Ackaert and het Vlaams Pleitgenootschap bij de balie te Brussel (eds.), *Proactief ondernemingsrecht*, Antwerp–Cambridge, Intersentia, 2013, (133) 147–148, no. 25.
102. Typical of the broad definitions is that they assume that the corporate interest is the product of the partial interests, in one way or the other. However, they do not give a conclusive answer as to how the corporate interest must be distilled from the partial interests in and around the company.
103. Considering the complexity and factuality of the corporate interest and the policy margin of the company contract executors which must be observed when it is concretised, this reference remains relative in the narrow interpretation. After all, the corporate interest is and remains a vague standard, regardless of its interpretation. And, of course, also the profit interests of the shareholders can be very heterogeneous.
104. Such action does not necessarily have to entail the passing of new mandatory legislation. See e.g. the proposed action plan by the Federal Government regarding the promotion of social corporate responsibility (*Federaal Actieplan. Maatschappelijk verantwoord ondernemen in België*, ICDO, 25 October 2006).
105. Indeed, we look at the discourse of business leaders and their (co-)authored corporate governance codes with the necessary scepticism, that the protection of stakeholder interests must occur through due consideration within the corporate interest (instead of across the corporate interest). Moreover, the question arises whether this discourse will be maintained, with the prospect that the infringement of the corporate interest (as a statutorily defined legal concept) and of corporate governance recommendations could lead to directors' liability under article 528 of the Belgian Companies Code (and not just indirectly via the rule of *comply or explain*) (see the legislative proposals of 2009, *supra* note 76).

ALL ANIMALS ARE EQUAL BUT SOME ARE MORE EQUAL THAN OTHERS*

Inequalities in (Re)financing Mechanisms

Régine Feltkamp**

1. INTRODUCTION

The financial crisis that started since the middle of 2007 has painfully demonstrated how lack of confidence can lead to interbank financing drying up and the serious consequences thereof for the financial system and the economy. To reinforce the financial system, diverse measures have since been taken or are in the course of being designed at a European and national level with a view to avoiding major disruption in the future caused by the failure of large financial institutions. The interventions range from prudential measures (increased capital and liquidity requirements, reorganisation of supervision, measures regarding recovery and resolution (including bail-in tools),[1] reinforcement of deposit protection, increased business organisation requirements, etc.) to private law measures such as tools to ensure better (re)financing conditions for financial institutions. As regards the latter, the Belgian legislator adopted in the summer of 2012 two acts both of which aim at facilitating for (certain) financial institutions the use of receivables in the context of financing transactions, whether as underlying value of other instruments or not. On the one hand a legal framework was adopted to enable the issue of Belgian covered bonds (the Belgian Covered Bonds Act, BCBA)[2] and, on the other hand, an act concerning different measures to facilitate the mobilisation of receivables in the financial sector was passed (the Mobilisation of Receivables Act, MRA).[3]

The BCBA aims at allowing credit institutions to improve their long-term financing sources and avoid liquidity problems due to maturity mismatch[4] by creating an adequate legal framework for the issue of a specific kind of debt instruments – covered bonds issued by credit institutions – and the protection of the holders of these instruments.[5] The MRA complements this framework by introducing specific provisions that favour transactions on receivables, which form – as explained later – an essential component of covered bond issues. However, the scope of the MRA is not limited to the mobilisation of receivables in the context of covered bonds. The MRA introduces a more general framework for the mobilisation of receivables to the benefit of certain financial institutions. The justification for this specific framework is that numerous legal obstacles still impede the use of receivables, which are the main assets of financial institutions, as collateral for refinancing transactions or only allow such use at less favourable conditions.[6] According to the Belgian legislator, the financial crisis has shown the necessity for financial institutions to be able to use to the maximum extent their assets as collateral for obtaining (long-term) financing in a swift manner and at the lowest possible costs. Such refinancing via central banks of the Eurosystem proved to be crucial when managing the negative effects of the financial crisis.[7] Long-term refinancing of credit institutions at a reasonable cost is, according to the Belgian legislator, a necessity for these institutions for them to be able, in the long term, to grant credits to companies and households at reasonable costs.[8] In other words, the measures taken were mainly considered necessary to guarantee, in times of crisis, access to refinancing by the Eurosystem for financial institutions and to ensure in the interest of the general economy, a better financing to all members of society. The BCBA and the MRA thus seem to have been adopted in view of safeguarding, albeit indirectly, the interest of the whole (Belgian) community.

Both acts take for granted that credit is an indispensable instrument for economic growth and thus for social welfare and that long-term refinancing mechanisms for those entities that systematically make credit to households or companies to fund economic activity should be favoured. The tool used to secure this long-term refinancing is the introduction of a specific legal framework that promotes and facilitates the mobilisation by financial institutions of receivables. Where trust is of essence for refinancing mechanisms and the provision of collateral reinforces such trust, the step of ensuring that the main assets of a financial institution – receivables – can be mobilised in a legally secure manner to secure such financing seems logic. At the same time tough, the approach causes eyebrows to rise. Has the use of receivables in the context of structured finance and securitisation – or at least the way the financial sector has made use thereof to develop and disperse complex investment instruments perceived[9] as high-yielding but nevertheless safe opportunities – not been denounced as one of the causes, or as amplifying factor, of the financial crisis?[10] Is it then wise, taking into account this experience, to facilitate even more financing structures based on the transfer of receivables?

Prior to the BCBA and the MRA, different legislative interventions already occurred with a view to facilitate the use of certain receivables as collateral specifically for financial institutions. Both the BCBA and the MRA further introduce specific provisions only and specifically for (certain) financial institutions in deviation from the normally applicable Belgian private law principles in this respect. Thus a specific private law regime further paves the way for financial institutions. Belgium is, especially as regards covered bonds, not the only country to follow such an approach, and is in fact 'obliged' to follow this route to enable Belgian financial institutions to compete on a level playing field with financial institutions of other European jurisdictions. This approach nevertheless raises the question of whether such a specific regime to the benefit of the financial sector is a sound choice. Will such measures really, as claimed, benefit the whole community or will the fruits thereof mainly be reaped by a limited group of already powerful persons, namely the financial institutions (and their shareholders)? Additionally, to the extent the underlying motive is that numerous legal obstacles prevent the use of receivables amongst other as collateral or only against more unfavourable conditions, is it justifiable to reserve the benefits of eliminating claimed private law obstacles *only* and *specifically* for those considered by some as the 'villains' of the crisis?

With the modest aim of stimulating a reflection in this respect, the purpose of this contribution is to show how, in my opinion, the specific regime introduced by the BCBA and the MRA creates questionable inequalities. It is impossible to capture this consequence of the BCBA and the MRA without providing an explanation of the new regimes and diving into some technicalities thereof (without however being comprehensive). This is why I will, after having briefly described the legal context prior to the BCBA and the MRA (section 2), set out for the BCBA (section 3) and then for the MRA (section 4) what the main features of the specific regime are, before assessing how they create questionable preferential treatment.

I highlight upfront two limitations of my contribution. The first is that it essentially concerns the aforementioned Belgian initiatives. One may question the merits of a contribution so limited. Ensuring financial stability and the reconstruction of the financial system are indeed fundamental global problems, which require a global approach. Additionally, the BCBA and the MRA provide a Belgian solution for only one of the 'defective' components of the complex machinery of the financial system and their consequences should be assessed against the full bundle of measures taken in response to the financial crisis. Nevertheless, lending practices and the use of receivables by, amongst others, credit institutions are key elements of the financial crisis and initiatives taken in respect of these elements merit specific attention. Comparing the Belgian approach with the approach followed in other European countries in this respect is undoubtedly of great interest for assessing the options taken by the Belgian legislator. The examination of other legal systems would however require a thorough knowledge and understanding of these other legal systems and their specificities, which as a Belgian legal expert I unfortunately do not have.

Secondly, my contribution may disappoint those that expect a detailed legal analysis of both texts in light of Belgian private law. The purpose is not to provide an in-depth and comprehensive legal analysis of all applicable principles and deviations therefrom but rather to distil those points of the BCBA and MRA that merit, in my view, specific interest in the context of the proposed discussion. By doing so, certain aspects are not addressed and certain nuances may not have been captured.

2. PRECEDENTS

2.1. 1952

It is not the first time that specific private law rules have been enacted to facilitate the use of receivables by financial institutions in the context of (re)financing transactions. The trend of foreseeing a more beneficial regime for the mobilisation of receivables by financial institutions already started in 1992 with a view to facilitating securitisation. In the Belgian Mortgage Credit Act[11] specific provisions were taken up to eliminate in the context of transactions giving rise to the issue of transferable securities (i.e. securitisation operations) the costly formality of registration (*kantmelding/inscription*) to which the transfer or pledging of receivables secured by mortgages is in principle subject to pursuant to article 5 of the Belgian Mortgage Act. Then followed an Act of 6 July 1994[12] by which – amongst other changes[13] – the common law rules regarding transfer and pledging of receivables were greatly simplified, again mainly with the aim of eliminating the costly formalities to which the enforceability towards third parties of these transactions was subject.[14] Although these adaptations of the common law regime were formulated in a general manner (i.e. regardless of the qualification of the involved parties), the main purpose of this change was to facilitate (at lesser cost) the privatisation by the Belgian Government of the *Office Central du Crédit Hypothécaire*[15] and to provide a regime that would be beneficial for securitisation operations.[16] With the same purpose, the Act of 6 July 1994 also introduced changes to the Belgian Mortgage Credit Act. A further change to the Belgian Mortgage Credit Act was implemented in 1995 to ensure enforceability of collateral granted to secure future receivables and to ensure that such collateral would benefit a possible transferee.[17]

2.2. 2002–2004

Following the Directive on Financial Collateral Arrangements (DFCA),[18] and with a view to guaranteeing the stability of the financial system and limiting potential systemic risk,[19] the possibility was granted to financial institutions by the Belgian Financial Collateral Act (FCA)[20] to use financial instruments and receivables for money deposits as collateral under a simplified regime as compared to the normally applicable common law rules. The main feature of this regime consists of eliminating the requirement of fulfilling certain formalities to ensure the creation, validity and enforceability of certain collateral mechanisms (pledge structures, ownership transfer as collateral and repurchase agreements (repos)) as well as the formalities related to the realisation of the collateral in the event of default, all considered as too cumbersome (and too costly). The overall goal was to secure as much as possible the effectiveness of collateral at the lowest possible cost. Whereas the scope of the DFCA was limited to the financial sector (collateral agreements with at least the collateral taker or the collateral provider being a financial institution under prudential supervision), the Belgian legislator decided to provide for a wider scope of application. The simplified regime has thus been made applicable without distinction as to the status of the persons concerned by the collateral transaction. However this regime remains specific since it is only applicable to 'financial collateral'. Belgian law is therefore since then characterised by the classic collateral law and a simplified collateral law for those persons that detain the financial assets envisaged by the FCA, being in practice mainly financial institutions and wealthy persons.[21]

2.3. 2011

By an Act of 26 September 2011[22] the type of financial assets covered by the FCA was expanded to include bank claims[23] (*bankvorderingen/créances bancaires*) following the adaptation of the DFCA[24] which was induced by a recommendation of the European Central Bank who decided to introduce these claims as eligible collateral for Eurosystem credit operations from 1 January 2007.[25] To facilitate the mobilisation of these receivables (and to maximise the economic impact thereof) it was considered necessary to abolish or prohibit any administrative rules, such as notification and registration obligations, which would make the assignments of such claims impracticable.[26] Additionally, it was considered necessary to provide the *possibility* for debtors to validly waive their set-off rights vis-à-vis creditors, in order not to compromise the position of collateral takers, and to waive bank secrecy rules to ensure that the collateral taker has sufficient information to properly assess the value of the underlying credit claims.[27] The expansion of the DFCA was predicted to be also beneficial for consumers and debtors, as the use of bank claims as collateral could ultimately lead to more intense competition and better availability of credit.[28]

Since the adaptation in 2011 of the FCA, holders of collateral consisting of bank claims – defined as claims arising out of a loan or a credit arrangement with credit institutions, mortgage companies or persons/companies granting consumer credits[29] – do not only benefit from the direct execution possibility and increased protection in the event of insolvency proceedings or other circumstances in which the creditors have competing rights (*concursus creditorum/samenloop*). Additionally, and consistently with the amendments to the DFCA, in order to secure the rights of the security taker the *possibility* was introduced for the debtor to waive its rights to set-off, without prejudice however to rules that prohibit such waiver by consumers, such as e.g. foreseen by article 27 of the Consumer Credit Act of 12 June 1991[30] or the Act of 6 April 2010 regarding market practices and the protection of the consumer.[31] To enhance the use of bank claims as collateral, the formality of mention in a public register (*kantmelding/inscription*)[32] required for the transfer or the pledging of a bank claim secured by a mortgage or a bank claim secured by a privilege on immovable assets, has been abolished for the transfer as collateral or pledging of bank claims. The determining motivation for the elimination of this formality was not the transposition of the amendments to the DFCA but the fact that this registration formality was too costly for the main persons concerned, the financial institutions.[33] The fear was expressed during the parliamentary debates that this simplification of the rules applicable to bank claims would facilitate the development of new complex financial products. This was nevertheless refuted with the consideration that the expansion would – although the text itself does in my reading not seem to infer this conclusion – only concern limited cases, that is only bank claims arising out of an agreement on the basis of which a credit institution grants a loan or a credit *to a company for consumer credits or a mortgage company.*[34]

Notably, whereas the Belgian legislator decided to give in principle a broad scope of application to the FCA, although the DFCA is limited to financial institutions, the same approach was not followed for the amendment of the FCA in 2011. The FCA was not expanded to receivables in general but only to bank claims as defined above. Other companies or persons than those mentioned above who grant credits or loans and whish to mobilise the receivables arising therefrom, must thus fall back on the common law rules for transfer and pledging of receivables and the general rules that apply to insolvency proceedings and other circumstances of *concursus creditorum*. The formality of mention in a public register (*kantmelding/inscription*) required for the transfer or the pledging of a bank claim secured by a mortgage or a bank claim secured by a privilege on immovable assets, considered too costly for credit institutions, was also not abolished in general, thus remaining applicable in cases where such claims are not mobilised as collateral, unless a specific derogation exists.

In the meantime the adaptation in 2011 of the FCA was still deemed insufficient to allow credit institutions and other companies to make maximal use of their receivables for financing operations. This is why the BCBA and the MRA have been enacted. As explained hereafter, both texts further introduce, specifically for financial institutions, deviations from applicable principles of estate, security and insolvency law as well as from the regime applicable to the transfer and pledging of receivables.

3. REFINANCING OF CREDIT INSTITUTIONS VIA COVERED BONDS ISSUES

3.1. THE BCBA IN A NUTSHELL

3.1.1. Reservation of the best assets

Under Belgian law, in principle a person's estate serves all creditors in case of failure of the debtor.[35] Belgian law however accepts the institution of security and foresees the possibility of creating privileged positions between creditors by contract either by using immovable assets (mortgage) or moveable assets (pledge or transfer of property as security) as collateral. The BCBA introduces a legal framework that specifically allows Belgian credit institutions to pool certain receivables as collateral for long-term debt instruments, i.e. bonds. As such, covered bonds are not a new technique in the financial sector. Covered bonds have existed since the 18th century in Germany under the name *Pfandbriefe*.[36] Covered bonds are bonds – i.e. long-term debt instruments issued by an entity in large scale to raise funds under the commitment towards each bondholder to reimburse the invested capital increased with a (fixed) interest – with as specific characteristic that the payment obligations of the issuer are secured ('covered') by specific assets (i.e. receivables), the so-called 'cover-pool' assets (*dekkingswaarden*).[37] Several elements ensure this covered position of the bondholders.

First of all it is typical for covered bonds that the pool of assets is *specifically reserved* to reimburse the bondholders, generally without such assets being transferred to another entity, as is the case in a securitisation operation. The covered bonds issuer thus remains owner of this pool of assets and keeps the related risks such as in particular the risk of credit default.

Secondly, the asset pool generally concerns *good quality assets*: not any assets are included in the pool but only those assets that comply with certain quality requirements.

The third characteristic is the *special privileged position* of the bondholder. The bondholder's claim to payment by the issuer is secured by a priority right on the proceeds of the quality assets in the pool. In addition:

(1) the value of the assets in the pool is in general higher than the amount for which the bond loan has been issued ('overcollateralisation');
(2) the asset pool is dynamic: it must at all times be supplemented with new quality assets if the value of the receivables taken up in the pool decreases

(e.g. as a result of default by the debtor or as a result of a decrease of the value of the collateral attached to the concerned receivable);

(3) the bondholders benefit from a so-called dual recourse: in case of insolvency they cannot only exercise a recourse on the reserved asset pool but they also have an unsecured claim on the rest of the estate of the credit institution; and

(4) the assets in the pool are 'ring-fenced': they are segregated in such a way that the other creditors cannot exercise any claim on the assets in the pool in the event of an insolvency proceeding of the issuer.

As such covered bonds were not impossible in Belgium prior to the BCBA. The preferred position of bondholders can also be achieved by contractual arrangements ('structured covered bonds') in which case the bondholders have to rely on general contract and commercial law for their validity and enforceability towards third parties. Based on the freedom to contract, such contractual constructions are in principle available for any legal entity that can issue bonds, without specific regard to its status.

Besides some insecurity on the enforceability of such contractual structures in the event of bankruptcy or insolvency of the issuer, the downside of structured covered bonds is the transactional (i.e. legal and negotiation) costs they entail. To remedy these inconveniences different countries have over the past years issued a specific legal framework for covered bonds, generally to the benefit of financial institutions.[38] These enactments were stimulated by regulatory initiatives whereby investment restrictions imposed on certain financial institutions are relieved[39] or equity requirements are assessed more favourably[40] if the investment concerns covered bonds issued in compliance with a legal framework that guarantees the protection of the bondholder. The importance of such a legal framework has also arisen in the context of the financing programs set up via the Eurosystem since the financial crisis, in the context of which covered bonds that comply with certain legal requirements have been purchased.[41] A specific legal regime for Belgian covered bonds was thus felt to be necessary to enable the Belgian issuers to 'compete' on a level playing field with issuers in other jurisdictions where such specific legal framework exists.[42] A legal framework for Belgian covered bonds[43] was therefore put into place which is composed, on the one hand, of a prudential framework introduced by the BCBA as a specific chapter in the Act of 22 March 1993 on the statute and supervision of credit institutions (Credit Institutions Act, CIA),[44] and, on the other hand, of specific private law rules introduced by the BCBA and the MRA. Three credit institutions have already made use of it.[45]

3.1.2. *Under strict conditions and supervision*

The specific regime for covered bonds does not apply without any restrictions. In brief, the following conditions must be met for the specific regime to apply:

(1) the issuer must be a *Belgian* credit institution in the sense of the CIA; the issuing credit institution may itself subscribe to the issued covered bonds, acquire them and hold them;[46]
(2) the cover assets must consist of the receivables indicated by the legislator. A list of different categories of cover assets that can be taken up in the pool has been established with indication of the required proportions between the different types of cover assets; the cover pool must e.g. be composed for 85% out of mortgage receivables or receivables on government institutions;[47]
(3) the cover assets must represent 105% of the nominal amount of the issued *covered bonds*;[48]
(4) the cover assets must resist a liquidity test: they must be sufficiently liquid to enable the credit institution to make the unconditional payments related to the issued covered bonds for a period of six months;[49]
(5) the covered bonds may only be issued with the prior approval of the competent authority, currently still the National Bank of Belgium (NBB). A double approval mechanism is foreseen. First, a general permission should be obtained, for which the NBB verifies in general the organisational capacity of the credit institution to issue Belgian covered bonds as well as whether the financial position of the issuer, in particular its solvency, is sufficient to guarantee the interests of creditors other than the covered bondholders.[50] A second specific permission should be obtained for each issue or issue programme. The specific permission may only be given if the NBB is satisfied that the issuing credit institution disposes of the general permission and that the cover assets consist of the assets admitted by law;[51, 52]
(6) during the lifetime of the issue each cover pool must continuously ensure an overcollateralisation of 105%;[53]
(7) the credit institution issuing covered bonds must appoint for each issue or issue programme a pool monitor (*portefeuille surveillant/surveillant de portefeuille*) who must, prior to the issue of covered bonds, report to the NBB on the credit institution's compliance with the conditions regarding the cover assets[54] and the registration of assets (see below

section 4) and, after the issue, report periodically to the NBB on the compliance with the requirements;[55] and

(8) the credit institution issuing covered bonds must periodically deliver proof to the NBB that the issued bonds still comply with the legal requirements, by reporting amongst others on the cover assets and their valuation.[56]

3.1.3. Special treatment

Holders of covered bonds, issued in compliance with the above-mentioned conditions, are granted by law a specific privileged status. Whereas in some countries such privileged status is guaranteed via the set up of a separate entity (special purpose vehicle, SPV), in Belgium this status is established via a particular technique: the introduction of so-called special estates of credit institutions that are reserved to secure the payment obligations of the bondholders. As soon as a credit institution has issued Belgian covered bonds, its estate is by operation of law split in different estates. In a deviation from the principle rules of unicity of the estate of a person and of equality between creditors, except in the case of a right of privilege provided by law, as laid down in articles 7 *et seq.* of the Belgian Mortgage Act,[57] the credit institution automatically becomes the titleholder of a so-called general estate (*algemeen vermogen/patrimoine general*) and, depending on the number of issues of bond loans, of one or more special estates (*bijzondere vermogens/patrimoine spécial*) which contain the cover assets for a specific bond issue and the collaterals related thereto.[58]

Since no SPV is in principle[59] to be set up, the peculiarity of the Belgium regime is the ring-fencing of the cover assets without them being legally transferred to another (legal) person. Nevertheless, for certain aspects, the special estate is – by way of a legal fiction – treated as a separate legal person. The rights and obligations regarding transactions between 'the credit institution and the special estate'[60] must for example, during the existence of the covered bonds, be established in writing as if the special estate were a separate legal person.[61] In addition, shifting assets between the general estate and the special estates is by way of a fiction – and thus in contradiction to the fact that the same legal person remains titleholder thereof – considered as a transfer of receivables so that, amongst other things, the beneficial regime of the MRA (see section 4) can apply.[62]

A special estate counts as exclusive security for the bondholders by virtue of a series of measures prescribed by the BCBA and the MRA as a result of which a special estate is made quasi immune in case of insolvency proceedings, reorganisation measures or other circumstances of *concursum creditorum* related to the issuing credit institution. These rules imply amongst other things that:

(1) deviating from normally applicable rules, the opening of a bankruptcy procedure or the opening of a winding up procedure[63] of a credit institution that has issued covered bonds is limited to the general estate and has no consequences for the special estate(s),[64] except that the credit institution loses the administration of such special estate which is taken over by the pool administrator (*portefeuillebeheerder/gestionnaire de portefeuille*);[65] the special estate continues to exist without the liabilities covered by the special estate becoming due (whereas normally an estate is to be liquidated as a whole in the event of bankruptcy or winding up) and payments that took place related to assets contained therein, are excluded from the bankruptcy estate (i.e. they are not taken into account for the liquidation procedure);[66]
(2) the covered bondholders benefit priority payment out of the proceeds of the special estate: the other creditors of the issuing credit institution do not have, in principle, a right of recourse on the special estate, except if the proceeds of the realisation of the assets contained therein exceed the payment obligations to be fulfilled by the credit institution. In the latter case, the non-secured creditors have a right of recourse on the positive balance that remains after closure of the liquidation of the special estate concerned.[67] In addition the bankruptcy administrator may, after consultation with the NBB, request from the pool administrator that the assets for which it can be established that they are no longer necessary as cover assets, are returned to the general estate;[68]
(3) the holders of covered bonds are granted a right of recourse on the general estate of the issuing credit institution.[69] They can thus have recourse on the special estate related to the bonds they hold and in addition on the general estate, should the special estate not be sufficient (so-called 'dual recourse');[70]
(4) deviating from the general rule that a transfer of receivables is subject to a notification to or recognition by the debtor to be enforceable towards the debtor[71] as well as to a registration (*kantmelding/inscription*)[72] if receivables out of mortgage loans are concerned in order for such a transfer to be enforceable towards third parties, the enforceability towards third parties of the attribution of an asset to a special estate or

the re-allocation of an asset from a special estate to the general estate is established by a simple registration respectively de-registration in a non-public register to be held by the credit institution;[73]

(5) in the event of insolvency or other circumstance of *concursus creditorum*, the enforceability towards third parties of the attribution of an asset to a special estate can only be challenged on the basis of the so-called common *actio pauliana* (fraudulent conveyance)[74] and the specific *actio pauliana* in the case of bankruptcy;[75] the rules that normally apply in the event of bankruptcy to set aside certain acts that have been accomplished in a given period prior to the bankruptcy declaration and thus are considered suspicious ('claw-back' provisions), do not apply;[76]

(6) in a deviation from the general rule that ownership of replaceable goods (such as cash) is subject to segregation, commingling of cash collected from the cover assets after the opening of the insolvency proceedings is excluded, as they are automatically allocated to the special estate[77] and all amounts and payments related to cover assets collected after the opening of a bankruptcy proceeding or of a liquidation procedure are excluded from the general estate and exclusively allocated to the specific estate.[78] To the extent the such amounts are not identifiable at the time it is requested to allocate them to the specific estate, the rights on these amounts are replaced by rights on other unencumbered assets of the general estate of the credit institution ('real subrogation');[79]

(7) the special estate must exclusively be used for the repayment of the bondholders or other creditors mentioned in the issue conditions; this exclusive use implies that any other creditor of the credit institution is excluded from the exercise of any right on the cover assets, including the right to seize these assets.[80] According to the preparatory work, the 'exclusive use' also implies that the debtors of the receivables in the asset pool are excluded from the right to invoke certain defences (set-off and right to withhold performance).[81] In any event, the right to set-off or to withhold performance is restricted by article 6 of the MRA (see below section 4).

In respect of the privileged position of the bondholders, due account is also to be given to the proposals formulated at EU level to grant additional protection to bondholders in case of winding up of the issuing credit institution. In the context of the currently discussed proposal of a directive for a framework for the recovery and resolution of credit institutions[82] and the bail-in tools proposed by this text, the covered bonds are excluded from the application of the bail-in tools foreseen by this text (as is for the time being also the case for guaranteed deposits and other secured liabilities).[83]

3.2. THE BCBA, SOURCE OF (UN)JUSTIFIED INEQUALITIES?

With the above-mentioned legal measures the Belgian legislator ensured that holders of Belgian covered bonds benefit from a very strong legal position that as such secures their claims to a greater extent than collateral would normally do.[84] From the perspective of the covered bondholder, covered bonds are thus a safe investment. Because of their safe nature funding via covered bonds is cheaper. As said, specific provisions also favour these instruments by allowing for certain financial institutions an increase of investment limits (UCITS and insurance companies) or by providing a preferential prudential risk weighting (credit institutions) if the investments concern regulated covered bonds. The attractiveness of these instruments is thus increased for these financial institutions. In this way, a strong incentive is created for credit institutions to use this kind of long-term (re)financing mechanism and for credit institutions and financial institutions to invest in covered bonds and to provide credit institutions with the necessary long-term funding. So far, so good. But how does this regime affect other concerned persons?

The BCBA deviates significantly from the existing private law rules that would normally apply to creditors. By doing so, not only is the covered bondholder granted a privileged position compared to other creditors that goes beyond what can be achieved with contractual securities, but Belgian credit institutions are also granted a beneficial financing mechanism. The BCBA thus creates, in my opinion, inequalities that relate, on the one hand, to the privileged position conferred to the bondholders in comparison to other creditors of the issuing credit institution and, on the other hand, to the privileged position conferred to Belgian credit institutions in comparison to other companies in the context of available financing mechanisms.

These inequalities create questions as to the appropriateness of the implemented framework from a policy perspective. In addition, the framework is also questionable from a legal perspective in light of the principles of non-discrimination and equal treatment as laid down in, amongst others, articles 10 and 11 of the Belgian Constitution against which the Belgian Constitutional Court may assess legal acts.[85] As such these principles do not exclude differentiation in treatment. However differences in treatment may only be introduced if they are based on a criterion for which an objective and reasonable justification exists, which is to be assessed in light of the purpose and consequences of the concerned act.[86] The means used, i.e. unequal treatment, must be reasonably proportional to the envisaged purpose, implying that the burden laid down on the disadvantaged category should not be too excessive. The Constitutional Court has already indicated that the mere fact that an act serves the general interest, such as ensuring financial stability, is not sufficient.[87]

To the extent that the enacted measures have the effect of granting competitive advantages, this may also raise questions as to their compatibility from a competition law perspective. Indeed, the question arises as to whether these measures taken by the Belgian State cannot be qualified as state aid to the extent that certain companies are granted an economic advantage (reduction of costs and better financing conditions which apparently cannot be achieved via normal commercial way), whereas others not.[88] If the answer is positive, such aid may raise concerns as to its compatibility with the internal market.[89]

3.2.1. Covered bondholders are more equal than other creditors?

3.2.1.1. Privileged position

For credit institutions that issue covered bonds, the BCBA introduces a legal mechanism to withdraw on a continuous basis (part of) the most reliable assets of a credit institution from the general pledge of the creditors of these credit institutions that do not benefit from the covered bond regime, such as the depositors or persons who are granted loans outside a bond scheme. To secure their rights, covered bondholders are granted a privileged position compared to other (secured) creditors.

3.2.1.2. Legal approach

As mentioned, privileged positions between creditors are valid if foreseen by law and parties can validly create such privileged positions via e.g. a mortgage or a pledge.[90] Belgian common law does not in principle foresee any limit on the amount of assets that can be used in this way as collateral. A person may thus collateralise all elements of his estate to privilege some creditors. Thus, also without a legal framework as set forth in the BCBA, a credit institution can privilege its creditors (e.g. bondholders) by using, via contractual mechanisms, all or a substantive part of its assets as collateral. In doing so, a similar privileged situation can be created, with the difference, however, that in that event the cover assets would remain part of the general estate and be subject to the consequences of insolvency proceedings or of other circumstances of *concursum creditorum*.

As regards the creation of special estates and deviations from general private law rules to guarantee the exclusive rights of the bondholders, any law with the same hierarchy can in principle deviate therefrom. The principle of unicity of estate only applies to the extent that no specific law has foreseen a deviation therefrom[91] and the rules regarding insolvency and concourse of creditors enacted by law can also be deviated from by another law with the same hierarchical status. From that perspective, the BCBA thus does not seem to be challengeable.

From a legal perspective it remains to be seen, however, whether the BCBA can resist the test of non-discrimination. In this context the question arises as to whether the BCBA does not create an unfair and disproportional inequality between the different creditors of a credit institution issuing covered bonds. The granting by law of a privileged position to holders of covered bonds undoubtedly creates a difference in treatment between these creditors and the other creditors. Indeed, holders of covered bonds are given the benefit of greater legal security at lesser cost compared to the other creditors who, in absence of a legal priority, must not only be able to impose, by contract, the granting of sufficient good quality collateral but also endure the rules and formalities of general contract and commercial law related to the validity, enforceability and realisation in case of insolvency of their collateral. In addition, the mechanism implies that, by operation of law, the burden of credit risk is shifted, to the other creditors and especially the non-secured creditors and *in fine*, if government intervention is necessary, the taxpayer.[92]

3.2.1.3. A questionable fair distribution

According to the Belgian legislator the BCBA efficiently contributes to the improvement of financing possibilities of credit institutions whilst securing a fair distribution between the different categories of creditors of a credit institution.[93] This view that the interests of the other creditors are sufficiently taken into account has been grounded on different arguments.

A first argument is that, by contrast to other surrounding countries, Belgian credit institutions are limited in their covered bond issues. They are allowed to issue covered bonds only up to 8%[94] of their assets, except if the NBB has consented to an exceeding of this limit.[95] Thus a restriction applies to the amount of assets that can be reserved for the covered bondholders. This restriction has been foreseen to ensure not only that credit institutions diversify their long-term financing sources, but also that they address the concern of the use of their assets to the detriment of the non-secured creditors.[96] The NBB indicated that it expects credit institutions to ensure an appropriate level of diversification of financing sources, the maintenance of a buffer containing non-collateralised assets to be able to face a potential crisis in the unsecured funding market and the maintenance of a buffer containing non-collateralised assets that can be used to comply with the obligations to replace or increase assets from the covered bond asset pool.[97]

Although the 8% limit ensures a restriction on the amount of assets of the credit institution that can be reserved for bondholders, this restriction is relative. It follows indeed from the Royal Decree of 11 October 2012, '*relatif à l'émission de covered bonds belges par des établissements de crédit de droit belge*'[98] that during the lifetime of the Belgian covered bonds, more than 8% of the assets can be attributed to the issued covered bonds to ensure the required coverage. Only *new* issues in excess of this limit seem not to be possible.[99] In addition, the NBB may consent to an exceeding of this 8% limit. This possibility is formulated as an exception to be used only temporarily and provided it is justified by exceptional circumstances on the financial markets that have an impact on the credit institution concerned and that justify the use of this financing source on a larger scale.[100] Such a justified circumstance would e.g. exist if the credit institution did not have access to unsecured financing.[101] The exceptional and temporary character of such measure should prevent a deviation being granted to allow a credit institution to further develop its activities through the issue of covered bonds.[102] Nevertheless, the foreseen possibility leaves the door open to further hollowing out the position of the non-secured creditors in critical situations.

A further guarantee for a fair equilibrium between the position of the covered bondholders and the other creditors (including the depositors) is seen in the supervision by the NBB. A closer look into the supervision powers, however, shows that these powers are mainly focussed on the verification of the quality of the cover assets and thus on the protection of the privileged holders of the covered bonds. Indeed the NBB is specifically to take into account the interests of the other creditors when it grants the general permission for the issue. It is less clear though whether the NBB should also take into account these interests when granting the specific permission for the issue.[103]

The NBB may also intervene by requiring an issuing credit institution to restrict the volume of issued covered bonds, in particular to protect the other creditors of the credit institution,[104] e.g. if the credit institution has already used other financing means with collateral or if the credit institution is in a situation of potential liquidation,[105] but such restriction is however without prejudice to the legal and contractual provisions related to the issued covered bonds.[106] As is the case with the 8% limit, this possible intervention by the NBB thus seems also to only concern *new* issues.

The NBB can during the lifetime of the covered bonds also supervise, in the context of its general supervision powers,[107] the solvency and liquidity of the credit institution in compliance with applicable regulation. However, the ultimate sanction to which non-compliance may lead in relation to covered bonds seems to be the removal of the credit institution from the list of credit institutions that can issue covered bonds, thus preventing such a credit institution from issuing new bonds, without having any consequences for the rights of the existing covered bondholders.[108]

More fundamentally the guarantee offered by supervision is dependent on the available means and quality of such supervision, and in respect of the supervision of the solvency and liquidity of credit institutions, on the efficiency of the new measures taken and to be taken in that respect. The recent financial crisis has shown that regulatory oversight is not exempt from failure. In this context, a specific point of concern may be the objectivity of the supervision performed. Indeed, the use of covered bonds has gained interest in the context of the refinancing programs set up via the Eurosystem, in which the NBB participates. To the extent that the covered bonds are (likely to be) purchased in the context of monetary policies established with the participation of the NBB, one may thus wonder whether the NBB's supervision is not biased by a conflict of interest. Due account is furthermore to be given to the fact that the liability of the NBB for negligent supervision is limited to fraud or gross misconduct.[109]

An additional argument that pleads in favour of the specific regime for covered bonds is that covered bonds would also imply better supervision by the credit institution itself and thus lead to better lending practices by credit institutions. The reasoning is that since, unlike the 'originate-to-distribute' model used in securitisation, the issuing credit institution remains (in principle) the owner of the assets in the cover pool, it remains exposed to the credit risk related to these assets. It will thus be required to continue to take the cover assets into account for the capital requirements and be inclined to exercise a better supervision over the credits it granted and act less recklessly (elimination of 'moral hazard').[110] This may however also result in the assets in the cover pool receiving too much attention given the specific requirements provided by the BCBA. The risk of 'bad' assets outside the cover pool remains and is concentrated with the other creditors. According to some, moreover, credit institutions with more covered bonds would even on the contrary be inclined to take on more risk,[111] knowing that the higher risks for the depositors will be secured via the deposit guarantee scheme and in the last resort by the government (i.e. the taxpayer).[112] Furthermore, the bondholders, who know that they are secured by the quality assets in the cover pool, will be less inclined to exercise control over the activity and the general creditworthiness of the credit institution concerned.[113] Securing their rights, whether or not the legal framework is complied with by the credit institution, increases this moral hazard in their respect.

It has furthermore been argued that the regime is not unbalanced since the depositor and savers are sufficiently protected by the more severe capital requirements[114] and the deposit guarantee scheme so that the consequences of the risk shifting are limited. However, will these mechanisms indeed provide sufficient guarantees? Are suffcient means available to monitor and ensure compliance with the new requirements? Does the legal framework on deposit guarantee schemes grant sufficient legal certainty as to the rights granted and are the available funds sufficient to cover potential claims? The expected new European framework on deposit guarantee schemes[115] will strengthen the depositors' protection via faster access and a robust financing regime based on increased contribution by participating credit institutions which will reflect their individual risk profiles. But will the financing regime be sufficiently flexible to take into account risk profile changes and occurring risk shifting to the depositors? To the extent that the deposit guarantee scheme is not (sufficiently) financed by the credit institutions themselves, an appeal to the deposit guarantee scheme will still imply risk-shifting to the taxpayer. Additionally, the guarantee provided under this scheme is limited to a fixed amount (currently in principle €100,000) and depositors still may incur losses if their deposits exceed this amount.[116] The scope of the beneficiaries is also limited (currently natural persons, certain SMEs and non-profit associations). The deposit guarantee scheme does thus not seem to compensate fully for the privileged position granted to the covered bondholders.

3.2.1.4. Compensation for burden

The foregoing shows that the arguments advanced to justify the unequal treatment of the other creditors of credit institutions that issue covered bonds, and in particular the deposit holder and saver, are challengeable. The burden laid upon the other creditors of credit institutions as a result of the risk shifting entailed by the covered bond mechanism could be considered justifiable if it is compensated – and the equilibrium is thus somehow restored – by direct or indirect advantages provided to the other creditors.

Provided they are aware of the risk shifting, professional financers of credit institutions might achieve to receive higher returns for uncovered or less covered financing and the credit risk shifting they undergo or decide not to grant any financing. But this is only valid if existing financing conditions can be adjusted or in case of new financing. In the first case they would be compensated for the disequilibrium and voluntarily undergo it.

The same cannot be said for deposit holders and savers. Deposit holders and savers primarily place their funds with credit institutions with a view to safely storing their funds and to using the payment services provided by the credit institutions. They are thus mainly recipients of a service, which nowadays has become indispensable in day-to-day life. Although the deposited funds are used by credit institutions to grant credits and thus also constitute a financing means for a credit institution, depositors and savers are not treated in the same way as professional financers: they receive some remuneration for the deposited funds (interests) but they are generally not in a position to demand an increase of return for increased risk. Deposit holders and savers do not have the same bargaining power as professional financers, unless they are very wealthy. In the context of covered bonds, deposit holders and savers are thus not likely to receive a higher return for the expropriation of value as a result of the involuntary subordination of their claims on the issuing credit institution. The only option (i.e. power) they have is to decide to deposit their savings at another credit institution or simply to use it for more secure investments (investment in immovable property). This option can however only be exercised provided they are actually aware of (the consequences of) covered bonds issues for their deposits and savings, which may be doubted,[117] and act accordingly. Information and education of depositors and savers in this respect and spontaneous transparent and understandable communication by credit institutions to their clients seems the minimum required to enable them to make a deliberate choice as to the risks they undertake and to limit the redistribution of value from the less to the better informed. Increased awareness of risk shifting might impact the attractiveness of deposits and savings and thus decrease the liquidity of credit institutions, at least of those that are involved in covered bonds issues.[118] In that way the possibility for depositors and savers to participate in disciplining ex ante a credit institution's risky behaviour, instead of reacting after a problem has become apparent, is increased. Of course, whether such possibility will in effect be used by depositors is another question.

Where no direct advantages are granted to those that carry the burden of the privileged position of the bondholder, the question then arises as to whether the created risk shifting can be outweighed by the indirect advantage that the specific regime seeks to achieve: ensuring long-term (re)financing mechanisms at lower costs for credit institutions to ensure better financing conditions to companies and households in general. The premise is that greater legal security for bondholders implies (re)financing at a lower cost for credit institutions that will in turn provide cheaper credits to companies and households. But is this a valid premise?

Whether this will in effect be the case depends in the first place on how the funding raised is used by the credit institution concerned. In this respect I have not found clear legal requirements or mechanisms that force credit institutions to use the cheaper funding only in the context of granting loans to companies and households and that ensure that the costs reduction is translated in more beneficial financial conditions for them.[119] In the absence of clear requirements, the use of the financing for the envisaged purposes thus depends on the willingness of the credit institution concerned. Requirements in this respect could be foreseen in the covenants agreed upon with the bondholders but this would imply social engagement and supervision responsibilities from these bondholders. That some scepticism is not out of place here seems to be confirmed by a press communication published on 28 September 2012 which quoted the following striking statement of the Belgian minister of finance at that time, Mr Van Ackere, on the BCBA: '*Le ministre espère que le monde bancaire ne se montrera pas ingrat. Cette décision "s'accompagne aussi d'attentes à l'égard du secteur financier: nous attendons qu'ils mobilisent cet argent pour l'économie réelle", a-t-il souligné.*'[120] As indicated by the minister, much will depend on the future behaviour of credit institutions.

Additionally, where covered bond issues may lead to an increase in the risk premium for uncovered covered financing this may render unsecured debt financing more expensive,[121] which may in turn have a negative effect on the liquidity of the market of unsecured financing and affect credit to companies and households.[122]

3.2.1.5. Proportionality

Finally, one may wonder in light of the preferential treatment instated by the BCBA whether the goal of ensuring long-term refinancing mechanisms for credit institutions could be achieved by less distortive measures. Different measures could have been implemented to ensure a better balance between the protection of the bondholders and of the unsecured creditors and especially the depositors and savers, and to ensure the overall goal of the BCBA, such as measures to ensure regular supervision of the interests of these creditors by the NBB and/or the pool monitor combined with adequate sanctions, measures that ensure a neutral assessment of the involved interests, measures to ensure that the proceeds of the covered bonds issues in effect serve the community and that the benefits of the refinancing at lower cost are effectively passed through, measures that make not only credit institutions, but also bondholders responsible for avoiding an unhealthy increase of risk for other creditors or additional guarantees for other creditors, and in particular deposit holders (e.g. increased deposit guarantee and increased contribution to the deposit guarantee scheme for credit institutions that have issued covered bonds,[123] or segregation of a proportion of assets to the exclusive benefit of other categories of creditors (e.g. a system of special estate to cover deposits),[124] and so on). Whether from this perspective the preferential treatment of bondholders under the BCBA can pass the test of non-discrimination, especially as regards the pertinence of the legal framework and the proportionality of the distortion created compared to other creditors remains to be seen.

3.2.2. (Belgian) (big) credit institutions are more equal than other debtors?

Whereas the previous considerations are situated at the level of the creditors of the credit institutions, a broader observation can more generally be formulated as to the beneficiaries of the new financing tool. The Belgian covered bonds regime is only available to Belgian credit institutions. This raises different concerns.

3.2.2.1. Belgian vs non-Belgian

First of all, since the covered bond regime is reserved to Belgian credit institutions, they are granted a competitive advantage compared to non-Belgian credit institutions that do not benefit from a similar regime. Additionally, it is to be noted that in practice probably only the bigger credit institutions will effectively be able to make use of the covered bond regime. The question thus arises as to whether the 'monopoly' on issuing covered bonds granted by the BCBA to undertakings that qualify as credit institutions is not likely to reinforce the dominance of the bigger credit institutions.

3.2.2.2. Credit institutions and the others

Besides the foregoing it can be observed that credit institutions are not the only persons interested in smooth and cheap(er) financing mechanisms backed by robust mechanisms that secure to the maximum their creditors' interests. Other companies whose assets consist mainly of receivables also have an interest in a regime whereby these assets can be pooled as collateral for financing transactions and are by operation of law ring-fenced from other creditors. One cannot only think of other companies in the financial sector, which hold similar illiquid assets as credit institutions, such as mortgage companies or finance companies (factoring, leasing), or other financial institutions, but also of any commercial company whose assets are composed of important portfolios of receivables that can be used in the context of financing transactions. More generally the question arises as to why these other companies (even those companies whose estate is composed by other assets than receivables) are not granted the option of creating special estates and must continue to rely on contractual mechanisms – considered too complex, too costly and too unsecure for credit institutions – to guarantee the rights of creditors in the context of comparable financing mechanisms. From that perspective the BCBA seems to create an inequality in access to (re)financing mechanisms and to reinforce the position of credit institutions.

3.2.2.3. Plea for a more general approach

Several Belgian legal scholars have already defended the view that the principle of unicity of estate of a person should be abandoned in favour of a more objective approach of the personal estate concept implying that a person can freely divide its estate and exclusively attribute the assets used for a specific purpose as general pledge for the liabilities undertaken for the same purpose.[125] Thus the technique of splitting up personal estates in special estates could efficiently be used in the context of syndicated loans to companies, where the collateral structure to the benefit of the consortium of lenders leads to complex legal constructions and diverse legal discussions[126] or more generally in the context of splitting up private and professional estates of physical persons engaging in economic activities. Given these discussions, and with the lessons learned form the financial crisis, a broader and fundamental reflection on the function of a general estate, the role and effect of collateral and of the organisation of special estates should in my opinion be conducted.

4. REFINANCING IN THE FINANCIAL SECTOR VIA MOBILISATION OF RECEIVABLES

4.1. THE MRA IN A NUTSHELL

The BCBA establishes a legal framework to facilitate credit institutions' use of receivables in the context of covered bond issues. The MRA complements this framework but also goes a step further. Based on the consideration that due to several legal constraints a great deal of the portfolio of credit receivables cannot be used as collateral for (re)financing or only under less favourable conditions,[127] the MRA adapts different aspects of the existing legal framework for the transfer of receivables that can be qualified as bank claims. Whereas these modifications are presented as necessary to ensure the success of covered bonds, the preparatory works also indicate that the modifications are aimed at facilitating the smooth mobilisation of bank claims in the context of collateral constructions.[128] The scope of the MRA is thus broader than governing the transfer of receivables in the context of covered bonds issues. In fact the MRA facilitates in general the transfer or pledging of the receivables falling within its scope without limitation to a specific transactional context, except where the provisions relate specifically to covered bond issues.

4.1.1. Bank claims

The MRA first of all contains a set of general provisions on the mobilisation of bank claims (Chapter 3 MRA). The provisions implemented by this chapter concern, broadly speaking, the following matters:

(1) the elimination of the existing constraints for the mobilisation of bank claims on the government out of public procurements: whereas in principle receivables on the government are not transferable before the provisory delivery of the works, this restriction no longer applies for the transfer of a bank claim arising out of a loan or a credit *by* or *to* a credit institution, a financial institution or a so-called mobilisation institution (*mobiliseringsinstelling/organisme de mobilisation*);[129]
(2) the explicit recognition of the possibility to transfer bank claims resulting from advance payments in the context of credit facilities which are not guaranteed by a mortgage, immovable privilege, mortgage promise or mortgage mandate;[130] advances granted after the transfer are subordinated to such transferred bank claims and advances granted prior

to or on date of the transfer have the same ranking unless the transferor and the transferee have agreed upon a ranking or a subordination;

(3) the clarification of the consequences of a transfer of a bank claim secured by collateral and guarantees vested for different bank claims ('all-sums collateral') or future bank claims:[131] unless otherwise agreed, each secured receivable may be transferred and each transferee benefits from the privileges and collateral pro rata the transferred receivable. In addition, arrangements may be made on the ranking and seniority of the receivables, including such arrangements to the benefit of a special estate in the context of covered bonds. These arrangements are enforceable on the debtor of the bank claim as soon as he has been notified thereof and on other third parties by operation of law. A ranking arrangement may however not prejudice the rights of third parties acquired prior to the transfer, unless otherwise agreed with that third party.

(4) the exclusion under certain conditions of the right to set-off claims and of the right to withhold performance (*exceptio non adimpleti contractus*) in the event of a transfer of a bank claim *by* or *to* a credit institution, a financial institution or a mobilisation institution;[132]

(5) the abolishment of certain formalities to which the transfer or pledging *to* or *by* a credit institution, a financial institution or mobilisation institution of bank claims and of the related accessories are subject;[133]

(6) specific provisions regarding covered bonds as also already mentioned above:
   (a) the transfer *to* or *by* a credit institution of bank claims, financial instruments and their accessories *by* or *to* a credit institution that issues covered bonds and the registration of cover assets in the context of the issue of covered bonds are valid and enforceable towards third parties even in the case of insolvency proceeding, seizure or other event of *concursum creditorum*, if the transfer occurred prior to such proceeding or event or, if it occurs afterwards, if the counterparty or such institution was lawfully unaware of such procedure or event after the opening of such proceedings;[134]
   (b) deviation of the generally applicable claw-back clauses provided by the Belgian Bankruptcy Act for transfer of receivables in the context of covered bond issues (whether via registration or not); and
   (c) the attribution of receivables to the specific estate through registration in the context of the issue of covered bonds is qualified (by fiction) as a transfer of receivables, as a result of which such registration benefits the favourable regime for transfer of receivables of the MRA.[135]

4.1.2. *Mortgage credits*

A second main part of the MRA (Chapter 4 MRA) is dedicated to adaptations of other legislation and in particular the adaptation of the Belgian Mortgage Credit Act.[136] The adaptation of the already favourable regime for the transfer of receivables out of mortgage credits as set forth in this Act concerns, amongst other things, the following:

(1) expansion of its scope of application to mobilisation institutions, credit institutions and financial institutions;[137] as a result the more favourable regime in respect of transfer of receivables out of mortgage credits previously limited to institutions for investment in receivables is expanded to these entities;[138]
(2) automatic enforceability on third parties without registration obligation of arrangements on the ranking and seniority of the receivables out of mortgage credits;[139] and
(3) facilitation of the use of receivables guaranteed by mortgage mandates or mortgage promises.[140]

These specific provisions apply without prejudice to the general rules of the MRA. Transfers of receivables out of mortgage loans or receivables to which a right on a mortgage (mortgage mandate or promise) is attached, are thus now governed by both the MRA and the Belgian Mortgage Credit Act. The MRA is indeed to be considered a *lex generalis* compared to the Belgian Mortgage Credit Act,[141] and since receivables secured by a mortgage or a right on a mortgage fall within the definition of the notion 'bank claims', the MRA's general rules on mobilisation of bank claims of the MRA apply to the extent the Belgian Mortgage Act does not foresee specific rules. Combining both texts into a single legal piece of work would have contributed to greater transparency.

4.2. THE MRA, SOURCE OF (UN)JUSTIFIED INEQUALITIES?

By eliminating certain constraints and formalities, explicitly allowing and clarifying the consequences of certain practices and excluding certain right of defence of the debtor of the transferred claim, the MRA implements measures that enhance the (legal) position of certain categories of persons concerned by the mobilisation of bank claims. First of all, the legal position of the transferee of a bank claim is reinforced, in particular by the implemented restrictions on certain rights of defences. The latter fundamentally affects the principles applicable to transfer of claims to the detriment of the debtor (as explained in section 4.2.1) below. In addition, due to its specific scope of application, the MRA entails a preferential treatment of transfers of bank claims to the benefit of the persons concerned by these transactions (section 4.2.2).

4.2.1. Transferees are more equal than debtors?

4.2.1.1. Defences of the debtor: an inconvenient obstacle for some

As mentioned above, the MRA introduces restrictions on the right for the debtor to invoke set-off and the right to withhold performance. In the context of relations with a credit institution, set-off implies that when a person is at the same time a creditor and a debtor of a credit institution, this person may, if the legal conditions for set-off are fulfilled, set-off its claim on the credit institution against the debt of the credit institution if the credit institution fails to reimburse its debt. Thus if a person is granted a loan by a credit institution (creating a reimbursement obligation on that person) and at the same time holds a deposit (implying a right of that person to claim reimbursement of the deposited amount) with the same credit institution, it can set-off his deposit against the loan if the credit institution fails to reimburse its debt. The right to withhold performance implies that the deposit holder can suspend paying back his loan as long as the credit institution does not pay back the deposit. Set-off, and more particularly close-out netting,[142] and the right to withhold performance are also relevant in the context of more complex financial transactions with or between credit institutions which involve high counterparty risk, such as derivatives transactions, repurchase and securities lending agreements. Credit institutions have an interest in ensuring that they can apply remedies such as set-off and the right to withhold performance to secure the receivables they have on their clients or counterparties. In that way they have a security in the event that their client or counterparty becomes insolvent. They have at the same time an interest in ensuring that their clients or counterparties cannot refuse payment of their debts by invoking these same remedies towards the credit institution. In practice, credit institutions often foresee in their general conditions a unilateral conventional right of set-off to their benefit and limit the client's set-off to the set-off by operation of law[143] or even exclude it.[144]

During the financial crisis the conditions under which these remedies, and especially set-off, can be invoked became a particular point of interest since it raised the question of whether depositors that also hold loans with the same failing credit institution could use this mechanism to avoid the loss of their deposits. The question was not only relevant in assessing the position of the deposit holders but also in assessing the consequences the application of set-off could have for the other creditors of credit institutions that granted e.g. credit facilities (inter banking financing) or liquidity facilities (operations in the context of the Eurosystem) secured by the receivables that could be the object of the set-off. The financial crisis also showed that, although set-off can contribute to a reduction of systemic risk to the extent that it reduces counterparty exposure for credit institutions and financial institutions, the decrease of value caused by massive application of set-off ('counterparty run') can accelerate insolvency of the failing credit institution and worsen its position in the context of its resolution or reorganisation.[145] The question thus arose as to whether in that context a stay should be imposed on the possibility of invoking set-off with a view to guaranteeing the success of reorganisation measures.[146]

The specific provisions of the MRA in respect of set-off and the right to withhold performance are to be situated in the context of the funding issues with which credit institutions were confronted as a result of the financial crisis. The premise is that financers of credit institutions will be more inclined to grant credit (and on better financial conditions) if they have good collateral to secure the reimbursement of these credits. If credit institutions wish to use receivables in this context e.g. as collateral, their financers will be inclined to accept these assets as collateral and grant better financing terms if they are sure of the value of these assets, i.e. if they are sure that the receivables will be paid out to them. The potentiality of set-off or withholding of performance, which could be invoked to avoid payment of the mobilised receivables, implies however a risk of loss of value for financers that accept these assets as collateral. Taking into account the legal insecurity that set-off and the right to withhold performance create in the context of (re)financing mechanisms where receivables are used as collateral and the impact these means of defence can thus have on the refinancing possibilities of credit institutions, the Belgian legislator decided to restrict the possibility to invoke these means of defence. Accepting such means of defence would, according to the Belgian legislator, imply that the transferee, pledgee or covered bondholder would not be able to attribute any value to the claims since he has no assurance that they will be paid.[147]

The rules introduced in respect of set-off and withholding performance modify in a quite fundamental manner the generally applicable rules in this respect in Belgium in the context of transfer of receivables and particularly raises concerns from the perspective of equal treatment.[148] To understand how, I will first briefly summarise the principles that apply in general (section 4.2.1.2) and then indicate how the MRA deviates from these principles (section 4.2.1.3).

4.2.1.2. Seeking a balance

4.2.1.2.1. Principle

In principle, Belgian law of obligations accepts that transfers of receivables are possible without the specific consent of the debtor, although as a result thereof the debtor is confronted with a new contract party, which he has not chosen himself. The reason for this acceptance is that a transfer implies a succession in rights. The transferee, the new creditor, succeeds as a result of the transfer in the rights of the transferor and the receivable passes on – unchanged – to the transferee. Since the new creditor takes over the legal position of the previous creditor and has the same rights – and no more – it is therefore considered that, from a legal perspective, the transfer does not prejudice the debtor. Consent of the debtor with the transfer is thus not required.[149] The debtor must however be made aware that the person towards whom he has to fulfil its payment obligations has changed and therefore article 1690 of the Belgian Civil Code subjects the enforceability of such a transfer towards the debtor to a specific condition: the notification of the transfer to the debtor or the recognition of the transfer by the debtor. Both were initially subject to a specific form, involving the intervention of a public servant (and thus costs), but since 1994 such specific form is no longer required.[150] The transfer is in principle enforceable towards other third parties as of the date of the conclusion of the transfer except (1) in case of conflicting transfers, in which case the first notified or recognised transfer will be preferred, and (2) in cases where specific formalities are to be performed to render the transfer enforceable to third parties, such as e.g. in principle in case of transfer of mortgage loans, for the enforceability of which a specific publicity measure (*kantmelding/inscription*) subject to specific formalities is to be performed.[151] Similar principles apply to the pledging of receivables.[152]

The above principle implies that in the case of a transfer of a receivable, such a receivable is transferred to the transferee with all the modalities, defaults, remedies and accessories[153] attached to it at time of the transfer. The debtor may thus invoke the nullity of the receivable (for lack or default in consent, lack of object, unlawful cause or incapacity), the terms and conditions to which the receivable is made subject, and all other possible reasons for extinction of his obligation (such as payment, prescription, novation, set-off, etc.) regardless the transfer.

With a view to finding equilibrium between the interests of the debtor and the transferee, article 1691 Belgian Civil Code modulates this fundamental principle somewhat. This provision first indicates that the debtor who has paid in good faith prior to any notification or acknowledgement of the transfer is liberated from his payment obligation. This provision provides in addition that the debtor may invoke towards the transferee, despite the transfer, all defences and remedies he has against the transferor, but if they originate from a legal act made against the transferor they may only be invoked if the debtor invokes them in good faith and if such legal act was made prior to the time at which the transfer became enforceable against the debtor by the notification or its acknowledgement of the transfer.

Some of the defences, such as the right to withhold performance and the right to set-off, require a certain reciprocity between the two parties involved. After a transfer of a receivable this reciprocity no longer exists, since one of the parties is in that case confronted with a new creditor. The question thus arises as to whether or not these defences remain possible if the conditions to which they are subject occur after the transfer of the receivable has taken place.

4.2.1.2.2. Right to withhold performance

The right to withhold performance (*exceptio non adimpleti contractus*) is a means of defence that allows a party to a reciprocal contract to suspend its own performance in the event of non-performance of its counter party. The remedy is based on the idea of interdependency between reciprocal obligations:[154] if A undertakes a performance towards B in exchange for which B has also committed a performance towards A, then A may suspend its performance if B does not (and as long as) B does not perform.[155] Under Belgian law, the following conditions should be fulfilled to invoke this means of defence:[156]

(1) the non-performance of the other party should relate to an obligation deriving from the same contract as the one the performance of which is withheld or at least both obligations should be interdependent;

(2) the party invoking it must itself be creditor of a debt which is certain and which becomes due before its own debt, i.e. its own performance should not be due first;
(3) the party invoking it should be able to prove that the other party has not performed as agreed;
(4) the party invoking it should have notified the non-performance;
(5) the party invoking it should not have caused the non-performance of the other party;
(6) the non-performance should be serious enough to justify the withholding of the performance.

If in the example above, B transfers its receivable against A to C, B remains bound to perform towards A, but A is as a result of the transfer no longer held to perform towards B but towards C. The conditions for invoking the right to withhold performance in the event B defaults thus no longer seem to be satisfied. The Belgian Supreme Court however considered that the debtor maintains his right to withhold performance in the event that the counterparty does not perform, even though this non-performance occurs after this counterparty has transferred its receivable against the debtor.[157] The reasoning is that in reciprocal relationships this remedy is *ab initio* available, regardless of the time at which the non-performance occurs.[158] So if B transfers its receivable against A but remains bound by obligations towards A, C may be frustrated in its right to claim performance from A if B does not perform its obligations towards A, since A is allowed to invoke B's non-performance to withhold its own performance towards C. A similar approach is upheld for the right to request the remedy available in reciprocal contracts to request rescission in the event of breach.[159]

4.2.1.2.3. Set-off

Set-off also requires a certain degree of reciprocity. Set-off implies that when two persons are each other's creditor their reciprocal receivables are extinguished for the smallest amount.[160] Set-off thus serves as payment mechanism and at the same time as security. In the event of set-off, payment no longer has to be made for that part of the debt that extinguishes as a result of the set-off.[161] If e.g. A is entitled to 100 from B and conversely B is entitled 60 from A, set-off implies that only 40 will need to be paid by B. At the same time, the person that may invoke set-off secures payment in the event of default of its debtor and thus reduces counterparty risk, since the debt of the debtor is reduced by the amount due from the person invoking set-off.[162] Taking the example above, the security function of the set-off implies that if B were to go bankrupt, A is at least ensured the payment of 60 and would only need to collect 40 from the bankruptcy estate. Normally[163] under Belgian law, set-off occurs automatically, by operation of law, if the following conditions are fulfilled:[164]

(1) two reciprocal debts exist between the same persons who are each personally (*in personam*) held by that debt; it is however in principle not necessary for these reciprocal debts to stem from the same cause;
(2) both debts should concern an amount of money or a certain amount of fungible goods;
(3) the existence and the amount of both debts must be certain;
(4) both debts must be due.

Set-off is however as a general rule excluded to the extent that it would affect acquired rights of third parties.[165] This rule implies that in principle set-off is not possible after the occurrence of an insolvency proceeding or another event of *concursum creditorum* in respect of one of the two parties to the set-off. This rule however does not apply if the receivables to be set-off are closely connected. If this is the case, set-off remains possible regardless of such insolvency proceeding or another event of *concursum creditorum*.[166]

In the event of a transfer of receivables, the condition of two reciprocal debts between two persons is no longer satisfied as soon as the transfer is effective towards the debtor. If in the example above, B transfers its receivable against A to C, B still owes a debt towards A, but A owes a debt towards C instead of B as soon as the transfer becomes effective towards A. Consistently with the rule of article 1690 of the Belgian Civil Code that the transfer is only enforceable towards the debtor if it has been notified to or acknowledged by him, article 1295 of the Belgian Civil Code thus foresees that the debtor who has been notified of a transfer of receivables or has recognised it, can no longer invoke the set-off by operation of law if the conditions for this set-off are only satisfied after such notification or recognition.[167] Some scholars are of the opinion that, as is the case for set-off in circumstances of *concursus creditorum*, an exception to this rule should be made for set-off between 'closely connected receivables' which should always be allowed, even after a transfer.[168] The Belgian Supreme Court first rejected this view[169] and then reversed its interpretation.[170] According to the latter decision of the Belgian Supreme Court, set-off remains possible for closely connected claims even after transfer of one of the concerned receivables, even though the conditions for the set-off are fulfilled after the transfer.

Parties may also conventionally organise the right to set-off and arrange e.g. when debts become due (acceleration clauses), the type of debts that can be set-off and what type of claims are closely connected. Whereas such conventional clauses are in principle not effective in the event of insolvency proceedings and other cases of *concursum creditorum*, the FCA enacts the validity and enforceability of conventional set-off clauses between or with traders (*kooplieden/commerçants*) in such cases and regardless of the transfer of receivables. The FCA thus transposes the DFCA, but has a broader scope of application since it applies more generally to traders.[171] According to article 14, §1 FCA, netting clauses or clauses or conditions organising early termination with a view to making conventional set-off possible are enforceable towards the creditors in the event of insolvency proceedings, seizure or other cases of *concursum creditorum*, without any default notice or judicial decision being required, regardless of the transfer of the rights to which such clauses relate, provided that the receivables to which the set-off is to be applied *exist* at the time the *concursum creditorum* circumstance arises. Article 15, §1 FCA adds that to be valid and enforceable towards third parties including in the event of insolvency proceedings, seizure or other cases of *concursum creditorum*, netting clauses should be concluded prior to the occurrence of the event of *concursum creditorum*, or after such event provided the counterparty can demonstrate that it was lawfully unaware of such event.[172] Two rules can be extrapolated from these provisions. First, that the conventional right to set-off remains available in the event of *concursum creditorum* regardless of the time at which the receivables become due and without any close connection being required between such receivables.[173] Thus article 1298 of the Belgian Civil Code is set aside. The second rule that can be extrapolated from these provisions is that conventional set-off remains possible even if the claim to be set-off against has been transferred. Although the formulation itself is not that clear in this respect,[174] the preparatory works indicate that the intention of article 14, §1 FCA is to set aside the application of article 1295 of the Belgian Civil Code for conventional set-off[175] which implies that the debtor can always invoke conventional set-off towards the transferee, even if the transfer was notified to or acknowledged by him.

A specific mandatory rule regarding the availability of defences and remedies exists in respect of the transfer of receivables out of consumer credits. In the event of transfer of receivables out of a consumer credit, the consumer maintains against the transferee all its means of defence, including the right to set-off, which he could invoke against the transferor.[176] The consumer can in this case always, regardless of any transfer, invoke towards the transferee all the defences and remedies he has against the transferor.

4.2.1.3. Trimming down debtors' rights

The MRA introduces important changes to the aforementioned principles. Article 6 MRA introduces a (complex) regime in respect of set-off and the right to withhold performance in the context of transfers and pledges of receivables. A distinction is made between the case where a *receivable on* a credit institution or a financial institution is transferred or pledged (hereafter referred to as the 'first rule')[177] and the case where a *bank claim* is transferred or pledged *by* or *to* a credit institution, financial institution or a mobilisation institution (hereafter referred to as the 'second rule').[178]

4.2.1.3.1. The first rule

If a *receivable on* a credit institution or a financial institution linked to an activity eligible for the mutual recognition in the context of the European passport as mentioned in article 3, §2 of the CIA has been transferred or pledged, this institution cannot – *regardless of whether any close connection exists* between the receivables to which the set-off is to be applied – invoke towards the transferee or pledgee the set-off by operation of law or the conventional set-off nor can it invoke the right to withhold performance by which the payment of the transferred or pledged receivable would be suspended or reduced if:

(1) the transfer or pledge has been notified to the concerned institution or the concerned institution has recognised the transfer; and
(2) if the conditions for these means of defence are satisfied after such notification or recognition.

The first rule does not however apply in the event that the transferor (i.e. the creditor of the credit institution or the financial institution) is a public or financial legal person and the credit institution or financial institution can invoke a netting agreement in the sense of the FCA, which forms part of a real collateral agreement or of an agreement containing a real collateral.[179] In addition, the first rule is without prejudice to set-off which can be invoked or is applied with a view to realising a pledge or any other real security that encumbers the receivable to be set-off.[180]

3.2.1.3.2. The second rule

Where a *bank claim* is transferred or pledged *by* or *to* a credit institution, a financial institution or a mobilisation institution, a similar exclusion of set-off and the right to withhold performance is provided. In that case the MRA excludes for the debtor both the right to withhold performance and the right to set-off (whether by operation of law or conventional), *regardless of whether any close connection exists* between the receivables to which the set-off is to be applied, if:

(1) the transfer or pledge has been notified to the debtor or the debtor has recognised the transfer; and
(2) if the conditions for these means of defence are satisfied after such notification or recognition.

In case the debtor of the bank claim is a public or financial legal person and can invoke a netting agreement in the sense of the FCA, which forms part of a real collateral agreement or of an agreement containing a real collateral, this second rule does equally not apply in respect of conventional set-off.[181] Set-off which can be invoked or is applied with a view to realising a pledge or any other real security that encumbers the receivable to be set-off remains also possible.[182] Furthermore, if the debtor qualifies as a consumer in the sense of the Consumer Credit Act (i.e. if the transferred receivable arises out of a consumer credit) all means of defence remain invocable as foreseen by article 27 of the Belgian Consumer Credit Act (i.e. no application of the second rule).[183]

As regards the limitation to invoke the right to withhold performance, the first and the second rule deviate from the applicable general principle. As indicated above, the right to withhold performance can under Belgian law always be invoked by the debtor, regardless of any transfer of the receivable. Thus the first and the second rule set aside, to the benefit of the concerned transferees, a basic rule of law of obligations.

As regards the right to set-off, the first and the second rule are a confirmation of the rule in article 1295 Belgian Civil Code.[184] However they also imply a rejection of set-off after transfer for closely connected claims. In addition, the first and the second rule deviate from what is provided for in article 14 FCA[185] to the extent that this provision is to be understood as granting the right to the debtor to invoke at all times conventional set-off against the transferee.

3.2.1.3.3. 'Good' things come in threes

The snag in the new regime of the MRA lies however most of all in an additional rule provided by the MRA *only* for the transfer of bank claims *by* or *to* a credit institution, a financial institution or a mobilisation institution (hereafter referred to as the 'third rule'). According to this third rule,[186] the right to set-off and the right to withhold performance can no longer be invoked towards the transferee or pledgee by the debtor after the transfer, *regardless of whether he was notified thereof or has recognised such transfer*, and *regardless of any close connection between the concerned bank claims*, if the conditions of the set-off or of the right to withhold performance are fulfilled following or as a result of an insolvency proceeding or of a circumstance of *concursum creditorum* related to the transferor or the pledgor. The same exceptions as mentioned above for the second rule apply to this rule.

Although this rule is formulated in quite a sibylline way, the intention of the legislator is clearly to exclude any possibility for the client of the concerned institutions to invoke set-off and the right to withhold performance based on its relation with such institution with a view to guaranteeing maximum legal certainty to the transferee (or the pledgee) of the bank claim as to his payment.[187] The preparatory works indicate that this denial of set-off after transfer or pledge of a bank claim is in line with the case law of the Belgian Supreme Court of 2003. However, as mentioned above (section 2) the Belgian Supreme Court at that time only denied the set-off between closely connected claims after notification or acknowledgement of the transfer. The third rule goes further than denying set-off in that case. The third rule excludes set-off even if the transfer has not been notified to or acknowledged by the debtor, i.e. even if the transfer is according to article 1690 Belgian Civil Code not enforceable to him. Thus the rule introduced by the MRA implies that article 1295 Belgian Code is completely set aside to the benefit of the transferee in the event of a transfer of a bank claim *by* or *to* a credit institution, a financial institution or a mobilisation institution in the cases where the conditions of the set-off or of the right to withhold performance are fulfilled following or as a result of an insolvency proceeding or of a circumstance of *concursum creditorum* related to the transferor or the pledgor.

3.2.1.3.4. Seeking balance

According to the Belgian legislator, the rules set forth above are the expression of a reasonable equilibrium between the parties. If I understand correctly that the first rule (transfer or pledge of a receivable) is intended to concern the case where a credit institution or financial institution is the debtor of the transferred receivable, whereas the rules related to the transfer or pledge of a bank claim are intended to concern cases where the debtor of the transferred bank claim is the client or the counterparty of a credit institution or financial institution, I am not fully convinced that such equilibrium is in effect achieved.

For the Belgian legislator the regime of the MRA is balanced since set-off is excluded in a reciprocal way. The restriction by the first rule of the right to set-off and the right to withhold compensation for credit institutions or financial institutions is indeed seen as a compensation for the restriction by the second and the third rule of the right to set-off and the right to withhold performance for debtors of bank claims.[188] The first rule would thus increase the value as guarantee of receivables of clients on their credit institution or financial institutions. However, this is only valid to the extent that (1) the receivables on a credit institution or a financial institution may in effect be mobilised and (2) these means of defence have not been excluded for or, as regards conventional set-off, have been granted to the benefit of clients. In practice the mobilisation of receivables envisaged by the first rule is limited. As regards for example loans or credit facilities granted by these entities, it is generally accepted that these are granted *intuitu personae* (that is taking into account the specific characteristics of the beneficiary of the loan or credit facility) and thus cannot be transferred without consent of the borrower.[189] As to deposits the general conditions of credit institutions often foresee the transfer as security and/or pledging to the credit institution of all amounts held for the account of the client (deposits) and any existing or future receivable[190] and the conventional right of set-off is also often only provided to the benefit of the credit institution. In the cases where a client would have pledged all his deposits to the credit institution, the latter will, based on the foreseen exception to the first rule, remain entitled to invoke set-off with a view to realising this pledge.[191] Credit institutions may also try to avoid application of the first rule by conventionally excluding for the client the right to mobilise the receivables or by subjecting it to prior consent or by excluding directly the application of the first rule.[192] Finally, the possibility for a client to apply the exceptions to the exclusion of set-off and the right to withhold performance in case of netting agreements, pledging or other real security on the concerned receivable is remote, since it is unlikely that a credit institution or a financial institution would grant such rights to its clients. Thus the reciprocity introduced by the MRA seems somewhat artificial[193] and the limitation of the means of defences in the event of transfer of receivables will in practice not apply in the same way.

In addition, it is to be noted that the elimination of the right of set-off and the right to withhold performance in case of a transfer without notification to or acknowledgement by the debtor (the third rule) only applies for the transfer of bank claims *by* or *to* a credit institution, a financial institution or a mobilisation institution. A similar rule to protect the transferee of a receivable *on* a credit institution or a financial institution linked to the licensed activities has not been foreseen.

The elimination of the right of set-off and the right to withhold performance has also been justified by the argument that the increased value of bank claims as collateral ensured by this regime will enable credit institutions to reinforce their liquidity position and their solvability, which will in turn benefit their clients and depositors and that the latter persons already benefit from substantial guarantees given the applicable prudential rules and the existing deposit guarantee scheme. This justification calls similar observations as made above in respect of covered bonds. In addition it is to be pointed out that whereas in the context of covered bonds, the transfer of receivables to the specific estate is subject to specific conditions and to the supervision of the NBB, which are – to a certain extent – aimed at securing the interests of the debtors, such specific conditions and supervision are not foreseen for the cases where the transfer or pledge of receivables takes place outside the context of the covered bonds.

The Belgian legislator also considered that sufficient balance between the interests of the transferee and potential debtors was ensured since the MRA does not deviate from article 27 of the Belgian Consumer Credit Act which reserves to debtors that qualify as a consumer in the sense of the Consumer Credit Act (i.e. if the transferred receivable arises out of a consumer credit) all means of defence, despite the transfer. Not all consumers are protected, however. Consumers that received credit outside of the Belgian Consumer Credit Act (e.g. mortgage credit)[194] from institutions falling within the scope *ratione personae* of the MRA are excluded from this protection. It is difficult to understand why an exemption should be granted to consumers who have been granted a consumer credit and not to other consumers.

As regards transfers or pledging of bank claims by or to a credit institution or a financial institution, the basic equilibrium organised by the generally applicable provisions between the position of the debtor and the position of the transferee seems to be substantially disrupted by the exclusion of set-off and the right to withhold performance.[195]

Especially to the extent that the right to withhold performance and the set-off for claims out of reciprocal (contractual) relations is no longer possible, the regime seems to favour an enrichment of the transferee. Indeed, in case of reciprocal relations the transferee knows that the transferor is only creditor to the extent that the transferor duly performs his obligations and only for the balance after deduction of the claims the debtor has against the transferor. Granting the transferee full payment in this case, even if the transferor does not perform and without the possibility of set-off for the debtor, implies that the debtor is prejudiced by the transfer. Thus the debtor will no longer be able to invoke basic means of defence available in reciprocal relations at a time where this remedy plays a crucial role for him: insolvency or other circumstance of *concursum creditorum* of the transferor. Some scholars have considered these basic means of defence in respect of transfer of reciprocal claims to be evident, although they now accept that it is not sound to maintain them in the context of the mobilisation of bank claims where receivables are used for obtaining liquidities.[196]

The exclusion of set-off and the right to withhold performance in case of insolvency of the transferor or the pledgor even though the transfer has not been notified seem to make things even worse for the debtor. It implies that the debtor, who is not even aware of the fact that the credit institution has transferred the claim against him, can suddenly be confronted with a transferee and be frustrated in his lawful expectations as to its legal position. Any debtor of a bank claim who is also a creditor of the same institution (i.e. holds deposits at the same credit institutions) faces the risk of being deprived of two principle defences in contractual relations as a result of the mobilisation over which he has no control (since his consent is not required) and without being informed of his legal situation being changed. This legal endorsement of the practice of 'occult' transfers has a perverse effect: it allows the parties concerned by the transfer to avoid the burden and cost of notification formalities and to reap the benefits of the legal security granted to the transferee, while at the same time causing an increased counterparty risk for the debtor.

Additionally the MRA may create wrong incentives. The mobilisation of receivables could now be seen by credit institutions not only as a way to eliminate credit risk for their clients/counterparties but also as a way to decrease possible claims of (certain) clients/counterparties (i.e. to decrease their own liabilities). At the same time, the safe feeling that the MRA may create – not fully justified, however, since not all defences that a debtor can invoke in the case of transfer to avoid payment are excluded – will reduce the incentive for transferees or pledgees to duly supervise the activities of the credit institution they finance. Adding to this the moral hazard[197] created by the expectation that the Belgian authorities will probably apply all means to avoid the insolvency of (critical) financial institutions[198] combined with the fact that the MRA does not set restrictions on the type of transaction in the context of which the receivables should be mobilised to benefit from the beneficial regime nor prescribes any quality requirements for the receivables or specific supervision, the MRA framework seems to facilitate more than before the further development by those financial institutions of complex products involving transfers of receivables.

4.2.2. Transfers of bank claims are more equal than others?

As is the case for the BCBA, the MRA also raises concerns related to the beneficiaries that can make use of the more favourable rules for the mobilisation of receivables. The title of the MRA makes no secret of it: the MRA is specifically conceived to serve the financial sector. The preparatory works do not explain what specific reasons underlie this limitation of scope. Since the preparatory works quite bluntly express the view that the general law rules related to the transfer or pledging of receivables, especially as regards the means of defence of the debtor, are inadequate and make these assets particularly unsuitable for mobilisation transactions (see footnote 147), the logical conclusion seems to be that the general framework, that serves all, should be adapted in a general way. As already mentioned above, other companies are interested in robust and smooth mechanisms for the mobilisation of receivables that would allow them to (re)finance themselves at a lower cost and with as much as possible legal security. Why should only the financial sector be given a more favourable regime and companies of other sectors be obliged to continue to work with a framework that has explicitly been qualified as unsuitable? If the rules implemented by the MRA are to be maintained it seems difficult to justify reserving them to the financial sector.

Even as concerns the financial sector, not all companies of this sector seem to be placed on the same level. Despite the expectation created by the title of the MRA that it benefits the financial sector to a large extent, the scope of application of the MRA is more limited than its title seems to imply, as a result of the combination of limitations in respect of the scope *ratione personae* and of the scope *ratione materiae* of the MRA.

The scope *ratione personae* of the provisions introduced by both chapters of the MRA generally concerns credit institutions, financial institutions and mobilisation institutions,[199] to the extent that the provisions of the MRA specifically refer to the aforementioned companies. As to the term credit institution, no specific definition is provided by the MRA. The term seems thus to be understood in its general meaning as provided by the CIA, meaning that the MRA applies to Belgian and foreign undertakings whose business is to receive deposits or other repayable funds from the public and to grant credits for their own account.[200] The term mobilisation institution has been defined by the MRA and covers, as a general matter, Belgian and foreign institutions involved in securitisation.[201] Financial institutions are defined with reference to the definition in article 3, 12° of the FCA and encompass any company that is not a credit institution and whose main activity consists in the acquisition of participations or in the exercise of one of the activities mentioned in article 3, §2 of the CIA. Article 3 FCA then lists as examples a mortgage company, a company granting consumer credits, a company specialised in leasing, a payment institution or an institution for electronic money. As this list of companies serving as examples is not exclusive, any company exercising an activity eligible for the mutual recognition in the context of the European passport as mentioned in article 3, §2 of the CIA can be considered a financial institution for the scope of application *ratione personae* of the MRA. Other companies than those listed above, such as for example factoring companies thus also fall within this definition of financial institution. However, some companies, despite generally being considered a financial institution,[202] like insurance companies, do not seem to qualify as a financial institution in the sense of the MRA since not mentioned in the examples listed in article 3, 12° FCA nor in article 3, §2 CIA.

Without going into the details of the given definitions, a closer look into the meaning of the terms 'credit institution', 'financial institution' and 'mobilisation institution' leads to the conclusion that the scope *ratione personae* is broad but does not seem to cover all institutions of the financial sector. This conclusion must however immediately be nuanced, taking into account the peculiar formulation of the MRA. Indeed, the rules of the MRA apply in principle to the transfer of pledging *by* or *to* the above-mentioned institutions. The MRA is thus applicable to transactions where (1) the transferor/pledgor qualifies as one of the mentioned institutions or (2) the transferee/pledgee qualifies as one of these three entities, the status of the transferor being irrelevant. Although thus e.g. insurance companies do not qualify as financial institution in the sense of the FCA and thus fall outside the scope of the MRA (since the MRA takes over the definition of the FCA),[203] a transfer or a pledge by insurance companies *to* a credit institution or a mobilisation institution would thus from a *ratione personae* perspective fall within the scope of the MRA. The same would be valid for transfers or pledges by commercial companies *to* one of the above companies.

To determine who can apply the favourable regime under the MRA, the scope of application *ratione personae* thus defined must however in addition be combined with the scope of application *ratione materiae* of the provisions introduced by the MRA. Whereas the title of the MRA refers in general to the mobilisation of receivables (*schuldvorderingen/créances*), the general provisions in the MRA do not concern receivables in general, but (save some exceptions)[204] bank claims defined with reference to the definition of this notion in the FCA. This means that where the term bank claim is used only claims arising out of a loan or a credit arrangement with a credit institution, a mortgage company or a person/company granting consumer credits are envisaged.[205] As a result, the scope of application of the MRA is significantly reduced. Thus for example, although factoring companies fall within the notion of financial institutions used by the MRA, transfers of commercial receivables to factoring companies and retransfer of such receivables by factoring companies to credit institutions in the context of refinancing operations do not fall under the scope of the MRA, since they do not qualify as bank claims. The same applies to transfers of receivables by leasing companies in the context of their refinancing operations. Whereas transfers of receivables by certain companies would fall within the scope *ratione personae* of the MRA (e.g. insurance companies), although they do not qualify as a financial institution, they will also fall outside the scope to the extent that these receivables cannot be considered bank claims.

Although the title of the MRA creates the expectation of a specific framework for the mobilisation of receivables applicable to the financial sector as a whole and of all entities of the financial sector being put on an equal footing in respect of the legal framework applicable to the mobilisation of receivables, this is thus not the case. The MRA introduces a beneficial regime for the mobilisation of receivables for a far more restricted number of companies in the financial sector than it seems to imply. By doing so, the MRA creates distortions as a result of which certain institutions of the financial sector are granted an important competitive advantage in the context of (re)financing operations, both as transferor (they can more easily transfer claims and receive financing at better conditions) and as transferee (they can take over claims under a more favourable regime and thus grant credits under better conditions than other companies with a similar business activity).

5. CONCLUSIONS

By subsequent legal acts, classical mechanisms of security law, insolvency law, law of obligations and also estate law have subsequently been set aside in Belgium to satisfy certain needs of the financial sector. As a response to the financial crises, the BCBA and the MRA further follow the path paved by the FCA of introducing specific private law deviations for certain financial institutions. Both aimed at ensuring better financing possibilities for certain institutions of the financial sector, the BCBA allows Belgian credit institutions to facilitate the use of receivables as collateral in the context of covered bonds issue and the MRA more generally eliminates to the benefit of certain financial institutions the legal obstacles that impedes the mobilisation of receivables.

The main ingredients to increase the attractiveness of the use of receivables in the context of financing transactions for the concerned institutions consist of increasing legal security for potential financers and decreasing transactional costs for those involved in the transaction. The examination of the BCBA and the MRA leads to the conclusion that these ingredients create questionable distortions as a result of:

(1) a risk shifting to (certain) creditors of those institutions seeking to be refinanced with application of the enacted regimes, in most cases occurring without these creditors being aware thereof and thus not being able to adjust their behaviour or receive an additional risk premium; and
(2) an imbalance between (re)financing mechanisms in general: the interventions benefit certain companies of the financial sector, to the exclusion of other companies within and outside the financial sector who equally need reliable and strong mechanisms to secure their (re)financing, thereby contributing to reinforcing the dominance of certain professional credit suppliers.

The financial crisis has shown that, given the serious grip the financial system has on society, ensuring a stable financial system is of interest to all.

But is it justified that the stability of financial companies is organised via measures that adversely affect others than those that are responsible for the good functioning of the financial system? To the extent that these others should contribute because of the benefits for the community derived from these measures, are sufficient guarantees and incentives in place to ensure that the fruits reaped from the advantages granted effectively flow to the community? The implemented measures offer support to certain actors of the financial sector by eliminating legal obstacles considered too complex, too costly and creating too much insecurity for credit institutions without sufficiently balancing the impact on depositors and other creditors. The costs reduction the new regime aims to realise will certainly benefit credit institutions. Whether the real economy will also benefit from it remains to be seen. It is to be hoped that other regulatory initiatives taken or to be taken contribute to achieving this goal, by ensuring sound lending practices and by preventing abuses of the mechanisms put in place by the BCBA and the MRA that would threaten the well-functioning of the financial system.

The BCBA and the MRA support in essence the credit supply activity of credit institutions. The interests of other financial and non-financial institutions in using the mobilisation of receivables as (re)financing technique are not considered by this text. Currently these other companies must continue to rely on the existing common legal framework. To the extent that the deviations introduced by the BCBA and the MRA are based on the consideration that the existing legal framework is not suitable for a legally secure mobilisation of receivables in the framework of financing operations, and to the extent that the mobilisation of receivables is considered an encourageable practice in financing context, a more general rethinking of this 'unsuitable' framework seems to be a logical conclusion, especially in a society where receivables and intangible assets increasingly form the main part of the estate of companies and estates in general. Taking into account the foregoing, a broader debate and reflection on the consequences and impact of the BCBA and the MRA than seems to have been conducted at the time these legal acts were enacted, is thus in my opinion to be encouraged.

Endnotes

* G. Orwell, *Animal Farm*.

** Régine Feltkamp is a Professor at the Free University of Brussels, an Attorney at the Brussels Bar and a Member of the Board of the European Association for Banking and Finance Law Belgium. This text was finalised at the beginning of 2014. It does not take into account the new banking law that was not yet enacted at that time.

1. Bail-in tools give authorities the power to impose losses of failing financial institutions on the unsecured creditors as part of a resolution process. Such tool is seen as a means to reduce the need for the taxpayer to support failing financial institutions.
2. See Act of 3 August 2012 '*Loi instaurant un régime légal pour les covered bonds belges*', *Belgian State Gazette*, 24 August 2012.
3. See Act of 3 August 2012 '*Loi relative à des mesures diverses pour faciliter la mobilisation de créances dans le secteur financier*', *Belgian State Gazette*, 24 August 2012.
4. Which can occur where long-term assets (such as mortgage credits) are financed by short-term liabilities, such as deposits which can be withdrawn at short notice or short-term repurchase agreements ('repos'), consisting of short-term lending structured via the sale of assets with the commitment to repurchase them. Prior to the outburst of the crisis certain financial institutions heavily relied on (overnight) repo financing. See inter alia M.K. Brunnermeier, 'Deciphering the liquidity and credit crunch 2007–08', NBER Working Paper Series, 2008, available at: www.nber.org/papers/w14612.pdf?new_window=1. According to Gorton and Metrick a run on the repo market as a result of concerns on the quality of the underlying assets contributed to the collapse of the banking system. See Gorton and Metrick, 'Securitized Banking and the Run on Repo, NBER Working Paper Series, issued in August 2009, available at www.nber.org/papers/w15223
5. See Explanatory memorandum (I), '*projet de loi du 6 juillet 2012 instaurant un regime legal pour les covered bonds belges – projet de loi relatif à des mesures diverses pour faciliter la mobilisation de créances dans le secteur financier*', *Doc. Parl. Chambre* 2011–12, n° 2341/001 (hereafter referred to as 'Explanatory memorandum (I)'), p. 4: '*S'inspirant des legislations étrangères, le présent projet entend ainsi faciliter les possibilités de refinancement des établissements de crédit tout en mettant en place les mécanismes juridiques adéquats destinés à protéger les titulaires des titres de créances ainsi émis*' (free translation: 'inspired by foreign legislation the present draft of law intends to facilitate the refinancing possibilities of credit institutions albeit implementing adequate legal mechanisms to protect the holders of the issued titles').
6. See the Report of 17 July 2012 in name of the Finance and Budget Commission prepared by G. Coëme, Draft BCBA/MRA, *Doc. Parl. Chambre* 2011–12, no. 2341/003 (hereafter referred to as 'Coëme Report') p. 5: '*De nombreuses entraves juridiques empêchent cependant une grande partie de ces portefeuilles de créances en Belgique de servir de garantie de refinancement ou alors de l'être à des conditions nettement moins avantageuses. Ce projet de loi permet donc de résoudre une série de problèmes juridico-techniques*' (free translation: 'due to many legal obstacles a great deal of (the portofolio of) credit claims in Belgium can however not be used as security for refinancing or at much unfavourable conditions').
7. See Explanatory memorandum (II), '*projet de loi du 6 juillet 2012 instaurant un regime legal pour les covered bonds belges – projet de loi relatif à des mesures diverses pour faciliter la mobilisation de créances dans le secteur financier*', *Doc. Parl. Chambre* 2011–12, n° 2341/001 (hereafter referred to as 'Explanatory memorandum (II)'), p. 37: '*La crise financière a mis en évidence la nécessité pour les institutions financières de pouvoir mobiliser au maximum leurs actifs à titre de garantie ("collateral") afin d'être en mesure de se financer de manière optimale et aux conditions les plus avantageuses. Ce mode de financement via les banques centrales de l'Eurosystème s'est même révélé déterminant dans la gestion des retombées de la crise financière actuelle*' (free translation: 'the financial crisis has shown that financial institutions must be able to use their assets

to a maximum extent as collateral to obtain themselves as smooth and cheaply possible financing. Such financing via central banks of the Eurosystem has even appeared crucial for controlling the negative effects of the actual financial crisis'); Coëme Report, p. 5.

8. See Coëme Report p. 3: '*Le projet de loi vise à faciliter le refinancement des établissements de crédit à long terme. Il est nécessaire, pour ces établissements de crédit, d'obtenir un refinancement à long terme à un coût raisonnable, afin qu'ils puissent, également à long terme, fournir des crédits à un coût raisonnable à nos entreprises et à nos ménages. En vue de stimuler l'activité économique, il est en effet d'une importance cruciale que nos entreprises et nos ménages puissent disposer d'un financement suffisant*' (free translation: 'the draft act aims at facilitating the long-term refinancing of credit institutions. The long-term refinancing of credit institutions at a reasonable cost is a necessity for these credit institutions, so that they are able to grant also long-term credits at reasonably cost to businesses and households. To stimulate economic activity it is indeed of crucial importance that businesses and households have access to sufficient financing').

9. Mainly as a result of the favourable ratings provided by the rating agencies.

10. In particular, securitisation via specific purpose vehicles, consisting of packaging up receivables out of loans in (complex) investment products (asset backed securities and collateral debt obligations) to be distributed to investors via the creation of separate entities ('special purpose vehicles') to whom the receivables were transferred. This structuring implied that the receivables out of loans could be kept off the balance sheet so that they would no longer count against the prudential capital requirements. Thus banks could expand their lending. Via this structure the risk associated with lending (default and interest risk) was, in slices, pushed through to the investors and the diminished responsibility it entailed encouraged banks to develop less cautious and even unhealthy lending practices. At the same time though the banks would grant back-up loans to these vehicles to ensure their funding liquidity and consequently still bore the financing risk of these vehicles. See in this respect amongst others Report of 25 February 2009 of the high-level group on financial supervision in the EU chaired by J. de Larosière (the so-called 'Larosière Report'), pp. 7–8, available at http://ec.europa.eu/internal_market/finances/docs/de_larosiere_report_en.pdf; F. Bellot, G. Coëme, H. De Croo, L. Van der Auwera and B. Collas, '*Rapport fait au nom de la Commission spéciale chargée d'examiner la crise financière et bancaire*', *Doc. Parl.* 2008–2009, Chambre 1642/002 / Senat 4–1100/1 and in particular pp. 43–45, 48, 176, 357 ff; Report of the Financial Stability Forum on enhancing market and institutional resilience, 7 April 2008, pp. 5 ff, available at www.financialstabilityboard.org/publications/r_0804.pdf; R. Ricol, Raport sur la crise financière, September 2008, available at www.ladocumentationfrancaise.fr/var/storage/rapports-publics/084000587/0000.pdf, pp. 25–29. See also amongst others J. Attali, *La crise et après*, Paris, Fayard, 2009, pp. 51 ff; K. Brunnermeier, 'Deciphering the liquidity and crédit craunch 2007–08', NBER Working Paper Series, 2008, pp. 3 ff, available at www.nber.org/papers/w14612.pdf?new_window=1; A. Brummer, *The Crunch, how greed and incompetence sparked the credit crisis*, London, Random House Business Books, 2009, pp. 36 ff; J. Stiglitz, *Free fall. Free markets and the sinking of the global economy*, London, Penguin Books, 2010, pp. 77 ff, in particular pp. 90–97.

11. Act of 4 August 1992 '*relative au crédit hypothécaire*', *Belgian State Gazette*, 19 August 1992, referred to as the 'Belgian Mortgage Credit Act'. R. Feltkamp, *Overdracht van schuldvordering, Naar een meer eenvormige tegenwerpbaarheidsregeling voor overdrachten in de burgerrechtelijke en handelsrechterlijke sfeer*, Antwerp, Intersentia, 2005, pp. 839 ff.

12. Act of 6 July 1994 '*modifiant la loi du 17 juin 1991 portant organisation du secteur public du crédit et de la détention des participations du secteur public dans certaines sociétés financières de droit privé, ainsi que la loi du 22 mars 1993 relative au statut et au contrôle des établissements de crédit*', *Belgian State Gazette,* 15 July 1994.
13. This act was initially intended to only modify the legal status of the A.S.L.K. Holding who could, since the privatisation of A.S.L.K- Bank and A.S.L.K Insurance no longer be considered as a public bank holding. The modification of the regime in respect of the transfer of receivables was introduced by an amendment to the initial draft of the act. See R. Feltkamp, *supra* note 11, pp. 361 ff.
14. R. Feltkamp, *supra* note 11, pp. 361 ff.
15. The central office for mortgage loans, a public credit institution created in 1936 to stimulate house construction in Belgium and to facilitate the acquisition of houses. Its activities have been transferred to Stater Belgium (in 2000) and to Argenta (2001).
16. R. Feltkamp, *supra* note 11, p. 355, no. 338.
17. R. Feltkamp, *supra* note 11, p. 844, no. 913.
18. Directive 2002/47/EC of the European Parliament and of the Council of 6 June 2002 on financial collateral arrangements, *OJ* L 168 of 27 June 2002, p. 43.
19. This is the risk that the insolvency of a particular credit institution entails, by domino effect, the insolvency of other banks.
20. Act of 15 December 2004 '*relative aux sûretés financières et portant des dispositions fiscales diverses en matière de conventions constitutives de sûreté réelle et de prêts portant sur des instruments financiers*', *Belgian State Gazette,* 1 February 2005.
21. The preparatory works to this Act specifically indicate that as regards physical persons this Act would only concern wealthy persons *since only they have securities or cash that can be given as collateral.* See Explanatory memorandum, '*projet de loi du 26 octobre 2004 'relatif aux sûretés financières et portant des dispositions fiscales diverses en matière de conventions constitutives de sûreté réelle et de prêts portant sur des instruments financiers*', *Doc. Parl.,* Chambre 2004–05, no 1407/001, p. 11.
22. See Act of 26 September 2011 '*transposant la Directive 2009/44/CE du Parlement européen et du Conseil du 6 mai 2009 modifiant la Directive 98/26/CE concernant le caractère définitif du règlement dans les systèmes de paiement et de règlement des opérations sur titres et la Directive 2002/47/CE concernant les contrats de garantie financière, en ce qui concerne les systèmes liés et les créances privées*', *Belgian State Gazette,* 10 November 2011.
23. Directive 2009/44/EC refers to credit claims, defined as 'pecuniary claims arising out of an agreement whereby a credit institution, as defined in Art. 4(1) of Directive 2006/48/EC, including the institutions listed in Art. 2 of that Directive, grants credit in the form of a loan' (see Art. 2(5)(a)(ii) of Directive 2009/44/EC amending Art. 2, §1, o) of the DFCA).
24. Directive 2009/44/EC of the European Parliament and of the Council of 6 May 2009 amending Directive 98/26/EC on settlement finality in payment and securities settlement systems and Directive 2002/47/EC on financial collateral arrangements as regards linked systems and credit claims, *OJ* L 146, 10 June 2009 (hereafter referred to as 'Directive 2009/44'), p. 37.
25. See Consideration (5) to the Directive 2009/44.
26. See Consideration (6) to the Directive 2009/44. In this respect, Art. 2(6)(a) of Directive 2009/44 amends Art. 3, §1 DFCA by adding the following subparagraph: 'Without

prejudice to Article 1(5), when credit claims are provided as financial collateral, Member States shall not require that the creation, validity, perfection, priority, enforceability or admissibility in evidence of such financial collateral be dependent on the performance of any formal act such as the registration or the notification of the debtor of the credit claim provided as collateral. However, Member States may require the performance of a formal act, such as registration or notification, for purposes of perfection, priority, enforceability or admissibility in evidence against the debtor or third parties'.

27. See Consideration (6) to the Directive 2009/44 and Art. 2(6)(b) of Directive 2009/44/EC amending Art. 3 DFCA.
28. See Consideration (5) to the Directive 2009/44.
29. Art. 3, 10° FCA.
30. Act of 12 June 1991 '*relative au crédit à la consommation*', *Belgian State Gazette*, 9 July 1991, hereafter the Credit Consumer Act.
31. Act of 6 April 2010 '*relative aux pratiques du marché et à la protection du consommateur*', *Belgian State Gazette*, 12 April 2010.
32. Art. 5 of the Belgian Mortgage Credit Act.
33. See Report of 9 September 2011 in name of the Finance and Budget Commission prepared by G. Rutten, '*projet de loi transposant la directive 2009/44/CE du Parlement européen et du Conseil du 6 mai 2009 modifiant la directive 98/26/CE concernant le caractère définitif du règlement dans les systèmes de paiement et de règlement des opérations sur titres et la directive 2002/47/CE concernant les contrats de garantie financière, en ce qui concerne les systèmes liés et les créances privées*', *Doc. Parl.* Chambre 2010–11, no. 1714/003, p. 13.
34. See Report of 9 September 2011 in name of the Finance and Budget Commission prepared by G. Rutten, '*projet de loi transposant la directive 2009/44/CE du Parlement européen et du Conseil du 6 mai 2009 modifiant la directive 98/26/CE concernant le caractère définitif du règlement dans les systèmes de paiement et de règlement des opérations sur titres et la directive 2002/47/CE concernant les contrats de garantie financière, en ce qui concerne les systèmes liés et les créances privées*', *Doc. Parl.* Chambre 2010–11, no. 1714/003, pp. 13 ff, in particular p. 14, second line: '*Par rapport à la crainte de voir se développer de nouveaux produits, il ne faut pas perdre de vue qu'il est ici question de créances bancaires, qui découlent d'un accord au terme duquel un prêt ou un crédit a été consenti par un établissement de crédit à un établissement de crédit à la consommation ou un établissement de crédit hypothécaire. Il s'agit donc de cas relativement limités.*'
35. Art. 7 Belgian Mortgage Act.
36. See amongst others for a description of the history of covered bonds S.L. Schwarz, 'The Conundrum of Covered Bonds', *The Business Lawyer* 2011, vol. 66, pp. 563 ff; also available at: http://papers.ssrn.com/sol3/papers.cfm?abstract_id=1661018 (last accessed in July 2013). See also S. Landuyt and L Anckaert, 'Nieuwe financieringstechnieken in de bancaire sector: covered bonds en de mobilisering van schuldvorderingen', *TBH* 2013, p. 161, no. 53.
37. S.L. Schwarz, *supra* note 36, p. 562.
38. For an overview see amongst others: S.L. Schwarz, *supra* note 36, p. 565, footnote 28. See also for a tool to compare the covered bond legislation implemented in Europe: www.ecbc.eu/framework/freeCompare/add_filter_chapter/1.
39. A specific deviation applies e.g. for the investment in these instruments for undertakings for collective investments in transferable securities (UCITS). Whereas in

principle a UCITS may not invest more than 5% of its assets in transferable securities or money market instruments issued by the same body, this limit may be raised to a maximum of 25% where bonds are issued by a credit institution which has its registered office in a Member State and is subject by law to special public supervision designed to protect bondholders. In particular, sums deriving from the issue of those bonds must be invested in accordance with the law in assets which, during the whole period of validity of the bonds, are capable of covering claims attaching to the bonds and which, in the event of failure of the issuer, would be used on a priority basis for the reimbursement of the principal and payment of the accrued interest. If this is the case, the foregoing implies that a UCITS can hold up to 25% of its assets in such regulated covered bonds issued by a single issuer, compared to only 5% in other bonds from a single issuer. It is also provided that if a UCITS invests more than 5% of its assets in these bonds, which are issued by a single issuer, the total value of these investments may not exceed 80% of the value of the assets of the UCITS. See Art. 52, §1 and §4 of Directive 2009/65/EG of the European Parliament and the Council of 13 July 2009 of 13 July 2009 on the coordination of laws, regulations and administrative provisions relating to undertakings for collective investment in transferable securities (UCITS), *OJ L* 302 17 November 2009, p. 32.

A specific deviation applies also for certain insurance institutions. See e.g. Art. 24.4 (rules for investment diversification) of Directive 2002/83/EC of the European Parliament and the Council of 5 November 2002 concerning life assurance (*PB L* 345 of 9 December 1992) according to which the investment limit of 5% for investments in instruments of certain issuers can be raised to 40% by the Member States 'in the case of certain debt securities when these are issued by a credit institution which has its head office in a Member State and is subject by law to special official supervision designed to protect the holders of those debt securities. In particular, sums deriving from the issue of such debt securities must be invested in accordance with the law in assets which, during the whole period of validity of the debt securities, are capable of covering claims attaching to debt securities and which, in the event of failure of the issuer, would be used on a priority basis for the reimbursement of the principal and payment of the accrued interest.'

40. Credit institutions e.g. that are subject to the Capital Requirements Directive must hold capital to cover possible losses on their assets *based* on the risk profile of those assets. The amounts of capital to be retained is determined on the basis of a risk weighting of these assets. Investments by credit institutions in regulated covered bonds benefit from a preferential treatment. See paragraph 71 of Annex VI of Directive 2006/48/EC of the European Parliament and of the Council of 14 June 2006 relating to the taking up and pursuit of the business of credit institutions (recast), *OJ* L 177, 30 June 2006. The BCBA distinguishes a specific type of covered bond, called the '*Belgische Pandbrief*', which are covered bonds that specifically comply with the specific conditions for benefitting the beneficial risk weighting enacted in the Belgian framework concerning capital requirements. See art. 64/7, §1 CIA as introduced by art. 15 BCBA.

41 See among others ECB, 'The ECB's response to the financial crisis', p. 66, www.ecb.europa.eu/pub/pdf/other/art1_mb201010en pp59–74en.pdf; ECB, 'The impact of the Eurosystem's covered bond purchase programme on the primary and secondary markets', 2011, www.ecb.europa.eu/pub/pdf/scpops/ecbocp122.pdf. See also www.ecb.europa.eu/press/pr/date/2009/html/pr090604_1.en.html for the conditions for the ECB purchase programme in 2009.

42. This was also the motivation for the urgency with which the Belgian covered bonds regime was introduced. See the Advice of 28 June of the Council of State on the BCBA, *Doc. Chambre* 2011–12, no. 2341/001, p. 91 and the Advice of 8 October 2012 of the Council of State on the Royal Decree of 11 October 2012 '*relatif à l'émission de covered bonds belges par des établissements de crédit de droit belge*', *Belgian State Gazette*, 18 October 2012, hereafter 'RD CB Issue'.
43. The term 'Belgian covered bonds' is protected. It may only be used for securities that are issued in compliance with the legal and regulatory provisions regarding the issue of Belgian covered bonds (see art. 64/1 CIA).
44. Act of 22 March 1993 '*relative au statut et au contrôle des établissements de crédit*', *Belgian State Gazette*, 19 April 1993.
45. Belfius, KBC and ING.
46. Art. 64/17, §1 CIA. In such case, as long as the covered bonds are held by the credit institution that issued them, the covered bonds do not enjoy the rights related to participation to the general assemblee of bondholders, except if the issue conditions provide otherwise.
47. See RD CB Issue. This Royal Decree further determines, amongst other things, the different categories of receivables and specifies that the cover pool must be composed for 85% of one of the first three listed categories of cover assets. See art. 3 RD CB Issue.
48. Art. 64/7, §2, al. 2 CIA and art. 5, §2 RD CB Issue. In practice an even higher collateralisation is often conventionally agreed upon.
49. Art. 7 RD CB Issue.
50. Art. 64/3, §1 CIA (as introduced by art. 10 BCBA) determines the conditions under which the general permission of the NBB may be granted. To obtain this permission the issuer must submit a file with information on the organisational capacity of the issuer. The file with information on the organisation capacity must contain the following information: (1) a description of the financial position of the issuer and especially its credit previsions, from which it appears it is sufficiently solvable to guarantee the interests of other creditors than the Belgian covered bond holders; (2) a description of the long-term strategy of the issuer, with particular attention for the liquidity and the place of the Belgian covered bonds in this strategy; (3) a description of the tasks and responsibilities within the issuer related to the issue of Belgian covered bonds; (4) a description of the risk management policy of the issuer for the Belgian covered bonds, with specific attention for interest risk, exchange rate risk, credit- and counterparty risk, liquidity risk and operational risk; (5) a description of the involvement of the internal audit in the issue procedure for Belgian covered bonds; and (6) a description of the IT systems necessary for the issue of Belgian covered bonds. The general permission of the NBB may only be granted if the NBB is satisfied that (1) the administrative and accounting organisation of the issuer is suitable to comply with the provisions regarding the issue of covered bonds and in particular the segregation of the covered assets and (2) proof is provided that the financial position of the issuer, in particular its solvability, is sufficient to guarantee the interests of the other creditors than the covered bondholders (see art. 64/3, §1 al. 2, CIA).
51. Art. 64/3, §3 CIA (as introduced by art. 10 BCBA) determines the conditions for the specific permission of the NBB of a given issue or issue programme. This specific permission also requires the submission of a file with information on the issue and the issue programme and in particular on the quality of assets by which the Belgian

covered bonds are covered. The NBB must determine which information should be provided and this information should at least concern: (1) the impact of the programme on the liquidity position of the credit institution; (2) the quality of the cover assets, in particular the nature of the debtors of these assets and of the real or personal collateral, guarantees or privileges by which they are covered, the diversification of the assets and their due date; (3) the extent to which the expiry date of the Belgian covered bond matches the due date of the cover assets; and (4) the elements on the basis of which it can be proven that the conditions to receive the general approval are still satisfied (art. 64/3, §2 CIA).

52. The NBB must publish on its website a list of the credit instructions that may issue Belgian covered bonds (art. 64/5, §3, 1° CIA is introduced by art. 12 BCBA) and per authorised credit institution a list of the issued covered bonds/issue programmes for which a specific permission is granted (art. 64/5, §3, 2° CIA).
53. Art. 5, §2 RD CB Issue.
54. Art. 64/21, §1 CIA (introduced by art. 32 BCBA). In particular the pool monitor should report on the compliance with the quality conditions to which the cover assets are subject, the limits regarding the cover assets, the conditions regarding the level of coverage and the liquidities at disposal as described in the RD CB Issue (see art. 11 RD CB Issue).
55. Art. 64/20, §2 CIA. Art. 11 RD CB Issue foresees a yearly verification duty and, only as regards the cover and liquidity test and the registration of the cover assets, a monthly verification duty.
56. Art. 64/20 CIA (introduced by art. 30 BCBA).
57. See in this respect R. Feltkamp, 'Een kredietinstelling, meerdere vermogens – Vermogensrechtelijke bedenkingen bij de regeling inzake Belgische covered bonds', in *Liber amicorum Hélène Casman*, Antwerp, Intersentia, 2013, pp. 194 ff and references cited.
58. See art. 64, §2 CIA for a description of the assets that form part of the special estate. As a general matter this special estate includes the cover pool assets themselves provided they have been registered as well as the collateral securing the cover pool assets and all amounts held by the issuing credit institution as a result of payments related to the cover pool assets.
59. The possibility is foreseen to structure the covered bond issue through the transfer of the cover pool assets in a separate company, in which case this separate company should also be a credit institution (whether or not from the same group). See art. 64/9 CIA.
60. According to the preparatory parliamentary works this is based on a fiction (see Explanatory memorandum (I), no. 2341/001, p. 26). Given that a person cannot in principle contract with itself, except if he acts in different capacities (acting for itself and acting on behalf of someone else), the question arises as to what the legislator intended here. To the extent that the issuing credit institution is responsible, by virtue of art. 64/12 CIA for the management of the special estate until a liquidation procedure is opened, or until a pool supervisor is appointed, if this is earlier, the aforementioned fiction could refer to a sort of trust construction according to which the special estate is held by the issuing credit institution for the account of the beneficiaries of the special estate. This would explain the fact that the credit institution can transact with itself.
61. Art. 64/12 CIA.
62. See art. 9, §1 MRA.
63. This is defined by art. 3, §1, 9° CIA as a collective procedure initiated and controlled by an administrative or judicial authority to realise the assets of a credit institution

under supervision of these authorities and for Belgian credit institutions bankruptcy is considered as such a procedure.

64. Art. 64/16 CIA (introduced by art. 24 BCBA).
65. Art. 64/13 CIA (introduced by art. 21 BCBA).
66. Art. 64/10 CIA (introduced by art. 18 BCBA).
67. This positive balance is by virtue of law part of the general estate of the issuing credit institution (art. 64/11, al. 7 CIA).
68. Art. 64/16, 8° CIA.
69. Art. 64/11, al. 7 CIA (introduced by art. 19 BCBA).
70. This is repeated by art. 64/16, 4° CIA for the opening of liquidation procedures against the issuing credit institution: the creditors of obligations and debts covered by a special estate, retain their rights in the liquidation procedure pursuant to art. 64/11, al. 8 CIA.
71. Art. 1690 Belgian Civil Code. See R. Feltkamp, *supra* note 11, pp. 361 ff.
72. Art. 5 Belgian Mortgage Act. See R. Feltkamp, *supra* note 11, pp. 492 ff.
73. Art. 9, §1 RD CB Issue and 8, §2 MRA (which specifically governs the enforceability of the registration in the event of an insolvency proceeding or another case of *concursum creditorum*).
74. Art. 1167 Belgian Civil Code.
75. Art. 20 Belgian Bankruptcy Act.
76. Art. 8, §3 and 4 MRA.
77. Art. 64/8, §2, al. 1, 4° CIA.
78. Art. 64/10 CIA.
79. Art. 64/8, §2, al. 2 CIA.
80. Art. 64/11 CIA.
81. Explanatory memorandum (I), p. 25.
82. Proposal for a directive of the European Parliament and of the Council establishing a framework for the recovery and resolution of credit institutions and investment firms and amending Council Directives 77/91/EEC and 82/891/EC, Directives 2001/24/EC, 2002/47/EC, 2004/25/EC, 2005/56/EC, 2007/36/EC and 2011/35/EC and Regulation (EU) No 1093/2010, COM/2012/0280 final – 2012/0150 (COD), available at: http://eur-lex.europa.eu/LexUriServ/LexUriServ.do?uri=CELEX:52012PC0280:EN:NOT.
83. See art. 38 of the draft directive that provides that resolution authorities shall not exercise the write down and conversion powers in relation to, amongst other things, deposits that are guaranteed in accordance with Directive 94/19/EC and secured liabilities. This exclusion of the bail-in tools does not, according to the same provision, prevent the resolution authorities, where appropriate, from exercising the write down and conversion powers in relation to any part of a secured liability or a liability for which collateral has been pledged that exceeds the value of the assets, pledge, lien or collateral against which it is secured. However Member States may be exempt from these provisions covered bonds as defined in Article 22 (44) of Council Directive 86/611/EEC of 20 December 1985 on the coordination of laws, regulations and administrative provisions relating to undertakings for collective investment in transferable securities (UCITS), *OJ* L 375, 31 December 1985, p. 3, as amended.
84. The implemented legal measures have been considered good protection for covered bondholders and privileged creditors to gain full first priority access to the cover assets. See Fichs' assessment of the covered bond issue programme by ING (available at: www.ing.be/xpedio/groups/internet/@public/@internet/@ingbe/@wholesale/documents/

portalcontent/611055_en.pdf) and of the covered bond issue programme of Belfius (available at: https://www.belfius.be/financial/NL/Media/FITCH%20PRESALE%20Belfius%20mortgage%20pandbrieven%20programme_tcm_35-46346.pdf). A reservation made by Fitch concerns the remote risk that the bankruptcy administrator would claim that cover assets are returned to the general estate of the issuer since not needed to repay the covered bondholders.

85. Such assessment can either be performed as a result of an appeal for annulment, which has to be introduced in principle by the interested party within six months after publication of the act in the *Belgian State Gazette* or a court's request for preliminary ruling. In the latter case, if the legal act is considered not compatible with the higher norm, the court may not apply the legal act for settling the dispute with which it is confronted. The legal act will thus not be annulled, but a new period of six months begins to run within which an appeal for annulment of the legal act can be filed. See the Special Act of 6 January 1989 regarding the Constitutional Court, *Belgian State Gazette*, 7 January 1989, as subsequently amended.
86. See amongst others Belgian Constitutional Court 20 April 1999, no. 47/99, role no. 1593; Belgian Constitutional Court 13 March 2002, no. 46/2002, role no. 2060.
87. Constitutional Court, 27 November 2008, no. 167/200, role no. 4345.
88. See Art. 107(1) TFEU: 'any aid granted by a Member State or through State resources in any form whatsoever which distorts or threatens to distort competition by favouring certain undertakings or the production of certain goods shall, in so far as it affects trade between Member States, be incompatible with the internal market.'
89. Thus according to Art. 107(3) TFEU aid to promote the execution of an important project of common European interest or to remedy a serious disturbance in the economy of a Member State or aid to facilitate the development of certain economic activities or of certain economic areas, where such aid does not adversely affect trading conditions to an extent contrary to the common interest, may be declared compatible with the internal market by the European Commission.
90. By their nature these privileged positions create inequalities to the benefit of the 'stronger' creditor that manages to obtain (contractual) securities. It could more generally be questioned whether these (contractual) privileged creditor positions leads to fair and righteous results.
91. The privileged situation created by a mortgage or a pledge is considered as such a deviation. See R. Feltkamp, 'Een kredietinstelling, meerdere vermogens – Vermogensrechtelijke bedenkingen bij de regeling inzake Belgische covered bonds', *Liber Amicorum Hélène Casman*, Antwerp, Intersentia, 2013, p. 197.
92. See amongst others Coëme Report, p. 7. This concern has also been raised in other countries see amongst others: P. Coy, 'Are Covered Bonds a Safe Way to Finance Mortgages? Not Likely', 29 July 2008, available at: www.businessweek.com/stories/2008-07-29/are-covered-bonds-a-safe-way-to-finance-mortgages-not-likely; De Nederlandse Bank, *Jaarverslag 2011*, p. 64, available at: www.jaarverslagdnb.nl/downloads/Jaarverslag_DNB_2011.pdf.; M. Sathy, 'Banks want covered bonds, but could taxpayers be left with the risk?', available at: http://theconversation.edu.au/banks-want-covered-bonds-but-could-taxpayers-be-left-with-the-risk-3877; A. Schwab, 'Covered bonds joy for banks: increased risk for taxpayers', 28 March 2011, available at: www.crikey.com.au/2011/03/28/covered-bonds-joy-for-banks-increased-risk-for-taxpayers/; A. Tarrant, 'MPs reviewing covered bonds law concerned about depositor

risk, and question why South Africa banned covered bonds to protect bank depositors', available at: www.interest.co.nz/bonds/60382/mps-reviewing-covered-bonds-law-concerned-about-depositor-risk-and-question-why-south-af; X., 'De Nederlandse Bank en covered bonds', available at: www.huizenmarkt-zeepbel.nl/de-nederlandsche-bank-en-covered-bonds/; X., Statement to Finance and Expenditure Select Committee on Reserve Bank (Covered Bonds) Amendment Bill, 25 July 2012, available at: http://www.geoffbertram.com/fileadmin/publications/Statement%20to%20Select%20Committee%20on%20Covered%20Bonds.pdf.

93. See Explanatory memorandum (I), p. 6.
94. Other countries apply a lower limit, e.g. 4% of the assets in Canada; 4% of the commitments in the United States. In Australia the issue is also limited to 8% of the assets. New Zealand applies a limit of 10% of the assets (see K. Anand, J. Chapman and P. Gai, 'Covered bonds, core markets, and financial stability', p. 3, available at: www.rbnz.govt.nz/research/workshops/dec2012/Session6_AnandChapmanGai_CoveredBonds.162849.pdf (last accessed in March 2013); see also Canada: www.fin.gc.ca/activty/consult/cb-os-eng.asp).
95. Art. 10 RD CB Issue implementing art. 64/3, §4, n° 6 CIA. The NBB determines which assets are taken into account to determine this limit.
96. See Report to the King, RD CB Issue.
97. See NBB, Circular letter of 29 October 2012 on the '*Modalités pratiques d'application de la loi du 3 août 2012 instaurant le régime légal pour les covered bonds*', p. 4, available at: www.nbb.be/doc/cp/fr/ki/circ/pdf/NBB_2012_10_12.pdf.
98. See Report to the King, RD CB Issue.
99. See Report to the King, RD CB Issue.
100. Art. 10, §1, al. 3 RD CB Issue.
101. See Report to the King, RD CB Issue.
102. See Report to the King, RD CB Issue.
103. Indeed, to obtain the specific permission of the NBB, the NBB must be satisfied that the credit institution disposes of the general permission of the NBB referred to in art. 64/3, §1 CIA and that the cover assets care composed of the statutory assets. It is not clear whether this reference implies that the NBB should, prior to granting the specific permission, verify again that the conditions to grant the general permission are satisfied and thus whether the financial situation of the credit institution is sufficient to guarantee the interest of other creditors than bondholders. To the extent that this reference implies that the aforementioned condition should be fulfilled (since otherwise the NBB should revoke the permission), it would have been more appropriate to foresee that the NBB can only grant the specific permission provided the conditions to obtain the general permission are still complied with and the general permission is to be maintained.
104. Art. 10, §2 RD CB Issue.
105. See Report to the King, RD CB Issue.
106. Art. 10, §2 RD CB Issue.
107. The preparatory works indicate that one may not deduce from the existence of a specific procedure that credit institutions may unilaterally adapt their activity program without the regulator being informed thereof beforehand. The specific approval procedure in other words does not prejudice the fact that the licence of the credit institution is granted on the basis of an activity program and that modifications thereof remain submitted to supervision. See Explanatory memorandum (I), pp. 11–12.

108. Art. 64/22 CIA (introduced by art. 33 BCBA).
109. Art. 12*bis* of the Act of 22 February 1998 on the constitutional statute of the National Bank of Belgium, *Belgian State Gazette,* 28 March 1998.
110. Moral hazard is used to refer to the situation where a party will have a tendency to take risks because the consequences in terms of liabilities and costs that could result from it, will not be borne by the party taking the risk. See also S. Landuyt and L. Anckaert, *supra* note 36, p. 164, footnote no. 149.
111. K. Schoors, '"Covered bonds" zijn niet de mirakeloplossing die de banksector er van maakt', *De Tijd,* 4 October 2012.
112. Ibid.
113. See e.g. R. Natter, 'Covered Bonds', 2011, available at: www.bsnlawfirm.com/newsletter/OP0511_3.pdf, p. 7. This is why some plead for bail-inable debt, i.e. financing instruments (bonds) that can be converted into equity (shares) under certain circumstances. See High-level Expert Group on reforming the structure of the EU banking sector ('Liikaden Report'), 2 October 2012, p. 92, available at: http://ec.europa.eu/internal_market/bank/docs/high-level_expert_group/report_en.pdf, in particular p. 103: 'The power to write down claims of unsecured creditors or convert debt claims to equity in a bank resolution process is crucial to ensure investor involvement in covering the cost of recapitalisation and/or compensation of depositors. It also reduces the implicit subsidy inherent in debt financing. This additionally improves the incentives of creditors to monitor the bank. […] In order to limit interconnectedness within the banking system and increase the likelihood that the authorities are eventually able to apply the bail-in requirements in the event of a systemic crisis, it is preferable that the bail-in instruments should not be held within the banking sector. This would be best accomplished by restricting holdings of such instruments to non-bank institutional investors (e.g. investment funds and life insurance companies). Bail-in instruments should also be used in remuneration schemes for top management so as best to align decision-making with longer-term performance in banks. The Group suggests that this issue should be studied further.' Nevertheless, it is proposed not to exempt covered bondholders from the bail-in tool. See *supra* note 83.
114. A question that arises in that respect is to what extent the capital requirements take into account the amount of assets tied up to covered bonds. Indeed, the more assets are in priority reserved for covered bonds holders, the smaller the 'general' buffer becomes.
115. See the proposal for a Directive on Deposit Guarantee Schemes (COD 2010/0207) available at: http://eur-lex.europa.eu/legal-content/EN/ALL/?uri=CELEX:52010PC0368 and the press release of 17 December 2013 in this respect: http://europa.eu/rapid/press-release_MEMO-13-1176_en.htm. See also C. Van Nieuwenhuyze and M.D. Zachary, 'Het Belgische depositogarantiestelsel vanuit een Europees perspectief', available at: www.nbb.be/doc/ts/publications/EconomicReview/2010/ecotijdIII2010_H5.pdf
116. See amongst others art. 3 et seq. of the Royal Decree of 14 November 2008 '*Arrêté royal portant exécution de la loi du 15 octobre 2008 portant des mesures visant à promouvoir la stabilité financière et instituant en particulier une garantie d'Etat relative aux crédits octroyés et autres opérations effectuées dans le cadre de la stabilité financière, en ce qui concerne la protection des dépôts, des assurances sur la vie et du capital de sociétés coopératives agréées, et modifiant la loi du 2 août 2002 relative à la surveillance du secteur financier et aux services financiers*', *Belgian State Gazette,* 17 November 2008, and the

terms applied by the Belgian protection fund for deposits and deposits and financial instruments of 1 January 2011, '*Modalités d'application de la protection des dépôts et des instruments financiers auprès d'établissements de crédit et d'entreprises d'investissement*', available at: www.beschermingsfonds.be/files/01.01.2011-Reglementation-des-systemes-de-protection.pdf.

117. De Nederlandse Bank, *Jaarverslag 2011, supra* note 92, p. 64. While working on this paper, I raised the question to several persons interested in knowing what I was writing about. Although these discussions cannot be seen as a duly scientific investigation, they revealed nevertheless that none of these persons was aware of the new measures and, what is more, did not feel concerned by this subject which they considered too technical to become part of their day-to-day worries.
118. See in the same way Coëme Report, p. 7.
119. The way in which a credit institution uses the means collected does not seem to fall under any specific supervision of the NBB, except for the general supervision related to the solvability and liquidity requirements. See in this respect also the Belfius prospectus for the issue of the Belgian *Pandbrieven* provide the following: 'The net proceeds of the sale of the Mortgage Pandbrieven will be used for the general funding purposes of the Issuer. If, in respect of any particular issuance, there is a particular identified use of proceeds, this will be stated in the applicable Final Terms'. See the Belfius prospectus of 8 November 2012, p. 19, available at: https://www.belfius.be/financial/NL/Media/Execution%20version%20Belfius%20Base%20Prospectus%2008%2011%202012_tcm_35-45972.pdf. Idem KBC prospectus. As mentioned above (see *supra* note 39) certain European directives require that the proceeds gained via the issue are invested in assets that can cover for the duration of the bonds the receivables related to such bonds and that can be used in priority in case of default of the credit institution for the payment of the bond holders. The BCBA does not seem to contain such an obligation, although the Belgian *Pandbrieven* are considered to be compliant with these directives.
120. X., 'Le cadre juridique des "covered bonds" finalisé', *Trends*, 28 September 2012, http://trends.levif.be/economie/actualite/politique-economique/le-cadre-juridique-des-covered-bonds-finalise/article-4000185494341.htm. Free translation: 'The minister hopes that the banking sector will not be ungratefull. This decision goes along with some other expectations from the financial sector: we expect that they will use this money for the real economy'.
121. De Nederlandse Bank, *Jaarverslag 2011, supra* note 92, p. 64.
122. K. Schoors, *supra* note 111.
123. K. Schoors, *supra* note 111.
124. See E. De Keuleneer, 'A better protection of bank depositors is necessary and easy', 16 August 2012, available at: www.itinerablog.org/article/a-better-protection-of-bank-depositors-is-necessary-and-easy; X., '"Gewaarborgde obligatie" in trek', *De Standaard*, 26 November 2012, available at: www.standaard.be/artikel/detail.aspx?artikelid=DMF20121125_00381306. This option was also mentioned in the preliminary text of a draft act for the revision of the Belgian Civil Code in relation to real collateral on moveable assets (Voorontwerp van wet tot wijziging van het burgerlijk wetboek wat betreft de zakelijke zekerheden op roerende goederen betreft, Verslag van de Expertengroep op de zekerheden opgericht door de Minister van Justitie, S. De Clerck, en voorgezeten door Professor E. Dirix, 14 October 2011, p. 10, available at: http://justitie.belgium.be/nl/binaries/loi_suretes_tcm265-150098.pdf, pp. 11–12) and was reiterated in the draft

of act submitted to the Belgian Parliament (see *Projet de loi modifiant le Code civil en ce qui concerne les sûretés réelles mobilières et abrogeant diverses dispositions en cette matière, Doc. Chambre.* 2012–13, no. 2463/001, p. 13).

125. See R. Feltkamp, 'Een kredietinstelling, meerdere vermogens – Vermogensrechtelijke bedenkingen bij de regeling inzake Belgische covered bonds', in *Liber amicorum Hélène Casman*, Antwerp, Intersentia, 2013, pp. 199 ff and references cited. See also for an analysis in this respect J. Rochfeld, *Les grandes notions du droit privé*, Paris, Presse Universitaires de France, 2011, pp. 357 ff.

126. See in this respect B. Broucke, 'Het structureren van zekerheden bij gesyndiceerde kredieten – Hoopvol uitkijken naar actieve hoofdelijkheid, parallel debt en trust?', *T.Fin.R.* 2002–2, p. 116; R. Janssens, 'Gesyndiceerde kredieten', *Jura Falconis* 2004–05, p. 87 ff; I. Peeters, 'De wet financiële zekerheden: netting, schuldvergelijking en overdracht tot zekerheid', *B.Fin.R.* 2005, pp. 111 ff.

127. Coëme Report., p. 5: '*De nombreuses entraves juridiques empêchent cependant une grande partie de ces portefeuilles de créances en Belgique de servir de garantie de refinancement ou alors de l'être à des conditions nettement moins avantageuses. Ce projet de loi permet donc de résoudre une série de problèmes juridico-techniques*' (free translation: 'Due to a multitude of legal constraints a great deal of (the) portofolios of receivables can however not be used as collateral for refinancing or only at less favourable conditions').

128. See Explanatory memorandum (II), p. 38: '*Aussi la présente proposition de loi entend-elle imposer les mesures qui doivent permettre que dans la pratique un volume suffisant de créances privées d'établissements de crédit et d'institutions financières belges puisse être affecté en garantie de "covered bonds" et de "collateral" (vis-à-vis de la BNB mais aussi à l'égard d'autres institutions financières par exemple). Il est primordial à cet égard que les solutions proposées ne se limitent pas aux crédits et créances futurs mais couvrent aussi les créances privées existantes*' (free translation: 'This proposal of act also intends to impose the measures that enable that in practice a sufficiant volume of private receivables of belgian credit institutions and financial institutions can be used as guarantee for "covered bonds" and as "collateral" (towards for example the NBB but also towards other financial institutions) It is crucial in this respect that the proposed solutions are not limited to future credits and receivables but cover also existing private receivables').

129. Art. 3 MRA.

130. Art. 4 MRA. A similar provision for claims arising out of advance payments in the context of credit facilities, which are guaranteed by a mortgage, immovable privilege, mortgage promise or mortgage mandate is foreseen by art. 51, §2 Belgian Mortgage Credit Act.

131. Art. 5 MRA.

132. Art. 6 MRA.

133. Art. 7 MRA.

134. Art. 8 MRA.

135. Art. 8, §2 MRA and art. 51*septies* Belgian Mortgage Act as introduced by art. 18 MRA (as regards mortgage receivables).

136. See art. 11 et seq. MRA. See for a more detailed analysis S. Landuyt and L. Anckaert, *supra* note 36, pp. 152 160.

137. Art. 51 Belgian Mortgage Credit Act as adapted by art. 12 MRA.

138. A specific form of collective investment institution.

139. Art. 51*bis*, §3 Belgian Mortgage Credit Act as adapted by art. 13 MRA.

140. Art. 51*ter* Belgian Mortgage Credit Act as adapted by art. 14 MRA.

141. See also S. Landuyt and L. Anckaert, *supra* note 36, p. 151, no. 7.
142. Close-out netting refers to contractual arrangements/processes that foresee amongst others the acceleration of debts under certain circumstances (e.g. default) with a view to allowing set-off and the subsequent combination of the debts of the involved parties to transform them a single net position.
143. See e.g. the general conditions (2013) of BNP Paribas Fortis available at: https://www.bnpparibasfortis.be/portal/start.asp or the general conditions (2013) of Belfius.
144. The validity of such exclusion is questionable towards consumers in light of the prohibitions regarding unfair contract terms contained in the Belgian law of 2 April 2010 regarding market practices and consumer protection (see e.g. art. 74, 16° and 74, 30°).
145. See amongst others D. Mengle, 'The importance of close-out netting', ISDA Research Notes 201/1, pp. 3 ff, available at: www.isda.org/researchnotes/pdf/Netting-ISDAResearchNotes-1–2010.pdf; Unidroit principles on the operation of close-out netting provisions, www.unidroit.org/english/studies/study78c/main.htm.
146. See amongst others D. Mengle, 'The importance of close-out netting', ISDA Research Notes 201/1, pp. 5 ff, available at: www.isda.org/researchnotes/pdf/Netting-ISDAResearchNotes-1–2010.pdf; P. Paech, 'Preliminary draft Report on the need for an international instrument on the enforceability of close-out netting in general and in the context of bank resolution', March 2011, www.unidroit.org/english/documents/2011/study78c/s-78c-02-e.pdf.
147. Explanatory memorandum (II), p. 44: '*En cas de mobilisation d'une créance privée (par exemple via une cession, une mise en gage ou une autre sûreté ou encore via des covered bonds), la valeur de la créance gagée est fixée par le fait que le débiteur de la créance est juridiquement tenu de payer l'intégralité de la créance majorée des intérêts au cessionnaire (après cession), au créancier gagiste (en cas de nantissement) ou auprès du patrimoine spécial d'un établissement de crédit émetteur d'un covered bond. Il est donc essentiel d'éviter que le débiteur de la créance privée ne puisse encore invoquer après la mobilisation d'autres moyens de défense pour refuser le paiement, pour autant du moins que ces moyens de défense (comme le droit à compensation ou l'exception d'inexécution) soient fondés sur sa relation avec l'établissement de crédit et non sur sa relation avec le cessionnaire, le créancier gagiste ou le patrimoine spécial (à savoir le pool de covered assets). Autoriser de tels moyens de défense signifierait que le cessionnaire, le créancier gagiste ou le détenteur de covered bonds ne peut pas accorder de valeur aux créances privées étant donné qu'il n'a (sur le plan juridique) absolument aucune certitude que celles-ci seront payées. Cette incertitude rend les créances privées inaptes à servir de nantissement*' (free translation: 'In case of a mobilisation of a private receivable (e.g. via a transfer, a pledge or another collateral mechanism or via covered bonds, the value of the collateralised receivable is determined by the fact that the debtor is legally held to pay the integrality of the receivable increased with the interest to the transferee (after transfer), or to the creditor holding the collateral (in case of pledge) or to the special estate of a credit institution that issued covered bonds. It is thus essential to avoid that a debtor of a receivable can still invoque after transfer the mobilisation of other means of defences to refuse payment, to the extent that these means of defense (such as the set-off or the right to withhold performance are based on the relationship with the credit institution and not on its relation with the transferee, the creditor holding the collateral or the special estate (i.e. the pool of covered assets). Authorising these

means of defenses would mean that transferee, the creditor holding the collateral or the "special estate" would not be able to grant any value to the private receivables since he has (from a legal perspective) absolutely no certainty that these will be paid. This insecurity renders private receivables unsuitable for pledging.')

148. P. Sobrana Gennari Curlo, 'La nouvelle loi sur les covered bonds est-elle illégale?', *L'Echo,* 14 August 2012.
149. See R. Feltkamp, *supra* note 11, p. 519, no. 526.
150. See R. Feltkamp, *supra* note 11, pp. 362 ff and pp. 398 ff.
151. Art. 5 Belgian Mortgage Act.
152. See art. 2075 Belgian Civil Code and art. 5 Belgian Mortgage Act. The rules in respect of pledging of receivables will in 2014 be replaced by a new regime installed by the Act of 11 July 2013. A similar rule is maintained for the pledging of receivables, see the new art. 60 of this Act.
153. For the accessories this is specifically stated in art. 1692 Belgian Civil Code.
154. See among others Cass. 13 September 1973, *Pas.* 1974, I, p. 31; Cass. 22 April 2002, *RGDC* 2004, p. 399; W. Van Gerven and S. Covemaeker, *Verbintenissenrecht*, Leuven, Acco, 2010, p. 209; P. Wéry, *Droit des obligations, Vol. 1, Théorie générale du contrat,* Brussels, Larcier, 2010, p. 672 ff, no. 775 et seq. and pp. 797, no. 947.
155. This remedy may be invoked without prior court intervention, but a court may however *a posteriori* verify its application.
156. W. Van Gerven and S. Covemaeker, *Verbintenissenrecht*, Leuven, Acco, 2010, pp. 210–212; P. Wéry, *Droit des obligations, Vol. 1, Théorie générale du contrat,* Brussels, Larcier, 2010, p. 675, no. 779.
157. R. Feltkamp, *supra* note 11, p. 527 and cited references.
158. R. Feltkamp, *supra* note 11, p. 526, no. 534 and references. See also E. Blomme, 'Mobilisering versus schuldvergelijking: artikel 6 van de wet van 3 augustus 2012', *Bank Fin. R.*, 2013, p. 157.
159. R. Feltkamp, *supra* note 11, p. 527 and cited references.
160. Art. 1289 Belgian Civil Code.
161. See amongst others L. Cornelis, *Algemene theorie van de verbintenis*, Antwerp, Intersentia, 2000, pp. 865 ff; R. Houben, 'Schuldvergelijking', *RW* 2010–11, p. 1370, no. 4.
162. See amongst others L. Cornelis, *supra* note 161, p. 867; R. Houben, *supra* note 161.
163. Article 1293 Belgian Civil Code excludes set-off for some debts.
164. See amongst others L. Cornelis, *supra* note 161, p. 869 ff; R. Houben, *supra* note 161, pp. 1371 ff.
165. Art. 1298 Belgian Civil Code.
166. Cass. 7 December 1961, *Pas.* 1962, I, 440. Where initially the required close connection was interpreted in the sense that the receivables to be set-off should find there origin in the same reciprocal agreement, the requirement has over time been interpreted more and more broadly, an objective connection (either stemming from a reciprocal agreement or from the same factual context) being sufficient. See amongst others R. Feltkamp, *supra* note 11, p. 539 and cited references; R. Houben, *supra* note 161, p. 1381 and cited references
167. The same rule applies in case a receivable is pledged.
168. R. Feltkamp, *supra* note 11, pp. 537 ff; R. Houben, *Schuldvergelijking*, Antwerp, Intersentia, 2010, pp. 216 ff.

169. Cass. 26 June 2003, *TBH* 2004, p. 476, note I. Peeters.
170. Cass. 5 October 2012, C.12.0073.N.
171. Initially the provision also applied to physical persons that are not traders. Following a decision of the Belgian Constitutional Court of 27 November 2008 according to which allowing the applicability of the clause with regard to natural persons would be discriminatory and contrary to articles 10 and 11 of the Belgian Constitution, the FCA was adapted in 2011 to explicitly specify that this provision does not apply to conventional set-off arrangements concluded with physical persons that do not qualify as a trader.
172. Art. 15, §1 FCA.
173. See also E. Blomme, *supra* note 158, p. 154. According to the Belgium Supreme Court the right of set-off exists regardless of the time as of which the receivable exists and regardless of whether there is or is not a close connection. Cass. 5 October 2012, C.12.0073.N.
174. To the extent art. 14, §1 FCA provides that the conventional set-off remains possible towards *the creditors* regardless the transfer of the rights to which such clauses relate, without specific reference to the transferee, it is less clear as to whether this provision is actually consistent with its *ratio legis*. Indeed, different scholars interpret the reference to 'the creditors' as a reference to the creditors of the counterparty against whom the set-off is invoked (I. Peeters, 'De wet financiële zekerheden: netting, schuldvergelijking en overdracht tot zekerheid', *Bank Fin. R.*, 2005, p. 168, no. 13; I. Peeters, 'De wet financiële zekerheden – Een stap te ver of de aanloop naar een totaal vernieuwd zekerheidsrecht?', *TBH* 2006, pp. 180–181, no. 38; V. Sagaert and H. Seeldrayers, 'De wet financiële zekerheden', *RW* 2004–05, p. 1543). In this interpretation the rule allows a party, in its status as creditor, to ensure that his payment has priority over the other creditors of the insolvent counterparty by applying set-off between his claim and the transferred receivables as if no transfer took place and despite the insolvency of the counterparty. Article 1295 of the Belgian Civil Code however concerns the question whether the debtor of the transferred claim (A in the example above) who is also creditor of the transferee (B in the example above) can still invoke set-off between his claim on the transferee and the transferred receivable towards the transferee. The transferee entitled to payment of the receivables by the debtor is however in that context not a creditor of the counterparty (i.e. the transferor) but of the debtor and thus seems not be covered by article 14, §1 FCA. Article 15, §1 FCA provides more generally that netting arrangements are valid and enforceable towards *third parties* (which would include the transferee) but this clause only contains an additional condition for such clauses to have effect in case of an insolvency and does not concern the specific situation of transfer of receivables.
175. See explanatory memorandum, draft of law of 26 October 2004 '*relatif aux sûretés financières et portant des dispositions fiscales diverses en matière de conventions constitutives de sûreté réelle et de prêts portant sur des instruments financiers*', *Doc. Chambre*, 2004–05, no. 1407/001, p. 46.
176. Art. 27 of the Act of 12 June 1991 on consumer credit, *Belgian State Gazette*, 9 June 1991.
177. Art. 6, §1 MRA.
178. Art. 6, §2, al. 1 and art. 6, §3, al. 1 MRA.
179. Art. 6, §4, 1° MRA.
180. Art. 6, §5 MRA.
181. Art. 6, §4, 3° MRA.

182. Art. 6, §5 MRA.
183. Art. 6, §4, 2° MRA.
184. See also S. Landuyt and L. Anckaert, *supra* note 36, p. 159, no. 47.
185. S. Landuyt and L. Anckaert, *supra* note 36, pp. 159–160, no. 48.
186. Art. 6, §2, al. 2 and art. 6, §3, al. 2 MRA.
187. Explanatory memorandum (II), p. 44 (see *supra* note 147).
188. See Explanatory memorandum (II), p. 45.
189. See amongst others A. De Wilde, *Boedelschulden in het insolventierecht*, Antwerp, Intersentia, 2005, p. 268, no. 285; W. Van Gerven, H. Cousy and J. Stuyck, *Handels en economisch recht, Ondernemingsrecht*, vol. B, in *Beginselen van Privaatrecht*, Ghent, Story Scientia 1989, p. 582.
190. See e.g. art. 19.6 and 19.8 of the General terms of Belfius (2013) available at: https://www.belfius.be/common/NL/multimedia/MMDownloadableFile/Info/About_Us/Regulations_and_rates/MMDF%20Algemeen%20Reglement%20der%20Verrichtingen.pdf.
191. Credit institutions and financial institutions can thus easily escape the first rule by foreseeing such a pledge. See also E. Blomme, *supra* note 158, pp. 159 and 161.
192. The question then arises whether such clause would be valid and opposable to the transferee. See more in detail E. Blomme, *supra* note 158, p. 161.
193. S. Landuyt and L. Anckaert, *supra* note 36, p. 160.
194. These mortgage credits are excluded from the scope of the Consumer Credit Act by art. 3, 7° of this Act.
195. See for a similar conclusion S. Landuyt and L. Anckaert, *supra* note 36, p. 171.
196. R. Houben, '(Contractuele) schuldvergelijking na cessie en de goede trouw van de gecedeerde schuldenaar (art. 1691, tweede lid BW)', note under Cass. 5 October 2012, *RW* 2012–13, p. 1340; R. Houben and I. Peeters, 'De zekerheidswaarde van schuldvergelijking in het Belgisch recht, mede in het licht van de financiële crisis. Pleidooi voor een genuanceerde maar verantwoorde aanpak', *TBH* 2011, p. 769–770.
197. J. Stiglitz, *Free fall. Free markets and the sinking of the global economy*, London, Penguin Books, 2010, pp. 83 and 164 ff.
198. Based on this expectation it has been argued that the prejudicial impact of the imbalances of the MRA should not be overestimated since the case that a non-professional would be confronted with the prejudicial effects of the MRA is rather limited. See S. Landuyt and L. Anckaert, *supra* note 36, p. 171.
199. This is not the case for all articles. Article 4 and 5 MRA apply without regard to whether or not a credit institutions, financial institutions or mobilisation institutions is concerned. Art. 8 and 9 MRA concerning covered bond concern specifically Belgian credit institutions.
200. Art. 1 CIA. See also S. Landuyt and L. Anckaert, *supra* note 36, p. 152, no. 13.
201. Art. 2, 5° MRA refers to institutions registered with the FSMA as public institution for collective investment in receivables, registered institutional institutions for collective investment in receivables and certain Belgian or foreign institutions that autonomously realise or accomplish securitisation to acquire receivables or other goods by issuing securities the value of which is dependent on such assets or which, being covered by those assets grant a guarantee to the holders of such securities.

202. See the overview of the institutional sectors according to the ESR95 provided by the NBB, available at: www.nbb.be/doc/dq/CIS/n/info.htm#S.12. For the application of the FCA they qualify as 'financial legal person' (see art. 3, 11° FCA).
203. But do qualify as a 'financial legal person' as defined in the FCA.
204. Article 6, §1 MRA refers in general to receivables.
205. See above §1.

FINANCIAL SUPERVISION IN PERSPECTIVE

Michel Flamée

'O, wonder!
How many goodly creatures are there here!
How beauteous mankind is! O brave new world,
That has such people in't!'
The Tempest, V, 1, William Shakespeare

– The tempest	The national authorities were insufficiently prepared for a crisis, and the importance of efficient international cooperation was greatly underestimated.
– Assessing the damage	The high quality of the supervisory staff and their performance does not exempt the supervisors from the need to permanently draw lessons from the crisis and to translate the conclusions into practical steps towards improving the efficiency and effectiveness of their actions.
– If the shoe doesn't fit…	The banking supervisory model had not often been called into question during the decade before the financial crisis. The supervisors have most often focused their supervisory actions on implementation of quantitative requirements, leaving aside the fundamental questioning of developments in the area of financial firms' risk management and strategic choices. Supervisors have to pay greater attention to developing a philosophy and setting priorities for overseeing financial institutions. With an iron hand in a velvet glove, the supervisor must intervene with a sure touch.
– Where is the compass?	Although this may to some extent restrict its discretionary freedom, a supervisory body ought to develop an explicit mission statement so as to provide a clearer framework for the work of its staff.
– Power game	The supervisor is granted considerable powers to act, the exercise of which demands an appropriate internal process of checks and balances as regards decision-making within the supervisory body.

– Together	It is essential for the executive of the supervisory authority to not only be collegial but also to work as a team in order to make optimal use of the complementary competences of each member and to develop a shared strategic vision that can realistically be put into practice.
– Sailing in the mist	It is advisable that the executive body of the supervisory authority proceeds to take internal organisational measures, which would enable it to devote priority attention and time to settling fundamental questions and evaluating the effectiveness of its choices.
– Standing on the shoulders of…	The job of supervising increasingly requires a combination of different perspectives, both macro- and microeconomic in nature. Experience of this evolution in insurance supervision, which is proving to have beneficial effects on the behaviour of firms in the sector, may serve as a source of inspiration in other areas of supervision.
– To twin peak or not to twin peak	Given the need to choose between the protection of insured parties and savers over the medium and long term, as is appropriate for a supervisor, and the promotion in the short term of more advantageous market conditions from the perspective of consumer interests or of the supervision of financial information and markets, there are good reasons for introducing a supervisory model in which these two functions operate independently from each other. This also prevents opaque internal decision-making. This organisational model is increasingly common in other countries, facilitating international cooperation both in setting and implementing standards and in developing joint prudential action on the part of multiple supervisors.
– Soft skills	Over and above the indispensable technical know-how, the executive of the supervisory authority must develop the competences necessary to equip the supervisory apparatus for a global approach to emerging risks, so that it can respond effectively or even anticipate these risks, among other things, by making judicious use of its signalling function to the sectors under supervision.
– The unreachable star	Although it is an illusion to think that supervisors can prevent every incident, they can still be expected to do everything possible in view of that goal, and thus continually evaluate their supervisory choices in order to try and improve them.

1. THE TEMPEST

In September–October 2008, a devastating whirlwind swept through the financial landscape. In my capacity as a board member of CEIOPS from 2002 to 2006 and then as Chairman of the International Association of Insurance Supervisors (IAIS), and as Vice Chairman of the Belgian Integrated Supervisor, I had the opportunity to observe at first hand the level of preparedness for such an occurrence among several types of supervisory authorities, including regional groupings, integrated banking and insurance supervisors, and central bankers. During this period, I was able more particularly to experience *ex officio* the work done by the G20 think tank, the FSF (Financial Stability Forum), precursor of the FSB (Financial Stability Board).

It is interesting to note how the considerations of international politics since late 2006 have made the discussion of emerging risks more difficult within the FSF. From the perspective of the IAIS, I repeatedly emphasised while Chairman the need to bear in mind the systemic importance of the failure of monoliners, and indeed of other businesses that provide financial services to the 'real' economy rather than primarily to other financial institutions. The FSF took up this concern as a significant element in the estimation of global stability.

By the end of my term as Chairman of the IAIS, the foundations were laid both within the IAIS and the FSF for devoting attention systematically to financial stability from the point of view of insurance supervision.

In the Belgian financial landscape, Fortis, Dexia and KBC banks one after the other were severely affected by the circumstances we are all familiar with, the two latter institutions' problems stemming partly from the consequences of the monoliner incidents; lastly, there was Ethias, to some extent a result of collateral damage from the banking vicissitudes, and Kaupthing. The way in which these financial institutions were handled by the Supervisor is described extensively in the reports of the Belgian special Parliamentary Commission charged with investigating the banking crisis.

Raising the level of preparedness for such incidents on the part of the Supervisors is now firmly on their agenda. Many foreign studies have reported similar findings. In the European context, the provisional target is for part if not all banking supervision to be applied or at least decided at the ECB level.

2. ASSESSING THE DAMAGE

Following various parliamentary commissions and expert reports, the question remains therefore as to how the Supervisors should continue to be structured in the future, be it at the ECB level itself, in order to be able to withstand these kinds of events.

Some expert reports highlighted as one of the Supervisor's inefficiencies, the practice of 'box-ticking' supervision that relied excessively on rules-based administration. This observation is without any doubt to be taken very seriously.

But there is no single Supervisor, just as there is no single financial institution, that can carry out its tasks without making use of checklists of action items, the processing of which inevitably involves ticking off the boxes labelled 'done'.

But what is essential is that when an estimate needs to be made, this is not a purely formal exercise but one in which the assessor makes a judgement with an added value based on his or her competence. Here, Supervisors must not allow themselves to be blinded by apparently convincing arguments. For example, in insurance supervision at EIOPA's level, a 'convincing' argument is currently being put forward in the analysis of the draft Solvency II Directive for developing a Long-Term Package that would correct the evident but generally undesirable volatility of assets by adjusting the scale of technical provisions. The stated reason is the specific character of the business which matches long-term liabilities with assets held in the long term. Interim volatility should therefore be neutralised. The solvency ratio would thus look better, but thus some volatility is introduced at the level of the technical provisions which, backed by appropriate covering assets, form the best guarantee for policy-holders, and should therefore always remain adequate. A solution that at first sight seems appropriate impairs in fact the robustness of the firm, while appropriate action on the assets can offer the same stability without affecting robustness. For example, intermittent volatility induced by rapid fluctuations in the spread risk concerning assets to be held long-term but which is irrelevant for solvency so long as those assets do not have to be realised, could be a more appropriate solution. Is it not time to produce other solutions by thinking outside the box in which the dispute over the Long-Term Package is confined? In such process, it must never be forgotten that the Supervisors must not allow beguiling figures to make them complacent.

You get what you measure. And in this business, nothing is more dangerous than trusting statistical results that create a false sense of security. Statistical results are based on assumptions, which must be constantly challenged. An initial validation of the set of instruments, however essential, should never throw you off-guard and prevent you from taking a sufficiently frequent, critical look at the instruments used.

The vast majority of the Supervisor's staff is university graduates; they are strongly committed to their tasks and endowed with a strong critical sense. They do tick off boxes, but also supplement these with comments, both in internal reports and in the reports addressed to the institutions under supervision, and they are also prepared to think outside the box and be innovative, if it can be demonstrated that this is more in line with the views of society.

3. IF THE SHOE DOESN'T FIT

Where even one shoe begins to pinch, that is where the overall supervisory technology has sometimes failed to keep pace with developments in the sector under supervision.

A supervisory body's management committee can opt to spend a great deal of time on formal decision-making, while ongoing discussion of evolving risks and therefore of supervisory requirements, and the associated managerial decisions and consequent operational action, are then given short shrift or may not even get on the agenda. When supervisory innovations are discussed, they are to be carefully brought up by the staff, and taken up at the top level of the organisation.

The philosophy of supervision relies within some supervisory bodies on the 'concentric circles' model developed more than a decade ago, when financial institutions still stuck quite closely to their traditional core business. The supervisory toolkit developed then was based on the analytical techniques in use at the time. It has partly fallen into disuse but without being replaced. Some aspects, although falling within the tasks of one of the concentric circles, namely that of the external auditors or appointed actuaries, have undergone such extensive changes that they can no longer really be considered to be an arm of the Supervisor extending into the institutions under supervision. This ought to result in modifications and expansion of the supervisory tasks, but instead, these are often postponed whenever voices calling for such changes are raised.

Moreover, since the beginning of 2000, a great deal of attention has been paid to implementing the Basel norms, prompting a good proportion of the staff to devote time to testing the banking function 'on site'. However, this is done largely from the perspective of compliance with the first pillar of the Basel rules, that is, by testing the robustness of the models used for determining capital requirements. Numerous inspections *in situ* have thus been carried out from that specific perspective, and therefore focusing only on certain items. Despite checking whether sufficient security measures were implemented in the cellar, however, no one considered the possibility of a fire breaking out in the kitchen.

The supervision that was conducted was thus principally quantitative in nature, with inspections intended to determine whether the capital requirements laid down for traditional activities would suffice to cover the 'usual' risks. Such a quantitative approach creates a feeling of security and offers comfort. Once it is established that the figures meet the requirements, the work is over, the conscience is clear, what was expected has been done, but a Supervisor is asked to look into the unexpected: to imagine the unimaginable.

Qualitative evaluation also requires the assumption of much greater personal responsibility in the assessments to be conducted. Further, making choices on qualitative issues, be it the appraisal of the business strategy or the governance structure, or the fit and proper character of individuals, requires the Supervisor to stick his neck out and in some cases stand up to fierce resistance. For instance, an on-site inspection can reveal a great deal of material that may cause headaches. It is thus correct to say that a great many on-site inspections were carried out, but it should be added that these inspections had a very narrow focus. Scarcely any time was left in which to test newly emerging risks.

Heisenberg's principle in the field of quantum mechanics has thus proved to be fully applicable in this area as well. The object being observed is influenced by the act of observation and by the parameters used for the purposes of that observation. Supervisory practice has had difficulty abandoning the logical box within which it had been developing since the end of the 1990s, and entering supervisory fields for which no Basel-level standards have so far been adopted. Less attention was paid to qualitative supervision (much was left up to the critical sense of the firms in question, relying, for instance with regard to MiFID, on a company's own compliance function) and to critical questioning during contact with those in charge at the firms under supervision than to the analysis of figures. True to the Heisenberg principle, the latter seemed to contain within it the limits of its own effectiveness.

Where the second shoe also seemed too tight a fit was in putting the new regulations into effect. A good deal of effort has been devoted in recent years to following up on the tsunami of standards laid down at international and European levels, and to implementing these in the national context. But weaving that mesh of rules took up much more staff time than elaborating the way in which the rules were to be transposed into daily supervisory practice. The operational departments were swamped with complex and detailed regulations that were not always accompanied by comprehensive explanations, so that the added value of the well-intentioned new regulations often could not be realised. There is also the question whether the proliferation of gold-plated rules, either nationally or within specific categories of cases (however good the intentions, e.g. out of respect for the principle of proportionality) – and the proliferation of individual interpretations, is beneficial to comparability, the level playing field and non-discrimination in supervision.

Supervision was thus afflicted by an accumulation of information that sufficed to appease the experts' hunger for quantitative data, but the resulting mass of individual expert reports did not help the manager to see the bigger picture of how the institution's risk profile was developing or to devote attention to newly emerging practices and the associated risks. The consequences of the tight-fitting shoes of inertia resulting from old habits and a flood of rules cannot be blamed on the supervisory staff. These matters fall within the purview of managerial oversight that ought to start with the executive of the supervisory authority, expressed in the way the latter makes known and carries out its mission. Here it is necessary to make sure that prudential activity means more than just amiably trying to convince the firms under supervision to change their ways: with an iron hand in a velvet glove, the Supervisor must intervene with a sure touch.

4. WHERE IS THE COMPASS?

A Supervisor cannot be expected to know – let alone evaluate – everything about the institutions under its supervision. Supervision of that sort would come with such an enormous social cost that it would impede every development of activities for the benefit of society and its members. By contrast, the Supervisor's executive must attend both to a clear description of the institution's tasks and to the teamwork that should exist among its staff in order to enhance the efficiency and the effectiveness of its action.

Here it must not be forgotten that financial supervision is not an end in itself, that a Supervisor must not aim to prove the reason for its own existence as an institution; instead, in an environment where anyone involved with financial intermediation is obliged to put their trust in it, the Supervisor should essentially aim to ensure that this trust is not betrayed. The Supervisor is not there to ensure compliance with the rule for the rule's sake, but compliance in order to achieve its socially useful purpose.

A good number of supervisors have duly drawn up a precise mission statement for their activity. The end result is, of course, that the scope for the executive's 'widely discretionary' policy freedom is thereby reduced to a 'narrowly discretionary' one. The latter structure also enables staff members to know more precisely what is expected of them.

5. POWER GAME

The broad policy freedom on the part of the Supervisor raises the question of how such policy is determined. The Supervisor's executive has links with the political authorities, if only due to the nature of its appointment by the government. It is striking that governments have to a large extent entrusted the task of financial legislation and regulation to the supervisory body, which therefore must make a number of political choices without any other legitimacy to do so than the nature of its appointment. In most cases where policy decisions have to be made, the Supervisor's executive is given no transparent indication from the government as regards these policy choices. The technical nature of the choices to be made only partly justifies entrusting the Supervisor with legislative and regulatory tasks. In some cases, the political authorities seek to protect themselves by leaving 'unpopular' regulations to their 'independent' executive arm. In other cases, the political authorities expect the regulation which is established to support or even bring about the choice of social structure that it stands for.

It is not always easy to distinguish here between 'regulatory' and 'supervisory' activity; between the establishment of rules and their enforcement. And it is clear that supervisory independence must meet absolute requirements, whereas it is more common to see links between political authorities and regulatory activity. In a context in which the political colours of the Supervisor's executive is an explicit factor in appointment, sufficient emphasis cannot be placed on the need to establish and honour adequate checks and balances within the executive in order to ensure that a variety of social visions are taken into consideration when drafting apparently technical regulatory texts.

Indeed, the structures in place should prevent individual inclinations from gaining the upper hand notably by forming a Management Committee in which checks and balances are provided. Yet the struggle for dominance remains a major driving force behind some people's actions. Global standards for supervisors consider independence to be one of the chief prerequisites. Implementing this requirement wisely by seeking to prevent incestuous relationships between supervisors and politics, while ensuring that the Supervisor is attuned to social reality, is one of the most difficult considerations when designing the supervisory toolkit.

6. TOGETHER

Teamwork on the executive board is particularly important insofar as it brings the necessary checks and balances, or at least the principle of 'two pairs of eyes' (the four-eyes principle), into that body. This is no different from what the firms under supervision are asked to do, in the interest of security. Why teams? Because the complexity of the financial sector has increased to such an extent that no one individual can master the totality of the knowledge necessary to grasp all the different aspects of financial institutions. It is therefore desirable for the executive to consist of a mix of people trained in various disciplines (financial analysis, economics, actuarial science, law, etc.). Moreover, it would be useful if there were space on such a team for strategic thinking as well as for research into the operationalisation of strategic outcomes.

Team-building however must not tend towards self-protection. Teams must be based on a strong internal structure, which is not afraid of an internal audit. Supervisors have obliged institutions under supervision to take a critical look at themselves. As complex organisations, supervisors must apply the same criteria to themselves, and that is true of all facets of their organisation and operation (such as governance and own risk management).

7. SAILING IN THE MIST

Experience shows that the call for devoting sufficient time to discussing strategic matters in prudential policy is a constant but often idle request.

Admittedly time has to be freed up for treating the cases that require a change in doctrine and for engaging in strategic thinking. Further, action plans prepared by the various operational departments, in which priority choices are proposed on account of the limited manpower, are to be put forward for collegial discussion. It is important that good executives understand that taking the time to address such problems and make choices will enhance teamwork at the top and thus help win consensus on sensitive political decisions.

However, ensuring that the findings resulting from work at the bottom get through to the top of the organisation must not lead to the top management just rubber-stamping ready-made drafts. The top management takes the decisions but must also give direction to the lower echelons on the items subject to various types of approach. In order to draw up regulations backed by broad consensus, the text must be the fruit of wide-ranging information gathering, dialogue, explicit description of alternatives, consequences of choices and questioning if it is to enjoy sufficient support. But to do so also requires allocating enough time to assessing all the potential consequences of introducing the regulations. The fact that preparatory sub-committees have already formulated a number of considerations on a subject cannot justify failing to give the rest of the team the chance to examine it thoroughly and contribute to the proposals put before them.

Finally, respect for limitations on the supervisor's powers is of paramount importance. Team spirit and transparency should not allow us to forget that a Supervisor is an administrative authority that must abide by the rules of sound governance applicable to every institution endowed with public authority. The rule of law in all its facets (competence, procedural rules, decision-making within the legally designated bodies of the supervisory authority) stands as the ultimate barrier against any arbitrary action and political intervention (with a small 'p', that is).

8. STANDING ON THE SHOULDERS OF...

The profession of supervisor in its modern incarnation requires close cooperation with all the specialised fields involved in supervision (macroprudential analysis, microprudential financial analysis, institutional supervision, technical analysis and, above all, audits in the form of on-site inspections). The resulting supervision gains in clout if all the departments involved in the various components of the task are closely involved in exchanging information and experience. But in order to be able to allow such exchanges to flourish among staff members, the example must be set, as just mentioned, by an executive that places a premium on teamwork. The Supervisor's executive must be prepared to listen to the experience of the staff and, instead of navel-gazing, be open to scrutiny and, where necessary, adjust its working methods by comparing them to those of fellow supervisors.

Comparative analysis reveals that the problems that in part lie at the source of less-than-optimal banking supervision were already present in Belgium to the same degree in insurance supervision in late 2002. The Belgian Insurance Supervisory Office (ISO), before its merger in 2004 with the Commission for Banking and Finance Supervision (CBF, which then became the CBFA, the Banking, Finance and Insurance Commission) had developed a supervisory toolkit based on the not-entirely-free market economy that had characterised the preceding period till the 1990s, in which the setting of tariffs for insurance products was the lynchpin of a regulatory arsenal. The European Solvency I Directive made such a development possible. The supervisory approach was not risk-minded, but consisted of *ex post* financial supervision with many formal traits.

The Law of 2 August 2002 made possible a reorientation of the ISO by merging it with the CBF. Despite the fact that the CBF executive was not at all keen on a merger at the time, the move was pushed through and a turn-around process was begun in legislation and supervisory methodology as well as in the upgrading of staff skills. The prospect of Solvency II gave impetus to this initiative. In the period between 2002 and mid-2007, legislation was gradually overhauled, giving a strong signal meanwhile to the firms under supervision.

Numerous meetings were held with industry leaders in order to raise their awareness of the changing financial environment in which they were operating. For the majority of firms, this policy led to a considerable redrawing of the signposts and revision of their internal structure, particularly in order to increase risk perception on the part of their staff and to introduce an adequate set of ALM instruments within the firm. In the implementation of the new supervisory philosophy, on-site inspections are of great importance. Inspections were intensified considerably and served as levers of change. Even if the legislation in question is still far from complete, it seems that for the majority of firms this approach has borne fruit. Within the supervisory authority, the merger provided the opportunity for cross-fertilisation of techniques from banking supervision that benefited insurance supervision. Further, a growing number of staff members from the banking side came to realise the utility of such cross-fertilisation for the supervision of banks as well.

9. TO TWIN PEAK OR NOT TO TWIN PEAK

It does seem that the effectiveness of the prudential function in supervision has suffered in some areas as a result of the integration of prudential supervision on the one hand, and consumer-sensitive market supervision on the other.

The tension between two perceptions of the mission statement within an integrated supervisory body renders decision-making more difficult: on the one hand, taking protective prudential action to benefit the consumer over the long term, and on the other hand favouring increased returns in response to consumer demand over the short term, with the attendant danger of generating long-term risks.

Thus, for instance, one and the same Supervisor must counterbalance the need for a financial institution to have sufficient regulatory capital, and the desirability of opting for such capital to consist of subordinated loans that could be more immediately risky for the consumer/policy-holder. Over and above other familiar reasons, this situation is an argument for a division along the lines of the 'twin peaks' model that has been adopted in a growing number of countries.

One of the most obvious reasons requiring a split between a market authority – which, among other things, exercises supervision over prospectuses – and the prudential authority is that the basis of assessment, and hence the nature and scale of the decision to be taken in supervising prospectuses differs fundamentally from prudential analysis. In fact, prospectus supervision entails a marginal assessment of the future prospects, which may be very optimistic and is essentially confined to warning the reader without being able to prohibit the operation if it is presented in an acceptable way. In contrast, prudential supervision entails a full appraisal of the feasibility of business plans, and well-designed prudential regulation provides the Supervisor with instruments which can be used to impose corrective measures.

If both aspects of the assessment are entrusted to one and the same body, it is difficult, if not impossible, to make it clear to the non-specialist investor that there are or should be impermeable barriers, Chinese walls, between the prudential authorities and the market supervision services. Those investors assume that a unified prudential authority uses the information available to it in full in making its decisions and when forming an opinion. If his investment fails, the investor will therefore assume that either the Supervisor did not have the necessary information, which implies that the supervision was not done properly, or the necessary information was available, in which case the Supervisor failed to perform his task of informing the investor correctly. He does not want to know about the subtleties of the internal allocation of functions or legal quibbling about the limits of intervention depending on which hat the Supervisor is wearing. It is therefore better to split these two functions between two different bodies.

Whether the performance of fully-fledged prudential functions should lead to absorption of the prudential body by the national central bank is a question that has been answered in the affirmative by a number of countries. That choice can be implemented in a wide variety of ways. There is a choice between less or more autonomy for the performance of the prudential functions, depending on whether less or more importance is attached to the inclusion of macroeconomic considerations in the design or operationalisation of supervisory policy, or to the risk of decisions being taken on account of the interests of the central bank itself, since it acts as lender of last resort, and may therefore have to incur a financial risk itself.

The twin peaks organisational model is becoming increasingly common in several countries, facilitating international cooperation both in setting and implementing standards, and in developing joint prudential activities on the part of multiple Supervisors. In the context of CRD IV and Solvency II, in the ESRB and the FSB, cooperation goes far beyond informal discussions. Joint risk analysis in supervisory colleges, joint assessment of models, governance structure and more generally the business strategies of institutions under supervision, and concerted action nowadays form part of standard supervision practice.

10. SOFT SKILLS

An additional aspect demands consideration, namely the need for 'soft skills' on the part of all the decisional levels within a supervisory body. The capacity to take a bird's-eye view from which to identify tendencies and risks, the skills to transpose these tendencies into operational action items and techniques for tackling the risks that have been identified, the willingness to do this as part of a team on which each member understands the importance of his or her contribution, are absolutely essential. What is the point of being able to predict a tsunami if no concrete measures to avoid the disaster are identified, put in place and, above all, implemented on the shore?

Motivating staff members, who should be made aware that their work is part of a team effort in which the contribution of each member together raises the quality of supervision exponentially, the willingness to put one's own ideas forward for discussion, to think outside the box, and to develop actions that are truly accepted by all those concerned, the need for transparency in the form of clear leadership and prioritisation, and a consistent stance both internally and vis-à-vis the press, are indispensable qualities for enhancing the effectiveness and efficiency of the Supervisor. Its credibility depends in part on such action, credibility that is essential if the supervisor's signalling function to the sectors under supervision is to have full effect.

11. THE UNREACHABLE STAR

It is an illusion to think that a Supervisor can be on top of everything and avoid all incidents. But it is no illusion to expect that it should strive to do so. '*Point n'est besoin d'espérer pour entreprendre, ni de réussir pour persévérer*' (William of Orange). Nevertheless, we ought to be able to expect the Supervisor to organise its work in such a way that it is more likely to succeed than to fail in performing its tasks. The new Belgian supervision structure is well underway in this respect. It will now face many new challenges at the European level with the setting up of a real European supervisory mechanism.

Endnotes

* Michel Flamée is a Former Vice-Chairman of the CBFA, Belgian Financial Supervisory Authority and a Former Chair of the IAIS, International Association of Insurance Supervisors.

(NO) CONCLUSION

Ludo CORNELIS

Does this book require a conclusion? Some may think it does. We do not share that point of view.

When our working group started, we were not concerned about conclusions to be reached.

And now, after the conference day has been held and the papers are presented in this book, we are even more convinced that a kind of a (general) conclusion would be a mistake.

In order to better understand how the emergence or the absence of a financial/economic crisis can be determined by institutions, mechanisms and/or instruments of private law, we joined forces. Even if every contribution is a world unto itself, they each point out and confirm that private law in many ways can do as much as public law to avoid the outbreak of a financial/economic crisis.

For none of the authors is this book the end of the story: our newly acquired insights will determine our future research work and teaching.

If they additionally can be of help to others interested or intrigued by the same questions, we will feel happy and grateful.